W9-CDV-204

ethernet networks

Third Edition

ethernet networks

Third Edition

- ◆ Design
- ◆ Implementation
- ◆ Operation
- ◆ Management

GILBERT HELD

WILEY COMPUTER PUBLISHING

John Wiley & Sons, Inc.

New York ◆ Chichester ◆ Weinheim ◆ Brisbane ◆ Singapore ◆ Toronto

ELMHURST COLLEGE LIBRARY

SEP   1999

Publisher: Robert Ipsen
Editor: Marjorie Spencer
Managing Editor: Angela Murphy
Text Design & Composition: North Market Street Graphics

Designations used by companies to distinguish their products are often claimed as trademarks. In all instances where John Wiley & Sons, Inc., is aware of a claim, the product names appear in initial capital or ALL CAPITAL LETTERS. Readers, however, should contact the appropriate companies for more complete information regarding trademarks and registration.

This book is printed on acid-free paper. ⊗

Copyright © 1998 by Gilbert Held. All rights reserved.

Published by John Wiley & Sons, Inc.

Published simultaneously in Canada.

No part of this publication may be reproduced, stored in a retrieval system or transmitted in any form or by any means, electronic, mechanical, photocopying, recording, scanning or otherwise, except as permitted under Sections 107 or 108 of the 1976 United States Copyright Act, without either the prior written permission of the Publisher, or authorization through payment of the appropriate per-copy fee to the Copyright Clearance Center, 222 Rosewood Drive, Danvers, MA 01923, (978) 750-8400, fax (978) 750-4744. Requests to the Publisher for permission should be addressed to the Permissions Department, John Wiley & Sons, Inc., 605 Third Avenue, New York, NY 10158-0012, (212) 850-6011, fax (212) 850-6008, E-Mail: PERMREQ@WILEY.COM.

Library of Congress Cataloging-in-Publication Data:
Held, Gilbert.
   Ethernet networks
  / Gilbert Held.—3rd ed.
     p.   cm.
   Includes index.
   ISBN 0-471-25310-3 (paper : alk. paper)
   1. Ethernet (Local area network system)   I. Title.
  TK5105.8.E83H45   1998
  004.6'8—dc21   98-3743

Printed in the United States of America.

10 9 8 7 6 5 4 3 2 1

contents

Chapter 7 Routers   281

Chapter 8 Gateway Methods   317

Chapter 9   Intelligent and Switching Hubs   371

preface

In a prior edition of this book the preface commenced with the paraphrase of an old adage in an era of evolving local area networking technology: Ethernet is dead—long live Ethernet!

Although advances in communications technology continue to occur at a rapid pace, that paraphrase continues to be valid. Within the past few years, the bandwidth of 10 Mbps Ethernet was advanced by a factor of ten with the introduction of Fast Ethernet. Now Fast Ethernet is being supplemented by Gigabit Ethernet, providing another leap in bandwidth that provides network managers and LAN administrators with the bandwidth to support emerging applications well into the next century.

This new edition provides a significant amount of additional material to most of the chapters of this book's previous edition. The importance of Internet connectivity and network backbone construction are recognized by two new major chapter sections that will guide you through these important topics. New information on Gigabit Ethernet is included in appropriate sections in chapters focused on different types of Ethernet networks and the composition and flow of Ethernet frames. Recognizing the importance of security in an era when networks are exposed to a virtually unlimited number of hackers when such networks are connected to the Internet, new information is included in this edition focused on securing your network through the creation of router access lists.

Other topics that were added or significantly revised in this new edition include the operation of Windows NT on Ethernet LANs, the operation and utilization of virtual LANs, new gateway methods you can consider to connect workstation users to mainframes, and the use of multitier switching to take advantage of Fast Ethernet and Gigabit Ethernet as network backbones. Thus, the scope and depth of material were significantly revised and updated to continue to provide you with detailed information concerning the design, implementation, operation, and management of different types of Ethernet networks.

This book incorporates into one reference source the material you will need to understand how Ethernet networks operate, the constraints and performance issues that affect their design and implementation, and how their growth and use can be managed both locally and as part of an enterprise network. Assuming readers have varied backgrounds in communications terms and technology, the first two chapters were written to provide a common foundation of knowledge. Those chapters cover networking concepts and network standards—two topics on which material in succeeding chapters is based. Succeeding chapters examine Ethernet concepts: frame operations; network construction; the use of bridges, routers, hubs, switches, and gateways; Internet connectivity; network backbone construction; and the management of Ethernet networks.

Chapter 3 covers Ethernet concepts. This chapter provides a detailed examination of different types of Ethernet networks, their hardware components, and the general methods by which this type of local area network is constructed. Recently developed high-speed Ethernet technology including isoENET, Fast Ethernet, 100VG-AnyLAN, and Gigabit Ethernet are covered in this chapter, as well as earlier developed 10BASE and 10BROAD networks. The following chapter examines the composition and flow of Ethernet frames that transport data on the network. This chapter provides a foundation for an in-depth examination of the use of bridges, routers, hubs, switches, and gateways, and of the tools and techniques you can use to expand and manage your network.

In writing this book, I attempted to incorporate practical information you can readily use in designing, operating, implementing, and managing an Ethernet network. Although Ethernet had its origins in the 1970s and can be considered a relatively "old" technology, in reality, the technology is anything but old. Only a few years ago, the standardization of what is now known as 10BASE-T (a twisted-wire version of Ethernet) resulted in a considerable expansion in the use of this type of local area network. By 1994 the use of intelligent switches greatly enhanced the operational capability of 10BASE-T networks, providing multiple simultaneous 10 Mbps connectivity. During 1995 high-speed Ethernet technology in the form of isoENET, Fast Ethernet, and 100VG-AnyLAN products provided users with the ability to upgrade their Ethernet networks to satisfy emerging multimedia requirements. Within a few years industry realized that emerging applications, as well as the growth in the use of the Internet, required higher-speed backbone LANs as a mechanism to support Internet access and similar high-speed networking requirements. This realization resulted in the deployment of Gigabit Ethernet hubs and switches during 1997. Thus, Ethernet technology can be expected to continue to evolve to satisfy the communications requirements of business, government, and academia.

For over 25 years I have worked as a network manager responsible for the design, operation, and management of an enterprise network in which local area networks throughout the United States are interconnected through the use of different wide area network transmission facilities. This challenging position has provided me with the opportunity to obtain practical experience in designing, operating, and interconnecting Ethernet networks to Token-Ring, SNA, the Internet, and other types of networks—experience which I have attempted to share with you. This book will help you consider the practicality of different types of routing protocols, LAN switches, and gateway methods. These and other network design issues are crucial to the efficient and effective expansion of a local Ethernet so that users on that network can access resources on other networks.

As a professional author, I very much value readers' comments. Those comments provide me with feedback necessary to revise future editions so that they better reflect the information requirements of readers. I look forward to receiving your comments, as well as suggestions for information you would like to see in a future edition of this book. You can write to me directly or through my publisher, whose address is on the back cover of this book or communicate with me directly via electronic mail at 235-8068@mcimail.com.

Gilbert Held
Macon, GA

acknowledgments

This book would not have been possible without the work of two people whose foresight and pioneering efforts were instrumental in the development of the technology upon which Ethernet is based.

One of the key concepts behind Ethernet—that of allocating the use of a shared channel—can be traced to the pioneering efforts of Dr. Norman Abramson and his colleagues at the University of Hawaii during the early 1970s. The actual development of Ethernet is due to the foresight of Dr. Robert Metcalfe. Working at the Xerox Palo Alto Research Center in Palo Alto, California, Dr. Metcalfe headed a development team that interconnected over 100 computers on a 1-km cable using a carrier sense multiple access collision detection (CSMA/CD) protocol. In addition to pioneering the technical development of Ethernet, Dr. Metcalfe coined its name, after the luminiferous ether through which electromagnetic radiation was once thought to propagate. I would be remiss if I did not thank Dr. Abramson, Dr. Metcalfe, and their colleagues for their visionary efforts in developing the technology through which millions of people now communicate.

Writing and producing a book about technology requires not only the technology itself, but also the efforts of many individuals. First and foremost, I would like to thank my family for their understanding for the nights and weekends I disappeared to write this book. Once again, I am indebted to Mrs. Linda Hayes for taking my notes and drawings and converting them into a manuscript. Last, but not least, I would like to thank Marjorie Spencer, Terri Hudson, Katherine Schowalter, and the many others at John Wiley & Sons who were instrumental in backing the three editions of this book, as well as in facilitating the conversion of my manuscript into the book you are reading.

ethernet
networks

Third Edition

chapter one

Introduction to Networking Concepts

One of the most logical assumptions an author can make is that readers will have diverse backgrounds of knowledge and experience. Making this book as valuable as possible to persons with different backgrounds requires an introductory chapter that covers basic networking concepts. Unfortunately, basic concepts for one person may not be the same as basic concepts for another person, which presents an interesting challenge for an author.

To meet this challenge, this book takes two courses of action. First, it assumes that some readers will have limited knowledge about the different types of communications systems available for transporting information, the relationship between wide area networks (WANs) and local area networks (LANs), and the relationships among different types of local area networks. Thus, this introductory chapter was written to provide those readers with a basic level of knowledge concerning these important topics. Secondly, readers who are already familiar with these basic concepts may wish to consult individual chapters separately, rather than reading through the entire book. To satisfy those readers, each chapter was written to be as independent as possible from preceding and succeeding chapters. Thus, readers who are familiar with wide and local area networking concepts, as well as the technical characteristics of LANs, may elect to skim or bypass this chapter. For other readers, information contained in this chapter will provide a level of knowledge that will make succeeding chapters more meaningful.

In this introductory chapter, we will first focus our attention on the key concepts behind the construction of wide area networks and local area networks. In doing so, we will examine each type of network to obtain an understanding of its primary design goal. Next, we will compare and contrast their operations and utilizations to obtain an appreciation for the rationale behind the use of different types of local area networks.

Although this book is about Ethernet networks, there are other types of local area networks that provide a viable data transportation highway for millions of users. By reviewing the technological characteristics of different types of LANs, we will obtain an appreciation for the governing characteristics behind the use of different local area networks. In addition, because many local area networks are connected to other LANs and WANs, we will conclude this chapter by focusing on the technological characteristics of local area networks. This will form a foundation for discussing a variety of Ethernet networking issues in succeeding chapters of this book.

1.1 Wide Area Networks

The evolution of wide area networks can be considered to have originated in the mid- to late 1950s, commensurate with the development of the first generation of computers. Based on the use of vacuum tube technology, the first generation of computers were large, power-hungry devices whose placement resulted in a focal point for data processing and the coinage of the term *data center.*

Computer-Communications Evolution

Originally, access to the computational capability of first-generation computers was through the use of punched cards. After an employee of the organization used a keypunch to create a deck of cards, that card deck was submitted to a window in the data center, typically labeled input/output (I/O) control. An employee behind the window would accept the card deck and complete a form that contained instructions for running the submitted job. The card deck and instructions would then be sent to a person in production control, who would schedule the job and turn it over to operations for execution at a predefined time. Once the job was completed, the card deck and any resulting output would be sent back to I/O control, enabling the job originator to return to the window in the data center to retrieve his or her card deck and the resulting output. With a little bit of luck, programmers might see the results of their efforts on the same day that they submitted their jobs.

Because the computer represented a considerable financial investment for most organizations, it was understandable that these organizations would be receptive to the possibility of extending their computers' accessibility. By the mid-1960s, several computer manufacturers had added remote access capabilities to one or more of their computers.

Remote Batch Transmission

One method of providing remote access was the installation of a batch terminal at a remote location. That terminal was connected via a telephone company–supplied analog leased line and a pair of modems to the computer in the corporate data center.

The first type of batch terminal developed to communicate with a data center computer contained a card reader, a printer, a serial communications adapter, and hard-wired logic in one common housing. The serial communications adapter converted the parallel bits of each internal byte read from the card reader into a serial data stream for transmission. Similarly, the adapter performed a reverse conversion process, converting a sequence of received serial bits into an appropriate number of parallel bits to represent a character internally within the batch terminal. Because the batch terminal was located remotely from the data center, it was often referred to as a *remote batch terminal,* while the process of transmitting data was referred to as *remote batch transmission.* In addition, the use of a remote terminal as a mechanism for grouping card decks of individual jobs, all executed at the remote data center, resulted in the term *remote job entry terminal* being used as a name for this device.

Figure 1.1 illustrates in schematic form the relationships between a batch terminal, transmission line, modems, and the data center computer. Because the transmission line connects a remote batch terminal in one geographic area to a computer located in a different geographic area, Figure 1.1 represents one of the earliest types of wide area data communications networks.

Paralleling the introduction of remote batch terminals was the development of a series of terminal devices, control units, and specialized communications equipment, which resulted in the rapid expansion of interactive computer applications. One of the most prominent collections of products was introduced by the IBM Corporation under the trade name *3270 Information Display System.*

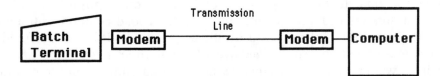

Figure 1.1 Remote batch transmission. The transmission of data from a remote batch terminal represents one of the first examples of wide area data communications networks.

IBM 3270 Information Display System

The IBM 3270 Information Display System was a term originally used to describe a collection of products ranging from interactive terminals that communicate with a computer, referred to as *display stations,* through several types of control units and communications controllers. Later, through the introduction of additional communications products from IBM and numerous third-party vendors and the replacement of previously introduced products, the IBM 3270 Information Display System became more of a networking architecture and strategy rather than a simple collection of products.

First introduced in 1971, the IBM 3270 Information Display System was designed to extend the processing power of the data center computer to remote locations. Because the data center computer typically represented the organization's main computer, the term *mainframe* was coined to refer to a computer with a large processing capability. As the mainframe was primarily designed for data processing, its utilization for supporting communications degraded its performance.

Communications Controller

To offload communications functions from the mainframe, IBM and other computer manufacturers developed hardware to sample communications lines for incoming bits, group bits into bytes, and pass a group of bytes to the mainframe for processing. This hardware also performed a reverse function for data destined from the mainframe to remote devices. When first introduced, such hardware was designed using fixed logic circuitry, and the resulting device was referred to as a *communications controller.* Later, minicomputers were developed to execute communications programs, with the ability to change the functionality of communications support by the modification of software—a considerable enhancement to the capabilities of this series of products. Because both hard-wired communications controllers and programmed minicomputers performing communications offloaded communications processing from the mainframe, the term *front-end processor* evolved to refer to this category of communications equipment. Although most vendors refer to a minicomputer used to offload communications processing from the mainframe as a front-end processor, IBM has retained the term *communications controller,* even though their fixed logic hardware products were replaced over 20 years ago by programmable minicomputers.

Control Units

To reduce the number of controller ports required to support terminals, as well as the amount of cabling between controller ports and terminals, IBM developed *poll and select* software to support its 3270 Information Display System. This software enabled the communications controller to transmit messages from one port to one or more terminals in a predefined group of devices. To share the communications controller port, IBM developed a product called a *control unit,* which acts as an interface between the communications controller and a group of terminals.

In general terms, the communications controller transmits a message to the control unit. The control unit examines the terminal address and retransmits the message to the appropriate terminal. Thus, control units are devices that reduce the number of lines required to link display stations to mainframe computers. Both local and remote control units are available; the key differences between them are the method of attachment to the mainframe computer and the use of intermediate devices between the control unit and the mainframe.

Local control units are usually attached to a channel on the mainframe, whereas remote control units are connected to the mainframe's front-end processor, which is also known as a communications controller in the IBM environment. Because a local control unit is within a limited distance of the mainframe, no intermediate communications devices, such as modems or data service units, are required to connect a local control unit to the mainframe. In comparison, a remote control unit can be located in another building or in a different city; it normally requires the utilization of intermediate communications devices, such as a pair of modems or a pair of data service units, for communications to occur between the control unit and the communications controller. The relationship of local and remote control units to display stations, mainframes, and a communications controller is illustrated in Figure 1.2.

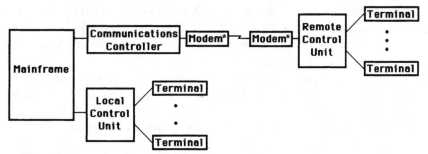

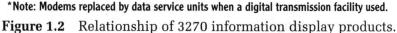
*Note: Modems replaced by data service units when a digital transmission facility used.

Figure 1.2 Relationship of 3270 information display products.

Network Construction

To provide batch and interactive access to the corporate mainframe from remote locations, organizations began to build sophisticated networks. At first, communications equipment such as modems and transmission lines was obtainable only from AT&T and other telephone companies. Beginning in 1974 in the United States with the well-known Carterphone decision, competitive non–telephone company sources for the supply of communications equipment became available. The divestiture of AT&T during the 1980s and the emergence of many local and long-distance communications carriers paved the way for networking personnel to be able to select from among several or even hundreds of vendors for transmission lines and communications equipment.

As organizations began to link additional remote locations to their mainframes, the cost of providing communications began to escalate rapidly. This, in turn, provided the rationale for the development of a series of line-sharing products referred to as *multiplexers* and *concentrators.* Although most organizations operated separate data and voice networks, in the mid-1980s communications carriers began to make available for commercial use high-capacity circuits known as T1 in North America and E1 in Europe. Through the development of T1 and E1 multiplexers, voice, data, and video transmission can share the use of common high-speed circuits. Because the interconnection of corporate offices with communications equipment and facilities normally covers a wide geographical area outside the boundary of one metropolitan area, the resulting network is known as a *wide area network* (WAN).

Figure 1.3 shows an example of a wide area network spanning the continental United States. In this example, regional offices in San Francisco and New York are connected with the corporate headquarters, located in Atlanta, via T1 multiplexers and T1 transmission lines operating at 1.544 Mbps. Assuming that each T1 multiplexer is capable of supporting the direct attachment of a *private branch exchange (PBX),* both voice and data are carried by the T1 circuits between the two regional offices and corporate headquarters. The three T1 circuits can be considered the primary data highway, or *backbone,* of the corporate network.

In addition to the three major corporate sites that require the ability to route voice calls and data between locations, let us assume that the corporation also has three smaller area offices located in Sacramento, California; Macon, Georgia; and New Haven, Connecticut. If these locations only require data terminals to access the corporate network for routing to the computers located in San Francisco and New York, one possible mechanism to provide network support is obtained through the use of tail circuits. These tail circuits could be

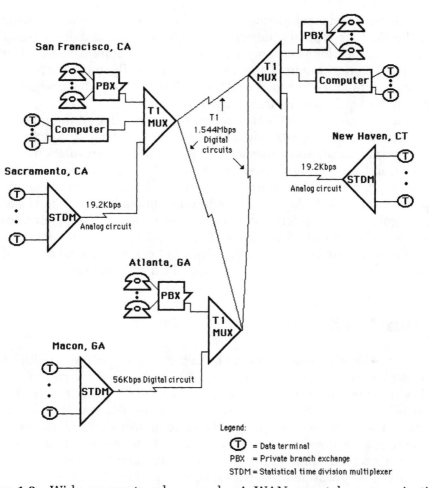

Figure 1.3 Wide area network example. A WAN uses telecommunications lines obtained from one or more communications carriers to connect geographically dispersed locations.

used to connect a *statistical time division multiplexer (STDM)* in each area office, each serving a group of data terminals to the nearest T1 multiplexer, using either analog or digital circuits. The T1 multiplexer would then be configured to route data terminal traffic over the corporate backbone portion of the network to its destination.

Network Characteristics

There are certain characteristics we can associate with wide area networks. First, the WAN is typically designed to connect two or more geographical areas. This connection is accomplished by the lease of transmission facilities from one or more communications vendors. Secondly, most WAN transmission occurs at or under a data rate of 1.544 Mbps or 2.048 Mbps, which are the operating rates of T1 and E1 transmission facilities.

A third characteristic of WANs concerns the regulation of the transmission facilities used for their construction. Most, if not all, transmission facilities marketed by communications carriers are subject to a degree of regulation at the federal, state, and possibly local government levels. Even though we now live in an era of deregulation, carriers must seek approval for many offerings before making new facilities available for use. In addition, although many of the regulatory controls governing the pricing of services were removed, the communications market is still not a truly free market. Thus, regulatory agencies at the federal, state, and local levels still maintain a degree of control over both the offering and pricing of new services and the pricing of existing services.

1.2 Local Area Networks

The origin of local area networks can be traced, in part, to IBM terminal equipment introduced in 1974. At that time, IBM introduced a series of terminal devices designed for use in transaction-processing applications for banking and retailing. What was unique about those terminals was their method of connection: a common cable that formed a loop provided a communications path within a localized geographical area. Unfortunately, limitations in the data transfer rate, incompatibility between individual IBM loop systems, and other problems precluded the widespread adoption of this method of networking. The economics of media sharing and the ability to provide common access to a centralized resource were, however, key advantages, and they resulted in IBM and other vendors investigating the use of different techniques to provide a localized communications capability between different devices. In 1977, Datapoint Corporation began selling its Attached Resource Computer Network (ARCNet), considered by most people to be the first commercial local area networking product. Since then, hundreds of companies have developed local area networking products, and the installed base of terminal devices connected to such networks has increased exponentially. They now number in the hundreds of millions.

Comparison to WANs

Local area networks can be distinguished from wide area networks by geographic area of coverage, data transmission and error rates, ownership, government regulation, and data routing—and, in many instances, by the type of information transmitted over the network.

Geographic Area

The name of each network provides a general indication of the scope of the geographic area in which it can support the interconnection of devices. As its name implies, a LAN is a communications network that covers a relatively small local area. This area can range in scope from a department located on a portion of a floor in an office building, to the corporate staff located on several floors in the building, to several buildings on the campus of a university.

Regardless of the LAN's area of coverage, its geographic boundary will be restricted by the physical transmission limitations of the local area network. These limitations include the cable distance between devices connected to the LAN and the total length of the LAN cable. In comparison, a wide area network can provide communications support to an area ranging in size from a town or city to a state, country, or even a good portion of the entire world. Here, the major factor governing transmission is the availability of communications facilities at different geographic areas that can be interconnected to route data from one location to another.

To better grasp the differences between LANs and WANs, today we can view the LAN as being analogous to our local telephone company, while the WAN can be compared with the long-distance communications carrier. However, this may not be true in the future when local telephone companies obtain permission to offer long-distance service and long-distance communications carriers obtain regulatory approval to offer local telephone service. However, for the present we will presume that telephone support in different cities is provided by the local telephone company in each city. Thus, for calls between cities, the local telephone companies must connect to the long-distance carrier. Similarly, we can have separate LANs in different cities or within different buildings in the same city; however, to interconnect those LANs we would normally require a wide area network.

Data Transmission and Error Rates

Two additional areas that differentiate LANs from WANs and explain the physical limitation of the LAN geographic area of coverage are the data transmission rate and error rate for each type of network. Older LANs, such as the original version of Ethernet and Token-Ring, normally operate at a low megabit-per-second rate, typically ranging from 4 Mbps to 16 Mbps. Recently introduced high-speed Ethernet networks, such as Fast Ethernet and 100VG-AnyLAN, as well as one recently standardized fiber optic–based LAN operate at 100 Mbps, while Gigabit Ethernet provides a transmission rate of 1 Gbps. In comparison, the communications facilities used to construct a major portion of most WANs provide a data transmission rate at or under the T1 and E1 data rates of 1.544 Mbps and 2.048 Mbps.

Because LAN cabling is primarily within a building or over a small geographical area, it is relatively safe from natural phenomena, such as thunderstorms and lightning. This safety enables transmission at a relatively high data rate, resulting in a relatively low error rate. In comparison, because wide area networks are based on the use of communications facilities that are much farther apart and always exposed to the elements, they have a much higher probability of being disturbed by changes in the weather, electronic emissions generated by equipment, or such unforeseen problems as construction workers accidentally causing harm to a communications cable. Because of these factors, the error rate on WANs is considerably higher than the rate experienced on LANs. On most WANs you can expect to experience an error rate between 1 in a million and 1 in 10 million (1×10^6 to 1×10^7) bits. In comparison, the error rate on a typical LAN may exceed that range by one or more orders of magnitude, resulting in an error rate from 1 in 10 million to 1 in 100 million bits.

Ownership

The construction of a wide area network requires the leasing of transmission facilities from one or more communications carriers. Although your organization can elect to purchase or lease communications equipment, the transmission facilities used to connect diverse geographical locations are owned by the communications carrier. In comparison, an organization that installs a local area network normally owns all of the components used to form the network, including the cabling used to form the transmission path between devices.

Regulation

Because wide area networks require transmission facilities that may cross local, state, and national boundaries, they may be subject to a number of governmental regulations at the local, state, and national levels. Most of those regulations govern the services that communications carriers can provide customers and the rates (*tariff*) they can charge for those services. In comparison, regulations affecting local area networks are primarily in the areas of building codes. Such codes regulate the type of wiring that can be installed in a building and whether the wiring must run in a conduit.

Data Routing and Topology

In a local area network data is routed along a path that defines the network. That path is normally a bus, ring, tree, or star structure, and data always flows on that structure. The topology of a wide area network can be much more complex. In fact, many wide area networks resemble a mesh structure, including equipment to reroute data in the event of communications circuit failure or excessive traffic between two locations. Thus, the data flow on a wide area network can change, while the data flow on a local area network primarily follows a single basic route.

Type of Information Carried

The last major difference between local and wide area networks is the type of information carried by each network. Many wide area networks support the simultaneous transmission of voice, data, and video information. In comparison, most local area networks are currently limited to carrying data. In addition, although all wide area networks can be expanded to transport voice, data, and video, many local area networks are restricted by design to the transportation of data. An exception to the preceding is asynchronous transfer mode (ATM), which can provide both a local and wide area network transmission capability. Asynchronous transfer mode was designed to support voice, data, and video from end-to-end, enabling different types of data to be transported from one LAN to another via an ATM WAN. Later in this book we will examine the use of Ethernet and ATM when the latter is used as a backbone for Ethernet. Table 1.1 summarizes the similarities and differences between local and wide area networks.

Utilization Benefits

In its simplest form, a local area network is a cable that provides an electronic highway for the transportation of information to and from different devices connected to the network. Because a LAN provides the capability to route data between devices connected to a common network within a relatively limited distance, numerous benefits can accrue to users of the network. These can include the ability to share the use of peripheral devices, thus obtaining common access to data files and programs, the ability to communicate with other people on the LAN by electronic mail, and the ability to access the larger processing capability of mainframes or minicomputers through common gate-

TABLE 1.1 Comparing LANs and WANs

Characteristic	Local Area Network	Wide Area Network
Geographic area of coverage	Localized to a building, group of buildings, or campus	Can span an area ranging in size from a city to the globe
Data transmission rate	Typically 4 Mbps to 16 Mbps, with high-speed Ethernet and fiber optic-based networks operating at 100 Mbps and 1 Gbps	Normally operate at or below T1 and E1 transmission rates of 1.544 Mbps and 2.048 Mbps
Error rate	1 in 10^7 to 1 in 10^8	1 in 10^6 to 1 in 10^7
Ownership	Usually with the implementor	Communications carrier retains ownership of line facilities
Data routing	Normally follows fixed route	Switching capability of network allows dynamic alteration of data flow
Topology	Usually limited to bus, ring, tree, or star	Virtually unlimited design capability
Type of information carried	Primarily data	Voice, data, and video commonly integrated

ways that link a local area network to larger computer systems. Here, the gateway can be directly cabled to the mainframe or minicomputer if they reside at the same location, or it may be connected remotely via a corporate wide area network.

Peripheral sharing allows network users to access color laser printers, CD-ROM jukebox systems, and other devices that may be needed only a small portion of the time a workstation is in operation. Thus, users of a LAN can obtain access to resources that would probably be too expensive to justify for each individual workstation user.

The ability to access data files and programs from multiple workstations can substantially reduce the cost of software. In addition, shared access to database information allows network users to obtain access to updated files on a real-time basis.

One popular type of application program used on LANs enables users to transfer messages electronically. Commonly referred to as *electronic mail* or *e-mail,* this type of application program can be used to supplement and, in many cases, eliminate the need for paper memoranda.

For organizations with mainframe or minicomputers, a local area network gateway can provide a common method of access to those computers. Without the use of a LAN gateway, each personal computer requiring access to a mainframe or minicomputer would require a separate method of access. This might increase both the complexity and the cost of providing access.

Perhaps the most popular evolving use of LANs is to provide a group of computer users with economical access to the Internet. Instead of having a large number of employees obtain individual modem dial-up or ISDN dial access accounts with an Internet service provider (ISP), it is often more economical to connect an organizational LAN to the Internet via a single connection to an ISP. In addition, the connection to the Internet will usually provide a higher transmission capability than obtainable on an individual user basis. In Chapter 10 we will turn our attention to methods that can be used to connect organizational LANs to the Internet, as well as the use of different products to protect organizational computer facilities from Internet users that have no business accessing those facilities.

Technological Characteristics

Although a local area network is a limited distance transmission system, the variety of options available for constructing such networks is anything but limited. Many of the options available for the construction of local area networks are based on the technological characteristics that govern their operation. These characteristics include different topologies, signaling methods, transmission media, access methods used to transmit data on the network, and the hardware and software required to make the network operate.

Topology

The *topology* of a local area network is the structure or geometric layout of the cable used to connect stations on the network. Unlike conventional data communications networks, which can be configured in a variety of ways with the addition of hardware and software, most local area networks are designed to operate based on the interconnection of stations that follow a specific topology. The most common topologies used in LANs include the loop, bus, ring, star, and tree, as illustrated in Figure 1.4.

Loop   As previously mentioned in this chapter, IBM introduced a series of transaction-processing terminals in 1974 that communicated through the use of a common controller on a cable formed into a loop. This type of topology is illustrated at the top of Figure 1.4.

Loop

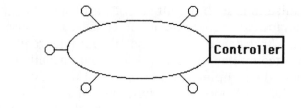

Bus

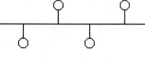

Ring

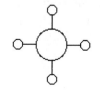

Star

Tree

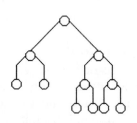

Figure 1.4 Local area network topology. The five most common geometric layouts of LAN cabling form a loop, bus, ring, star, or tree structure.

Because the controller employed a poll-and-select access method, terminal devices connected to the loop required a minimum of intelligence. Although this reduced the cost of terminals connected to the loop, the controller lacked the intelligence to distribute the data flow evenly among terminals. A lengthy exchange between two terminal devices or between the controller and a terminal would thus tend to bog down this type of network structure. A second problem associated with this network structure was the centralized placement of network control in the controller. If the controller failed, the entire network would become inoperative. Due to these problems, the use of loop systems is restricted to several niche areas, and they are essentially considered a derivative of a local area network.

Bus In a bus topology structure, a cable is usually laid out as one long branch, onto which other branches are used to connect each station on the network to the main data highway. Although this type of structure permits any station on the network to talk to any other station, rules are required for recovering from such situations as when two stations attempt to communicate at the same time. Later in this chapter, we will examine the relationships among the network topology, the method employed to access the network, and the transmission medium employed in building the network.

Ring In a ring topology, a single cable that forms the main data highway is shaped into a ring. As with the bus topology, branches are used to connect stations to one another via the ring. A ring topology can thus be considered to be a looped bus. Typically, the access method employed in a ring topology requires data to circulate around the ring, with a special set of rules governing when each station connected to the network can transmit data.

Star The fourth major local area network topology is the star structure, illustrated in the lower portion of Figure 1.4. In a star network, each station on the network is connected to a network controller. Then, access from any one station on the network to any other station can be accomplished through the network controller. Here, the network controller functions like a telephone switchboard, because access from one station to another station on the network can occur only through the central device.

Tree A tree network structure represents a complex bus. In this topology, the common point of communications at the top of the structure is known as the *headend.* From the headend, feeder cables radiate outward to nodes, which in turn provide workstations with access to the network. There may also be a feeder cable route to additional nodes, from which workstations gain access to the network.

Mixed Topologies   Some networks are a mixture of topologies. For example, as previously discussed, a tree structure can be viewed as a series of intercon- nected buses. Another example of the mixture of topologies is a type of Ether- net known as 10BASE-T, which is described in detail in Chapter 3. That network can actually be considered a *star-bus* topology, because up to 16 or 24 devices known as *stations* are first connected to a common device known as a *hub,* which in turn can be connected to other hubs to expand the network.

Comparison of Topologies

Although there are close relationships among the topology of the network, its transmission media, and the method used to access the network, we can examine topology as a separate entity and make several generalized observa- tions. First, in a star network, the failure of the network controller will render the entire network inoperative. This is because all data flow on the network must pass through the network controller. On the positive side, the star topol- ogy normally consists of telephone wires routed to a LAN switch. A local area network that can use in-place twisted-pair telephone wires in this way is sim- ple to implement and usually very economical.

In a ring network, the failure of any node connected to the ring normally inhibits data flow around the ring. Due to the fact that data travels in a circu- lar path on a ring network, any cable break has the same effect as the failure of the network controller in a star-structured network. Because each network sta- tion is connected to the next network station, it is usually easy to install the cable for a ring network. In comparison, a star network may require cabling each section to the network controller if existing telephone wires are not available, and this can result in the installation of very long cable runs.

In a bus-structured network, data is normally transmitted from a single sta- tion to all other stations located on the network, with a destination address appended to each transmitted data block. As part of the access protocol, only the station with the destination address in the transmitted data block will respond to the data. This transmission concept means that a break in the bus affects only network stations on one side of the break that wish to communi- cate with stations on the other side of the break. Thus, unless a network sta- tion functioning as the primary network storage device becomes inoperative, a failure in a bus-structured network is usually less serious than a failure in a ring network. However, some local area networks, such as Token-Ring and FDDI, were designed to overcome the effect of certain types of cable failures.

Token-Ring networks include a backup path which, when manually placed into operation, may be able to overcome the effect of a cable failure between hubs (referred to as *multistation access units* or *MAUs*). In an FDDI network, a second ring can be activated automatically as part of a self-healing process to overcome the effect of a cable break.

A tree-structured network is similar to a star-structured network in that all signals flow through a common point. In the tree-structured network, the common signal point is the headend. Failure of the headend renders the network inoperative. This network structure requires the transmission of information over relatively long distances. For example, communications between two stations located at opposite ends of the network would require a signal to propagate twice the length of the longest network segment. Due to the propagation delay associated with the transmission of any signal, the use of a tree structure may result in a response time delay for transmissions between the nodes that are most distant from the headend.

Although the first type of Ethernet network was based on a bus-structured topology, other types of Ethernet networks incorporate the use of different topologies. Today you can select bus-based, star-bus, or tree-structured Ethernet networks. Thus, you can select a particular type of Ethernet network to meet a particular topology requirement.

Signaling Methods

The *signaling method* used by a local area network refers to both the way data is encoded for transmission and the frequency spectrum of the media. To a large degree, the signaling method is related to the use of the frequency spectrum of the media.

Broadband versus Baseband

Two signaling methods used by LANs are broadband and baseband. In *broadband signaling,* the bandwidth of the transmission medium is subdivided by frequency to form two or more subchannels, with each subchannel permitting data transfer to occur independently of data transfer on another subchannel. In *baseband signaling,* only one signal is transmitted on the medium at any point in time.

Broadband is more complex than baseband, because it requires information to be transmitted via the modulation of a carrier signal, thus requiring the use of special types of modems, as discussed later in this chapter.

Figure 1.5 illustrates the difference between baseband and broadband signaling with respect to channel capacity. It should be noted that although a twisted-pair wire system can be used to transmit both voice and data, the data

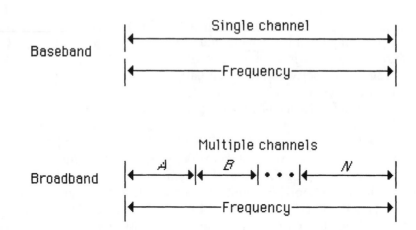

Figure 1.5 Baseband versus broadband signaling. In baseband signaling the entire frequency bandwidth is used for one channel. In comparison, in broadband signaling the channel is subdivided by frequency into many subchannels.

transmission is baseband, because only one channel is normally used for data. In comparison, a broadband system on coaxial cable can be designed to carry voice and several subchannels of data, as well as fax and video transmission.

Broadband Signaling   A broadband local area network uses analog technology, in which high-frequency (HF) modems operating at or above 4 kHz place carrier signals onto the transmission medium. The carrier signals are then modified—a process known as *modulation,* which impresses information onto the carrier. Other modems connected to a broadband LAN reconvert the analog signal block into its original digital format—a process known as *demodulation.*

Figure 1.6 illustrates the three primary methods of data encoding used by broadband analog systems: amplitude, frequency, and phase modulation. The most common modulation method used on broadband LANs is *frequency shift keying (FSK),* in which two different frequencies are used, one to represent a binary 1 and another frequency to represent a binary 0.

Another popular modulation method uses a combination of amplitude and phase shift changes to represent pairs of bits. Referred to as *amplitude modulation phase shift keying (AM PSK),* this method of analog signaling is also known as *duobinary signaling* because each analog signal represents a pair of digital bits.

Because it is not economically feasible to design amplifiers that boost signal strength to operate in both directions, broadband LANs are unidirectional. To provide a bidirectional information transfer capability, a broadband LAN uses

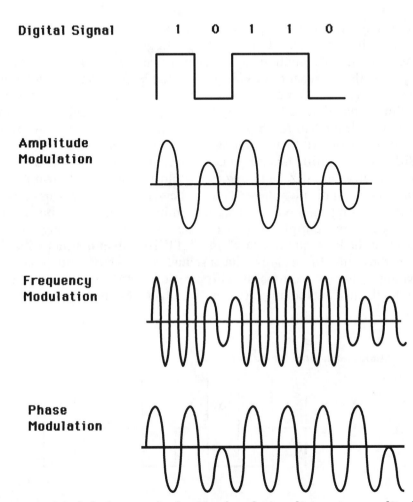

Figure 1.6 Modulation methods. Baseband signaling uses amplitude, frequency, or phase modulation, or a combination of modulation techniques to represent digital information.

one channel for inbound traffic and another channel for outbound traffic. These channels can be defined by differing frequencies or obtained by the use of a dual cable.

Baseband Signaling In comparison to broadband local area networks, which use analog signaling, baseband LANs use digital signaling to convey information.

To understand the digital signaling methods used by most baseband LANs, let us first review the method of digital signaling used by computers and terminal devices. In that signaling method, a positive voltage is used to represent a binary 1, while the absence of voltage (0 volts) is used to represent a binary 0. If two successive 1 bits or 0 bits occur, two successive bit positions then have a similar positive voltage level or a similar zero voltage level. Because the signal goes from 0 to some positive voltage and does not return to 0 between successive binary 1s, it is referred to as a *unipolar nonreturn to zero signal (NRZ)*. This signaling technique is illustrated at the top of Figure 1.7.

Although unipolar NRZ signaling is easy to implement, its use for transmission has several disadvantages. One of the major disadvantages associated with this signaling method involves determining where one bit ends and another begins. For example, if you examine the top portion of Figure 1.7 you will note that the bit sequences "00" and "111" remain at distinct voltage levels. Thus, the ability to recognize that a sequence of two or more pulses of the same value occurred requires synchronization between a transmitter and receiver by the use of clocking circuitry, which can be relatively expensive.

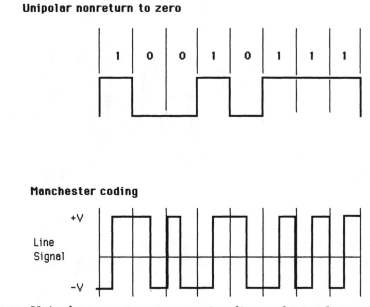

Figure 1.7 Unipolar nonreturn to zero signaling and Manchester coding. In Manchester coding, a timing transition occurs in the middle of each bit and the line code maintains an equal amount of positive and negative voltage.

To overcome the need for clocking, baseband LANs use *Manchester* or *Differential Manchester encoding.* In Manchester encoding, a timing transition always occurs in the middle of each bit, while an equal amount of positive and negative voltage is used to represent each bit. This coding technique provides a good timing signal for clock recovery from received data, due to its timing transitions. In addition, because the Manchester code always maintains an equal amount of positive and negative voltage, it prevents direct current (DC) voltage buildup, enabling repeaters to be spaced farther apart from one another.

The lower portion of Figure 1.7 illustrates an example of Manchester coding. Note that a low to high voltage transition represents a binary 1, while a high to low voltage transition represents a binary 0. Under Differential Manchester encoding, the voltage transition is used only to provide clocking. The encoding of a binary 0 or 1 is represented by the presence or absence of a transition at the beginning of each bit period. Refer to Chapter 4 for specific information concerning Manchester encoding on different types of Ethernet networks.

Along with providing users with a choice of topologies, Ethernet also provides a choice of signaling methods. Although most types of Ethernet networks use baseband signaling, a broadband Ethernet is also available. In fact, you can connect baseband- and broadband-based Ethernet networks to satisfy different organizational requirements. Refer to Chapter 3 for specific information concerning the signaling methods used by different Ethernet networks and the hardware components used to construct and interconnect such networks.

Transmission Medium

The transmission medium used in a local area network can range in scope from twisted-pair wire, such as is used in conventional telephone lines, to coaxial cable, fiber-optic cable, and electromagnetic waves such as those used by FM radio and infrared. Each transmission medium has a number of advantages and disadvantages. The primary differences between media are their cost and ease of installation; the bandwidth of the cable, which may or may not permit several transmission sessions to occur simultaneously; the maximum speed of communications permitted; and the geographic scope of the network that the medium supports.

Twisted-Pair Wire

In addition to being the most inexpensive medium available for LAN installations, twisted-pair wire is very easy to install. Since this wiring uses the same RJ11 and RJ45 modular connectors as a telephone system, once a wire is cut and a connector fastened, the attachment of the connector to network devices is extremely simple. Normally, a screwdriver and perhaps a pocket knife are the only tools required for the installation of twisted-pair wire. Anyone who has hooked up a pair of speakers to a stereo set has the ability to install this transmission medium.

Although inexpensive and easy to install, unshielded twisted-pair (UTP) wire is very susceptible to noise generated by fluorescent light ballasts and electrical machinery. In addition, a length of twisted-pair wire acts as an antenna; however, the twists serve as a mechanism to partially counteract this antenna effect. Unfortunately, due to the law of physics, the longer the wire length, the greater the noise it gathers. At a certain length, the received noise will obliterate the signal, which attenuates or decreases in strength as it propagates along the length of the wire. This noise can affect the error rate of data transmitted on the network, although lead-shielded twisted-pair (STP) cable can be employed to provide the cable with a high degree of immunity to the line noise and enable extended transmission distances. In Chapter 3 we will examine a building cabling standard and the various categories of twisted-pair that can support different transmission rates which, in turn, enable different types of Ethernet networks to be supported.

Because the bandwidth of twisted-pair cable is considerably less than coaxial or fiber-optic cable, normally only one signal is transmitted on this cable at a time. As previously explained, this signaling technique is known as baseband signaling and should be compared with the broadband signaling capability of coaxial and fiber-optic cable.

Although a twisted-pair wire system can be used to transmit both voice and data, the data transmission is baseband because only one channel is normally used for data. In comparison, a broadband system on coaxial or fiber-optic cable can be designed to carry voice and several subchannels of data, as well as fax and video transmission. Other constraints of unshielded twisted-pair wire are the rate at which data can flow on the network and the distance it can flow. Although data rates up to 1 gigabit per second (Gbps) can be achieved, normally local area networks employing UTP wiring operate at a lower data rate. In addition, UTP systems normally cover a limited distance, measured in terms of several hundred to a few thousand feet, while coaxial and fiber-optic cable–based systems may be limited in terms of miles. Extending transmission distances over twisted-pair wire requires the periodic insertion of repeaters into the cable. A repeater receives a digital signal and then regenerates it; hence, it is also known as a *data regenerator*.

Coaxial Cable

At the center of a coaxial cable is a copper wire, which is covered by an insulator known as a *dielectric*. An overlapping woven copper mesh surrounds the dielectric, and the mesh, in turn, is covered by a protective jacket consisting of polyethylene or aluminum. Figure 1.8 illustrates the composition of a typical coaxial cable; however, it should be noted that over 100 types of coaxial cable are currently marketed. The key differences between such cables involve the number of conductors contained in the cable, the dielectric employed, and the type of protective jacket and material used to provide strength to the cable so it can be pulled through conduits without breaking.

Two basic types of coaxial cable are used in local area networks. The type of cable used is based on the transmission technique employed: baseband or broadband signaling. Both cable types are much more expensive than twisted-pair wire; however, the greater frequency bandwidth of coaxial cable permits higher data rates for longer distances than you can obtain over twisted-pair wire.

Normally, 50-ohm coaxial cable is used in baseband networks, while 75-ohm cable is used in broadband networks. The latter coaxial is identical to that used in cable television (CATV) applications, including the coaxial cable used in a home. Data rates on baseband networks using coaxial cable range from 50 to 100 Mbps. With broadband transmissions, data rates up to and including 400 Mbps are obtainable.

A coaxial cable with a polyethylene jacket is normally used for baseband signaling. Data is transmitted from stations on the network to the baseband cable in a digital format, and the connection from each station to the cable is accomplished by the use of a simple coaxial T-connector. Because data on a baseband network travels in a digital form, those signals can be easily regen-

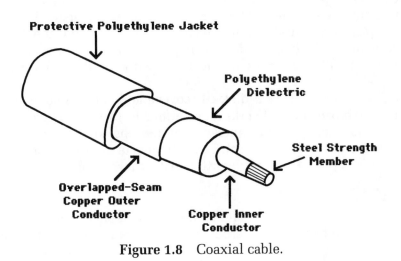

Figure 1.8   Coaxial cable.

erated by the use of a device known as a *line driver* or *data regenerator*. The line driver or data regenerator is a low-cost device that is constructed to look for a pulse rise, and upon detecting the occurrence of the rise, it will disregard the entire pulse and regenerate an entirely new pulse. Thus, you can install low-cost line drivers into a baseband coaxial network to extend the distance over which transmission can occur on the cable. Typically, a coaxial cable baseband system can cover an area of several miles, and may contain hundreds to thousands of stations on the network.

Obtaining independent subchannels defined by separate frequencies on coaxial cable broadband transmission requires the translation of the digital signals from workstations into appropriate frequencies. This translation process is accomplished by the use of radio-frequency (RF) modems, which modulate the digital data into analog signals and then convert or demodulate received analog signals into digital signals. Because signals are transmitted at one frequency and received at a different frequency, a headend or frequency translator is also required for broadband transmission on coaxial cable. This device is also known as a *remodulator,* as it simply converts the signals from one subchannel to another subchannel.

The need for modems and frequency translators normally makes broadband transmission more expensive than baseband. Although the ability of broadband to support multiple channels provides it with an aggregate data transmission capacity that exceeds baseband, baseband transmission generally permits a higher per-channel data flow. While this is an important consideration for mainframe-to-mainframe communications when massive amounts of data must be moved, for most personal computer interactive screen sessions and file transfer operations, the speed of either baseband or broadband transmission should be sufficient. This fact may be better understood by comparing the typical transmission rates obtainable on baseband and broadband networks to drive a high-speed dot matrix printer and the differences between the time required to transmit data on the network and the time required to print the data.

Typical transmission speeds on the first generation of commonly employed baseband and broadband networks range from 2 to 16 Mbps. In comparison, a high-speed dot matrix printer operating at 120 cps would require approximately 200 seconds to print 1 second's worth of data transmitted at 2 Mbps, or 1600 seconds to print 1 second's worth of data transmitted at 16 Mbps.

Fiber-Optic Cable

Fiber-optic cable is a transmission medium for light energy, and as such, provides a very high bandwidth, permitting data rates ranging up to billions of bits per second. The fiber-optic cable has a thin core of glass or plastic, which is surrounded by a protective shield. Several of these shielded fibers are bundled in a jacket, with a central member of aluminum or steel employed for tensile strength.

Digital data represented by electrical energy must be converted into light energy for transmission on a fiber-optic cable. This is normally accomplished by a low-power laser, or through the use of a light-emitting diode and appropriate circuitry. At the receiver, light energy must be reconverted into electrical energy. Normally, a device known as a *photo detector,* as well as appropriate circuitry to regenerate the digital pulses and an amplifier, are used to convert the received light energy into its original digital format.

In addition to their high bandwidth, fiber-optic cables offer users several additional advantages over conventional transmission media. Because data travels in the form of light, it is immune to electrical interference and to the building codes that often require expensive conduits for conventional cables. Similarly, fiber-optic cable can be installed through areas where the flow of electricity could be dangerous.

Because most fibers provide only a single, unidirectional transmission path, a minimum of two cables is normally required to connect all transmitters to all receivers on a network built using fiber-optic cable. Due to the higher cost of fiber-optic cable, the dual cable requirement of fiber cables can make them relatively expensive in comparison with other types of cable. In addition, until recently it was very difficult to splice fiber-optic cable, and sophisticated equipment and skilled installers were required to implement a fiber-optic-based network. Similarly, once this type of network was installed, until recently it was difficult to modify the network. Recent advances in fiber transmission through the use of wavelength division multiplexing enables two or more transmission paths separated by the frequency of light to be carried on a common optical cable. Although wavelength division multiplexing is being used in the long-distance fiber backbones of communications carriers to increase the transmission capacity of their infrastructure, the cost of electro-optical transmitter receivers to support this technology usually precludes its use with local area networks.

Currently, the cost of the cable and the degree of difficulty of installation and modification make the utilization of fiber-optic-based local area networks impractical for many commercial applications. Today, the primary use of fiber-optic cable is to extend the distance between stations on a network or to connect two distant networks to one another. The device used to connect a length of fiber-optic cable into the LAN or between LANs is a *fiber-optic repeater.* The repeater converts the electrical energy of signals flowing on the

LAN into light energy for transmission on the fiber-optic cable. At the end of the fiber-optic cable, a second repeater converts light energy back into electrical energy.

Another common use of fiber-optic cable occurs in constructing FDDI networks. Such networks are now primarily used to function as a backbone data highway, connecting two or more local area networks. Although a few organizations have extended fiber to the desktop, its cost as well as the cost of FDDI components currently precludes its widespread adoption as a replacement for other types of local area networks. With the declining cost of the fiber-optic cable and fiber-optic components, and the continued introduction of improvements that simplify the installation and modification of networks using this type of cable, the next few years may bring a profound movement toward the utilization of fiber optics throughout local area networks.

Ethernet can be categorized as a network for everyone, because of its support of multiple topologies, signaling methods, and transmission media. In addition to twisted-pair and coaxial cable–based Ethernet networks, you can also extend the transmission distance of such networks by the use of fiber-optic cable. Thus, the old adage from a presidential campaign, "a choice not an echo," is highly relevant to Ethernet networks.

Access Method

If the topology of a local area network can be compared with a data highway, then the access method might be viewed as the set of rules that enable data from one workstation to successfully reach its destination via the data highway. Without such rules, it is quite possible for two messages sent by two different workstations to collide, with the result that neither message reaches its destination. The three access methods primarily employed in local area networks are carrier-sense multiple access/collision detection (CSMA/CD), carrier-sense multiple access/collision avoidance (CSMA/CA), and token passing. Each of these access methods is uniquely structured to address the previously mentioned collision and data-destination problems. A fourth access method, referred to as *demand priority,* is applicable to a high-speed Ethernet network referred to as 100VG-AnyLAN. Through the use of a demand-priority access method you can support either existing Ethernet CSMA/CD or token passing networks at 100 Mbps.

Before discussing how access methods work, let us first examine the two basic types of devices that can be attached to a local area network to gain an appreciation for the work that the access method must accomplish.

Listeners and Talkers

We can categorize each device by its operating mode as being a *listener* or a *talker*. Some devices, like printers, only receive data, and thus operate only as listeners. Other devices, such as personal computers, can either transmit or receive data and are capable of operating in both modes. In a baseband signaling environment where only one channel exists, or on an individual channel on a broadband system, if several talkers wish to communicate at the same time, a collision will occur. Therefore, a scheme must be employed to define when each device can talk and, in the event of a collision, what must be done to keep it from happening again.

For data to reach its destination correctly, each listener must have a unique address, and its network equipment must be designed to respond to a message on the net only when it recognizes its address. The primary goals in the design of an access method are to minimize the potential for data collision, to provide a mechanism for corrective action when data does collide, and to ensure that an addressing scheme is employed to enable messages to reach their destinations.

Carrier-Sense Multiple Access with Collision Detection (CSMA/CD)

CSMA/CD can be categorized as a *listen-then-send* access method. CSMA/CD is one of the earliest developed access techniques and is the technique used in Ethernet. Ethernet represents a local area network developed by Xerox Corporation; its technology is now licensed to many companies, and was standardized by the Institute of Electrical and Electronics Engineers (IEEE) under its 802.3 standard.

Under the CSMA/CD concept, when a station has data to send, it first listens to determine whether any other station on the network is talking. The fact that the channel is idle is determined in one of two ways, based on whether the network is broadband or baseband.

In a broadband network, the fact that a channel is idle is determined by *carrier sensing,* or noting the absence of a carrier tone on the cable.

Ethernet, like other baseband systems, uses one channel for data transmission and does not employ a carrier. Instead, Ethernet encodes data using a Manchester code, in which a timing transition always occurs in the middle of each bit, as illustrated in Figure 1.7. Although Ethernet does not transmit data via a carrier, the continuous transitions of the Manchester code can be considered as equivalent to a carrier signal. Carrier sensing on a baseband network is thus performed by monitoring the line for activity. Manchester coding is used by Ethernet at data rates up to 10 Mbps. At operating rates above 10

Mbps, different encoding techniques are used, which provide a higher level of efficiency than Manchester's 50-percent level of efficiency.

In a CSMA/CD network, if the channel is busy, the station will wait until it becomes idle before transmitting data. Because it is possible for two stations to listen at the same time and discover an idle channel, it is also possible that the two stations could then transmit at the same time. When this situation arises, a collision will occur. Upon sensing that a collision has occurred, a delay scheme will be employed to prevent a repetition of the collision. Typically, each station will use either a randomly generated or a predefined time-out period before attempting to retransmit the message that collided. Because this access method requires hardware capable of detecting the occurrence of a collision, additional circuitry required to perform collision detection adds to the cost of such hardware.

Figure 1.9 illustrates a CSMA/CD bus–based local area network. Each workstation is attached to the transmission medium, such as coaxial cable, by a device known as a *bus interface unit (BIU)*. To obtain an overview of the operation of a CSMA/CD network, assume that station A is currently using the channel and stations C and D wish to transmit. The BIUs connecting stations C and D to the network listen to the channel and note that it is busy. Once station A completes its transmission, stations C and D attempt to gain access to the channel. Because station A's signal takes longer to propagate down the

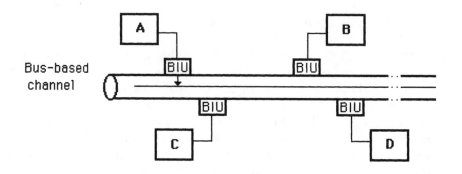

BIU = Bus interface unit

Figure 1.9 CSMA/CD network operation. In a CSMA/CD network, as the distance between workstations increases, the resulting increase in propagation delay time increases the probability of collisions.

cable to station D than to station C, C's BIU notices that the channel is free slightly before station D's BIU. However, as station C gets ready to transmit, station D now assumes that the channel is free. Within an infinitesimal period of time, C starts transmission, followed by D, resulting in a collision. Here, the collision is a function of the propagation delay of the signal and the distance between two competing stations. CSMA/CD networks therefore work better as the main cable length decreases.

The CSMA/CD access technique is best suited for networks with intermittent transmission, because an increase in traffic volume causes a corresponding increase in the probability of the cable being occupied when a station wishes to talk. In addition, as traffic volume builds under CSMA/CD, throughput may decline, because there will be longer waits to gain access to the network, as well as additional time-outs required to resolve collisions that occur.

Carrier-Sense Multiple Access with Collision Avoidance (CSMA/CA)

CSMA/CA represents a modified version of the CSMA/CD access technique. Under the CSMA/CA access technique, each of the hardware devices attached to the talkers on the network estimates when a collision is likely to occur and avoids transmission during those times. Because this technique eliminates the requirement for collision-detection hardware, the cost of hardware to implement this access technique is usually less than CSMA/CD hardware. Unfortunately, time delays associated with collision avoidance usually result in a lower level of throughput than that obtainable with CSMA/CD-based networks, and this limitation has made CSMA/CA-based networks less popular.

Token Passing

In a *token-passing* access method, each time the network is turned on, a token is generated. The token, consisting of a unique bit pattern, travels the length of the network, either around a ring or along the length of a bus. When a station on the network has data to transmit, it must first seize a free token. On a Token-Ring network, the token is then transformed to indicate that it is in use. Information is added to produce a frame, which represents data being transmitted from one station to another. During the time the token is in use, other stations on the network remain idle, eliminating the possibility of collisions. Once the transmission is completed, the token is converted back into its original form by the station that transmitted the frame, and becomes available for use by the next station on the network.

Figure 1.10 illustrates the general operation of a token-passing Token-Ring network using a ring topology. Because a station on the network can only transmit when it has a free token, token passing eliminates the requirement

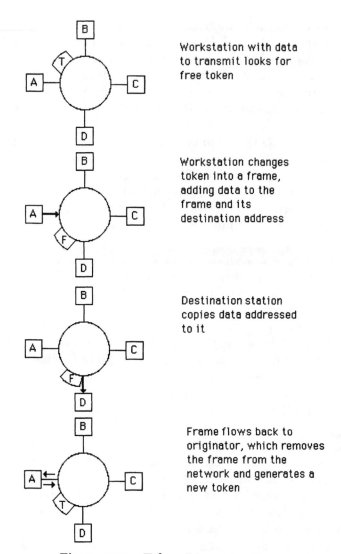

Workstation with data
to transmit looks for
free token

Workstation changes
token into a frame,
adding data to the
frame and its
destination address

Destination station
copies data addressed
to it

Frame flows back to
originator, which removes
the frame from the
network and generates a
new token

Figure 1.10   Token-Ring operation.

for collision detection hardware. Due to the dependence of the network on the token, the loss of a station can bring the entire network down. To avoid this, the design characteristics of Token-Ring networks include circuitry that automatically removes a failed or failing station from the network, as well as other self-healing features. This additional capability is costly: a Token-Ring

TABLE 1.2 Technical Characteristics of LANs

Characteristic	Transmission Medium			
	Twisted-pair wire	Baseband coaxial cable	Baseband coaxial cable	Fiber-optic cable
Topology	Bus, star, or ring	Bus or ring	Bus or ring	Bus, star, or ring
Channels	Single channel	Single channel	Multichannel	Single, multichannel
Data rate	Normally 4 to 16 Mbps; up to 1000 Mbps obtainable	Normally 2 to 10 Mbps; up to 100 Mbps obtainable	Up to 400 Mbps	Up to GMbps
Maximum nodes on net	Usually <255	Usually <1024	Several thousand	Several thousand
Geographical coverage	Thousands of feet	Miles	Tens of miles	Tens of miles
Major advantages	Low cost; may be able to use existing wiring	Low cost; simple to install	Supports voice, data, video applications simultaneously	Supports voice, data, video applications simultaneously
Major disadvantages	Limited bandwidth; requires conduits; low immunity to noise	Low immunity to noise	High cost; difficult to install; requires RF modems and headend	Cable cost; difficult to splice

adapter card is typically priced at two to three times the cost of an Ethernet adapter card.

Due to the variety of transmission media, network structures, and access methods, there is no one best network for all users. Table 1.2 provides a generalized comparison of the advantages and disadvantages of the technical characteristics of local area networks, using the transmission medium as a frame of reference.

1.3 Why Ethernet

After reviewing the basic characteristics of various local area networks, you will note that they present a considerable range of technological characteristics. You can select a network based on its topology, access method, signaling method, and/or support of a particular type of transmission medium.

Although there is no one best network for all users, Ethernet represents a diverse mixture of technological characteristics. As such, it provides many more potential networking solutions to user communications requirements than other types of local area networks.

In addition to supporting a broad range of technological characteristics, Ethernet is a declining-cost network. Due to economies of manufacture, as well as the recent support of twisted-pair wiring, Ethernet networks can be established for a fraction of the cost of other types of local area networks. In fact, by early 1998, adapter cards supporting 10 Mbps Ethernet that were designed for use in IBM PCs and compatible personal computers could be obtained for under $20, while 10/100 Mbps adapter cards could be obtained for under $125. In addition, several notebook and laptop computer vendors were incorporating Ethernet chip sets into their portable computers, enabling computer users who want to transfer files to other computers and printers connected to the network to simply plug their computer into a telephone jack upon returning to the office.

Although the previously mentioned reasons are significant, the scalability of Ethernet and the product development effort of industry provide two additional reasons to use Ethernet. Concerning scalability, you can obtain interoperable Ethernet equipment that enables you to operate a network originally at 10 Mbps and have the option of using a variety of vendor products to upgrade your network to 100 Mbps or even 1 Gbps. Concerning product development, over the past decade a large number of products reached the market that enable Ethernet users to boost the performance and management of their networks. Perhaps the most versatile product is actually a series of Ethernet switches that enable multiple cross-connections between workstations and servers to occur simultaneously, as well as enable the transmission on multiple ports to be aggregated, a technique referred to as a *fat pipe.* Although your organization may not currently require the ability to transmit data at 100 Mbps or 1 Gbps nor require the ability to aggregate multiple paths at those data rates, the capability is there if you should need it in the future. For other organizations such as Internet service providers that use a local area network as a gateway for subscribers to access the Internet, the ability to upgrade to 1 Gbps can be a significant benefit. Due to this capability Ethernet is truly a "people's network," able to satisfy the networking requirements of the small business, large corporation, university, and government.

chapter two

Networking Standards

Standards can be viewed as the "glue" that binds hardware and software from different vendors so they can operate together. The importance of standards and the work of standards organizations have proved essential for the growth of both local and worldwide communications. In the United States and many other countries, national standards organizations have defined physical and operational characteristics that enable vendors to manufacture equipment compatible with line facilities provided by communications carriers, as well as equipment produced by other vendors. At the international level, standards organizations have promulgated several series of communications-related recommendations. These recommendations, while not mandatory, have become highly influential on a worldwide basis for the development of equipment and facilities, and have been adopted by hundreds of public companies and communications carriers.

In addition to national and international standards, a series of de facto standards has evolved through the licensing of technology among companies. These de facto standards have facilitated, for example, the development of communications software for use on personal computers. Today, communications software can control modems manufactured by hundreds of vendors, because most modems are now constructed to respond to a core set of uniform control codes.

2.1 Standards Organizations

In this chapter, we will first focus our attention on two national and two international standards organizations. The national standards organizations we will briefly discuss in this section are the American National Standards Institute (ANSI) and the Institute of Electrical and Electronics Engineers (IEEE). The work of both organizations has been a guiding force in the rapid expansion in the use of local area networks due to a series of standards they have developed. Due to the importance of the work of the IEEE in developing LAN standards, we will examine those standards as a separate entity in the next section in this chapter. In the international arena, we will discuss the role of the International Telecommunications Union (ITU), formerly known as the Consultative Committee for International Telephone and Telegraph (CCITT), and the International Standards Organization (ISO), both of which have developed numerous standards to facilitate the operation of local and wide area networks.

Because of the importance of the ISO's Open Systems Interconnection (OSI) Reference Model and the IEEE's 802 Committee lower layer standards, we will examine each as a separate entity in this chapter. Because we must understand the OSI Reference Model before examining the effect of the efforts of the IEEE and ANSI upon the lower layers of that model, we will look at the OSI Reference Model before examining the Reference Model layer subdivisions performed by the IEEE and ANSI.

National Standards Organizations

The two national standards organizations we will briefly discuss are the American National Standards Institute and the Institute of Electrical and Electronics Engineers. In the area of local area networking standards, both ANSI and the IEEE work in conjunction with the ISO to standardize LAN technology.

The ISO delegated the standardization of local area networking technology to ANSI. The American National Standards Institute, in turn, delegated lower-speed LAN standards—initially defined as operating rates at and below 50 Mbps—to the IEEE. This resulted in ANSI's developing standards for the 100-Mbps fiber distributed data interface (FDDI), while the IEEE developed standards for Ethernet, Token-Ring, and other LANs. Because the IEEE developed standards for 10-Mbps Ethernet, that organization was tasked with the responsibility for modifications to that LAN technology. This resulted in the IEEE becoming responsible for the standardization of high-speed Ethernet to include isoENET, 100BASE-T, and 100VG-AnyLAN, the latter two representing 100-Mbps LAN operating rates. In addition, when this book revision occurred the IEEE was in the process of finalizing its 802.3z standard for Gigabit Ethernet.

Once the IEEE develops and approves a standard, that standard is sent to ANSI for review. If ANSI approves the standard, it is then sent to the ISO. Then, the ISO solicits comments from all member countries to ensure that the standard will work at the international level, resulting in an IEEE- or ANSI-developed standard becoming an ISO standard.

ANSI

The principal standards-forming body in the United States is the American National Standards Institute (ANSI). Located in New York City, this nonprofit, nongovernmental organization was founded in 1918 and functions as the representative of the United States to the ISO.

American National Standards Institute standards are developed through the work of its approximately 300 Standards Committees, and from the efforts of associated groups such as the Electronic Industry Association (EIA). Recognizing the importance of the computer industry, ANSI established its X3 Standards Committee in 1960. That committee consists of 25 technical committees, each assigned to develop standards for a specific technical area. One of those technical committees is the X3S3 committee, more formally known as the Data Communications Technical Committee. This committee was responsible for the ANSI X3T9.5 standard that governs FDDI operations, and that is now recognized as the ISO 9314 standard.

IEEE

The Institute of Electrical and Electronics Engineers (IEEE) is a U.S.-based engineering society that is very active in the development of data communications standards. In fact, the most prominent developer of local area networking standards is the IEEE, whose subcommittee 802 began its work in 1980 before they had even established a viable market for the technology.

The IEEE Project 802 efforts are concentrated on the physical interface between network devices and the procedures and functions required to establish, maintain, and release connections among them. These procedures include defining data formats, error control procedures, and other control activities governing the flow of information. This focus of the IEEE actually represents the lowest two layers of the ISO model, physical and link, which are discussed later in this chapter.

International Standards Organizations

Two important international standards organizations are the International Telecommunications Union (ITU), formerly known as the Consultative Committee for International Telephone and Telegraph (CCITT), and the International Standards Organization (ISO). The ITU can be considered a governmental body, because it functions under the auspices of an agency of the United Nations. Although the ISO is a nongovernmental agency, its work in the field of data communications is well recognized.

ITU

The International Telecommunications Union (ITU) is a specialized agency of the United Nations headquartered in Geneva, Switzerland. The ITU has direct responsibility for developing data communications standards and consists of 15 study groups, each with a specific area of responsibility. Although the CCITT was renamed as the ITU in 1994, it continues to be recognized by its former mnemonic. Thus, the remainder of this book will refer to this standards organization by its new set of commonly recognized initials.

The work of the ITU is performed on a four-year cycle known as a study period. At the conclusion of each study period, a plenary session occurs. During the plenary session, the work of the ITU during the previous four years is reviewed, proposed recommendations are considered for adoption, and items to be investigated during the next four-year cycle are considered.

The ITU's tenth plenary session met in 1992 and its eleventh session occurred during 1996. Although approval of recommended standards is not intended to be mandatory, ITU recommendations have the effect of law in some Western European countries, and many of its recommendations have been adopted by communications carriers and vendors in the United States. Perhaps the best-known set of ITU recommendations is its V-series, which describes the operation of many different modem features—for example, data compression and transmission error detection and correction.

ISO

The International Standards Organization (ISO) is a nongovernmental entity that has consultative status within the UN Economic and Social Council. The goal of the ISO is to "promote the development of standards in the world with a view to facilitating international exchange of goods and services."

The membership of the ISO consists of the national standards organizations of most countries. There are approximately 100 countries currently participating in its work.

Perhaps the most notable achievement of the ISO in the field of communications is its development of the seven-layer Open Systems Interconnection (OSI) Reference Model.

2.2 The ISO Reference Model

The International Standards Organization (ISO) established a framework for standardizing communications systems called the Open Systems Interconnection (OSI) Reference Model. The OSI architecture defines the communications process as a set of seven layers, with specific functions isolated and associated with each layer. Each layer, as illustrated in Figure 2.1, covers lower layer processes, effectively isolating them from higher layer functions. In this way, each layer performs a set of functions necessary to provide a set of services to the layer above it.

Layer isolation permits the characteristics of a given layer to change without impacting the remainder of the model, provided that the supporting services remain the same. One major advantage of this layered approach is that users can mix and match OSI-conforming communications products, and thus tailor their communications systems to satisfy particular networking requirements.

The OSI Reference Model, while not completely viable with many current network architectures, offers the potential to connect networks and networking devices together to form integrated networks, while using equipment from different vendors. This interconnectivity potential will be of substantial benefit to both users and vendors. For users, interconnectivity will remove the shackles that in many instances tie them to a particular vendor. For vendors, the ability to easily interconnect their products will provide them with access to a larger market. The importance of the OSI model is such that it was adopted by the ITU as Recommendation X.200.

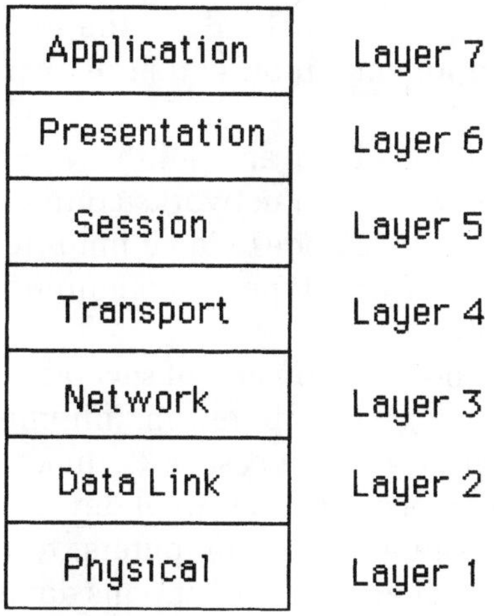

Application	Layer 7
Presentation	Layer 6
Session	Layer 5
Transport	Layer 4
Network	Layer 3
Data Link	Layer 2
Physical	Layer 1

Figure 2.1   ISO Reference Model.

Layered Architecture

As previously discussed, the OSI Reference Model is based on the establishment of a layered, or partitioned, architecture. This partitioning effort is derived from the scientific process, in which complex problems are subdivided into several simpler tasks.

As a result of the application of a partitioning approach to communications network architecture, the communications process was subdivided into seven distinct partitions, called *layers*. Each layer consists of a set of functions designed to provide a defined series of services. For example, the functions associated with the physical connection of equipment to a network are referred to as the *physical layer.*

With the exception of layers 1 and 7, each layer is bounded by the layers above and below it. Layer 1, the physical layer, is bound below by the interconnecting medium over which transmission flows, while layer 7 is the upper layer and has no upper boundary. Within each layer is a group of functions that provide a set of defined services to the layer above it, resulting in layer n using the services of layer $n - 1$. Thus, the design of a layered architecture enables the characteristics of a particular layer to change without affecting the rest of the system, assuming that the services provided by the layer do not change.

OSI Layers

The best way to gain an understanding of the OSI layers is to examine a network structure that illustrates the components of a typical wide area network. Figure 2.2 illustrates a network structure that is typical only in the sense that it will be used for a discussion of the components upon which networks are constructed.

The circles in Figure 2.2 represent nodes, which are points where data enters or exits a network or is switched between two networks connected by one or more paths. Nodes are connected to other nodes via communications cables or circuits and can be established on any type of communications medium, such as cable, microwave, or radio.

From a physical perspective, a node can be based on any of several types of computers, including a personal computer, minicomputer, mainframe computer, or specialized computer, such as a front-end processor. Connections to network nodes into a wide area network can occur via terminal devices, such as PCs and fixed logic devices, directly connected to computers, terminals connected to a node via one or more intermediate communications devices, or

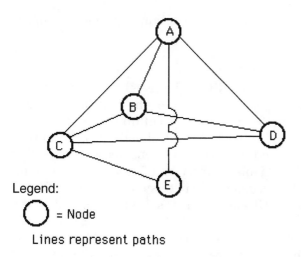

Legend:

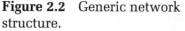

⬤ = Node

Lines represent paths

Figure 2.2 Generic network structure.

paths linking one network to another network. In fact, a workstation on an Ethernet local area network that provides access into a wide area network can be considered a network node. In this situation, the workstation can be a bridge, router, or gateway, and provides a connectivity mechanism between other stations on the Ethernet local area network and the wide area network.

The routes between two nodes—such as C-E-A, C-D-A, C-A, and C-B-A, all of which can be used to route data between nodes A and C—are *information paths.* Due to the variability in the flow of information through a wide area network, the shortest path between nodes may not be available for use, or may be inefficient in comparison to other possible paths. A temporary connection between two nodes that is based on such parameters as current network activity is known as a *logical connection.* This logical connection represents the use of physical facilities, including paths and temporary node-switching capability.

The major functions of each of the seven OSI layers are described in the following seven paragraphs.

Layer 1—The Physical Layer

At the lowest or most basic level, the physical layer (level 1) is a set of rules that specifies the electrical and physical connection between devices. This level specifies the cable connections and the electrical rules necessary to transfer data between devices. Typically, the physical link corresponds to previously established interface standards, such as the RS-232/V.24 interface. This interface governs the attachment of data terminal equipment, such as the serial port of personal computers, to data communications equipment, such as modems.

Layer 2—The Data Link Layer

The next layer, which is known as the data link layer (level 2), denotes how a device gains access to the medium specified in the physical layer. It also defines data formats, including the framing of data within transmitted messages, error control procedures, and other link control activities. Because it defines data formats, including procedures to correct transmission errors, this layer becomes responsible for the reliable delivery of information. Two examples of data link control protocols that can reside in this layer are IBM's Binary Synchronous Communications (BSC) and the ITU's High-Level Data Link Control (HDLC).

Because the development of OSI layers was originally targeted toward wide area networking, its applicability to local area networks required a degree of modification. Under the IEEE 802 standards, the data link layer was initially divided into two sublayers: *logical link control (LLC)* and *media access control (MAC)*. The LLC layer is responsible for generating and interpreting commands that control the flow of data and perform recovery operations in the event of errors. In comparison, the MAC layer is responsible for providing access to the local area network, which enables a station on the network to transmit information.

With the development of high-speed local area networks designed to operate on a variety of different types of media, an additional degree of OSI layer subdivision was required. First, the data link layer required the addition of a reconciliation layer (RI) to reconcile a medium-independent interface (MII) signal added to a version of high-speed Ethernet, commonly referred to as Fast Ethernet. Next, the physical layer used for Fast Ethernet required a subdivision into three sublayers. One sublayer, known as the *physical coding sublayer (PCS)* performs data encoding. A *physical medium attachment* sublayer (PMA) maps messages from the physical coding sublayer to the transmission media, while a *medium-dependent interface (MDI)* specifies the connector for the media used. Similarly, Gigabit Ethernet implements a gigabit media-independent interface (GMII), which enables different encoding and decoding methods to be supported that are used with different types of media. Later in this chapter, we will examine the IEEE 802 subdivision of the data link and physical layers, as well as the operation of each resulting sublayer.

Layer 3—The Network Layer

The network layer (level 3) is responsible for arranging a logical connection between the source and destination nodes on the network. This responsibility includes the selection and management of a route for the flow of information between source and destination, based on the available data paths in the network. Services provided by this layer are associated with the movement of data packets through a network, including addressing, routing, switching, sequencing, and flow control procedures. In a complex network, the source and destination may not be directly connected by a single path, but instead require a path that consists of many subpaths. Thus, routing data through the network onto the correct paths is an important feature of this layer.

Several protocols have been defined for layer 3, including the ITU X.25 packet switching protocol and the ITU X.75 gateway protocol. X.25 governs the flow of information through a packet network, while X.75 governs the flow of information between packet networks. Other popular examples of layer 3 protocols include the Internet Protocol (IP) and Novell's Internet Packet Exchange (IPX), both of which represent layers in their respective protocol suites that were defined before the ISO Reference Model was developed.

Layer 4—The Transport Layer

The transport layer (level 4) is responsible for guaranteeing that the transfer of information occurs correctly after a route has been established through the network by the network level protocol. Thus, the primary function of this layer is to control the communications session between network nodes once a path has been established by the network control layer. Error control, sequence checking, and other end-to-end data reliability factors are the primary concern of this layer, and they enable the transport layer to provide a reliable end-to-end data transfer capability. Examples of popular transport layer protocols include the Transmission Control Protocol (TCP), User Datagram Protocol (UDP), and Novell's Sequence Packet Exchange (SPX).

Layer 5—The Session Layer

The session layer (level 5) provides a set of rules for establishing and terminating data streams between nodes in a network. The services that this session layer can provide include establishing and terminating node connections, message flow control, dialogue control, and end-to-end data control.

Layer 6—The Presentation Layer

The presentation layer (level 6) services are concerned with data transformation, formatting, and syntax. One of the primary functions performed by the presentation layer is the conversion of transmitted data into a display format appropriate for a receiving device. This can include any necessary conversion between ASCII and EBCDIC codes. Data encryption/decryption and data compression/decompression are additional examples of the data transformation that can be handled by this layer.

Layer 7—The Application Layer

Finally, the application layer (level 7) acts as a window through which the application gains access to all of the services provided by the model. Examples of functions performed at this level include file transfers, resource sharing, and database access. While the first four layers are fairly well defined, the top three layers may vary considerably, depending on the network protocol used. For example, the TCP/IP protocol, which predates the OSI Reference Model, groups layer 5 through layer 7 functions into a single application layer. In Chapter 10 when we examine Internet connectivity and the construction and operation of virtual private networks (VPNs) via the Internet, we will also examine the relationship of the TCP/IP protocol stack to the seven-layer OSI Reference Model.

Figure 2.3 illustrates the OSI model in schematic format, showing the various levels of the model with respect to a terminal device, such as a personal

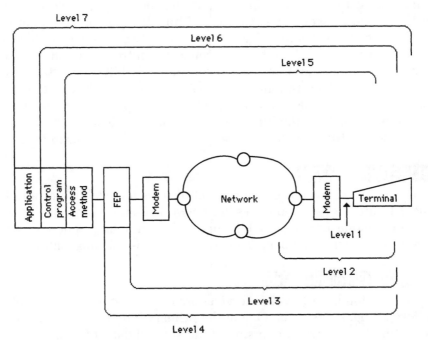

Figure 2.3   OSI model schematic.

computer accessing an application on a host computer system. Although Figure 2.3 shows communications occurring via a modem connection on a wide area network, the OSI model schematic is also applicable to local area networks. Thus, the terminal shown in the figure could be replaced by a workstation on an Ethernet network while the front-end processor (FEP) would, via a connection to that network, become a participant on that network.

Data Flow

As data flows within an ISO network, each layer appends appropriate heading information to frames of information flowing within the network, while removing the heading information added by a lower layer. In this manner, layer n interacts with layer $n - 1$ as data flows through an ISO network.

Figure 2.4 illustrates the appending and removal of frame header information as data flows through a network constructed according to the ISO Reference Model. Because each higher level removes the header appended by a lower level, the frame traversing the network arrives in its original form at its destination.

As you will surmise from the previous illustrations, the ISO Reference Model is designed to simplify the construction of data networks. This simplification is due to the potential standardization of methods and procedures to append appropriate heading information to frames flowing through a network, permitting data to be routed to its appropriate destination following a uniform procedure.

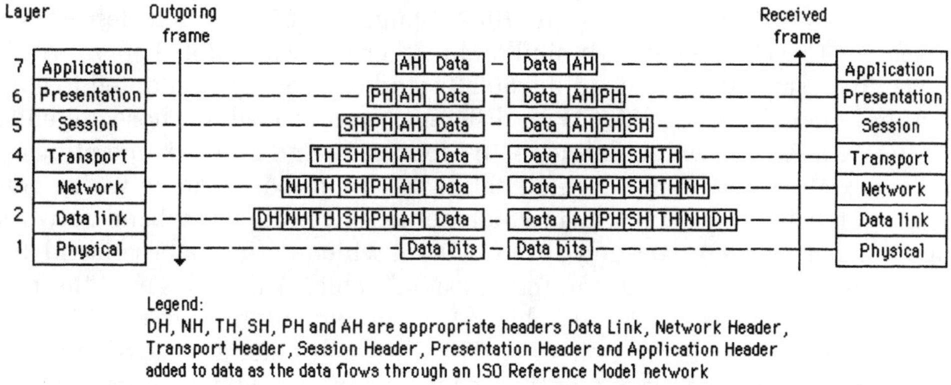

Legend:
DH, NH, TH, SH, PH and AH are appropriate headers Data Link, Network Header, Transport Header, Session Header, Presentation Header and Application Header added to data as the data flows through an ISO Reference Model network

Figure 2.4 Appending and removal of frame header information.

2.3 IEEE 802 Standards

The Institute of Electrical and Electronics Engineers (IEEE) Project 802 was formed at the beginning of the 1980s to develop standards for emerging technologies. The IEEE fostered the development of local area networking equipment from different vendors that can work together. In addition, IEEE LAN standards provided a common design goal for vendors to access a relatively larger market than if proprietary equipment were developed. This, in turn, enabled economies of scale to lower the cost of products developed for larger markets.

The actual committee tasked with the IEEE Project 802 is referred to as the IEEE Local and Metropolitan Area Network (LAN/WAN) Standards Committee. Its basic charter is to create, maintain, and encourage the use of IEEE/ANSI and equivalent ISO standards primarily within layers 1 and 2 of the ISO Reference Model. The committee conducts a plenary meeting three times a year and currently has 13 working groups, each of which may have several meetings per year at locations throughout the world.

802 Committees

Table 2.1 lists a portion of the organization of IEEE 802 committees involved in local and metropolitan area networks. In examining the lists of committees in Table 2.1, it is apparent that the IEEE early on noted that a number of different systems would be required to satisfy the requirements of a diverse end-user population. Accordingly, the IEEE adopted the CSMA/CD, Token-Bus, and Token-Ring as standards 802.3, 802.4, and 802.5, respectively.

The IEEE Committee 802 published draft standards for CSMA/CD and Token-Bus local area networks in 1982. Standard 802.3, which describes a baseband CSMA/CD network similar to Ethernet, was published in 1983. Since then, several addenda to the 802.3 standard have been adopted to govern the operation of CSMA/CD on different types of media. Those addenda include 10BASE-2, which defines a 10-Mbps baseband network operating on thin coaxial cable; 1BASE-5, which defines a 1-Mbps baseband network operating on twisted-pair; 10BASE-T, which defines a 10-Mbps baseband network operating on twisted-pair; and 10BROAD-36, which defines a broadband 10-Mbps network that operates on thick coaxial cable. Although Fast Ethernet, which is denoted as 802.3μ in Table 2.1, is an addendum to the 802.3 standard, it was not finalized until 1995. Thus, we will defer a discussion of the 802.3μ standard until the end of this section. Similarly, 802.3z represents the 802 committee developing the Gigabit Ethernet standard, which should be

TABLE 2.1   IEEE Series 802 Committees/Standards

802.1	High-Level Interface
802.1Q	Virtual Bridged LANs
802.2	Logical Link Control
802.3	CSMA/CD
802.3μ	Fast Ethernet
802.3x	Full Duplex
802.3z	Gigabit Ethernet
802.4	Token-Passing Bus
802.5	Token-Passing Ring
802.6	Metropolitan Area Networks
802.7	Broadband Technical Advisory Group
802.8	Fiber Optic Technical Advisory Group
802.9	Integrated Voice and Data Networks
802.9a	IDoENET (proposed)
802.10	Network Security
802.11	Wireless LANs
802.12	100VG-AnyLAN

finalized by the time you read this book and which is discussed at the end of this section.

The next standard published by the IEEE was 802.4, which describes a token-passing bus–oriented network for both baseband and broadband transmission. This standard is similar to the Manufacturing Automation Protocol (MAP) standard developed by General Motors.

The third LAN standard published by the IEEE was based on IBM's specifications for its Token-Ring network. Known as the 802.5 standard, it defines the operation of token-ring networks on shielded twisted-pair cable at data rates of 1 and 4 Mbps. That standard was later modified to acknowledge three IBM enhancements to Token-Ring network operations. These enhancements include the 16-Mbps operating rate, the ability to release a token early on a 16-Mbps network, and a bridge routing protocol known as *source routing*.

Two relatively recent Ethernet standards are 802.3μ and 802.12, both of which have their foundation in IEEE efforts that occurred during 1992. In that year the IEEE requested proposals for "Fast Ethernet," designed to raise the Ethernet operating rate from 10 Mbps to 100 Mbps. This request resulted in two initial proposals. One proposal, now referred to as a series of 100BASE proposals, was developed by a consortium that included Synoptics Communications, Inc., 3Com Corporation, and Ungermann-Bass, Inc. This proposal retained the CSMA/CD access proposal, which formed the basis for the operation of earlier versions of Ethernet. Now included in 802.3μ are 100BASE-TX, 100BASE-FX, and 100BASE-T4.

100BASE-TX defines the specifications for 100-Mbps CSMA/CD over two pairs of category 5 unshielded twisted-pair (UTP) cable. 100BASE-FX specifies 100-Mbps Ethernet over two pairs of optical fiber cable, while 100BASE-T4 defines the operation of 100-Mbps Ethernet over four pairs of category 3, 4, and 5 UTP or shielded twisted-pair (STP) cable.

The second 100-Mbps proposal, which is now referred to as 100VG-AnyLAN, was initially developed by AT&T Microelectronics and Hewlett-Packard Company. This proposal replaced the CSMA/CD access protocol by a demand-priority scheme that enables the support of Ethernet, Token-Ring, FDDI, and other types of local area networks. Since this proposal described operations on voice grade (VG) twisted pair, it received the mnemonic 100VG-AnyLAN.

During 1994, the IEEE 802.9 working group completed a document that creates a 16.384-Mbps physical layer for operation on UTP category 3 or higher cable. Referred to as isoENET, the draft document is technically referred to as 802.9a. Readers are referred to Chapter 3, Section 4 for information concerning this higher-speed version of Ethernet.

The CSMA/CD protocol requires stations to listen for activity before transmitting data. This means that a four-wire connection with separate pairs for transmit and receive cannot be operated simultaneously to transmit and receive data, precluding true full-duplex operations from occurring. However, when an Ethernet station is connected to a port on a LAN switch, the two wire pairs between the station enable the switch port and workstation to simultaneously transmit and receive data without the possibility of a collision occurring. This method of full duplex CSMA/CD transmission was standardized by the IEEE as the 802.3x standard during 1996.

In addition to the briefly described 802.3z standard that will be discussed later in this chapter, another standard that warrants attention is 802.1Q. This standard, whose title is "Standard for Virtual Bridged Local Area Networks," was scheduled for completion during 1998 and defines how port-based virtual LANs (vLANs) operate. Because vLANs are based on the use of switches, we will cover both topics in Chapter 9.

Data Link Subdivision

One of the more interesting facets of IEEE 802 standards was the initial subdivision of the ISO Open System Interconnection Model's data link layer into two sublayers: logical link control (LLC) and medium access control (MAC). Figure 2.5 illustrates the relationship between IEEE 802 local area network standards and the first three layers of the OSI Reference Model.

The separation of the data link layer into two entities provides a mechanism for regulating access to the medium that is independent of the method for establishing, maintaining, and terminating the logical link between workstations. The method of regulating access to the medium is defined by the MAC portion of each LAN standard. This enables the LLC standard to be applicable to each type of network.

Medium Access Control

The MAC sublayer is responsible for controlling access to the network. To accomplish this, it must ensure that two or more stations do not attempt to transmit data onto the network simultaneously. For Ethernet networks, this is accomplished through the use of the CSMA/CD access protocol.

In addition to network access control, the MAC sublayer is responsible for the orderly movement of data onto and off of the network. To accomplish this,

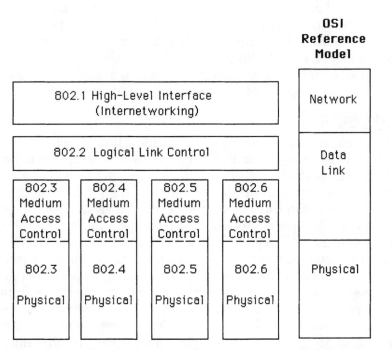

Figure 2.5 Relationship between IEEE standards and the OSI Reference Model.

the MAC sublayer is responsible for MAC addressing, frame type recognition, frame control, frame copying, and similar frame-related functions.

The MAC address represents the physical address of each station connected to the network. That address can belong to a single station, can represent a predefined group of stations (group address), or can represent all stations on the network (broadcast address). Through MAC addresses, the physical source and destination of frames are identified.

Frame type recognition enables the type and format of a frame to be recognized. To ensure that frames can be processed accurately, frame control prefixes each frame with a preamble, which consists of a predefined sequence of bits. In addition, a frame check sequence (FCS) is computed by applying an algorithm to the contents of the frame; the results of the operation are placed into the frame. This enables a receiving station to perform a similar operation. Then, if the locally computed FCS matches the FCS carried in the frame, the frame is considered to have arrived without error.

Once a frame arrives at a station that has the same address as the destination address in the frame, that station must copy the frame. The copying operation moves the contents of the frame into a buffer area in an Ethernet adapter card. The adapter card removes certain fields from the frame, such as the preamble and start of frame delimiter, and passes the information field into a predefined memory area in the station into which the adapter card is inserted.

Refer to Chapter 4 for detailed information concerning Ethernet frame formats, as well as information concerning how the MAC layer controls the transmission and reception of data on an Ethernet local area network.

Logical Link Control

Logical link control frames are used to provide a link between network layer protocols and media access control. This linkage is accomplished through the use of service access points (SAPs), which operate in much the same way as a mailbox. That is, both network layer protocols and logical link control have access to SAPs and can leave messages for each other in them.

Like a mailbox in a post office, each SAP has a distinct address. For the logical link control, a SAP represents the location of a network layer process, such as the location of an application within a workstation as viewed from the network. From the network layer perspective, a SAP represents the place to leave messages concerning the network services requested by an application.

LLC frames contain two special address fields, known as the destination services access point and the source services access point. The destination services access point (DSAP) is one byte in length and specifies the receiving network layer process. The source services access point (SSAP) is also one byte in length. The SSAP specifies the sending network layer process. Both DSAP and SSAP addresses are assigned by the IEEE. Refer to Chapter 4 for detailed information concerning LLC frame formats and data flow.

Additional Sublayering

As previously mentioned, the standardization of high-speed Ethernet resulted in an additional sublayer at the data link layer, and the subdivision of the physical layer. Figure 2.6 illustrates the relationship between the first two layers of the ISO Reference Model and the IEEE 802.3μ Fast Ethernet sublayers. The additional sublayering illustrated in Figure 2.6 became necessary, as it was desired to support different media with one standard. To accomplish this required the physical layer to be independent from the data link layer, because there can be different coding schemes used to support transmission on different types of media.

To retain the CSMA/CD access protocol while supporting the use of different media required the use of different connectors, resulting in the introduction of a physical medium-dependent (PMD) sublayer. Because different data coding schemes are required to support 100 Mbps on different types of media, a physical coding sublayer was introduced. This sublayer defines the coding method used for transmission on different types of media. To map messages from the physical coding sublayer onto the transmission media resulted in those functions being performed by the physical medium attachment sublayer. Thus, the physical layer was subdivided into three sublayers.

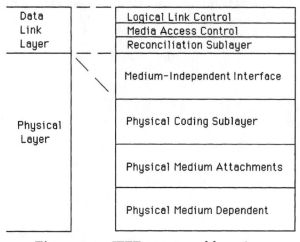

Figure 2.6   IEEE 802.3μ sublayering.

Data Link Layer	Logical Link Control	
	Media Access Control	
		Gigabit Media Independent Interface (optional)
Physical Layer	Physical Coding	Physical Coding
	Physical Medium	Physical Medium

Figure 2.7   IEEE 802.3z gigabit sublayering.

At the data link layer an additional sublayer, known as the *reconciliation sublayer,* was introduced. This sublayer is responsible for reconciling the MII from the physical layer, with the MAC signal.

Recognizing that Gigabit Ethernet would operate on different types of media also resulted in the subdivision of its physical layer. Under the 802.3z standard, several coding methods are defined to support the use of two types of fiber and two types of copper media. Although the Fiber Channel 8B/10B coding method is used for supporting two types of fiber and one type of copper media, an optional gigabit media-independent interface (GMII) functions as a logical interface between the media access control and physical layers, which enables other coding schemes to be used. The GMII will be primarily used to support transmission on unshielded twisted-pair; however, it is possible that it will also allow transmission on other types of media. Figure 2.7 provides a general indication of the sublayering of Gigabit IEEE 802.3z standard.

chapter three

Ethernet Networks

From the title of this chapter, it is apparent that there is more than one type of Ethernet network. From a network access perspective, there is actually only one Ethernet network. However, the CSMA/CD access protocol used by Ethernet, as well as its general frame format and most of its operating characteristics, were used by the IEEE to develop a series of Ethernet-type networks under the IEEE 802.3 umbrella. Thus, this chapter will first focus on the different types of Ethernet networks by closely examining the components and operating characteristics of Ethernet and then comparing its major features with the different networks defined by the IEEE 802.3 standard. Once this is accomplished, we will focus our attention on the wiring, topology, and hardware components associated with each type of IEEE 802.3 Ethernet network. This will enable us to examine the construction of several types of 802.3 networks using a variety of hardware devices and then illustrate how those networks can be connected to one another—a process referred to as *internetworking*.

3.1 Ethernet

One of the key concepts behind Ethernet—that of allocating the use of a shared channel—can be traced to the pioneering efforts of Dr. Norman Abramson and his colleagues at the University of Hawaii during the early 1970s. Using a ground-based radio broadcasting system to connect different locations through the use of a shared channel, Abramson and his colleagues developed the concept of listening to the channel before transmission, transmitting a frame of information, listening to the channel output to determine whether a collision occurred, and, if it did, waiting a random period of time before retransmission. The resulting University of Hawaii ground-based radio broadcasting system, called ALOHA, formed the basis for the development of numerous channel contention systems, including Ethernet. In addition, the subdivision of transmission into frames of data was the pioneering work in the development of packet-switching networks. Thus, Norman Abramson and his colleagues can be considered the forefathers of two of the most important communications technologies, contention networks and packet-switching networks.

Evolution

The actual development of Ethernet occurred at the Xerox Palo Alto Research Center (PARC) in Palo Alto, California. A development team headed by Dr. Robert Metcalfe had to connect over 100 computers on a 1-km cable. The resulting system, which operated at 2.94 Mbps using the CSMA/CD access protocol, was referred to as "Ethernet" in a memorandum authored by Metcalfe. He named it after the luminiferous ether through which electromagnetic radiation was once thought to propagate.

During its progression from a research-based network into a manufactured product, Ethernet suffered several identity crises. During the 1970s, it endured such temporary names as the "Alto Aloha Network" and the "Xerox Wire." After reverting to the original name, Xerox decided, quite wisely, that the establishment of Ethernet as an industry standard for local area networks would be expedited by an alliance with other vendors. A resulting alliance with Digital Equipment Corporation and Intel Corporation resulted in the development of a 10-Mbps Ethernet network. It also provided Ethernet with a significant advantage over Datapoint's ARCNet and Wang Laboratories' Wangnet, proprietary local area networks that were the main competitors to Ethernet during the 1970s.

The alliance between Digital Equipment, Intel, and Xerox resulted in the publication of a "Blue Book Standard" for Ethernet Version 1. An enhancement to that standard occurred in 1982 and is referred to as Ethernet Version 2 or Ethernet II in many technical publications. Because the IEEE used Ethernet Version 2 as the basis for the 802.3 CSMA/CD standard, and Ethernet Version 1 has been obsolete for over a decade, we will refer to Ethernet Version 2 as Ethernet in the remainder of this book.

Network Components

The 10-Mbps Ethernet network standard originally developed by Xerox, Digital Equipment Corporation, and Intel was based on the use of five hardware components. Those components include a coaxial cable, a cable tap, a transceiver, a transceiver cable, and an interface board (also known as an Ethernet controller). Figure 3.1 illustrates the relationships among Ethernet components.

Coaxial Cable

One of the problems faced by the designers of Ethernet was the selection of an appropriate medium. Although twisted-pair wire is relatively inexpensive and easy to use, the short distances between twists serve as an antenna for receiving electromagnetic and radio frequency interference in the form of noise. Thus, the use of twisted-pair cable restricts the network to relatively short distances. Coaxial cable, however, has a dielectric shielding the conductor. As long as the ends of the cable are terminated, coaxial cable can transmit over greater distances than twisted-pair cable. Because the original development of Ethernet was oriented toward interconnecting computers located in different buildings, the use of coaxial cable was well suited for this requirement. Thus, the initial selection for Ethernet transmission medium was coaxial cable.

There are two types of coaxial cable that can be used to form the main Ethernet bus. The first type of coaxial cable specified for Ethernet was a relatively thick 50-ohm cable, which is normally colored yellow and is commonly referred to as "thick" Ethernet. This cable has a marking every 2.5 meters to indicate where a tap should occur, if one is required to connect a station to the main cable at a particular location. These markings represent the minimum

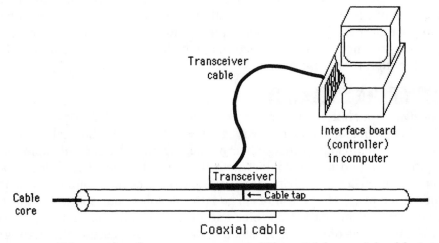

Figure 3.1 Ethernet hardware components. When thick coaxial cable is used for the bus, an Ethernet cable connection is made with a transceiver cable and a transceiver tapped into the cable.

distance one tap must be separated from another on an Ethernet network. The outer insulation or jacket of the yellow-colored cable is constructed using PVC. A second popular type of 50-ohm cable has a Teflon jacket and is colored orange-brown. The Teflon jacket coax is used for plenum-required installations in air-handling spaces, referred to as plenums, to satisfy fire regulations. When installing a thick coaxial segment the cable should be rolled from a common cable spool or cable spools manufactured at the same time, referred to as a similar cable lot, to minimize irregularities between cables. Under the Ethernet specifications when the use of cable from different lots cannot be avoided, cable sections should be used that are either 23.4 m, 70.2 m, or 117 m in length. Those cable lengths minimize the possibility of excessive signal reflections occurring due to variances in the minor differences in cable produced by different vendors or from different cable lots from the same vendor.

A second type of coaxial cable used with Ethernet is smaller and more flexible; however, it is capable of providing a transmission distance only one-third of that obtainable on thick cable. This lighter and more flexible cable is referred to as "thin" Ethernet and also has an impedance of 50 ohms. When the IEEE standardized Ethernet, the thick coaxial cable–based network was assigned the designation 10BASE-5, while the network that uses the thinner cable was assigned the designator 10BASE-2. Later in this chapter we will examine IEEE 802.3 networks under which 10BASE-5, 10BASE-2, and other Ethernet network designators are defined.

Two of the major advantages of thin Ethernet over thick cable are its cost and its use of BNC connectors. Thin Ethernet is significantly less expensive than thick Ethernet. Thick Ethernet requires connections via taps, whereas the use of thin Ethernet permits connections to the bus via industry standard BNC connectors that form T-junctions.

Transceiver and Transceiver Cable

Transceiver is a shortened form of *transmitter-receiver.* This device contains electronics to transmit and receive signals carried by the coaxial cable. The transceiver contains a tap that, when pushed against the coaxial cable, penetrates the cable and makes contact with the core of the cable. Ethernet transceivers are used for broadband transmission on a coaxial cable and usually include a removable tap assembly. The latter enables vendors to manufacture transceivers that can operate on thick and thin coaxial cable, enabling network installers to change only the tap instead of the entire device and eliminating the necessity to purchase multiple types of transceivers to accommodate different media requirements. In books and technical literature the transceiver, its tap, and its housing are often referred to as the *medium attachment unit (MAU).*

The transceiver is responsible for carrier detection and collision detection. When a collision is detected during a transmission, the transceiver places a special signal, known as a *jam,* on the cable. This signal, described in Chapter 4, is of sufficient duration to propagate down the network bus and inform all of the other transceivers attached to the bus node that a collision has occurred.

The cable that connects the interface board to the transceiver is known as the *transceiver cable.* This cable can be up to 50 meters (165 feet) in length and contains five individually shielded twisted pairs. Two pairs are used for data in and data out, and two pairs are used for control signals in and out. The remaining pair, which is not always used, permits the power from the computer in which the interface board is inserted to power the transceiver.

Because collision detection is a critical part of the CSMA/CD access protocol, the original version of Ethernet was modified to inform the interface board that the transceiver collision circuitry is operational. This modification resulted in each transceiver's sending a signal to the attached interface board after every transmission, informing the board that the transceiver's collision circuitry is operational. This signal is sent by the transceiver over the collision pair of the transceiver cable and must start within 0.6 microseconds after each frame is transmitted. The duration of the signal can vary between 0.5 and 1.5 microseconds. Known as the *signal quality error* and also referred to as the *SQE* or *heartbeat,* this signal is supported by Ethernet Version 2.0, published as a standard in 1982, and by the IEEE 802.3 standard. Although the heartbeat (SQE) is between the transceiver and the system to which it is attached, under the IEEE 802.3 standard transceivers attached to a repeater must have their heartbeat disabled.

The SQE signal is simply a delayed response by a few bit times to the transmission of each frame, informing the interface card that everything is working normally. Because the SQE signal only flows from the transceiver back to the interface card, it does not delay packet transmission nor does it flow onto the network. Today most transceivers have a switch or jumper that enables the SQE signal, commonly labeled SQE Test, to be disabled. Because repeaters must monitor signals in real time and cannot use the Ethernet time gap of 9.6 ms between frames (which we will discuss later in this book), this means that they are not capable of recognizing a heartbeat signal. It should be noted that a twisted-pair 10BASE-T Ethernet hub is also a repeater. If you fail to disable the SQE Test signal, the repeater electronics to include hub ports will misinterpret the signal as a collision. This will result in the transmission of a jam signal on all hub ports other than the port receiving the SQE Test signal, significantly degrading network performance.

Interface Board

The *interface board,* or *network interface card (NIC),* is inserted into an expansion slot within a computer and is responsible for transmitting frames to and receiving frames from the transceiver. This board contains several special chips, including a controller chip that assembles data into an Ethernet frame and computes the cyclic redundancy check used for error detection. Thus, this board is also referred to as an *Ethernet controller.*

Most Ethernet interface boards contain a DB-15 connector for connecting the board to the transceiver. Once thin Ethernet cabling became popular, many manufacturers made their interface boards with both DB-15 and BNC connectors. The latter was used to permit the interface board to be connected to a thin Ethernet cable through the use of a T-connector. Figure 3.2 illustrates the rear panel of a network interface card containing both DB-15 and BNC connectors. With the development of twisted-pair-based Ethernet, such as 10BASE-T, modern Ethernet interface boards, which are commonly referred to as network interface cards (NICs), also include an RJ 45 connector to accommodate a connection to wire-based networks.

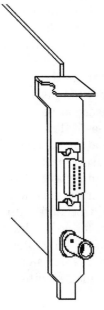

Figure 3.2 Ethernet interface board connectors. Many Ethernet interface boards (network interface cards) contain both DB-15 and BNC connectors to support the use of either thick or thin coaxial cable.

Cabling Restrictions

Under the Ethernet standard developed by Xerox, Digital Equipment Corporation, and Intel Corporation, a thick coaxial cable is permitted a maximum length of 500 meters (1640 feet). Multiple cable segments can be joined together through the use of repeaters; however, the maximum cable distance between two transceivers is limited to 2.5 km (8200 feet), and no more than four repeaters can be traversed on any path between transceivers.

Each thick trunk cable segment must be terminated with what is known as an *N-series connector* on each end of the cable. The terminator "terminates" the network and blocks electrical interference from flowing onto what would otherwise be exposed cable. One N-series connector also serves as a ground, when used with an attached grounding wire that can be connected to the middle screw of a dual AC electrical power outlet.

Figure 3.3 illustrates a thick Ethernet cable segment after an installer fastened N-series plugs to each cable end. This is normally accomplished after the desired length of coaxial cable is routed to form the required network bus. Next, an N-series terminator connector is fastened onto one N-series plug,

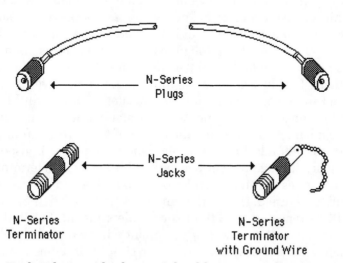

Thick Ethernet Cable Segment

N-Series Plugs

N-Series Jacks

N-Series Terminator

N-Series Terminator with Ground Wire

Figure 3.3 Each Ethernet thick coaxial cable segment has N-series plugs on each end. They are terminated through the use of N-series terminators, one of which contains a ground wire or ground wire connection.

while an N-series terminator with ground wire is fastened onto the N-series plug at the opposite end of the cable segment.

In addition, as previously mentioned, attachments to the common bus must be separated by multiples of 2.5 meters. The latter cabling restriction prevents reflections caused by taps in the main cable from adding up in phase and being mistaken by one transceiver for another's transmission. For the total network, up to 1024 attachments are allowed, including all cable sections connected through the use of repeaters; however, no more than 100 transceivers can be on any one cable segment.

Repeaters

A *repeater* is a device that can be used to connect two network segments together to form a larger local area network topology. The repeater receives, amplifies, and retransmits signals, restoring the symmetry and position of each signal. Signal amplification results in the restoration of the original amplitude characteristics of the data signal. The restoration of signal symmetry results in each output signal pulse matching the shape of the originally transmitted signal. The last function performed by a repeater is the restoration of the signal position. More formally referred to as *retiming,* this repeater function results in the data signal output in its correct position by time, removing any prior shift or displacement in the placement of the received signal. That shift or displacement is known as *jitter,* while a very small shift or displacement of a transmitted signal is referred to as a *wander.*

Because a repeater operates at the physical layer, it is transparent to data and simply regenerates signals. Figure 3.4 illustrates the use of a repeater to connect two Ethernet cable segments. As indicated, a transceiver is taped to each cable segment to be connected, and the repeater is cabled to the transceiver. When used to connect cable segments, a repeater counts as one station on each connected segment. Thus, a segment capable of supporting up to 100 stations can support only 99 additional stations when a repeater is used to connect cable segments. Although not shown, each cable segment is terminated at each end with an N-series terminator and grounded at one end of one segment.

In examining Figure 3.4, note that any data traffic carried on the top cable segment will be repeated onto the lower cable segment. Similarly, any cable traffic transported on the lower cable segment will be repeated onto the upper cable segment. Thus, the use of a repeater simply provides a mechanism to extend transmission between cable segments and should not be confused with the use of a bridge that normally isolates traffic to different segments unless data is destined to a station on a different segment.

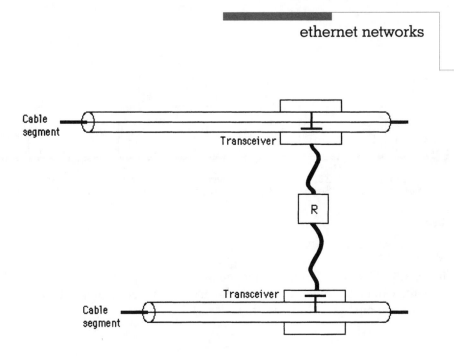

Legend: R = Repeater

Figure 3.4 Using a repeater. Cable segments can be joined together by a repeater to expand the network. The repeater counts as a station on each cable segment.

The 5-4-3 Rule

When Ethernet was developed it was recognized that the use of repeaters to connect segments to form a larger network would result in pulse regeneration delays that could adversely affect the probability of collisions. Thus, a limit was required on the number of repeaters that could be used to connect segments together. This limit in turn limited the number of segments that could be interconnected. A further limitation involved the number of populated segments that could be joined together, because stations on populated segments generate traffic that can cause collisions, whereas nonpopulated segments are more suitable for extending the length of a network of interconnected segments. A result of the preceding was the "5-4-3 rule." That rule specifies that a maximum of five Ethernet segments can be joined through the use of a maximum of four repeaters. In actuality, this part of the Ethernet rule really means that no two communicating Ethernet nodes can be more than two repeaters

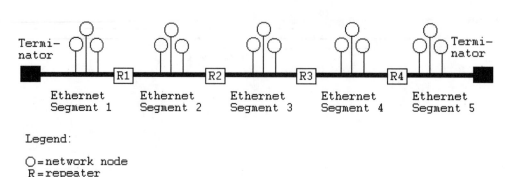

Figure 3.5 The 5-4-3 rule. Under the 5-4-3 Ethernet rule a maximum of five segments can be connected through the use of four repeaters, with a maximum of three segments populated with nodes.

away from one another. Finally, the "three" in the rule denotes the maximum number of Ethernet segments that can be populated. Figure 3.5 illustrates an example of the 5-4-3 rule for the original bus-based Ethernet. Note that this rule is also applicable to hub-based Ethernet LANs, such as 10BASE-T, which we will examine later in this chapter.

3.2 IEEE 802.3 Networks

The IEEE 802.3 standard is based on Ethernet. However, it has several significant differences, particularly its support of multiple physical layer options, which include 50- and 75-ohm coaxial cable, unshielded twisted-pair wire, and the use of optical fiber. Other differences between various types of IEEE 802.3 networks and Ethernet include the data rates supported by some 802.3 networks, their methods of signaling, the maximum cable segment lengths permitted before the use of repeaters, and their network topologies.

Network Names

The standards that define IEEE 802.3 networks have been given names that generally follow the form "s type l." Here, s refers to the speed of the network in Mbps, *type* is BASE for baseband and BROAD for broadband, and *l* refers to the maximum segment length in 100-meter multiples. Thus, 10BASE-5 refers to an IEEE 802.3 baseband network that operates at 10 Mbps and has a maximum segment length of 500 meters. One exception to this general form is 10BASE-T, which is the name for an IEEE 802.3 network that operates at 10 Mbps using UTP wire.

Although recently introduced high-speed Ethernet networks do not exactly follow the preceding form, they continue to resemble prior naming conventions. For example, 100BASE-TX, 100BASE-T4, and 100BASE-FX represent three physical layer versions of the Fast Ethernet standard. Each version operates at 100 Mbps and uses baseband signaling; however, the suffix now represents different types of media instead of a maximum segment length in 100-meter multiples.

Table 3.1 compares the operating characteristics of five IEEE 802.3 networks with Ethernet. Note that the comparisons indicated in Table 3.1 do not consider differences in the composition of Ethernet and IEEE 802.3 frames. Those differences preclude compatibility between Ethernet and IEEE 802.3 networks, and are discussed in detail in Chapter 4.

Also note that Table 3.1 does not include IEEE 802.3μ (Fast Ethernet) and IEEE 802.12 (100VG-AnyLAN) Ethernet networks nor any of the emerging Gigabit Ethernet networks specified under the IEEE 802.z standard. The first standard actually represents three standards for 100-Mbps CSMA/CD operations. The second standard supports 100-Mbps operations using a demand-priority scheme in place of the CSMA/CD access protocol. Fast Ethernet,

TABLE 3.1 Ethernet and IEEE 802.3 1-Mbps and 10-Mbps Network Characteristics

Operational Characteristics	Ethernet	10BASE-5	10BASE-2	1BASE-5	10BASE-T	10BROAD-36
Operating rate (Mbps)	10	10	10	1	10	10
Access protocol	CSMA/CD	CSMA/CD	CSMA/CD	CSMA/CD	CSMA/CD	CSMA/CD
Type of signaling	Baseband	Baseband	Baseband	Baseband	Baseband	Broadband
Data encoding	Manchester	Manchester	Manchester	Manchester	Manchester	Manchester
Maximum segment length (meters)	500	500	185	250	100	1,800
Stations/segment	100	100	30	12/hub	12/hub	100
Medium	50-ohm coaxial (thick)	50-ohm coaxial (thick)	50-ohm coaxial (thin)	Unshielded twisted pair	Unshielded twisted pair	75-ohm coaxial
Topology	Bus	Bus	Bus	Star	Star	Bus

100VG-AnyLAN, and Gigabit Ethernet networks are covered at the end of this chapter when we turn our attention to high-speed Ethernet networks. Thus, the networks compared in Table 3.1 are limited to a 10-Mbps operating rate.

10BASE-5

As indicated in Table 3.1, the IEEE 10BASE-5 standard resembles Ethernet more closely than the other 802.3 standards. In fact, an examination of the operating characteristics of Ethernet and 10BASE-5 indicates that these networks are exactly the same. Similarities between Ethernet and 10BASE-5 include the use of DB-15 connectors on interface boards and transceivers (MAUs) and the termination of 10BASE-5 cable segments with N-series terminators.

However, there are differences in the frame format used by each network, and these differences preclude compatibility between Ethernet and all IEEE 802.3 standards. In addition, under the IEEE 802.3 specification, several network components have different names.

Figure 3.6 illustrates the major terminology changes between Ethernet and the IEEE 802.3 10BASE-5 network. These changes are in the media interface: the transceiver cable is referred to as the *attachment unit interface (AUI),* and the transceiver, including its tap and housing, is referred to as the *medium attachment unit (MAU).* The Ethernet controller, also known as an interface board, is now known as the *network interface card (NIC).* Other similarities between Ethernet and 10BASE-5 include the use of DB-15 connectors on network interface cards and MAUs and the termination of 10BASE-5 cable segments with the use of N-series 50-ohm terminators at each cable segment end. In addition, the 802.3 standard requires one end of the thick coax segment to be grounded for electrical safety. All other metal portions on the coax should be insulated and fastened in place using plastic or other nonmetallic cable ties to avoid accidentally connecting to the electrical ground.

The actual connection between the NIC and the MAU is limited to a maximum of 50 meters (164 feet). The 15-pin AUI connector is a socket (female) receptacle while the connector on the MAU is a 15-pin AUI connector with a pin (male) receptacle. The AUI cable consists of four pairs of shielded twisted wires, three of which transport data signals while one pair carries 12-volt DC power from the Ethernet interface to the MAU. The three data signal wire pairs include transmit data that go from the Ethernet interface to the network, receive data that carry data from the network to the interface, and a collision indicator signal wire pair that transports collision indications to the interface.

Although a standard AUI cable is approximately 0.4 inches in diameter and has a limited degree of flexibility, many cable manufacturers market thinner

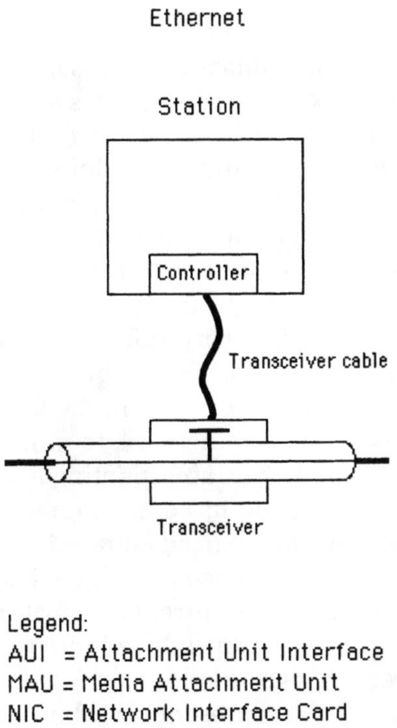

Ethernet   IEEE 10BASE-5

Station   Station

Controller   NIC

Transceiver cable   AUI

Transceiver   MAU

Legend:
AUI = Attachment Unit Interface
MAU = Media Attachment Unit
NIC = Network Interface Card

Figure 3.6 Ethernet and 10BASE-5 media interface differences. Terminology changes under the IEEE 10BASE-5 standard resulted in the transceiver being called the *media attachment unit,* while the transceiver cable is known as the *attachment unit interface.*

and more flexible cable. However, the trade-off when using such cable is a lower allowable cabling length from the interface to the MAU, because thinner cable has a higher amount of signal attenuation.

Both Ethernet and the IEEE 802.3 10BASE-5 standards support a data rate of 10 Mbps and a maximum cable segment length of 500 meters. 10BASE-5, like Ethernet, requires a minimum spacing of 2.5 meters between MAUs and supports a maximum of five segments in any end-to-end path through the traversal of up to four repeaters in any path. Within any path, no more than three cable segments can be *populated*—have stations attached to the cable—and the maximum number of attachments per segment is limited to 100. As previously discussed in our coverage of Ethernet, these restrictions are sometimes referred to as the 5-4-3 rule, referencing a maximum of five segments linked through four repeaters, with no more than three segments populated.

Advantages and Disadvantages

Similar to any technology there are various advantages and disadvantages associated with the use of a 10BASE-5 network. Major advantages associated with the use of 10BASE-5 include the span distance of 500 m (1650 feet), which makes it extremely useful for connecting multiple locations within a building without the use of repeaters, its ability to span up to 2.5 km (8200 feet) by connecting multiple segments together to form an extended backbone, and its heavily shielded media, making it suitable for use in electrically noisy environments.

The thick coax required by 10BASE-5 makes it a very inflexible network where the movement of a node can be difficult, if not impossible, to accomplish without a major restructuring of the network. In addition, the failure of any part of the cable or any node can cause the entire network to fail, resulting in 10BASE-T being fault-intolerant. This makes troubleshooting a failure, difficult and time-consuming, because each node and its connection has to be checked until the point of failure is located. A fourth disadvantage is the fact that power from different sources results in a difference in voltage between points on the network. This voltage differential causes current to flow through the shields of the cable, which can cause noise to be introduced into the center conductor, a situation referred to as creating a ground loop. 10BASE-5 networks are very susceptible to ground loops, which represent a weakness of the technology. Although common during the early 1980s, most new network requirements only consider 10BASE-T as a backbone to connect multiple 10BASE-T hubs to create one large network as illustrated in Figure 3.7.

10BASE-2

10BASE-2 is a smaller and less expensive version of 10BASE-5. This standard uses a thinner RG-58 coaxial cable, more commonly referred to as RG-58 A/U or RG-58 C/U, thus earning the names of *cheapnet* and *thinnet,* as well as *thin Ethernet.* Although 10BASE-2 cable is both less expensive and easier to use than 10BASE-5 cable, it cannot carry signals as far as 10BASE-5 cable.

The coaxial cable used by 10BASE-2 is approximately 0.5 cm or 3/16 inch in diameter. This cable must have a 50-ohm impedance rating and a stranded center conductor. Although those specifications are met by RG-58 A/U and RG-58 C/U cable, it is important to note that vendors sometimes use those nomenclatures for cables with impedance ratings different from 50 ohms. Thus, it is important to verify both the nomenclature and impedance rating of the coaxial cable.

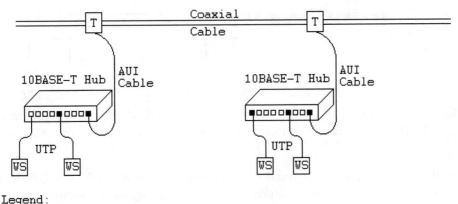

Legend:
```
T   = Transceiver
WS  = Workstation
UTP = Unshielded twisted pair
```

Figure 3.7 Using 10BASE-5 as a backbone. The use of 10BASE-T as a backbone enables 10BASE-T hubs to be located further from one another than if they were wired together using unshielded twisted-pair cable.

Under the 10BASE-2 standard, the maximum cable segment length is reduced to 185 meters (607 feet), with a maximum of 30 stations per segment. This length limitation is often confused by persons that assume the *2* in the network nomenclature allows a 200-meter cable length. Perhaps the IEEE should have used the designator 10BASE-1.85, but it used 10BASE-2 even though the cable length limit is 185 meters.

Unlike 10BASE-5 that has spacing rules for MAUs, there are none for 10BASE-2. However, because the minimum length of coaxial cable required for a 10BASE-2 segment cannot be shorter than 0.5 meters (1.64 feet), this indirectly provides a minimum spacing between MAU connections of 0.5 meters.

Another difference between 10BASE-5 and 10BASE-2 concerns the integration of transceiver electronics into the network interface card under the 10BASE-2 standard. This permits the NIC to be directly cabled to the main trunk cable. In fact, under 10BASE-2 the Thin Ethernet cable is routed directly to each workstation location and routed through a BNC T-connector, one end of which is pressed into the BNC connector built into the rear of the network interface card. Figure 3.8 illustrates the cabling of a one-segment 10BASE-2 network, which can support a maximum of 30 nodes or stations. BNC barrel connectors can be used to join two lengths of thin 10BASE-2 cable to form a cable segment, as long as the joined cable does not exceed 185 meters in

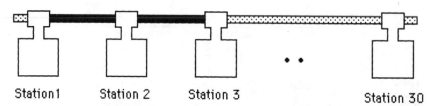

Station1   Station 2   Station 3   Station 30

Figure 3.8 Cabling a 10BASE-2 network. A 10BASE-2 cable segment cannot exceed 185 meters and is limited to supporting up to 30 nodes or stations.

length. A BNC terminator must be attached to each end of each 10BASE-2 cable segment. One of the two terminators on each segment contains a ground wire that should be connected to a ground source, such as the screw on an electrical outlet.

The Thinnet Tap

The coaxial cable that forms the network bus must be routed directly into each T-connector, which in turn is mated to a node or station. This means it is not possible to locate a node away from the BNC T-connector by connecting a single coaxial stub or drop cable between the T-connector and the node, limiting the flexibility of this network unless you employ a thinnet tap. Otherwise, the use of a single coaxial drop cable can result in the occurrence of signal reflections that can generate transmission errors.

A thinnet tap was developed by vendors to enable individual nodes to be located at a distance from the main 10BASE-2 network cable. This tap consists of a tap assembly that connects to the main coaxial 10BASE-2 cable and a drop cable with two coaxial cables and the equivalent of a BNC T-adapter. When the drop cable is connected to a tap assembly it triggers a switch in the tap, which electrically connects each side of the tap to one of the cables in the drop cable. This action loops the signal from the top of the node and back to the other side of the tap, resulting in an unbroken network, which from an electrical perspective, is the same as connecting the node via a conventional BNC T-connector. Figure 3.9 illustrates a schematic diagram of a tap assembly.

Multifunction Transceivers

Because of the similarities between 10BASE-5 and 10BASE-2, several vendors have introduced transceivers that support both thick and thin coaxial cable. Figure 3.10 illustrates the Universal Ethernet Transceiver manufactured by Transition Engineering of Edina, Minnesota. The transceiver illustrated in the upper left corner of Figure 3.10 is a 10BASE-2 transceiver. It can be converted

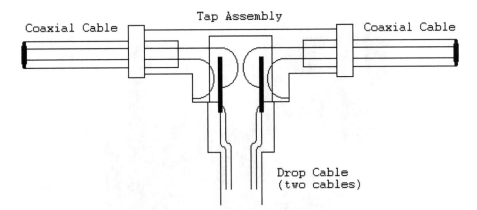

Figure 3.9   A 10BASE-2 tap assembly. Through the use of a 10BASE-2 tap assembly, it becomes possible to locate nodes at a distance from the backbone network.

into a 10BASE-5 transceiver with an adapter that converts the BNC on the thin-net transceiver into a *vampire* tap–type connector, as illustrated in the lower right corner of Figure 3.10.

Grounding

Depending upon the type of coaxial-based Ethernet installed, you may require the cable to be grounded. The 10BASE-5 specification indicates that the coaxial cable should be grounded at one, and only one, point. In comparison, the 10BASE-2 specification indicates that thin coaxial cable may be grounded at one, and only one, point.

Regardless of the type of coaxial cable–based network you are using, it is normally a good idea to ground the cable at one location. Doing so alleviates the potential for static electricity to build up. In addition, many local electrical codes require network cabling to be grounded at one location. When grounding a coaxial-based network, it is also important to ensure you do so at only one location. Otherwise, multiple grounds on an Ethernet segment can result in a risk to equipment, shock to people, and network errors.

You can ground a network segment through the use of a coaxial cable terminator with ground wire, similar to the terminator illustrated in the lower right portion of Figure 3.3. If you install a repeater on one end of a segment, it is important to note that most repeaters can be set up to ground or *not* ground. Thus, you may be able to use a repeater to ground a segment.

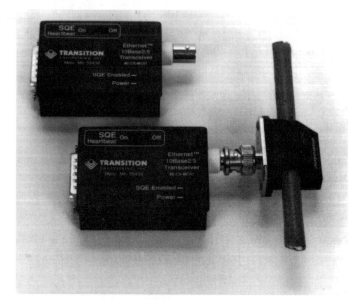

Figure 3.10 Universal Ethernet Transceiver. The Universal Ethernet Transceiver manufactured by Transition Engineering of Edina, Minnesota, supports both 10BASE-2 and 10BASE-5 coaxial cable connections. (Photograph courtesy of Transition Engineering, Inc.)

Expanding a 10BASE-2 Network

You can increase the number of stations that can be attached to a 10BASE-2 network, the total network distance, or both through the use of repeaters. As with a 10BASE-5 network, between any two nodes there can be up to five cable segments connected through four repeaters. Like a 10BASE-5 segment, each end of every 10BASE-2 segment must be terminated with a 50-ohm terminator, with one end of each segment grounded.

Figure 3.11 illustrates an expanded 10BASE-2 network consisting of three populated cable segments; two segments are used to extend the network span by simply connecting two repeaters. The latter segments are also commonly referred to as *interrepeater cable segments* (IRCS). Each cable segment shown in Figure 3.11 requires one MAU connection to a repeater. Because there are a maximum of 30 stations or MAU connections per segment, this means that segments connected by a repeater are limited to actually supporting 29 workstations.

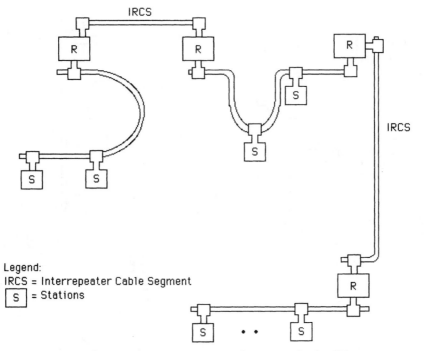

Figure 3.11 Expanding a 10BASE-2 network. Up to five cable segments connected through the use of four repeaters can be used to expand a 10BASE-2 network.

Two-Tier Cabling You can further expand a 10BASE-2 network by establishing a two-tier method of cabling. Under this cabling concept, the upper tier can consist of up to 30 repeaters, connected to one another through the use of interrepeater cable segments. These form a backbone network without direct station attachments, so populated segments on the backbone have to be connected on each segment end to a repeater. The lower tier then consists of repeaters connected to populated cable segments, with the lower-tier repeater cabled to the upper-tier repeater to obtain a connection to the backbone. Figure 3.12 illustrates the use of a two-tier cabling hierarchy that can be used to extend a 10BASE-2 network. As in Figure 3.11, between any pair of workstations there can be a maximum of five cable segments and four repeaters. Of the five cable segments, up to three can be populated, and each populated segment is limited to a maximum of 30 connections, of which one or two will be repeater connections depending upon where the cable segment resides with

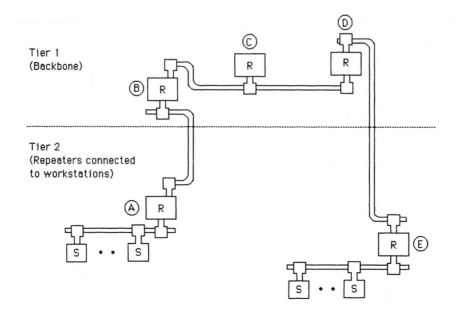

Legend:
R = Repeater
S = Workstation

Figure 3.12 Two-tier thin 10BASE-2 network. A two-tier network permits expansion of a 10BASE-2 network by adding another level of repeaters to the backbone. The segment between repeaters B, C, and D is considered to be populated, because repeater C is counted as one connection on the segment.

respect to the interconnected network. In addition, the maximum distance between any two stations is limited to 100 meters (328 feet), while the minimum distance between BNC T-connectors is 0.5 meters (1.6 feet).

Advantages and Disadvantages

Similar to a 10BASE-5 network, the use of coaxial cable for a 10BASE-2 network makes it suitable for use in locations that require a high degree of immunity from electrical noise. Two additional advantages associated with 10BASE-2 include the fact that it is easy to establish because devices are daisy-chained together, and it is relatively inexpensive. Disadvantages of 10BASE-2 are also similar to the disadvantages associated with 10BASE-5. That is, a 10BASE-2 network is difficult to reconfigure; a single device failure or cable break can bring down the entire network, making it fault-intolerant, and the isolation of a failure can be very time-consuming due to the need to check every device and cable section.

Normally 10BASE-2 is well-suited for small networks that are relatively static with respect to node relocations. Similar to 10BASE-5, the use of a 10BASE-2 network is often used as a backbone technology for interconnecting 10BASE-T hubs that must be located at cable distances beyond the range of that twisted-pair network. Although a 10BASE-2 backbone length is considerably less than that of a 10BASE-5 backbone, thinnet cable is cheaper and easier to install, making it popular for backbones that must span distances up to 185 meters per segment.

Combining 10BASE-5 and 10BASE-2 Networks

There are many situations in which a combination of thick and thin coaxial cable can better satisfy your cabling requirements than the exclusive use of one type of cable. For example, you may have several clusters of terminals located in different geographically separated areas within a large office complex. Instead of connecting the two clusters through the use of several thin 10BASE-2 cable segments and multiple repeaters, it may be easier to install one or more thick 10BASE-5 cable segments to serve as a backbone network for attachment to two 10BASE-2 cable segments. Thus, the ability of thick coaxial cable to support a longer transmission distance can eliminate or reduce the number of repeaters required in a combined network. In addition, a network built using thin 10BASE-2 cable, which was originally designed for a network span under 925 meters, cannot cover greater distances without mixing network media. Thus, the use of thick coaxial cable may provide the span of coverage not obtainable from the exclusive use of thin coaxial cable.

When thick and thin coaxial cable are combined to form a single cable segment, you must consider the length of each type of cable you anticipate using to develop a combined media cable segment. If the segment is entirely made up of thin cable, its maximum length is 607 feet, while a cable segment made up of thick cable has a maximum length of 1640 feet. Thus, a combined thin and thick cable segment should vary in length between 607 and 1640 feet. If L represents the length of a combined media cable you wish to construct, you can use the following equation to determine the maximum length of thin cable:

$$\text{thin cable} = \frac{1640 - L \text{ feet}}{3.28}$$

For example, suppose you want to construct a cable segment 1400 feet long. Then, the maximum length of thin 10BASE-2 cable you can use becomes:

$$\frac{1640 - 1400}{3.28} = 73 \text{ feet}$$

Thus, you could use 73 feet of 10BASE-2 cable and route that cable through T-connectors, which are fastened to the BNC connectors on the rear of network interface cards. Then, you could use thick cable for the remaining 1327 feet of cable required in the cable segment.

Figure 3.13 shows an example of a combined 10BASE-5 and 10BASE-2 cable segment that connects two groups of stations located at opposite ends of a building without using repeaters. At one end of the building, 10BASE-2 cable is used with BNC T-connectors to connect a large number of stations clustered together. At the other end of the building, we will assume there are only a few stations. Thus, we would use 10BASE-5 cable and connect each station to the thick cable through the use of an MAU (transceiver) and an AUI (transceiver cable).

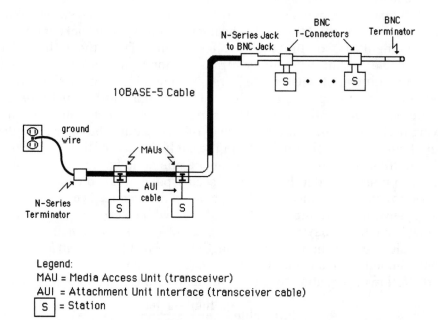

Figure 3.13 Combined 10BASE-5 and 10BASE-2 cable segment. A combined thick and thin coaxial segment can be used to economically connect a group of stations clustered in one area of a building to a few stations located a relatively long distance away from the cluster.

In examining Figure 3.13, note that the end of the thin cable is terminated with a BNC terminator. The connection of thick and thin cable is accomplished through the use of an N-series jack to BNC jack, while the thick cable is terminated with an N-series terminator that has a ground wire.

10BROAD-36

10BROAD-36 is the only broadband network based on the CSMA/CD access protocol standardized by the IEEE. Unlike a baseband network, in which Manchester-encoded signals are placed directly onto the cable, the 10BROAD-36 standard requires the use of radio frequency (RF) modems. Those modems modulate nonreturn to zero (NRZ)–encoded signals for transmission on one channel at a specified frequency, and they demodulate received signals by listening for tones on another channel at a different frequency.

Cable

A 10BROAD-36 network is constructed with a 75-ohm coaxial cable, similar to the cable used in modern cable television (CATV) systems. Under the IEEE 802.3 broadband standard, either single or dual cables can be used to construct a network. If a single cable is used, the end of the cable (referred to as the *headend*) must be terminated with a frequency translator. That translator converts the signals received on one channel to the frequency assigned to the other channel, retransmitting the signal at the new frequency. Because the frequency band for a transmitted signal is below the frequency band 10BROAD-36 receivers scan, we say the frequency translator *upconverts* a transmitted signal and retransmits it for reception by other stations on the network. If two cables are used, the headend simply functions as a relay point, transferring the signal received on one cable onto the second cable.

Advantages

A broadband transmission system has several advantages over a baseband system. Two of the primary advantages of broadband are its ability to support multiple transmissions occurring on independent frequency bands simultaneously, and its ability to support a tree structure topology carrying multiple simultaneous transmissions. Using independent frequency bands, you can establish several independent networks. In fact, each network can be used to carry voice, data, and video over a common cable. As for topology, broadband permits the use of a tree structure network, such as the structure shown in Figure 3.14. In this example, the top of the tree would be the headend; it would contain a frequency translator, which would regenerate signals received at one frequency back onto the cable at another predefined frequency.

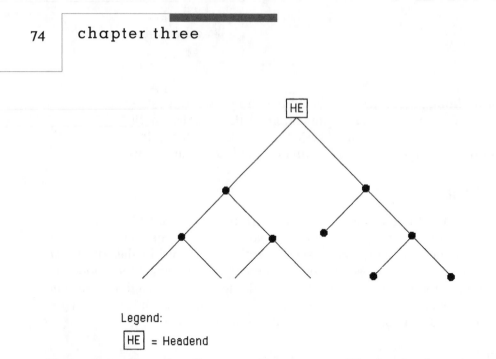

Legend:

HE = Headend

Figure 3.14 Broadband tree topology support. The headend receives transmissions at one frequency and regenerates the received signals back onto the network at another predefined frequency.

Disadvantages

Like the 10BASE-5 network, the 10BROAD-36 system uses an MAU. However, this MAU is more intelligent than a 10BASE-5 MAU, as it is responsible for modifying the 802.3 frame slightly for broadband transmission via a modulator. These frame modifications include the scrambling of the preamble, so that the modulation of the preamble does not result in a loss of clocking, and the addition of a postamble to each frame. The latter assists in the detection of the end-of-frame. Although a 10BASE-5 AUI cable can be connected to a 10BROAD-36 MAU, a 10BROAD-36 MAU obviously cannot be used with a 10BASE-5 network. However, the design specifications of the 10BROAD-36 network enable this network to support the connection of CSMA/CD baseband equipment, and also provide a large degree of compatibility and interoperability with baseband systems.

The higher noise immunity of 75-ohm coaxial cable permits a 10BROAD-36 network to span 3600 meters, making this medium ideal for linking buildings on a campus. In addition, the ability of 10BROAD-36 to share channel space on a 75-ohm coaxial cable permits organizations that have an existing CATV system, such as one used for video security, to use that cable for part or all of their broadband CSMA/CD network. Although these advantages can be significant, the cost associated with more intelligent MAUs and RF modems has limited the use of broadband primarily to campus environments that require an expanded network span. In addition, the rapid development and acceptance of 10BASE-T and the decline in the cost of fiber cable to extend the span of 10BASE-T networks have severely limited what many people once anticipated as a promising future for 10BROAD-36 networks.

1BASE-5

The 1BASE-5 standard was based on AT&T's low-cost CSMA/CD network, known as StarLan. Thus, 1BASE-5 is commonly referred to as StarLan, although AT&T uses that term to refer to CSMA/CD networks operating at both 1 and 10 Mbps using unshielded twisted-pair cable. The latter is considered the predecessor to 10BASE-T.

The 1BASE-5 standard differs significantly from Ethernet and 10BASE-5 standards in its use of media and topology, and in its operating rate. The 1BASE-5 standard operates at 1 Mbps and uses UTP wiring in a star topology; all stations are wired to a hub, which is known as a *multiple-access unit* (MAU). To avoid confusion with the term *media access unit,* which also has the same abbreviation, we will refer to this wiring concentrator as a *hub.*

Topology

Each station in a 1BASE-5 network contains an NIC, cabled via UTP on a point-to-point basis to a hub port. The hub is responsible for repeating signals and detecting collisions.

The maximum cabling distance from a station to a hub is 250 meters; up to five hubs can be cascaded together to produce a maximum network span of 2500 meters. The highest-level hub is known as the *header hub,* and it is responsible for broadcasting news of collisions to all other hubs in the network. These hubs, which are known as *intermediate hubs,* are responsible for reporting all collisions to the header hub.

Usage

AT&T's 1-Mbps StarLan network, along with other 1BASE-5 systems, initially received a degree of acceptance for use in small organizations. However, the introduction of 10BASE-T, which provided an operating rate ten times that obtainable under 1BASE-5, severely limited the further acceptance of 1BASE-5 networks.

The growth in the acceptance of 10BASE-T resulted in economies of scale in the manufacture of 10BASE-T hubs and network interface cards. This, in turn, enabled vendors to match or exceed price cuts of other vendors. One key result of this situation was the ability of end users to obtain a low-cost, high-performance local area networking capability through the use of 10BASE-T equipment. Needless to say, 10BASE-T became the preferred network technology of both small and large organizations during the early 1990s, and it essentially replaced the use of 1BASE-5.

10BASE-T

In the late 1980s, a committee of the IEEE recognized the requirement of organizations for transmitting Ethernet at a 10-Mbps operating rate over low-cost and readily available unshielded twisted-pair cable. Although several vendors had already introduced equipment that permitted Ethernet signaling via UTP cabling, such equipment was based on proprietary designs and was not interoperable. Thus, a new task of the IEEE was to develop a standard for 802.3 networks operating at 10 Mbps using UTP cable. The resulting standard was approved by the IEEE as 802.3i in September 1990, and is more commonly known as 10BASE-T, with the *T* referencing the use of twisted-pair wire.

UTP Use

The 10BASE-T standard supports an operating rate of 10 Mbps at a distance of up to 100 meters (328 feet) over UTP cable without the use of a repeater. The UTP cable requires two pairs of twisted wire. One pair is used for transmitting, while the other pair is used for receiving. Each pair of wires is twisted together, and each twist is 180 degrees. Any electromagnetic interference (EMI) or radio frequency interference (RFI) is therefore received 180 degrees out of phase; this theoretically cancels out EMI and RFI noise while leaving the network signal. In reality, the wire between twists acts as an antenna and receives noise. This noise reception resulted in a 100-meter cable limit, until repeaters were used to regenerate the signal.

Because UTP cable previously installed in commercial buildings contains either three or four wire pairs, the RJ-45 jack used with 10BASE-T has eight-pin connectors. However, only four pins are actually used. Table 3.2 compares the 10BASE-T pin numbers with the RJ-45 jack numbers and indicates the signal names of the pins used with 10BASE-T UTP cable.

Although 10BASE-T was designed to support transmission distances of up to 100 meters under the Electronic Industry Association/Telecommunications Industry Association (EIA/TIA) cabling standard (described later in this chapter), the cabling distance consists of three segments. The first segment, which can be up to 90 meters in length, runs from a patch panel in a wiring closet to

TABLE 3.2   10BASE-T Wiring Sequence

10BASE-T Pin #	RJ-45 Jack #	10BASE-T Signal Name
1	1	Transmit Data +
2	2	Transmit Data −
3	3	Receive Data +
—	4	Not used
—	5	Not used
6	6	Receive Data −
—	7	Not used
—	8	Not used

a wall plate in an office. The second and third segments, which can be up to a total of 10 meters in length, allow patch cables at each end of the link while restricting signal loss on the total of three interconnected segments. The actual cable standard defined by the EIA/TIA for 10BASE-T is based upon the signaling rate of the network and not the type of network. Under EIA/TIA cable standards, which are described later in this chapter, category 3 cable, which provides support for a signaling rate up to 16 MHz, must be used in a 10BASE-T network. However, it is quite common for most organizations installing 10BASE-T today to use category 5 cabling, which supports transmission up to 100 MHz. This allows an organization to upgrade to a higher-speed LAN without having to replace their cabling infrastructure.

Network Components

A 10BASE-T network can be constructed with network interface cards, UTP cable, and one or more hubs. Each NIC is installed in the expansion slot of a computer and wired on a point-to-point basis to a hub port. When all of the ports on a hub are used, one hub can be connected to another to expand the network, resulting in a physical star, logical bus network structure.

The design of a 10BASE-T hub centric–based network provides a wiring scheme that can tolerate wiring failures much better than a bus-based coaxial cable network. For example, if a coaxial cable is broken at any point, the entire network segment fails. In comparison, the star-wiring topology of a 10BASE-T hub-based network eliminates the single point of failure of a common cable. This is because the failure of a cable between a hub port and a workstation will not affect other workstations. Although the hub is a central point of failure, it is normally a very reliable device, and you can probably expect numerous cable failures from everyday office activity to occur before a hub failure occurring.

Network Interface Cards   Most 10BASE-T network interface cards contain multiple connectors, which enable the card to be used with different types of 802.3 networks. For example, the NIC illustrated in Figure 3.15 includes an RJ-45 jack as well as BNC and DB-15 connectors. The RJ-45 jack supports the direct attachment of the NIC to a 10BASE-T network, while the BNC connector permits the NIC to be mated to a 10BASE-2 T-connector. The DB-15 connector enables the NIC to be cabled to a transceiver, and is more commonly referred to as the NIC's attachment unit interface (AUI) port.

Depending on the type of connectors built into your NIC, you may have several options to consider for connecting the NIC to a specific type of IEEE 802.3 network. For example, assume that your NIC is limited to supporting a thick

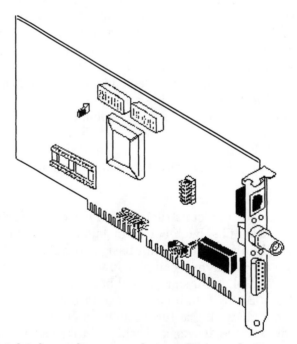

Figure 3.15   Multiple-media network interface card. Some multiple-media network interface cards, such as the one illustrated, support the direct attachment to UTP and thin coaxial cable, while the DB-15 connector permits the card to be cabled to an MAU connected to thick coaxial cable.

or thin coaxial cable connection. In that case, you can still use the NIC to connect to a 10BASE-T network, using a transceiver similar to the one illustrated in Figure 3.16.

Figure 3.16 illustrates a 10BASE-T Ethernet transceiver manufactured by Transition Engineering, Inc. This transceiver allows you to connect an existing thick or thin 10BASE-5 or 10BASE-2 NIC's DB-15 AUI port to a 10BASE-T network. To do this, you would cable the NIC's DB-15 AUI port to the DB-15 connector at the left of the transceiver. Then, you would cable the transceiver to a hub port using UTP.

Hub The wiring hub in a 10BASE-T network functions as a multiport repeater: it receives, retimes, and regenerates signals received from any attached station. The hub also functions as a filter: it discards severely distorted frames.

All hubs that conform to IEEE 10BASE-T specifications perform a core set of tasks in addition to receiving and regenerating signals. 10BASE-T hubs test each port connection, detect and handle excessive collisions, and ignore data that exceeds the maximum 802.3 frame size.

A 10BASE-T hub tests the integrity of the link from each hub port to a connected station by transmitting a special signal to the station. If the device doesn't respond, the hub will automatically shut down the port and may illuminate a status light-emitting diode (LED) to indicate the status of each port.

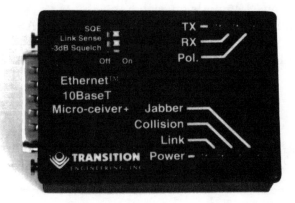

Figure 3.16 Transition 10BASE-T transceiver. With a 10BASE-T transceiver, you can connect existing thick or thin 10BASE-5 or 10BASE-2 NICs to a 10BASE-T network. (Photograph courtesy of Transition Engineering, Inc.)

Hubs monitor, record, and count consecutive collisions that occur on each individual station link. Because an excessive number of consecutive collisions will prevent data transfer on all of the attached links, hubs are required to cut off or partition any link on which too many collisions have occurred. This partitioning enables the remainder of the network to operate in situations where a faulty NIC transmits continuously. Although the IEEE 802.3 standard does not specify a maximum number of consecutive collisions, the standard does specify that partitioning can be initiated only after 30 or more consecutive collisions occur. Thus, some hub vendors initiate partitioning when 31 consecutive collisions occur, while other manufacturers use a higher value.

Another operating function of 10BASE-T hubs is to ignore continuous data transmissions in which the frame length exceeds the maximum length of 1518 bytes. Such excessive length frames usually result from collisions and are referred to as *jabbering*. Most hubs also partition a jabbering port, and some hubs include a jabber indicator LED in addition to a partition status LED on each port.

Although a wiring hub is commonly referred to as a *concentrator*, this term is not technically correct. A 10BASE-T wiring hub is a self-contained unit that typically includes 8, 10, or 12 RJ-45 ports for direct connection to stations, and a BNC and/or DB-15 AUI port for expanding the hub to other network equipment. The BNC and AUI ports enable the 10BASE-T hub to be connected to 10BASE-2 and 10BASE-5 networks, respectively. For the latter, the AUI port is cabled to a 10BASE-5 MAU (transceiver), which is tapped into thick 10BASE-5 coaxial cable. One 10BASE-T hub can be connected to another with a UTP link between RJ-45 ports on each hub.

Figure 3.17 illustrates the connectors on a typical 10BASE-T hub. On some hubs, one RJ-45 jack is labeled uplink/downlink for use in cascading hubs, while other vendors permit any RJ-45 port to be used for connecting hubs.

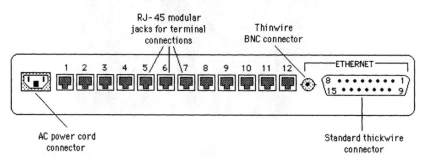

Figure 3.17 10BASE-T hub connectors. In addition to 8, 10, or 12 RJ-45 modular jacks for terminal connections, most 10BASE-T hubs contain a BNC and DB-15 port to permit attachment to thin and thick backbone networks.

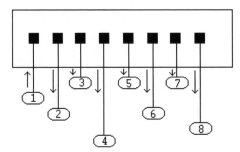

Figure 3.18 A 10BASE-T single hub–based network. A hub functions as a multiport repeater, regenerating data received on one port to all other ports.

Figure 3.18 illustrates the use of a 10BASE-T hub to form a single 10BASE-T network segment. Note that the twisted-pair connections allow workstations to be connected from different locations with respect to the hub, providing more cabling flexibility than bus-based Ethernet networks.

In examining Figure 3.18 note that station 1 is shown transmitting data to the hub. As previously mentioned, the hub functions as a repeater. Thus, it is shown retransmitting data received on one port back to all stations connected to other ports on the hub.

Wiring Requirements There are two types of wiring used with 10BASE-T networks—straight-through and crossover. Each type of wiring is used to support a different type of equipment connection, thus it is important to understand where each type of wiring is used.

Straight-through Wiring The wiring used with UTP cable for connecting a 10BASE-T hub to the network interface card consists of straight-through wiring. That is, each RJ-45 pin used by 10BASE-T would be routed directly from the connector at one end of the cable to the RJ-45 connector at the opposite end of the cable. Figure 3.19 indicates the 10BASE-T hub to NIC wiring requirements.

Crossover Wiring When one hub is connected to another, a special cable must be used. In that cable, the transmit and receive wire pairs have to be crossed over; that is, the receive pair at one end (pins 1 and 2) must be connected to the transmit pair (pins 3 and 6) at the other end of the cable and vice versa. Figure 3.20 illustrates the routing of crossover wiring used to connect two UTP hub ports to one another.

The only exception to using a crossover cable is when a special hub port containing the crossover function is provided. On some hubs this type of port is labeled *crossover,* and it enables a straight-through cable to be used to cas-

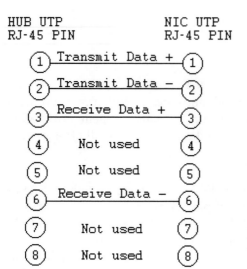

Figure 3.19 10BASE-T hub to NIC wiring.

cade one hub to another. On other hubs an *X* is placed on the crossover, functioning port as a label to indicate pin reversals.

Unlike a hub, a concentrator consists of a main housing into which modular cards are inserted. Although some modular cards may appear to represent hubs, and do indeed function as 10BASE-T hubs, the addition of other mod-

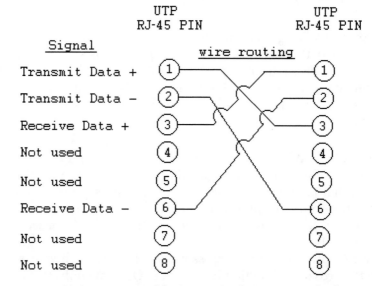

Figure 3.20 A crossover cable is required to connect hubs together.

ules permits the network to be easily expanded from one location and allows additional features to be supported. For example, the insertion of a fiber-optic interrepeater module permits concentrators to be interconnected over relatively long distances of approximately 3 km.

Expanding a 10BASE-T Network

A 10BASE-T network can be expanded with additional hubs once the number of stations serviced uses up the hub's available terminal ports. In expanding a 10BASE-T network, the wiring that joins each hub together is considered to represent a cable segment, while each hub is considered as a repeater. Thus, under the 802.3 specification, no two stations can be separated by more than four hubs connected together by five cable segments. In addition, two of the five segments cannot be populated, which results in 10BASE-T adhering to the previously described 5-4-3 rule.

Figure 3.21 illustrates the expansion of a 10BASE-T network through the use of five hubs. Note that the connection between station A and station B traverses five segments and four hubs, and does not violate IEEE 802.3 connection rules.

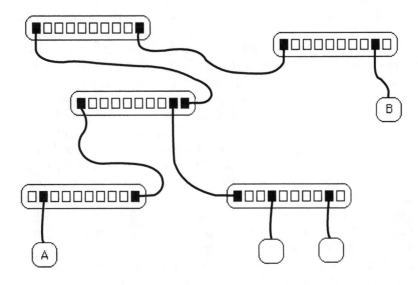

Legend: ◯ = Stations

Figure 3.21 Expanding a 10BASE-T network. No two stations can be separated by more than four hubs in a 10BASE-T network.

Because the maximum span of a 10BASE-T network is 100 meters per segment times five segments, or 500 meters, it is quite common for 10BASE-T networks to use a 10BASE-5 or even a 10BASE-2 cable backbone. As in Figure 3.12, in which a 10BASE-5 cable provided a backbone for a 10BASE-2 network, either 10BASE-2 or 10BASE-5 cable can be used to support an extension of a 10BASE-T network. In such situations, the AUI port of a 10BASE-T hub is connected to a MAU (transceiver) connected to the 10BASE-5 (thick coaxial) cable, or the BNC connector is mated to a thin coaxial cable's T-connector. Another reason for using a thin or thick coaxial cable for a backbone is that you can thereby avoid the four-hub cascading limit of 10BASE-T. For example, if you cabled ten hubs to a 10BASE-5 coaxial cable backbone, each station would traverse at most two hubs, and would thus comply with the IEEE rules. In comparison, you could not connect more than five hubs together in a conventional 10BASE-T network because of IEEE 802.3 rules.

3.3 Use of Fiber-Optic Technology

An addition to Ethernet, which allows transmission via pulses of light instead of electrical current, is known as FOIRL, an acronym that stands for *fiber-optic repeater link.* Although FOIRL is not an Ethernet network, this specification governs the transmission of Ethernet across dual-fiber cable—one fiber is used for the transmission of data in the form of light pulses, while the second fiber is used for the reception of data in the form of light pulses.

Fiber-optic repeater link represents one of two fiber-optic specifications developed to support different types of Ethernet networks operating at 10 Mbps. The second standard, referred to as 10BASE-F, is designed to interoperate with older FOIRL-based equipment and provides backward compatibility with the older specification. Both standards provide immunity from electrical hazards to include electromechanically generated noise and lightning, enabling networks to be extended through gasoline refineries and other areas where metallic media would be banned.

The use of fiber permits you to support multiple Ethernet segments at distances up to 2000 meters (6600 feet) from one another. At a remote location connected through the use of fiber-optic technology, you can connect a single station directly using a fiber transceiver, or you can connect a 10BASE-T or fiber hub and support multiple stations. You would use the AUI port of the hub to provide a connection via a standard transceiver to different types of Ethernet networks, while you would use an optical transceiver to provide a connection to the dual-fiber cable.

FOIRL

The older IEEE 802.3 FOIRL standard enables a fiber link segment to be up to 1000 meters between two repeaters while the more recent 10BASE-F standard doubles the distance to 2000 meters. The greater distance is, however, only obtainable when 10BASE-F repeaters are used at both ends. When 10BASE-F is mixed with FOIRL, the maximum length of the segment is reduced to 1000 meters.

Other differences between FOIRL and 10BASE-F include the names associated with different fiber-optic components associated with each network technology and the optical transmit power levels, receive sensitivity, and power loss associated with each optical technology. In our examination of the use of 10-Mbps fiber-optic media, we will first turn our attention to the use of FOIRL components and, when appropriate, discuss its similarities and differences with respect to the more modern 10BASE-F standard. Once we complete our examination of FOIRL, we will then turn our attention to 10BASE-F.

Optical Transceiver

The optical transceiver is common to both FOIRL and 10BASE-F, with only the optical power transmit and receive levels differing between the two specifications. An optical transceiver consists of a pulse-generating LED, a photodetector, and associated transmit and receive circuitry. Transmit circuitry turns the LED on and off to convert electrical voltages representing data into a series of light pulses for transmission over the fiber. The photodetector recognizes received light pulses, while the receive circuitry generates electrical voltages and shapes pulses to correspond to the received light pulses.

Today, you can purchase a fiber network access unit (NAU), an optical transceiver mounted on an adapter card for installation in the system unit of a personal computer, for less than $200. A second type of optical transceiver used on Ethernet networks is built into fiber hubs, the use of which will be covered next in this section. This type of optical transmitter may be designed to share the use of a common power source and circuitry, resulting in a per-port hub cost usually less than the cost of a fiber adapter.

Fiber Hubs

Under the original FOIRL specification the use of a fiber-optic segment was only applicable between repeaters. This meant that you could not actually connect a distant station directly to a port on a hub. While industry waited for the development of 10BASE-FL standards several vendors, including AT&T, incorporated FOIRL capability into hubs to provide network customers with additional capabilities while awaiting the ability to manufacture 10BASE-FL products once appropriate standards were promulgated. Thus, when we discuss the operation of FOIRL ports in hubs, you should note that this actually references proprietary equipment, because that standard only governed transmission on fiber between repeaters.

A fiber hub is a special type of hub that contains a number of FOIRL ports, one AUI port, and usually one or more 10BASE-T ports. For example, AT&T's original StarLan fiber hub contained six FOIRL ports, one 10BASE-T port, and one AUI port. In comparison, Transition Engineering's Model 1050 fiber-optic hub contains 12 FOIRL ports and one AUI interface port.

In effect, a fiber hub is a grouping of fiber NAUs and one or more 10BASE-T and/or AUI ports. Thus, you can use a fiber hub to support several extended-distance Ethernet connections, and then link those connections directly to a 10BASE-T network with a 10BASE-T port built into the fiber hub, or indirectly to any type of Ethernet network with an AUI port built into the fiber hub. A more modern 10BASE-F hub consists of a series of fiber link (10BASE-FL) ports, with the key difference between 10BASE-F and FOIRL hubs being the optical transmit power and optical receiver sensitivity supported by each port on each hub.

Fiber Adapter

A third type of hardware product used with FOIRL is a fiber adapter. The fiber adapter is a media conversion device that converts between twisted-pair and fiber-optic cable. This device extends the transmission distance between a wire hub and an attached workstation—or another 10BASE-T wire hub—from 100 meters (328 feet) to 1000 meters. If a 10BASE-F fiber adapter is used with a 10BASE-F-compliant hub port, the transmission distance is extended to 2000 meters. For both FOIRL and 10BASE-F, unless the fiber adapter is connected directly to a fiber hub, an adapter is required at each end of an extended fiber link.

Wire and Fiber Distance Limits

Figure 3.22 illustrates the transmission distance limits associated with the use of 10BASE-T and FOIRL-compliant fiber hubs and fiber adapters. Note that a fiber network access unit installed in the system unit of a PC can communicate up to 1000 meters via fiber-optic cable, either directly into a fiber hub or to a fiber adapter connected to a wire hub. Also note that in the upper right corner of Figure 3.22, it was assumed that three 10BASE-T wire hubs were installed in a wire closet. If that wire closet is located on a low floor in a building and your organization leases another floor hundreds of feet above the wire closet floor, the use of fiber-optic cable provides a mechanism to link two network segments together. Similarly, the wire closet shown in the illustration could be in one building on a university campus, with fiber used to connect that building to another building. This use of fiber-optic cable not only extends the transmission distance of the network, but also eliminates the possibility of electromagnetic interference (EMI), because fiber cable is immune to EMI.

The distance limitation associated with the use of FOIRL has nothing to do with the transmission constraints associated with optical signals. Instead, the FOIRL distance limitation is related to the timing constraints in the IEEE 802.3 standard.

Because the FOIRL standard is limited to point-to-point connections, when used to interconnect two 10BASE-2 networks you must consider the cable length of each segment. For example, assume you have two 10BASE-2 networks located in different areas on a large factory floor, as illustrated in Figure 3.23. If segment A has a cable length of 300 meters and segment B has a cable

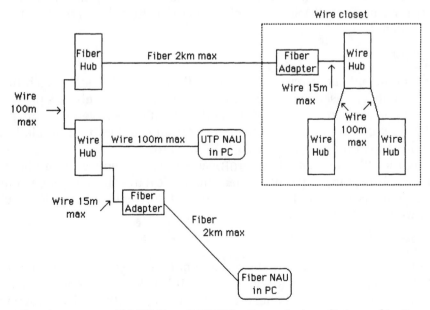

Figure 3.22   10BASE-T and FOIRL transmission distance limits.

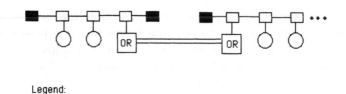

Legend:

◯ = Workstation

OR = Optical repeater

Figure 3.23 Connecting 10BASE-2 networks using a fiber-optic interrepeater link.

length of 500 meters, what is the maximum FOIRL cable length? Because the maximum cabling distance of a 10BASE-2 network is 2500 meters, subtracting the sum of the cable lengths from that cable constraint (2500 − (300 + 500)) results in a maximum fiber-optic link of 1700 meters.

Another constraint you must consider is the Ethernet repeater limitation. Ethernet limits any interconnected network to a maximum of four repeaters between any two nodes. Thus, when considering the use of fiber-optic repeaters, you must take into consideration the maximum network length as well as the number of repeaters that can be placed between nodes. As we will shortly note, under 10BASE-F a mechanism exists that allows the 5-4-3 rule to be exceeded.

10BASE-F

The development and promulgation of the IEEE 10BASE-F standard officially provided network users with the ability to use fiber-optic hubs. As previously noted in the section covering the FOIRL specification, vendors integrated FOIRL capability into hubs; however, the actual standard that officially provided this capability was the 10BASE-F standard.

Under the 10BASE-F standard, which actually represents a set of fiber-optic media standards, three types of segments for optical transmission were defined. Those segments include 10BASE-FL, 10BASE-FB, and 10BASE-FP, each of which we will now examine.

10BASE-FL

The 10BASE-FL standard provides a fiber-optic link segment that can be up to 2000 meters in length, providing that only 10BASE-FL equipment is used at both ends of the segment. Otherwise, the mixing of 10BASE-FL and FOIRL equipment reduces the maximum length of the optical segment to 1000 meters.

The development of the 10BASE-FL standard was intended as a replacement for the older FOIRL specification. Unlike FOIRL that was restricted to providing an optical connection between repeaters, 10BASE-FL enables an optical segment to be routed between two workstations, two repeaters, or between a workstation and a repeater port.

The actual connection of a copper-based network node to a 10BASE-FL segment can be accomplished in one of two ways. First, a stand-alone fiber-optic MAU (FOMAU) can be connected via the 15-pin AUI connector on a network adapter to provide an electrical-to-optical conversion capability. A second method is to use a 10BASE-T/FL converter. The latter is used when only a 10BASE-T port is available on a NIC. Both the 10BASE-FL FOMAU and the 10BASE-T/FL converter include two fiber-optic connectors, one for transmitting and one for receiving data. Some 10BASE-T/FL converters include two RJ-45 connectors that provide a high degree of cabling flexibility. One RJ-45 connector functions as a crossover cable and allows hub-to-hub communications via optical media, while the second connector is for workstations that use a straight-through connection.

The top portion of Figure 3.24 illustrates the connection of a workstation to a 10BASE-FL FOMAU via a 15-pin AUI connector. The lower portion of that illustration shows the use of a 10BASE-T/FL converter. Both devices provide you with the ability to transmit up to 2000 meters via a fiber link when a 10BASE-F-compliant optical device is at the other end of the optical link.

In addition to the use of a 10BASE-FL FOMAU and 10BASE-T/FL converter, other types of converters have been developed to extend a fiber-optic transmission capability to other types of Ethernet networks. For example, a 10BASE-2/FL converter enables you to extend the transmission distance of a 10BASE-2 network via a fiber-optic connection.

The creation of a 10BASE-F optical hub is accomplished by the inclusion of two or more FOMAUs in the hub. This results in the hub becoming an optical repeater, which retransmits data received on one port onto all other ports. Under the 10BASE-F standard you can use multiple 10BASE-FL connections to connect several individual workstations at distances up to 2000 meters to a common hub equipped with FOMAU ports.

When examining the potential use of a converter or a FOMAU, it is important to verify the type of optical media supported. Multimode fiber (MMF) is commonly used, with the most popular type of fiber having a 62.5-micron (μ) fiber-optic core and a 125-μ outer cladding. This type of multimode fiber is referenced by the numerics 62.5/125 μ. The wavelength of light used on a 62.5/125-μ MMF fiber link is 850 nanometers (nm), and the *optical loss budge,* a term used to reference the amount of optical power lost through attenuation,

a. Using a fiber-optic MAU (FOMAU)

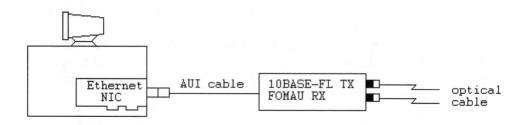

b. Using a 10BASE-T/FL converter

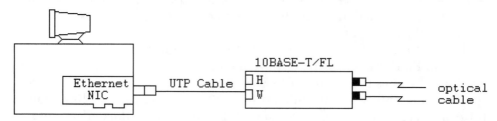

Figure 3.24   Options for connection of a workstation to a 10BASE-FL segment.

should not exceed the range 9.7 to 190 dB, with the exact amount dependent upon the type of fiber used. Table 3.3 provides a comparison of the optical attenuation for 10BASE-FL and FOIRL for six types of multimode fiber. In examining the entries in Table 3.3, you will note that 10BASE-FL has a higher loss budge than FOIRL for each type of multimode fiber. This explains why the transmission distance of 10BASE-FL optical repeaters exceeds the distance obtainable using FOIRL repeaters.

10BASE-FB

A second 10BASE-F specification is 10BASE-FB, with the *B* used to denote a synchronous signaling backbone segment. The 10BASE-FB specification enables the limit on the number of repeaters previously described in the 5-4-3 rule section to be exceeded. A 10BASE-FB signaling repeater is commonly used to connect repeater hubs together into a repeated backbone network infrastructure that can span multiple 2000-m links.

TABLE 3.3 Comparing the Loss Budget (Optical Attenuation) of 10BASE-FL and FOIRL

Multimode, graded index fiber size (μm)	50/125	50/125	50/125	62.5/125	83/125	100/140
Numerical aperture	.20	.21	.22	.275	.26	.30
10BASE-FL Loss budget (dB)	9.7	9.2	9.6	13.5	15.7	19.0
FOIRL Loss budget (dB)	7.2	6.7	7.1	11.0	13.2	16.5

10BASE-FP

A third 10BASE-F specification was developed to support the connection of multiple stations via a common segment that can be up to 500 meters in length. Referred to as 10BASE-FP, the P references the fact that the end segment is a fiber-passive system. Under the 10BASE-FP specification a single fiber-optic passive-star coupler can be used to connect up to 33 stations. Those stations can be located up to 500 meters from a hub via the use of a shared fiber segment.

Although 10BASE-FP provides a clustering capability that might represent a practical networking solution to the requirements of some organizations, as well as reduce the cost associated with the use of multiple individual optical cables, most organizations prefer to link hubs together. Doing so also allows the use of a single pair of optical cables; however, the transmission distance to the cluster is then extended to 2000 meters.

3.4 High-Speed Ethernet

To differentiate Gigabit Ethernet from other versions of Ethernet whose operating rates exceed 10 Mbps but have a maximum operating rate one-tenth that of Gigabit, those versions of Ethernet that operate at or below 100 Mbps were classified as high-speed Ethernet and are covered in this section. This enables Gigabit Ethernet to be covered as a separate entity in Section 3.5.

There are three broad categories into which high-speed Ethernet networks fall. The first two types of high-speed Ethernet networks are represented by de jure standards for operations at 100 Mbps, while the third standard represents an extension to 10BASE-T that operates at 16 Mbps. As discussed in Chapter 2, the IEEE standardized two general types of 100-Mbps Ethernet networks, with the 802.3µ standard defining three types of 100-Mbps CSMA/CD networks, while the 802.12 standard defines a demand-priority operation that replaces the CSMA/CD access protocol. The third high-speed Ethernet network is considered as a high-speed network only when compared with the operating rate of Ethernet networks developed before 1992. This type of network, referred to as *isochronous Ethernet* (isoENET), operates at 16 Mbps. This section will focus upon obtaining a detailed overview of the operation and use of each of these three types of Ethernet networks.

Isochronous Ethernet

Isochronous Ethernet, or isoENET, represents an extension to 10BASE-T technology. Isochronous Ethernet adds time-sensitive multimedia support through an addition of 6.144 Mbps of isochronous bandwidth to existing 10-Mbps 10BASE-T Ethernet. Here, the term *isochronous* references a series of repetitive time slots used for the transmission of constant bit-rate services at the physical bit-transmission level. Because multimedia applications transporting audio or video are time sensitive, an isochronous transmission scheme provides an ideal mechanism to support this application.

Isochronous Ethernet dates to 1992, when National Semiconductor and IBM, with support from Apple Computer, submitted the basics of isoENET to the IEEE 802.9 Integrated Services Local Area Networks working group. Better known by its trade names isoEthernet and isoENET, this technique was standardized by the IEEE as standard 802.9a, with the official designation Integrated Service Local Area Network (ISLAN16-T). Here, the *T* in the abbreviation denotes its capability to operate over twisted-pair wiring, while the *16* references its operating rate. In comparison with other Ethernet LANs that are asynchronous, isoENET was developed to support the 8-KHz sampling clock used as a worldwide standard for voice transmission. This synchronization capability was layered on top of the 10-Mbps 10BASE-T operating rate, enabling isoENET to support real-time communications in addition to conventional 10BASE-T asynchronous LAN transmission.

Isochronous Ethernet can be considered to represent a hybrid type of Ethernet network, combining standard 10-Mbps 802.3 10BASE-T with a 6.144-Mbps isochronous networking capability. The 6.144 Mbps of additional bandwidth is designed to accommodate 96 integrated services digital network (ISDN) B-channels, either individually or in multiple combinations of $N \times 64$ Kbps. For example, a videoconference requiring 128 Kbps of bandwidth would be assigned two 64-Kbps channels, while digitized voice that requires 64 Kbps when pulse code modulation (PCM) is used for digitization would be assigned one channel.

In addition to supporting 96 ISDN B-channels, the isochronous bandwidth supports one 64-Kbps ISDN D-channel that is used for signaling and one 96-Kbps ISDN M-channel that is used to support ISDN maintenance functions. Figure 3.25 illustrates the allocation of isoENET bandwidth. In examining Figure 3.25, note that isoENET was developed to operate over the existing 10BASE-T wiring infrastructure, enabling the large installed base of Category 3 UTP cabling to be used to support this hybrid network.

The key to the operation of isoENET is the replacement of Manchester encoding used by 10BASE-T to a 4B/5B encoding scheme, which represents the data encoding method used by the ANSI X3T9.5 FDDI standard. Under 4B/5B coding, each octet of data is split into two four-bit nibbles (4B). Each nibble is then coded using five bits (5B), resulting in an 80-percent level of utilization of the 20-MHz IEEE 802.3 clock signal. In comparison, Manchester encoding provides a 50-percent utilization of the 20-MHz clock. The change in the method of data coding provides an additional 6.144-Mbps bandwidth on existing 10BASE-T wiring, connector, and hub facilities. However, the use of the additional bandwidth requires the installation of an isoENET hub and isoENET adapter cards for each local area network node that requires an isochronous communications capability. Users who do not require an isochronous communications capability can continue to use their existing 10BASE-T adapter cards, and 802.3 traffic will not notice any change to the operation of a 10BASE-T network. Figure 3.26 illustrates an isoENET hub supporting conventional 10BASE-T and isoENET network nodes.

An isoENET network provides a mechanism to add multimedia support to users who require that capability, while enabling your investment in 10BASE-T wiring, adapter cards, and hubs to be maintained. For example, if users connected to hubs do not require multimedia support, you can leave that portion

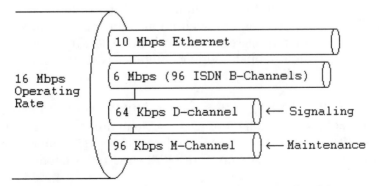

Figure 3.25   Allocation of isoENET bandwidth.

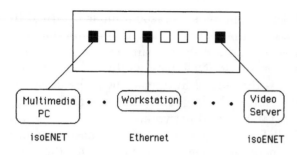

isoENET   Ethernet   isoENET

Figure 3.26   isoENET supports the addition of 6.155 Mbps to nodes equipped with isoENET adapter cards.

of a 10BASE-T network as is. Thus, isoENET provides you with a mechanism to selectively upgrade a 10BASE-T network.

One of the key advantages associated with the use of isoENET is its ability to support multimedia on the LAN, and to and from the LAN and a WAN. A multimedia dial tone, which represents the signaling protocol required to establish and tear down multimedia calls, is built into isoENET on a supplementary 64-Kbps signaling channel previously illustrated in Figure 3.25. In addition, because the hybrid ISDN extension supports ISDN and PSTN (public switched telephone network) telephone numbers, isoENET users can originate and receive calls to and from ISDN and PSTN subscribers. Thus, it becomes possible for a group of isoENET users to obtain an intra- and inter-LAN communications capability and a distant PSTN and ISDN communications capability by connecting an isoENET hub to a PBX or a telephone company central office. Figure 3.27 illustrates an example of how an ISDN PRI (primary rate interface) line, capable of supporting 23 bearer channels, each operating at 64 Kbps and a 64-Kbps signaling channel (D-channel), could be routed from an isoENET hub to a telephone company control office, providing inter- and intra-LAN voice and data communications. In examining Figure 3.27, note that conventional 10BASE-T hubs can be connected to an isoENET hub; however, this precludes the ability of stations connected to the 10BASE-T hub from using the isochronous transmission capability of the network. Also note that by aggregating two or more 64-Kbps B-channels, each isoENET station could establish a videoconference with another isoENET station on the same or a distant LAN or connect to a videoconference room that uses ISDN.

One of the first isoENET applications was IBM's Person-to-Person videoconferencing software, which became available in mid-1995. Providing users with the ability to perform personal conferencing at 15 frames per second, this application, which was sold with OS/2, was redesigned to work with isoENET.

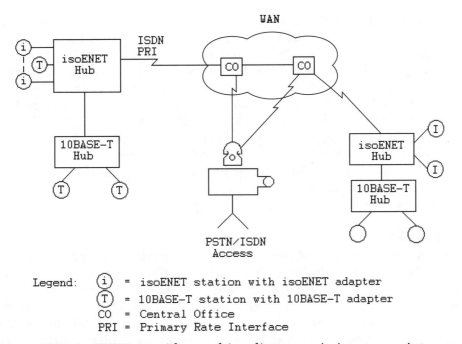

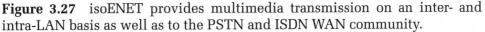

Legend: (i) = isoENET station with isoENET adapter
           (T) = 10BASE-T station with 10BASE-T adapter
           CO   = Central Office
           PRI = Primary Rate Interface

Figure 3.27 isoENET provides multimedia transmission on an inter- and intra-LAN basis as well as to the PSTN and ISDN WAN community.

Although at one time about a dozen vendors manufactured isoENET products and its use provides a mechanism to extend multimedia to the desktop, other Ethernet technologies dulled the demand for its 16-Mbps communications capability. The introduction of 100BASE-T and Gigabit Ethernet appears to resolve the bandwidth crunch experienced by many networks that added Internet connections and graphics-intensive applications. Because it appears that greater bandwidth was more important than obtaining a videoconferencing capability to the desktop, a majority of vendor and customer interest became focused upon faster Ethernet solutions than that provided by iso-ENET.

Fast Ethernet

Fast Ethernet is not actually a local area network, but a term commonly used to reference a series of three 100-Mbps physical-layer LAN specifications in the IEEE 802.3µ addendum. Those specifications include 100BASE-TX,

100BASE-FX, and 100BASE-T4. Each specification maintains the use of the MAC protocol used by earlier Ethernet/IEEE 802.3 standards, CSMA/CD.

100BASE-T specifies 100-Mbps operations using the CSMA/CD protocol over two pairs of category 5 UTP cable. 100BASE-FX changes the LAN transport media to two pairs of fiber, while 100BASE-T4 supports four pairs of category 3, 4, and 5 UTP or STP cable. Table 3.4 provides a summary of the three types of Fast Ethernet with respect to their IEEE media specification designation, types of media supported, types of connectors supported, and the coding scheme used. Because an understanding of Fast Ethernet requires knowledge of the LAN transport media, we will first focus upon the characteristics of UTP and STP cable. In doing so, we will examine the EIA/TIA-568 standard that defines different building cabling parameters.

EIA/TIA-568

The Electronics Industry Association/Telecommunications Industries Association "Commercial Building Telecommunications Standard," commonly referred to as EIA/TIA-568, was ratified in 1992. This standard specifies a variety of building cabling parameters, ranging from backbone cabling used to connect a building's telecommunication closets to an equipment room, to horizontal cabling used to cable individual users to the equipment closet. The standard defines the performance characteristics of both backbone and horizontal cables as well as different types of connectors used with different types of cable.

Backbone Cabling   Four types of media are recognized by the EIA/TIA-568 standard for backbone cabling. Table 3.5 lists the media options supported by the EIA/TIA-568 standard for backbone cabling.

TABLE 3.4   Fast Ethernet Functionality

IEEE Media Specifications	Cable Support	Connector Support	Coding Scheme
100BASE-TX	Category 5 UTP (2-pair wire)	RJ-45	4B/5B
	100-ohm STP (2-pair wire)	DB-9	
100BASE-FX	62.5/125-micron fiber-optic cable (2 multimode fibers)	SC or ST	4B/5B
100BASE-T4	Category 3, 4, or 5 UTP (4-pair wire)	RJ-45	8B6T

Legend: UTP, unshielded twisted pair; STP, shielded twisted pair.

TABLE 3.5   EIA/TIA-568 Backbone Cabling Media Options

Media Type	Maximum Cable Distance
100-ohm UTP	800 meters (2624 feet)
150-ohm STP	700 meters (2296 feet)
50-ohm thick coaxial cable	500 meters (1640 feet)
62.5/125-µ multimode optical fiber	2000 meters (6560 feet)

Horizontal Cabling   As previously indicated, horizontal cabling under the EIA/TIA-568 standard consists of cable that connects equipment in a telecommunications closet to a user's work area. The media options supported for horizontal cabling are the same as specified for backbone cabling, with the exception of coaxial cable for which 50-ohm thin cable is specified; however, cabling distances are restricted to 90 meters in length from equipment in the telecommunications closet to a telecommunications outlet. This permits a patch cord or drop cable up to 10 meters in length to be used to connect a user workstation to a telecommunications outlet, resulting in the total length of horizontal cabling not exceeding the 100-meter restriction associated with many LAN technologies that use UTP cabling.

UTP Categories

One of the more interesting aspects of the EIA/TIA-568 standard is its recognition that different signaling rates require different cable characteristics. This resulted in the EIA/TIA-568 standard classifying UTP cable into five categories. Those categories and their suitability for different types of voice and data applications are indicated in Table 3.6.

In examining the entries in Table 3.6, note that categories 3 through 5 support transmission with respect to indicated signaling rates. This means that the ability of those categories of UTP to support different types of LAN trans-

TABLE 3.6   EIA/TIA-568 UTP Cable Categories

Category 1	Voice or low-speed data up to 56 Kbps; not useful for LANs.
Category 2	Data rates up to 1 Mbps.
Category 3	Supports transmission up to 16 MHz.
Category 4	Supports transmission up to 20 MHz.
Category 5	Supports transmission up to 100 MHz.

mission will depend upon the signaling method used by different LANs. For example, consider a LAN encoding technique that results in 6 bits encoded into 4 signaling elements that have a 100-MHz signaling rate. Through the use of category 5 cable, a data transmission rate of 150 Mbps ((6/4) × 100) could be supported.

Category 3 cable is typically used for Ethernet and 4 Mbps Token-Ring LANs. Category 4 is normally used for 16-Mbps Token-Ring LANs, while category 5 cable supports 100-Mbps Ethernet LANs, such as 100VG-AnyLAN and 100BASE-T, and will support ATM to the desktop at a 155-Mbps operating rate.

Cable Specifications

There are two metrics that define the capability of EIA/TIA-568 cable with respect to the signaling rate they support, which in turn defines the cable category. Those metrics are attenuation and near-end crosstalk (NEXT).

Attenuation Attenuation represents the loss of signal power as a signal propagates from a transmitter at one end of a cable toward a receiving device located at the distant end of the cable. Attenuation is measured in decibels (dB) as indicated:

$$\text{Attenuation} = 20 \log_{10} \frac{\text{(transmit voltage)}}{\text{receive voltage}}$$

For those of us a little rusty with logarithms, let's examine a few examples of attenuation computations. First, let's assume the transmit voltage was 100, while the receive voltage was 1. Then,

$$\text{Attenuation} = 20 \log_{10} \frac{(100)}{1} = 20 \log_{10} 100$$

The value of $\log_{10} 100$ can be obtained by determining the power to which 10 should be raised to equal 100. Because the answer is 2 ($10^2 = 100$), $\log_{10} 100$ has a value of 2, and $20 \log_{10} 100$ then has a value of 40.

Now let's assume the transmit voltage was 10 while the receiver voltage was 1. Then,

$$\text{Attenuation} = 20 \log_{10} \frac{(10)}{1} = 20 \log_{10} 10$$

Because the value of $\log_{10} 10$ is 1 ($10^1 = 10$), then $20 \log_{10} 10$ has a value of 20. From the preceding, note that a lower level of signal power loss results in a lower level of attenuation.

NEXT   Crosstalk represents the electromagnetic interference caused by a signal on one wire pair being emitted onto another wire pair, resulting in the generation of noise. Because transmit and receive pairs are twisted and the transmit signal is strongest at its source, the maximum level of interference occurs at the cable connector and decreases as the transmit signal traverses the cable. Recognizing this fact of physics, crosstalk is measured at the near end, hence the term near-end crosstalk (NEXT).

NEXT denotes the induced or coupled signal flowing from the transmit pair to the receive pair even though the two pairs are not interconnected. Mathematically, NEXT is defined in decibels (dB) as follows:

$$\text{NEXT} = 20 \, \log_{10} \frac{\text{(transmitted voltage)}}{\text{coupled voltage}}$$

In the preceding equation the transmit voltage represents the power placed on the transmit pair, while the coupled signal is measured on the receive pair at the location where the transmit voltage was generated. Note that a larger dB NEXT measurement is better as it indicates a lower level of crosstalk and is the opposite of attenuation, because a lower attenuation reading indicates less signal loss and is better than a higher reading for that parameter. Table 3.7 indicates the EIA/TIA-568 specification limits for categories 3, 4, and 5 UTP cable. In examining Table 3.7, note that both attenuation and NEXT must be measured over a range of frequencies. That range is based upon the cable category. For example, because category 3 cable is designed to support signaling

TABLE 3.7   EIA/TIA-568 Attenuation and NEXT Limits in dB

Frequency (MHz)	Category 3		Category 4		Category 5	
	Attenuation	NEXT	Attenuation	NEXT	Attenuation	NEXT
1.0	4.2	39.1	2.6	53.3	2.5	60.3
4.0	7.3	29.3	4.8	43.3	4.5	50.6
8.0	10.2	24.3	6.7	38.2	6.3	45.6
10.0	11.5	22.7	7.5	36.6	7.0	44.0
16.0	14.9	19.3	9.9	33.1	9.2	40.6
20.0	—	—	11.0	31.4	10.3	39.0
25.0	—	—	—	—	11.4	37.4
31.2	—	—	—	—	12.8	35.7
62.5	—	—	—	—	18.5	30.6
100.0	—	—	—	—	24.0	27.1

rates up to 16 MHz, attenuation and NEXT should be measured up to and including the highest signaling rate supported by that type of cable, which is 16 MHz.

100BASE-T Overview

The standardization of 100BASE-T required an extension of previously developed IEEE 802.3 standards. In the definition process of standardization development, both the Ethernet media access control (MAC) and physical layer required adjustments to permit 100-Mbps operational support. For the MAC layer, scaling its speed to 100 Mbps from the 10BASE-T 10-Mbps operational rate required a minimal adjustment, because in theory the 10BASE-T MAC layer was developed independently of the data rate. For the physical layer, more than a minor adjustment was required, because Fast Ethernet was designed to support three types of media. Using work developed in the standardization process of FDDI in defining 125-Mbps full-duplex signaling to accommodate optical fiber, UTP, and STP through physical media-dependent (PMD) sublayers, Fast Ethernet borrowed this strategy. Because a mechanism was required to map the PMD's continuous signaling system to the start-stop *half-duplex* system used at the Ethernet MAC layer, the physical layer was subdivided. This subdivision is illustrated in Figure 3.28. The PMD sublayer supports the appropriate media to be used, while the convergence sublayer (CS), which was later renamed the physical coding sublayer, performs the mapping between the PMD and the Ethernet MAC layer.

Although Fast Ethernet represents a tenfold increase in the LAN operating rate from 10BASE-T to ensure proper collision detection, the 100BASE-T network span was reduced to 200 meters, with a maximum of 100 meters permitted between a network node and a hub. The smaller network diameter reduces potential propagation delay. When coupled with a tenfold operating

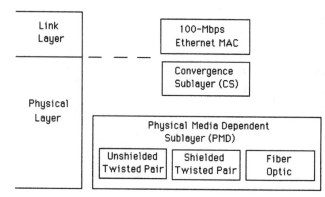

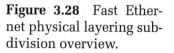

Figure 3.28 Fast Ethernet physical layering subdivision overview.

rate increase and no change in network frame size, the ratio of frame duration to network propagation delay for a 100BASE-T network is the same as for a 10BASE-T network.

Physical Layer

The physical layer subdivision previously illustrated in Figure 3.28, as indicated in the title of the figure, presents an overview of the true layer subdivision. In actuality, a number of changes were required at the physical layer to obtain a 10-Mbps operating rate. Those changes include the use of three wire pairs for data (the fourth is used for collision detection), 8B6T ternary coding (for 100BASE-T4) instead of Manchester coding, and an increase in the clock signaling speed from 20 MHz to 25 MHz. As indicated in Table 3.8, in comparison to 10BASE-T the differences at the physical layer resulted in a tenfold increase in the 100BASE-T operating rate.

When the specifications for Fast Ethernet were being developed, it was recognized that the physical signaling layer would incorporate medium-dependent functions if support was extended to two-pair cable (100BASE-TX) operations. To separate medium-dependent interfaces to accommodate multiple physical layers, a common interface referred to as the medium–independent interface (MII) was inserted between the MAC layer and the physical encoding sublayer. The MII represents a common point of interoperability between the medium and the MAC layer. The MII can support two specific data rates, 10 Mbps and 100 Mbps, permitting older 10BASE-T nodes to be supported at Fast Ethernet hubs. To reconcile the MII signal with the MAC signal, a reconciliation sublayer was added under the MAC layer, resulting in the subdivision of the link layer into three parts—a logical link control layer, a media access control layer, and a reconciliation layer. The top portion of Figure 3.29 illustrates this subdivision.

That portion of Fast Ethernet below the MII, which is the new physical layer, is now subdivided into three sublayers. The lower portion of Figure 3.29 illustrates the physical sublayers for 100BASE-T4 and 100BASE-TX.

TABLE 3.8 100BASE-T System Throughput Compared with 10BASE-T

Transmit on 3 pairs vs. 1 pair	×3.00
8B6T coding instead of Manchester	×2.65
20 to 25 MHz clock increase	×1.25
Total throughput increase	10.00

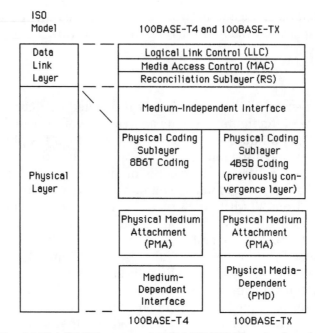

ISO
Model   100BASE-T4 and 100BASE-TX

Data Link Layer		Logical Link Control (LLC)
		Media Access Control (MAC)
		Reconciliation Sublayer (RS)

Medium-Independent Interface

Physical Layer	Physical Coding Sublayer 8B6T Coding	Physical Coding Sublayer 4B5B Coding (previously con- vergence layer)
	Physical Medium Attachment (PMA)	Physical Medium Attachment (PMA)
	Medium- Dependent Interface	Physical Media- Dependent (PMD)

100BASE-T4   100BASE-TX

Figure 3.29 100BASE-T4 versus 100BASE-TX physical and link layers.

The physical coding sublayer performs the data encoding, transmit, receive, and carrier sense functions. Because the data coding method differs between 100BASE-T4 and 100BASE-TX, this difference requires distinct physical coding sublayers for each version of Fast Ethernet.

The physical medium attachment (PMA) sublayer maps messages from the physical coding sublayer (PCS) onto the twisted-pair transmission media, and vice versa.

The medium-dependent interface (MDI) sublayer specifies the use of a standard RJ-45 connector. Although the same connector is used for 100BASE-TX, the use of two pairs of cable instead of four results in different pin assignments.

100BASE-T4

As previously discussed at the beginning of this section covering Fast Ethernet, 100BASE-T4 supports a 100-Mbps operating rate over four pairs of category 3, 4, or 5 UTP wiring. Figure 3.30 illustrates the RJ-45 pin assignments of wire pairs used by 100BASE-T4. Note that wire pairs D1 and D2 are unidirectional. As indicated in Figure 3.30, three wire pairs are available for data transmission and reception in each direction, while the fourth pair is used for

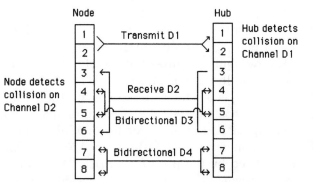

Figure 3.30 100BASE-T4 pin assignments.

collision detection. Because 100BASE-T4 can operate on category 3, which is used for 10BASE-T, this feature enables many organizations to migrate to a 100-Mbps network without changing their wiring infrastructure.

The 100BASE-T4 physical coding sublayer implements 8B6T block coding. Under this coding technique, each block of eight input bits is transformed into a unique code group of six ternary symbols. Figure 3.31 provides an overview of the 8B6T coding process used by 100BASE-T4.

The output code groups resulting from 8B6T coding flow out to three parallel channels that are placed on three twisted pairs. Thus, the effective data rate on each pair is 100 Mbps/3, or 33.33 Mbps. Because 6 bits are represented by 8 bit positions, the signaling rate or baud rate on each cable pair becomes 33 Mbps × 6/8, or 25 MHz, which is the clock rate used at the MII sublayer.

100BASE-TX

As previously discussed, 100BASE-TX represents the use of two pairs of category 5 UTP cabling with RJ-45 connectors or two pairs of category 5 STP cable terminated with the common DB-9 communications connector used on the serial port of many notebook computers. A 100BASE-TX network requires a hub, and the maximum cable run is 100 meters from hub port to node, with a maximum network diameter of 200 meters.

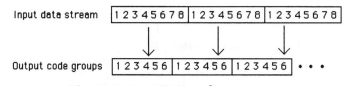

Figure 3.31 8B6T coding process.

Figure 3.32 illustrates the cabling of two pairs of UTP wires between a hub and node to support 100BASE-TX transmission. One pair of wires is used for transmission, while the second pair is used for collision detection and reception of data. The use of a 125-MHz frequency requires the use of a *data grade* cable. Thus, 100BASE-TX is based upon the use of category 5 UTP and STP.

Although the 100BASE-TX physical layer structure resembles the 100BASE-T4 layer, there are significant differences between the two to accommodate the differences in media used. At the physical coding sublayer, the 100-Mbps start-stop bit stream from the MII is first converted to a full-duplex 125-Mbps bit stream. This conversion is accomplished by the use of the FDDI PMD as the 100BASE-TX PMD. Next, the data stream is encoded using a 4B5B coding scheme. The 100BASE-TX PMD decodes symbols from the 125-Mbps continuous bit stream and converts the stream to 100-Mbps start-stop data bits when the data flow is reversed.

4B5B Coding

The use of a 4B5B coding scheme enables data and control information to be carried in each symbol represented by a 5-bit code group. In addition, an inter-Stream fill code (IDLE) is defined, as well as a symbol used to force signaling errors. Because 4 data bits are mapped into a 5-bit code, only 16 symbols are required to represent data. The remaining symbols not used for control or to denote an IDLE condition are not used by 100BASE-TX and are considered as invalid.

Table 3.9 lists the 4B5B 100BASE-TX code groups. Because an explanation of the use of the control codes and IDLE code requires an examination of the MAC frame, we will defer our discussion of those symbols until Chapter 4, as frame formats are discussed in that chapter.

100BASE-FX

100BASE-FX represents the third 100BASE-T wiring scheme, defining Fast Ethernet transmission over fiber-optic media. 100BASE-FX requires the use of two-strand 62.5/125-micron multimode fiber media and supports the 4B5B coding scheme, identical to the one used by 100BASE-TX.

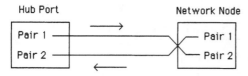

Figure 3.32   100BASE-TX cabling.

TABLE 3.9   4B/5B Code Groups

PCS Code Group		MII (TXD/RXD)	
4 3 2 1 0	Name	3 2 1 0	Interpretation
DATA			
1 1 1 1 0	0	0 0 0 0	Data 0
0 1 0 0 1	1	0 0 0 1	Data 1
1 0 1 0 0	2	0 0 1 0	Data 2
1 0 1 0 1	3	0 0 1 1	Data 3
0 1 0 1 0	4	0 1 0 0	Data 4
0 1 0 1 1	5	0 1 0 1	Data 5
0 1 1 1 0	6	0 1 1 0	Data 6
0 1 1 1 1	7	0 1 1 1	Data 7
1 0 0 1 0	8	1 0 0 0	Data 8
1 0 0 1 1	9	1 0 0 1	Data 9
1 0 1 1 0	A	1 0 1 0	Data A
1 0 1 1 1	B	1 0 1 1	Data B
1 1 0 1 0	C	1 1 0 0	Data C
1 1 0 1 1	D	1 1 0 1	Data D
1 1 1 0 0	E	1 1 1 0	Data E
1 1 1 0 1	F	1 1 1 1	Data F
IDLE			
1 1 1 1 1	I		IDLE:
			Used as inter-Stream fill code
CONTROL			
1 1 0 0 0	J		Start-of-stream delimiter, part 1 of 2; always used in pairs with K.
1 0 0 0 1	K		Start-of-stream delimiter, part 2 of 2; always used in pairs with J.
0 1 1 0 1	T		End-of-stream delimiter, part 1 of 2; always used in pairs with R.
0 0 1 1 1	R		End-of-stream delimiter, part 2 of 2; always used in pairs with T.
INVALID			
0 0 1 0 0	H		Transmit error; used to force signaling errors.
0 0 0 0 0	V		Invalid code
0 0 0 0 1	V		Invalid code
0 0 0 1 0	V		Invalid code

TABLE 3.9 (*Continued*)

PCS Code Group		MII (TXD/RXD)	
4 3 2 1 0	Name	3 2 1 0	Interpretation
0 0 0 1 1	V		Invalid code
0 0 1 0 1	V		Invalid code
0 0 1 1 0	V		Invalid code
0 1 0 0 0	V		Invalid code
0 1 1 0 0	V		Invalid code
1 0 0 0 0	V		Invalid code
1 1 0 0 1	V		Invalid code

100BASE-FX provides an extended network diameter of up to 400 meters. However, in a mixed 100BASE-T4 and 100BASE-FX environment, the collision domain should not exceed 231 meters, consisting of 100 meters for 100BASE-T4 and 131 meters for 100BASE-FX. Concerning connectors, 100BASE-FX supports both ST and SC fiber connectors, which were originally defined for FDDI.

Network Construction and Use

Similar to 10-Mbps Ethernet networks, you can use adapter cards, cable, and hubs to construct a variety of Fast Ethernet networks to satisfy different organizational network requirements. However, when doing so, it is important to understand the role of repeaters in a Fast Ethernet environment, as the standard defines two types, each having a different effect upon network construction.

Repeater Rules

When we examined Ethernet we discussed the 5-4-3 rule, which applied to a common type of repeater. When we discuss Fast Ethernet we must consider two types of repeaters, referred to as Class I and Class II repeaters.

A Class I repeater has a greater budget for timing delay, enabling it to be used to support dissimilar physical media segments that use dissimilar signaling such as 100BASE-T4 and 100BASE-TX. This support is possible because the greater budget of the Class I repeater enables it to translate the line signal received on one port to a different type of signal for transmission onto other ports. Only one Class I repeater can be installed in a segment. In comparison, a Class II repeater has a lower budget for timing delay, resulting in it being faster than a Class I repeater. This enables up to two Class II repeaters to be used in a segment; however, in doing so the interrepeater cable length is limited to 5 meters when data terminal equipment are 100 meters from repeaters. Because a Class II repeater immediately repeats an incoming signal onto all other ports other than the port data was received on without a translation process being possible, it can only be used to interconnect segment types that use the same signaling method, such as 100BASE-TX and 100BASE-FX.

The actual span distance obtainable through the use of repeaters depends upon the type of repeater used and the media cable. Figure 3.33 illustrates the cable restrictions associated with Fast Ethernet. In examining the entries in Figure 3.33, note that the repeater references a Fast Ethernet hub, because the hub receives information on one port and rebroadcasts the received data onto all other ports. To exceed the cable limits shown in Figure 3.33, you must connect the workstation or hub port to a switch, bridge, or router, which results in a new segment being established. Concerning those cable limits, although all

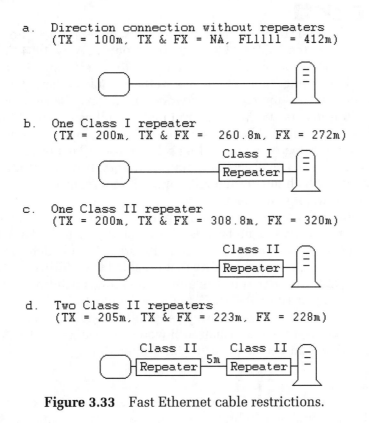

Figure 3.33   Fast Ethernet cable restrictions.

vendors support the first two cabling distances shown in Figure 3.33a and 3.33b, there are minor differences in the construction of Class II–type repeaters between some vendors that may reduce the span distance from that shown in Figure 3.33c for a mixture of TX and FX or FX usage. In addition, the use of two Class II repeaters manufactured by different vendors can also result in a slight reduction from the span distances shown in Figure 3.33d for a mixture of TX and FX and FX repeater use. Thus, it is highly recommended to check vendor specification sheets concerning the network guidelines associated with a particular type of repeater.

Because 100BASE-T4 and 100BASE-TX preserve the 10BASE-T MAC layer, both standards are capable of interoperability with existing 10BASE-T networks as well as with other low-speed Ethernet technology. Through the use of NWay autosensing logic, Fast Ethernet adapters, hub, and switch ports can determine if attached equipment can transmit at 10 or 100 Mbps and adjust to the operating rate of the distant device.

NWay Autonegotiation

NWay is a cable and transmission autosensing scheme proposed by National Semiconductor to the IEEE 802.3 standards group in May 1994. The NWay autosensing scheme permits Ethernet circuits to detect both the cable type and speed of incoming Ethernet data, as well as enables Ethernet repeaters to configure themselves for correct network operations. Because NWay can detect 10-Mbps versus 100-Mbps operations, as well as half- and full-duplex transmission, it permits Ethernet circuits to be developed to automatically adjust to the operating rate and cabling scheme used. This in turn simplifies the efforts of network managers and administrators, because products incorporating NWay will be self-configurable and will not require the setting of DIP switches or software parameters.

Autonegotiation can operate on an individual end basis or with autonegotiation-compliant devices at both ends of a twisted-pair link. An example of this autonegotiation capability is shown in Figure 3.34 in which station A has a NIC with autonegotiation capability that is cabled to a 10BASE-T/100BASE-TX switching hub whose port has an autonegotiation capability, while station B has a conventional 10BASE-T NIC. In this example, the hub port connected to station A would operate at 100 Mbps as 100BASE-TX devices. In comparison, the hub port connection to station B would recognize the 10BASE-T signals from station B and switch to 10BASE-T operations.

Operation

The key to the ability of NWay to provide an autonegotiation capability is through the encoding of a 16-bit word which, when transmitted, is known as

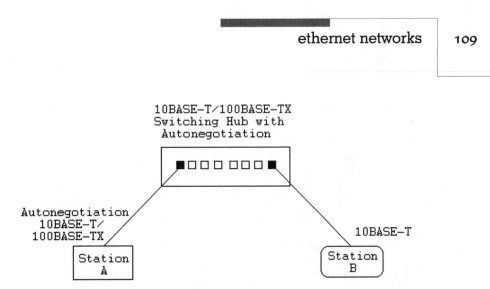

Figure 3.34 Autonegotiation. Through the use of autonegotiation, the 10BASE-T/100BASE-TX switching hub will operate at 100 Mbps with station A and at 10 Mbps with station B.

a fast link pulse (FLP). The FLP is transmitted as a FLP burst comprised of 17 to 33 link pulses. FLP bursts occur at the same interval as link pulses used in 10BASE-T, 16.8 ms, with a nominal duration of 2 ms. This enables a 100-Mbps node to recognize the presence of a 10-Mbps node.

The 16-bit word is subdivided into a 5-bit selector field, an 8-bit technology ability field, and 3 bit positions used for special purposes. The 5-bit selector field allows 32 different definitions of the technology ability field to be developed, with the latter incorporating bits that advertise a specific IEEE 802.3 or 802.9 technology, such as 100BASE-TX Full Duplex, 100BASE-T4, 100BASE-TX, 100BASE-T Full Duplex, and 10BASE-T. Because a selector field value of 1 is used for IEEE 802.3 and a value of 2 for 802.9, it becomes possible to use an additional available code to support Gigabit Ethernet, which can be expected to extend autonegotiation to that technology by the time you read this book.

There are several network configurations you can consider for Fast Ethernet operations. First, you can construct a 100BASE-TX network similar to a 10BASE-T network, using an appropriate hub and workstations that support the specific network type. This type of network, commonly referred to as a *shared-media hub-based* network, should be considered when most, if not all, network users access servers to perform graphic-intensive or similar bandwidth-intensive operations, and the sharing of the 100-Mbps transmission capability provides an acceptable average bandwidth per network node. Figure 3.35a illustrates a Fast Ethernet shared-media hub network configuration.

Another common use for Fast Ethernet is in its incorporation into one or more ports in an Ethernet switch. An Ethernet switch can be viewed as a sophisticated hub that can be programmed to transmit packets arriving on one

a. Shared-media hub.

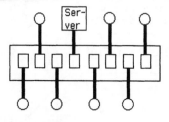

All connections operate at 100 Mbps.

b. 10/100 Mbps Ethernet switch.

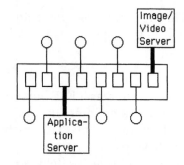

Some connections operate at 100 Mbps
and some at 10 Mbps.

Legend:

○ = Workstation
▬ = Fat pipe

Figure 3.35   Fast Ethernet network applications.

input port to a predefined output port. This is accomplished by the switch reading the destination address in the frame and comparing that address to a table of preconfigured address-port relationships. Readers are referred to Chapter 5 for specific information concerning the operation and use of Ethernet switches. In the interim, in examining the use of Fast Ethernet switches, note that most switches contain one or two 100-Mbps operating ports, while the other ports are conventional 10BASE-T ports. Typically you would connect servers that have a heavy workload to 100-Mbps Fast Ethernet ports, such as an image/video server and a database server. Figure 3.35 illustrates the use of a 10/100-Mbps Ethernet switch. In examining Figure 3.35 a and b, note that the heavily shaded connections to all workstations in Figure 3.35a and to the servers in Figure 3.35b represent 100-Mbps Fast Ethernet ports requiring Fast Ethernet adapter cards to be installed in each server or workstation connected to a 100-Mbps port. A common term used to reference the 100-Mbps connection is *fat pipe.*

Because a Fast Ethernet port provides downward compatibility with 10BASE-T, you can interconnect conventional 10BASE-T hubs to a Fast Ethernet shared-media hub or Fast Ethernet switch. Additional network configurations concerning the use of Fast Ethernet technology will be covered in Chapter 5 when switching hubs are covered.

In addition to having to consider the type or types of NIC connectors, it is also extremely important to consider the bus they are designed to work with along with driver support for different operating systems. Some NICs are limited to one type of connector, requiring the purchase of a separate converter if you decide to use a different media other than the media the NIC was manufactured to directly support.

Concerning computer bus support, in the DOS/Windows world you can select NICs that work with the original IBM PC 8- and 16-bit industry-standard architecture (ISA) bus, the 32-bit extended industry-standard architecture (EISA) bus, IBM's proprietary and essentially now obsolete microchannel architecture (MCA) 16- and 32-bit buses, and the relatively recent 32- and 64-bit peripheral-component interconnect (PCI) bus. The key difference between adapters supporting different computer buses is in their ability to transmit and receive sustained bursts of traffic such as file transfers. The ISA bus has a throughput between 4 Mbytes/sec and 5 Mbytes/sec, while the first-generation EISA bus has a throughput of 16 Mbytes/sec, later modified to support burst speeds up to 33 Mbytes/sec. IBM's 16-bit MCA bus can reach 20 Mbytes/sec, with its 32-bit bus slightly exceeding 36 Mbytes/sec. While all of the preceding buses can normally support small bursts of traffic onto a network operating at 10 Mbps, when used for sustained transfers onto a 100-Mbps network those buses cannot keep up with the network, resulting in a suboptimal level of performance. However, the use of a PCI-based NIC can resolve such problems. This is because the 32-bit PCI bus can support data bursts up to 132 Mbytes/sec while a 64-bit PCI bus can reach 264 Mbytes/sec, sufficient for operations at 100 Mbps.

Figures 3.36 through 3.38 illustrate three 3Com Corporation Fast Ethernet NICs manufactured to support different computer buses. Figure 3.36 shows the 3Com 3C515-TX NIC, which supports the ISA bus. Figure 3.37 shows the 3Com Corporation's Fast Etherlink PT adapter, which supports the EISA bus. The third 3Com NIC shown in Figure 3.38 is the Fast Etherlink XL, designed to support the PCI bus.

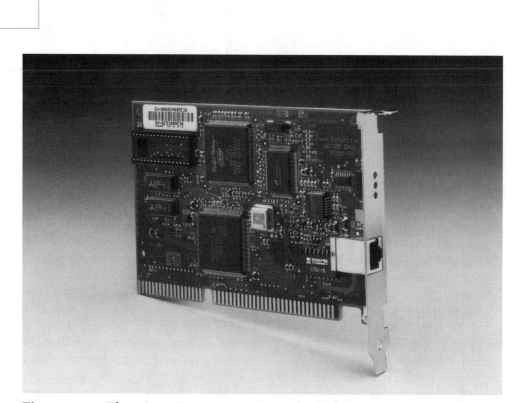

Figure 3.36 The 3Com Corporation Fast Etherlink TX NIC supports the use of the ISA bus. (Photograph courtesy of 3Com Corporation.)

A third NIC-related item that warrants careful consideration when selecting an appropriate NIC is the drivers available for use with the adapter. Today, in addition to different versions of NetWare and Windows NT, there are other operating systems ranging from DOS to SCO UNIX and OS/2 you may need to support. Although support for many NICs and protocols is built into many operating systems, such support is not all-inclusive. This means you may have to obtain one or more files from the NIC manufacturer to be able to use the NIC with a particular operating system. Figure 3.39 illustrates how under Windows NT Version 4.0 you would select the "Have Disk" option if your NIC wasn't directly supported, resulting in the display of the "Insert Disk" dialog box to enable NT to recognize your adapter.

One of the more interesting aspects concerning the use of NIC drivers, obtained from firsthand experience, is to ensure you have the appropriate driver. On occasion, it was found that the diskette packaged with the NIC manual and shipped with a newly purchased computer did not contain the

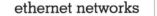

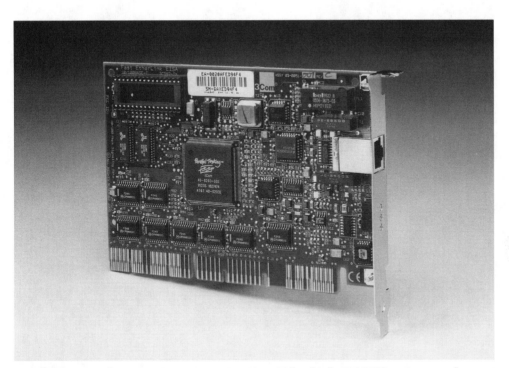

Figure 3.37   The 3Com Corporation Fast Etherlink PT NIC supports the use of the EISA bus. (Photograph courtesy of 3Com Corporation.)

appropriate driver for the computer. Although the operating system would use the driver, the computer would freeze about once a month, a situation corrected when it was determined that the computer manufacturer had a Web site with updated drivers for the NIC shipped with their computer.

100VG-AnyLAN

100VG-AnyLAN was originally proposed by AT&T Microelectronics and Hewlett-Packard Company as a mechanism to support evolving LAN-based multimedia applications. To accomplish this, the proposal, which became the IEEE 802.12 standard, replaced the CSMA/CD access protocol by a demand-priority scheme. This scheme enables the transmission of time-sensitive video and voice associated with multimedia applications in preference to conventional data that is relatively time-insensitive. In addition, the use of a demand-priority scheme extends 100VG-AnyLAN beyond Ethernet,

Figure 3.38 The 3Com Corporation Fast Etherlink XL NIC supports the use of the PCI bus. (Photograph courtesy of 3Com Corporation.)

enabling this network to support Token-Ring, FDDI, and other types of local area networks.

Now that we have an appreciation for the advantages associated with this technology, let's focus upon the architecture of 100VG-AnyLAN and how this network is interconnected to other types of LANs as well as wide area network transmission facilities. To accomplish this we will examine both the physical 100VG-AnyLAN network structure as well as its demand-priority access method. Once this is accomplished, we will turn our attention to the sublayer functions of the standard to include the technology used to enable a 100-Mbps data rate.

Architecture

100VG-AnyLAN was designed as a hub-centric network architecture. A central hub, known as a level-1 or *root* hub, functions as an inverted tree base in

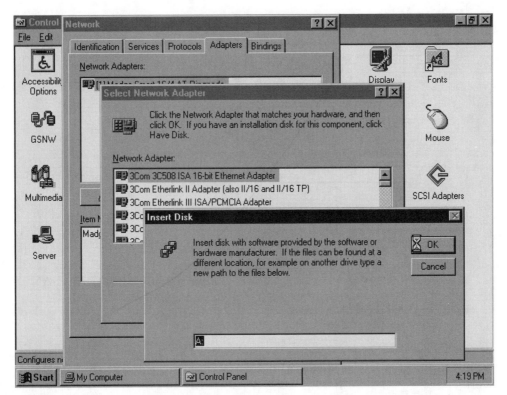

Figure 3.39   When using Windows NT you can specify a "Have Disk" option to use a NIC adapter not directly supported by that operating system.

establishing a 100VG-AnyLAN network. From this hub other hubs and/or nodes form a star topology, fanning out underneath the root hub, as illustrated in Figure 3.40. All hubs located in the same network segment must be configured to support the same frame format—IEEE 802.3 Ethernet or IEEE 802.5 Token-Ring. Through the attachment of a bridge or router to a hub port you can extend the 100VG-AnyLAN network to interconnect with other Ethernet or Token-Ring networks, FDDI- and ATM-based networks, or a wide area network transmission facility.

Each hub in a 100VG-AnyLAN network has one up-link port, labeled *up* in Figure 3.40; and *n* down-link ports, labeled 1 through *N*. The up-link port on each hub is reserved for connecting lower-level hubs to an upper-level hub, while the down-link ports are used to connect an upper-level hub to workstations, bridges, routers, and other network devices to include lower-level

Level-1 *Root* Hub

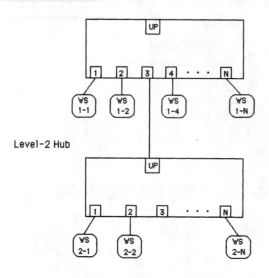

Figure 3.40   100VG-AnyLAN topology.

Legend: ws l-p = workstation hub level-port

hubs. Up to three levels of cascading can be used on a 100VG-AnyLAN network.

Hub Operation

Each hub port can be configured to operate in one of two modes—normal or monitor. Ports configured to operate in their normal mode are forwarded only those packets specifically addressed to the attached node. In comparison, ports configured to operate in the monitor mode are forwarded every packet received by the hub.

Devices connected to nodes gain access to a 100VG-AnyLAN network through the use of a centrally controlled access method, referred to as demand-priority. Under the demand-priority access method a node issues a request, referred to as a demand, to the hub it is connected to, to transmit a packet onto the 100VG-AnyLAN network. Each request includes a priority label assigned by the upper-layer application. The priority label is either normal, for normal data packets, or high, for packets carrying time-critical multimedia information. As you might expect, high-priority requests are granted access to the network before normal-priority requests are granted.

The level 1 or root hub continuously scans its ports using a round-robin sequence for requests. Lower-level hubs connected as nodes also perform a round-robin scanning process and forward node requests to the root hub. The root hub determines which nodes are requesting permission to transmit a packet as well as the priority level associated with the packet. Each hub maintains a separate list for both normal- and high-priority requests.

Normal-priority requests are serviced in their port order until a higher-priority request is received. Upon receipt of a higher-priority request the hub will complete any packet transmission in progress and then service the high-priority packet before returning to service the normal-priority list.

To prevent a long sequence of high-priority requests from abnormally delaying low-priority requests from being serviced, the hub also monitors node request-to-send response times. If the delay exceeds a predefined time, the hub automatically raises the normal-priority level to a high-priority level.

Round-Robin Scanning

Figure 3.41 illustrates an example of the 100VG-AnyLAN hub round-robin scanning process. Assume all ports initially have normal-priority requests pending. Then, the round-robin sequence at the root or level 1 hub results in the packet service order commencing at the level 1 hub's first port (1-1). Next, the level 1 hub's second port is serviced (1-2). When the third port is examined, it inserts the round-robin sequence generated by the level 2 hub. That is, it inserts the packet order sequence 2-1, 2-2, 2-3, . . . , 2-N. This sequence is then followed by adding the remaining level 1 hub ports. Thus, the inserted packet order sequence is followed by the sequence 1-4, . . . , 1-N. Now let's assume at time t = 0 nodes 2-1 and 1-4 generate high-priority requests. Then, the packet service order at the level 1 hub would be revised, becoming 2-1, 1-4, 1-1, 1-2, 2-2, . . . , 2-N, 1-5, . . . , 1-N.

Network Layers

As 100VG-AnyLAN was developed to comply with IEEE network modes, its design resulted in the separation of network functions into sublayers. Figure 3.42 illustrates the relationship of the IEEE 802.12 Data Terminal Equipment (DTE) Reference Model to the well-known ISO Open Systems Reference Model.

Similar to other IEEE LAN standards, 802.12 subdivides the ISO data link layer into two sublayers—logical link control (LLC) and media access control (MAC). The LLC sublayer results in the transmission of information in either IEEE 802.3 or 802.5 frame formats, while the MAC sublayer uses the previously described demand-priority mechanism as the access method to the network. Where the 802.12 model differs from the well-known Ethernet and Token-Ring models is in its subdivision of the physical layer into four sublayers.

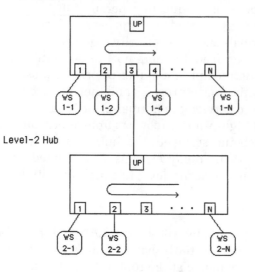

If all ports have normal-priority requests pending, then:
Level-1 scan 1-1,1-2,1-3,1-4,...1-N

Level-2 scan 2-1,2-2,2-3,...2-N

Level-1 resulting packet order sequence
1-1,1-2,2-1,2-2,2-3,...2-N,1-4,...1-N

Figure 3.41 100VG-AnyLAN hub round-robin scanning.

PMI Sublayer Functions

The PMI sublayer is responsible for performing four key functions before passing data to the PMD sublayer. Those functions are quartet channeling, data scrambling, 5B6B encoding, and the addition of a preamble and start and end frame delimiters to frames, which prepares them for transmission by the lower sublayer. Figure 3.43 illustrates the functions performed at the PMI and PMD sublayers.

Quartet Channeling

Quartet channeling is the process of first sequentially dividing MAC frame data octets into 5-bit data quintets. Next, each 5-bit quintet is distributed sequentially among four channels. Figure 3.44 illustrates the quartet channeling process. In examining Figure 3.44, note that each sequence of 5 bits in the MAC frame is transmitted on channel nMOD4. Thus, the first 5 bits are transmitted

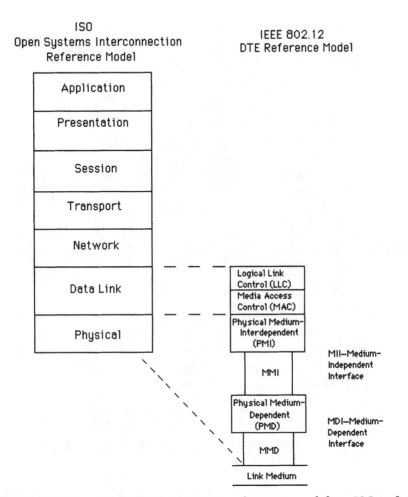

Figure 3.42   Relationship of IEEE 802.12 reference model to ISO reference model.

on channel 0, the second 5 bits on channel 1, the fifth set of 5 bits on channel 0, and so forth. Also note that the bits sent to each channel are placed on the channel sequentially. The rationale for the use of four channels is that they represent a transmission pair for a 4-UTP demand-priority network. As indicated in Figure 3.43, channel 0 data is transmitted on twisted-pair wires 1 and 2, channel 1 data winds up being transmitted on wires 3 and 6, and so on. When 2-pair or fiber-optic cable is used, 100VG-AnyLAN specifies the use of a multiplexing scheme which is incorporated at the PMD sublayer. Through the use of

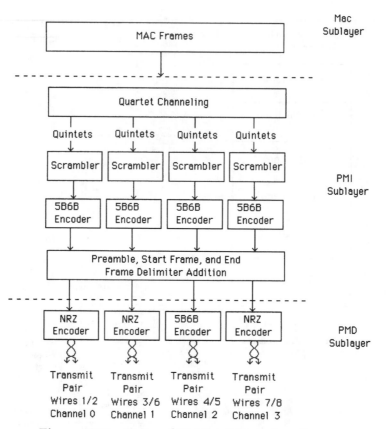

Figure 3.43 PMI and PMD sublayer functions.

multiplexing, the four channels illustrated in the lower portion of Figure 3.43 are converted into two channels for transmission on 2-pair wire, or to one channel for transmission on fiber-optic cable. Thus, the addition of multiplexing tailors the PMD sublayer to the physical medium used by the network.

Scramblers

The scramblers used at the PMI layer are employed to reduce the potential effect of radio frequency interference and signal crosstalk between cable pairs. To accomplish this the scramblers randomize the bit patterns on each transmission pair, eliminating the potential of long, repetitious strings of 0s and 1s from occurring. Each of the four scramblers uses a different scrambling mechanism, which ensures the randomness of the resulting data.

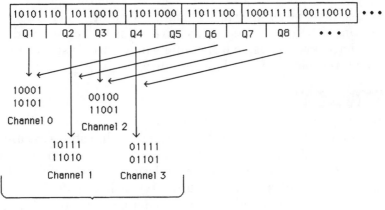

Figure 3.44   Quartet channelization process.

5B6B Encoding

The mapping of scrambled 5-bit data quintets into 6-bit symbols is performed by the 5B6B encoders shown in Figure 3.43. The encoding process results in the creation of a balanced data pattern that will contain equal numbers of 0s and 1s, providing guaranteed clock transition synchronization for receiver circuits. In addition, the 5B6B encoding process provides an added error-checking capability. This results from the fact that 5B6B encoding supports the use of only 16 symbol patterns. Thus, invalid symbols can be detected as error conditions.

Data Addition

As previously discussed, the last function performed by the PMI layer is to add the preamble and starting and ending frame delimiters to each channel. This results in the data being preprocessed into a format that facilitates the transmission of data onto the network. The actual placement of data onto the network is performed by the PMD sublayer.

PMD Sublayer

The PMD sublayer functions include NRZ encoding, link medium operation, and link status control. In addition, as previously discussed, if the transmission medium is 2-pair or fiber-optic cable, the PMD sublayer will also perform channel multiplexing.

NRZ Encoding

Nonreturn to zero (NRZ) encoding is a two-level signaling mechanism (0 and + voltage) used to represent the values of data transmitted on the copper 4-pair UTP cable. Under NRZ encoding, successive 1 bits are represented by a continuous + voltage level. Thus, to differentiate one *1* from a succeeding *1*, NRZ encoding requires the use of clocking circuitry.

Link Medium Operation

Link medium operation permits a 4-UTP 100VG-AnyLAN network to operate in both full- and half-duplex. Full-duplex communications results in two channels being used for transmission from the hub to a node, while the remaining two channels are used for transmission from the node to the hub.

Full-duplex communications is required when link status information is transmitted between a hub and a node. In comparison, normal data flow is accomplished via a half-duplex operating mode. In this mode of operation, all four channels are used to transmit data from the node to the hub, or from the hub to the node.

Link Status Control

As previously mentioned, link status control requires a full-duplex transmission mode of operation. When operating in full-duplex, two frequency tones, referred to as Tone 1 and Tone 2, are used to communicate the link status between the hub and the node. In actuality, the tones are generated by producing a pattern of 1s and 0s at a specific signaling rate to produce a tone. For example, Tone 1 is generated by transmitting a 30-MHz alternating pattern of 16 1s followed by 16 0s, resulting in a frequency of approximately 0.9375 MHz. In comparison, Tone 2 is generated by transmitting a 30-MHz alternating pattern of 8 1s followed by 8 0s, resulting in a frequency of approximately 1.875 MHz.

Through the use of a combination of tones, control signals are transmitted by the hub and the node. Table 3.10 lists the link status control signals supported at the PMD sublayer.

The IDLE status when received by a node indicates that the hub has no pending packets. When received by the hub an Idle status indicates no requests are pending.

An incoming data packet status indicates to a node that data may be destined to that port from the hub. This instructs the node to stop sending control tones on channels 2 and 3 so that it can receive the packet. The normal-priority request indicates to the hub that the node is requesting to transmit a normal-priority packet. In comparison, the high-priority request indicates to the hub that the node is requesting to send a high-priority packet. The last sig-

TABLE 3.10   PMD Link Status Control Signaling

Tone Pattern	Meaning When Received by a Node	Meaning When Received by a Hub
1-1	Idle	Idle
1-2	Incoming Data Packet	Normal Priority Request
2-1	Reserved	High-Priority Request
2-2	Link-Training Request	Link-Training Request

nal permissible, link-training request, indicates to the node or hub that link initialization is being requested.

Cabling Requirements

100VG-AnyLAN products currently marketed provide a 100-Mbps data rate using 4-pair category 3, 4, or 5 unshielded twisted-pair cable. 100VG-AnyLAN also supports 2-pair UTP, 2-pair STP, and fiber-optic cabling. The cabling medium required for 4-pair 100VG-AnyLAN is 4-pair UTP that meets the specifications of the EIA/TIA-568 standard for 100-ohm category 3, 4, or 5 cable. Such cable connects to RJ-45 wall jacks and can go through punch-down blocks or patch panels in a wiring closet.

Figure 3.45 indicates the RJ-45 modular plug pin assignments for 4-UTP 100VG-AnyLAN. In addition, this illustration indicates for comparison purposes the pairs used by 10BASE-T and Token-Ring cable.

Comparing Technologies

Both 100BASE-T and 100VG-AnyLAN provide users with a tenfold increase in network operating rates with respect to 10BASE-T. However, the 100-Mbps operating rate represents one of the few common operating characteristics between the two technologies.

100BASE-T was designed as a mechanism to provide a growth path from 100BASE-T while enabling organizations to retain the invested base of 10BASE-T adapter cards and cabling for workstations that do not require a 100-Mbps operational capability. In doing so, no provision was made to prioritize traffic. Thus, while a lightly loaded 100BASE-T network can transport multimedia data, this may not be true as the network load increases.

The replacement of the CSMA/CD access protocol by a demand-priority protocol results in 100VG-AnyLAN being more suitable for multimedia applications. Unfortunately, there is a cost associated with the additional technology incorporated into 100VG-AnyLAN, which resulted in network adapters costing 50 percent more than 100BASE-T adapters. Table 3.11 pro-

100VG-AnyLAN (4-UTP)

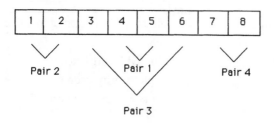

Token-Ring

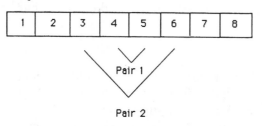

10BASE-T

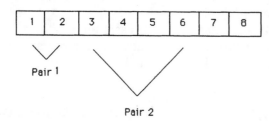

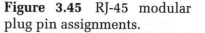
Figure 3.45 RJ-45 modular plug pin assignments.

vides a comparison of the operating characteristics of 100BASE-T and 100VG-AnyLAN.

A comparison of 100VG-AnyLAN to 100BASE-T is probably similar to a comparison of Beta to VHS. While Beta was a superior technology, the VHS extended record and playback time better satisfied consumer requirements. If we turn our focus back to LANs, 100BASE-T better interoperates with 10BASE-T through an NWay autonegotiation capability. This makes it easier to construct interoperable networks. Based upon the preceding, 100BASE-T products dominate the high-speed Ethernet marketplace, with 100VG-AnyLAN now essentially restricted to niche markets where consumers require a higher-speed networking capability with priority to transmit time-sensitive data but do not want to upgrade to ATM nor consider replacing existing equipment with IEEE 802.1p devices that recognize different levels of priority.

TABLE 3.11 Operating Characteristics Comparison

	100BASE-T	100VG-AnyLAN
Data rate	100 Mbps	100 Mbps
Access protocol	CSMA/CD	Demand-priority
Frame support	802.3 Ethernet 802.5 Token-Ring	802.3 Ethernet
Physical topology	Star	Star
Cable support		
2-pair Category 5 UTP	100BASE-TX	Not planned
4-pair Category 3, 4, or 5 UTP	100BASE-T4	Yes
2-pair STP	100BASE-TX	Yes
Fiber	100BASE-FX	Yes
Maximum UTP drive distance	100 meters on Category 5 UTP	100 meters Category 3, 4, UTP
Maximum repeaters allowed	2	4
Maximum UTP network diameter	200 meters	4,000 meters
Other cabling	2-pair Type 1 STP; optical fiber; 4-pair Category 3, 4, 5 UTP	2-pair Type 1 STP; optical fiber; 2-pair Category 5 UTP
Full duplex support	Yes	Yes

3.5 Gigabit Ethernet

Gigabit Ethernet represents an extension to the 10-Mbps and 100-Mbps IEEE 802.3 Ethernet standards. Providing a data transmission capability of 1000 Mbps, Gigabit Ethernet supports the CMSA/CD access protocol, which makes various types of Ethernet networks scalable from 10 Mbps to 1 Gbps.

Components

Similar to 10BASE-T and Fast Ethernet, Gigabit Ethernet can be used as a shared network through the attachment of network devices to a 1-Gbps repeater hub providing shared use of the 1-Gbps operating rate or as a switch, the latter providing 1-Gbps ports to accommodate high-speed access to servers while lower operating rate ports provide access to 10-Mbps and 100-Mbps workstations and hubs. Although very few organizations can be expected to require the use of a 1-Gbps shared media network as illustrated in Figure 3.46a, the use of Gigabit switches can be expected to play an important role in providing a high-speed backbone linking 100-Mbps network users to large databases, mainframes, and other types of resources that can tax lower-speed networks. In addition to hubs and switches, Gigabit Ethernet operations require workstations, bridges, and routers to use a network interface card to connect to a 1-Gbps network. The few Gigabit Ethernet NICs introduced when this book was written were designed for PCI bus operations and use an SC fiber connector to support 62.5/125 and 50/125 micron fiber. Such adapters provide 1 Gbps of bandwidth for shared media operations and 2 Gbps aggregate bandwidth when used for a full-duplex connection to a switch port. In Chapter 5, when we review switching, we will examine in more detail how Gigabit switches can be used to provide a backbone network capability.

Media Support

Similar to the recognition that Fast Ethernet would be required to operate over different types of media, the IEEE 802.3z committee recognized that Gigabit Ethernet would also be required to operate over multiple types of media. This recognition resulted in the development of a series of specifications, each designed to accommodate different types of media. Thus, any discussion of Gigabit Ethernet involves an examination of the types of media the technology supports and how it provides this support.

There are five types of media supported by Gigabit Ethernet—single-mode fiber, multimode fiber, short runs of coaxial cable or shielded twisted pair, and longer runs of unshielded twisted pair. Figure 3.47 illustrates the relationship of Gigabit Ethernet's MAC and physical layers to include the drive distances supported for each type of media.

Table 3.12 summarizes the flavors of Gigabit Ethernet indicating the IEEE designator used to reference Gigabit operations on a specific type of media and the maximum transmission distance associated with the use of each type of media. The actual relationship of the Gigabit 802.3z Reference Model to the ISO Reference Model is very similar to Fast Ethernet and 100VG-AnyLAN, the latter previously shown in Figure 3.43. Instead of a MII, Gigabit Ethernet uses a GMII. The GMII provides the interconnection between the MAC sublayer and the physical layer to include the use of an 8-bit data bus that operates at 125 MHz, plus such control signals as transmit and receiver clocks, carrier indicators, and error conditions.

Single-Mode Fiber

The specification that governs the use of single-mode fiber is referred to as 1000BASE-LX, where L represents recognition of the use of long-wave light pulses. The maximum distance obtainable for Gigabit Ethernet when trans-

a. Shared media hub use

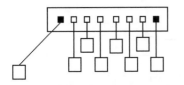

In a shared media environment the 1-Gbps bandwidth provided by Gigabit Ethernet is shared among all users.

b. Switching hub use

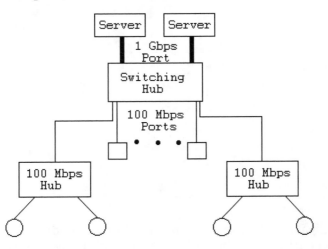

In a switch environment each 1-Gbps port can provide a full—duplex 2-Gbps data transfer capability.

Legend: ◯ =workstations

Figure 3.46 Using Gigabit Ethernet.

mission occurs using a 1330-nanometer (nm) frequency on single-mode fiber is 3000 meters. In examining Figure 3.47, note that the 8B/10B coding scheme used for both single-mode and multimode fiber represents the coding scheme used by the Fibre Channel. Due to the importance of Fibre Channel technology incorporated into Gigabit Ethernet, a short digression to discuss that technology is warranted.

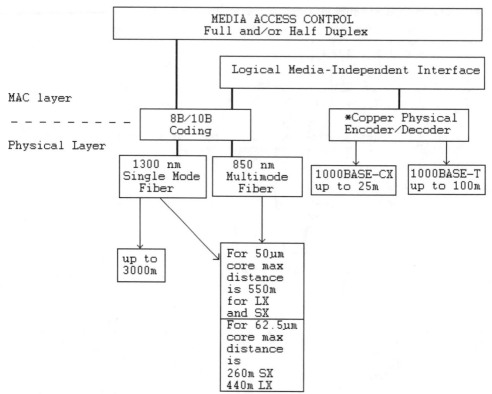

*8B/10B used for 1000BASE-CX

Figure 3.47 Gigabit Ethernet media support. Encoding method for 1000BASE-T to be defined by the IEEE 802.3ab Task Force, probably during late 1998.

The Fibre Channel The Fibre Channel actually represents a rather old technology, dating back to 1988 when the American National Standards Institute charted a working group to develop a high-speed data transfer capability for supporting data transfers between computers and peripheral devices. Initially, the Fibre Channel was developed to support fiber-optic cabling. When support for copper media was added, an ISO task force renamed the spelling of fiber to reduce the association of fiber optics while maintaining the name recognition of the technology. Today both optical and electrical copper-based media are supported by the Fibre Channel, with operating rates ranging from 133 Mbps to 1.062 Gbps provided by most equipment. In 1995 ANSI approved 2.134- and 4.25-Gbps speed rates as enhancements to the previously developed Fibre Channel specifications.

TABLE 3.12   The Flavors of Gigabit Ethernet

Media Designator	Media Type	Transmission Distance
1000BASE-LX	SMF	3 km
1000BASE-LX	MMF, 50 μ	550 m
1000BASE-LX	MMF, 62.5 μ	440 m
1000BASE-SX	MMF, 50 μ	550 m
1000BASE-SX	MMF, 62.5 μ	260 m
1000BASE-CX	Shielded balanced copper (coax or STP)	25 m
1000BASE-T	UTP, Category 5	100 m

SMF, single-mode fiber; MMF, multimode fiber; UTP, unshielded twisted pair; STP, shielded twisted pair.

The Fibre Channel supports point-to-point, shared media, and switch network topologies, with Fibre Channel hubs, switches, loop access controllers, and NICs installed on computers used to provide different network structures. The Fibre Channel supports a five-layer protocol stack from FC-0 through FC-4. The three lower layers form the Fibre Channel physical standard, while the two upper layers provide the interface to network protocols and applications. The FC-0 layer defines the physical characteristics of the media, transmitters, receivers, and connectors available for use, transmission rates supported, electrical and optical characteristics, and other physical layer standards. The second layer, FC-1, defines the 8B/10B encoding and decoding method used, a serial physical transport, timing recovery, and serial line balance. The 8B/10B encoding and decoding scheme was patented by IBM and is the same technique used in that vendor's 200-Mbps ESCON channel technology. Under 8B/10B coding eight data bits are transmitted as a 10-bit group. The two extra bits are used for error detection and correction.

To enable 1-Gbps operations the transmission rate of the Fibre Channel was raised to 1.25 Gbps. Then, the use of an 8B/10B coding technique permits data transfer at 80 percent of the operating rate or 1.256 ∗ 80, resulting in the modified Fibre Channel technology being capable of supporting the 1-Gbps data transfer of Gigabit Ethernet.

The third layer, FC-2, functions as the transport mechanism. This layer defines the framing rules of data transmitted between devices and how data flow is regulated. Although Ethernet frames are encapsulated within Fibre Channel frames for transmission between devices, the encapsulation is transparent to the Ethernet frame. Thus, the use of a modified Fibre Channel technology enabled the IEEE to use a proven technology as a transport mechanism for connecting Gigabit Ethernet devices while enabling the CSMA/CD protocol and Ethernet frame to be retained.

Multimode Fiber

The support of multimode fiber is applicable to both long-wave (LX) and short-wave (SX) versions of Gigabit Ethernet. When transmission occurs on multimode fiber the short-wave version of Gigabit Ethernet, which is referred to as 1000BASE-SX, uses an 850-nm frequency, providing a 260-meter maximum distance when transmission occurs over a 62.5-micron (μm) core. Note that in some trade publications and books the maximum transmission distance may be indicated as 300 meters; however, in September 1997, the IEEE task force working on the development of Gigabit Ethernet standards lowered the maximum distance to 260 meters from 300 meters. When a 1300-nm frequency is used on a 62.5-μm core, which represents 1000BASE-LX, a maximum transmission distance of 440 meters becomes possible. This distance was formerly 500 meters and was also reduced by the IEEE Gigabit Ethernet task force. When a 50-micron core fiber is used, the maximum distance is 550 meters for both LX and SX specifications.

Copper Media

Gigabit Ethernet supports three types of copper media—category 5 STP, coaxial cable, and UTP. The use of the first two types of copper media are defined by the 1000BASE-CX standard, which governs the use of patch cords and jumpers that provide a maximum cabling distance of 25 meters. This standard also uses the Fibre Channel–based 8B/10B coding method at a serial line operating rate of 125 Gbps, and runs over a 150-ohm balanced, shielded, cable assembly, referred to as twinax cable as well as on STP. The 25-meter maximum cabling distance makes 1000BASE-CX suitable for use in a wiring closet or a computer room as a short jumper interconnection cable. In comparison, the 1000BASE-T standard defines the use of four-pair HTP cable, with each wire expected to carry a 125-MHz signal in each direction. When this book was written, a separate IEEE organization, referred to as the 802.3ab task force, was in the process of defining and resolving several significant technical issues to enable transmission to occur at 1 Gbps at distances up to 100 meters on UTP. The task force was examining three encoding schemes referred to as QAM25 (quadrature amplitude modulation), PAM25 (pulse amplitude modulation), and CAP12 (carrierless amplitude phase modulation). Each coding scheme uses a different procedure and operates between 75 and 125 MHz in frequency. Both the selection of an encoding scheme and method for manufacturers of NICs to block frequencies above 30 MHz under FCC regulations remain to be addressed. Due to those issues, this standard may be delayed from the release of other Gigabit Ethernet standards that are scheduled for publication in 1998.

Duplex Capability

Gigabit Ethernet supports a full-duplex operating mode for switch-to-switch and switch-to-end station connections, while a half-duplex operating mode is used for shared connections using repeaters. Although not supported in the current draft version of the 802.3z standards, several vendors announced full-duplex, multiport, hublike devices to be used to interconnect two or more 802.3 links operating at 1 Gbps. Referred to as a buffered distributor, this device functions as a repeater, forwarding all incoming data received on one port onto all ports other than the original port. However, unlike conventional repeaters, the buffered distributor has the ability to buffer one or more inbound frames on each port before forwarding them.

In addition to having memory, the buffered distributor supports the IEEE 802.3z flow control standard. These two features enable each port on a buffered distributor to provide transmission support at a rate that matches the maximum rate of the 1-Gbps shared bus used to broadcast frames received on one port to all other ports. Because the buffered distributor supports 802.3z full-duplex flow control, the situation where an offered load exceeds the bandwidth of the shared bus is easily handled. This is accomplished by a port transmitting a flow control frame to the transmitting system, indicating that the port cannot accommodate additional data. The 802.3z-compliant transmitting device will then cease transmission until the port forwards a frame indicating it can accept additional data.

To illustrate the operation of a buffered distributor, consider Figure 3.48, which illustrates the use of a four-port buffered distributor. Let's assume that at a certain point in time devices connected to ports 1 and 3 are transmitting data to the buffered distributor at 700 Mbps and 400 Mbps, respectively. It should be noted that those data rates represent traffic carried and not the operating rate of those devices which would be 1 Gbps. Because the aggregate rate exceeds 1 Gbps, a normal repeater would not be able to support this traffic load. However, a buffered repeater includes a memory buffer area into which the excessive 100-Mbps transmission (1100 − 1000) rapidly fills. To insure that its buffers do not overflow, the buffered repeater will issue a flow control signal telling the transmitters to reduce their transmission rate. This flow control signal will occur once the occupancy of the buffer reaches a predefined level of occupancy, as indicated in the right portion of Figure 3.48. Once data from the buffer is serviced to the point where occupancy is at a predefined low level, the buffered distributor will use flow control to enable transmission to the distributor by disabling flow control.

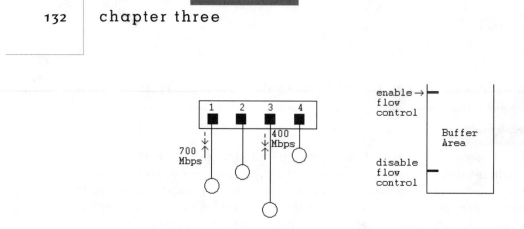

Legend: -→=enable/disable flow control frames

Figure 3.48 A buffered distributor uses IEEE 802.3z flow control whenever the offered traffic exceeds the bandwidth of its shared bus.

To provide an equitable method for sharing the 1-Gbps bus, the buffered distributor uses a round-robin algorithm to determine which port can transmit onto the bus. This round-robin method occurs one frame at a time, with port 1 serviced, followed by port 2, and so on. Through the use of a buffered distributor, it becomes possible to support applications that require a many-to-one transmission capability, such as a LAN with a local server used for graphic database queries, e-mail, and similar applications. Instead of migrating the LAN to a switch environment, a buffered distributor may represent another possible network solution to network bottlenecks for power users.

chapter four

Frame Operations

In this chapter, we will first focus our attention on the composition of different types of Ethernet frames. In reality, there is only one physical Ethernet frame. However, the composition of the frame was altered by the IEEE when the CSMA/CD original Ethernet frame format was standardized by that organization as the 802.3 frame. In addition, the logical composition of the data field within the 802.3 frame can vary based upon the protocol transported.

Once we obtain an understanding of the composition of Ethernet and IEEE 802.3 frames, we will examine the function of fields within each frame, as well as the manner in which the placement of frames on the media is controlled—a process known as *media access control.* After this is accomplished, we will turn our attention to the manner by which protocol information is carried within an IEEE 802.3 frame to include logical link control (LLC), NetWare, TCP/IP, and other protocols.

Although the composition of the IEEE 802.3 frame remains the same from 10-Mbps through 1-Gbps operations, there are certain restrictions on the framing of frames and the minimum size of the information field at different network operating rates. Thus, in the last two sections in this chapter, we will examine certain modifications and restrictions on frames transported on Fast Ethernet and Gigabit Ethernet networks.

4.1 Frame Composition

Figure 4.1 illustrates the general frame composition of Ethernet and IEEE 802.3 frames. You will note that they differ slightly. An Ethernet frame contains an eight-byte preamble, while the IEEE 802.3 frame contains a seven-byte preamble followed by a one-byte start-of-frame delimiter field. A second difference between the composition of Ethernet and IEEE 802.3 frames concerns the two-byte Ethernet type field. That field is used by Ethernet to spec-

Ethernet

Preamble	Destination Address	Source Address	Type	Data	Frame Check Sequence
8 bytes	6 bytes	6 bytes	2 bytes	46-1500 bytes	4 bytes

IEEE 802.3

Preamble	Start of Frame Delimiter	Destination Address	Source Address	Length	Data	Frame Check Sequence
7 bytes	1 byte	2/6 bytes	2/6 bytes	2 bytes	46-1500 bytes	4 bytes

Figure 4.1 Ethernet and IEEE 802.3 frame formats.

ify the protocol carried in the frame, enabling several protocols to be carried independently of one another. Under the IEEE 802.3 frame format, the type field was replaced by a two-byte length field, which specifies the number of bytes that follow that field as data.

The differences between Ethernet and IEEE 802.3 frames, while minor, make the two incompatible with one another. This means that your network must contain either all Ethernet-compatible NICs or all IEEE 802.3–compatible NICs. Fortunately, the fact that the IEEE 802.3 frame format represents a standard means that most vendors now market 802.3-compliant hardware and software. Although a few vendors continue to manufacture Ethernet or dual functioning Ethernet/IEEE 802.3 hardware, such products are primarily used to provide organizations with the ability to expand previously developed networks without requiring the wholesale replacement of NICs. Although the IEEE 802.3 frame does not directly support a type field within the frame, as we will note in section 4 in this chapter, the IEEE defined a special type of frame to obtain compatibility with Ethernet LANs. That frame is referred to as an Ethernet Subnetwork Access Protocol (Ethernet-SNAP) frame, which enables a type subfield to be included in the data field. While the IEEE 802.3 standard has essentially replaced Ethernet, because of their similarities and the fact that 802.3 was based upon Ethernet, we will consider both to be Ethernet.

Now that we have an overview of the structure of Ethernet and 802.3 frames, let's probe more deeply and examine the composition of each frame field. We will take advantage of the similarity between Ethernet and IEEE 802.3 frames to examine the fields of each frame on a composite basis, noting the differences between the two when appropriate.

Preamble Field

The preamble field consists of eight (Ethernet) or seven (IEEE 802.3) bytes of alternating 1 and 0 bits. The purpose of this field is to announce the frame and to enable all receivers on the network to synchronize themselves to the incoming frame. In addition, this field by itself (under Ethernet) or in conjunction with the start-of-frame delimiter field (under the IEEE 802.3 standard) ensures that there is a minimum spacing period of 9.6 ms between frames for error detection and recovery operations.

Start-of-Frame Delimiter Field

This field is applicable only to the IEEE 802.3 standard and can be viewed as a continuation of the preamble. In fact, the composition of this field continues in the same manner as the format of the preamble, with alternating 1 and 0 bits used for the first six bit positions of this one-byte field. The last two bit positions of this field are 11—this breaks the synchronization pattern and alerts the receiver that frame data follows.

Both the preamble field and the start-of-frame delimiter field are removed by the controller when it places a received frame in its buffer. Similarly, when a controller transmits a frame, it prefixes the frame with those two fields (if it is transmitting an IEEE 802.3 frame) or a preamble field (if it is transmitting a true Ethernet frame).

Destination Address Field

The destination address identifies the recipient of the frame. Although this may appear to be a simple field, in reality its length can vary between IEEE 802.3 and Ethernet frames. In addition, each field can consist of two or more subfields, whose settings govern such network operations as the type of addressing used on the LAN, and whether the frame is addressed to a specific station or more than one station. To obtain an appreciation for the use of this field, let's examine how this field is used under the IEEE 802.3 standard as one of the two field formats applicable to Ethernet.

Figure 4.2 illustrates the composition of the source and destination address fields. As indicated, the two-byte source and destination address fields are applicable only to IEEE 802.3 networks, while the six-byte source and destination address fields are applicable to both Ethernet and IEEE 802.3 networks. A user can select either a two- or six-byte destination address field; however, with IEEE 802.3 equipment, all stations on the LAN must use the same ad-

a. 2 byte field (IEEE 802.3)

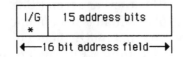

b. 6 byte field (Ethernet and IEEE 802.3)

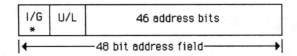

I/G bit subfield   '0' = individual address   '1' = group address
U/L bit subfield   '0' = universally administrated addressing
                   '1' = locally administrated addressing

* Set to '0' in source address field

Figure 4.2   Source and destination address field formats.

dressing structure. Today, almost all 802.3 networks use six-byte addressing, because the inclusion of a two-byte field option was designed primarily to accommodate early LANs that use 16-bit address fields.

Both destination and source addresses are normally displayed by network monitors in hexadecimal, with the first three bytes separated from the last three by a colon (:) when six-byte addressing is used. For example, the source address 02608C876543 would be displayed as 02608C:876543. As we will shortly note, the first three bytes identify the manufacturer of the adapter card, while the following three bytes identify a specific adapter manufactured by the vendor identified by the first three bytes or six hex digits.

I/G Subfield

The one-bit I/G subfield is set to a 0 to indicate that the frame is destined to an individual station, or 1 to indicate that the frame is addressed to more than one station—a *group address.* One special example of a group address is the assignment of all 1s to the address field. Hex "FFFFFFFFFFFF" is recognized as a broadcast address, and each station on the network will receive and accept frames with that destination address.

An example of the use of a broadcast destination address is the service advertising packet (SAP) transmitted every 60 seconds by NetWare servers. The SAP is used to inform other servers and workstations on the network of the presence of that server. Because the SAP uses a destination address of FF-FF-FF-FF-FF-FF, it is recognized by every node on the network.

When a destination address specifies a single station, the address is referred to as a *unicast address*. A group address that defines multiple stations is known as a *multicast address,* while a group address that specifies all stations on the network is, as previously mentioned, referred to as a *broadcast address*.

U/L Subfield

The U/L subfield is applicable only to the six-byte destination address field. The setting of this field's bit position indicates whether the destination address is an address that was assigned by the IEEE (universally administered) or assigned by the organization via software (locally administered).

Universal versus Locally Administered Addressing

Each Ethernet NIC contains a unique address burned into its read-only memory (ROM) at the time of manufacture. To ensure that this universally administered address is not duplicated, the IEEE assigns blocks of addresses to each manufacturer. These addresses normally include a three-byte prefix, which identifies the manufacturer and is assigned by the IEEE, and a three-byte suffix, which is assigned by the adapter manufacturer to its NIC. For example, the prefix 02608C identifies an NIC manufactured by 3Com, while a prefix of hex 08002 identifies an NIC manufactured by Digital Equipment Company.

Although the use of universally administered addressing eliminates the potential for duplicate network addresses, it does not provide the flexibility obtainable from locally administered addressing. For example, under locally administered addressing, you can configure mainframe software to work with a predefined group of addresses via a gateway PC. Then, as you add new stations to your LAN, you simply use your installation program to assign a locally administered address to the NIC instead of using its universally administered address. As long as your mainframe computer has a pool of locally administered addresses that includes your recent assignment, you do not have to modify your mainframe communications software configuration. Because the modification of mainframe communications software typically requires recompiling and reloading, the attached network must become inoperative for a short period of time. Because a large mainframe may service hundreds to thousands of users, such changes are normally performed late in the evening or on a weekend. Thus, the changes required for locally administered addressing are more responsive to users than those required for universally administered addressing.

Source Address Field

The source address field identifies the station that transmitted the frame. Like the destination address field, the source address can be either two or six bytes in length.

The two-byte source address is supported only under the IEEE 802.3 standard and requires the use of a two-byte destination address; all stations on the network must use two-byte addressing fields. The six-byte source address field is supported by both Ethernet and the IEEE 802.3 standard. When a six-byte address is used, the first three bytes represent the address assigned by the IEEE to the manufacturer for incorporation into each NIC's ROM. The vendor then normally assigns the last three bytes for each of its NICs.

Table 4.1 lists the NIC identifiers for 85 Ethernet card manufacturers. Note that many organizations including Cisco Systems, 3Com, IBM, MIPS, Ungermann-Bass, and Data General were assigned two or more blocks of addresses by the IEEE. Also note that organizations listed in Table 4.1 range in scope from well-known communications and computer manufacturers to universities and even a commercial firm probably best known for its watch commercials. The entries in Table 4.1 represent a portion of three-byte identifiers assigned by the IEEE over the past decade and do not include obsolete identifiers or identifiers currently assigned to all vendors. For a comprehensive list of currently assigned three-byte identifiers, readers should contact the IEEE.

Many software- and hardware-based network analyzers include the capability to identify each station on a LAN, count the number of frames transmitted by the station and destined to the station, as well as identify the manufacturer of the NIC used in the station. Concerning the latter capability, this is accomplished by the network analyzer containing a table of three-byte identifiers assigned by the IEEE to each NIC manufacturer, along with the name of the manufacturer. Then the analyzer compares the three-byte identifier read from frames flowing on the network and compares each identifier with the identifiers stored in its identifier table. By providing information concerning network statistics, network errors, and the vendor identifier for the NIC in each station, you may be able to isolate problems faster or better consider future decisions concerning the acquisition of additional NICs.

TABLE 4.1 Ethernet NIC Manufacturer IDs

NIC Manufacturer	Three-Byte Identifier
Cisco	00-00-0C
Fujitsu	00-00-0E
Cabletron	00-00-1D
NeXT	00-00-0F
TRW	00-00-2A
Hughes LAN Systems (formerly Sytek)	00-00-10
Tektronix	00-00-11
Datapoint Corporation	00-00-15
Olicom	00-00-24
AT&T	00-00-3D
NEC	00-00-4C
Network General	00-00-65
MIPS	00-00-6B
Madge Networks	00-00-6F
MIPS	00-00-77
Proteon	00-00-93
Cross Com Communications (now part of Olicom)	00-00-98
Wellfleet (now Bay Networks)	00-00-A2
Xerox	00-00-AA
RND (RAD Network Devices)	00-00-B0
Western Digital	00-00-C0
Emulex	00-00-C9
Develcon Electronics, Ltd.	00-00-D0
Adaptec, Inc.	00-00-D1
Gandalf Data Ltd.	00-00-F3
Allied Telesis, Inc.	00-00-F4
Racal Datacom	00-07-01
XYlan	00-20-DA
Crescendo (now owned by Cisco)	00-40-0B
Ascom	00-40-15
AST Research	00-40-1C

TABLE 4.1 (*Continued*)

NIC Manufacturer	Three-Byte Identifier
Netcomm	00-40-28
Nokia Data Communications	00-40-43
Cable and Wireless	00-40-74
AMP Incorporated	00-40-76
DigiBoard	00-40-9D
Cray Research, Inc.	00-40-A6
Mocom Communications Corp.	00-40-C5
PlainTree Systems, Inc.	00-40-EA
3Com	00-60-08
Cisco Systems, Inc.	00-60-09
Cisco Systems, Inc.	00-60-2F
Cisco Systems, Inc.	00-60-3E
Cisco Systems, Inc.	00-60-5C
Cisco Systems, Inc.	00-60-70
Cisco Systems, Inc.	00-60-83
3Com	00-60-8C
3Com	00-60-97
Hewlett-Packard	00-60-BO
Thomas Conrad Corporation	00-80-13
Bell Atlantic	00-80-1A
Newbridge Networks Corporation	00-80-21
Kalpana (acquired by Cisco)	00-80-24
University of Toronto	00-80-46
Compaq Computer Corporation	00-80-5F
Nippon Steel Corporation	00-80-6E
Xircom, Inc.	00-80-C7
Shiva	00-80-D3
Zenith Communications Products	00-80-F7
Azure Technologies, Inc.	00-80-FE
Bay Networks	00-A0-00
National Semiconductor	00-A0-D1
Allied Telesyn	00-A0-D2
Intel	00-AA-00
Ungermann-Bass	00-DD-00

TABLE 4.1 (*Continued*)

NIC Manufacturer	Three-Byte Identifier
Ungermann-Bass	00-DD-01
Racal Interlan	02-07-01
3Com	02-60-8C
BBN	08-00-08
Hewlett Packard	08-00-09
Unisys	08-00-0B
Tektronix	08-00-11
Data General	08-00-A
Data General	08-00-1B
Sun	08-00-20
DEC	08-00-2B
Bull	08-00-38
Sony	08-00-46
Sequent	08-00-47
Stanford University	08-00-56
IBM	08-00-5A
Silicon Graphics	08-00-69
Silicon Graphics	08-00-79
Seiko	08-00-83
Excelan	08-00-6E
Danish Data Elektronix	08-00-75
AT&T	80-00-10

An example of the use of NIC manufacturer IDs can be obtained by examining two monitoring screen displays of the Triticom EtherVision network monitoring and analysis program. Figure 4.3 illustrates the monitoring screen during the program's autodiscovery process. During this process the program reads the source address of each frame transmitted on the segment that the computer executing the program is connected to. Although obscured by the highlighted bar, the first three bytes of the adapter address first discovered is 00-60-8C, which represents a block of addresses assigned by the IEEE to 3 Com Corporation. If you glance at the first column in Figure 4.3, you will note that the second row, fourth row, ninth row, and a few additional rows also have NIC addresses that commence with hex 00-60-8C. By pressing the F2 key

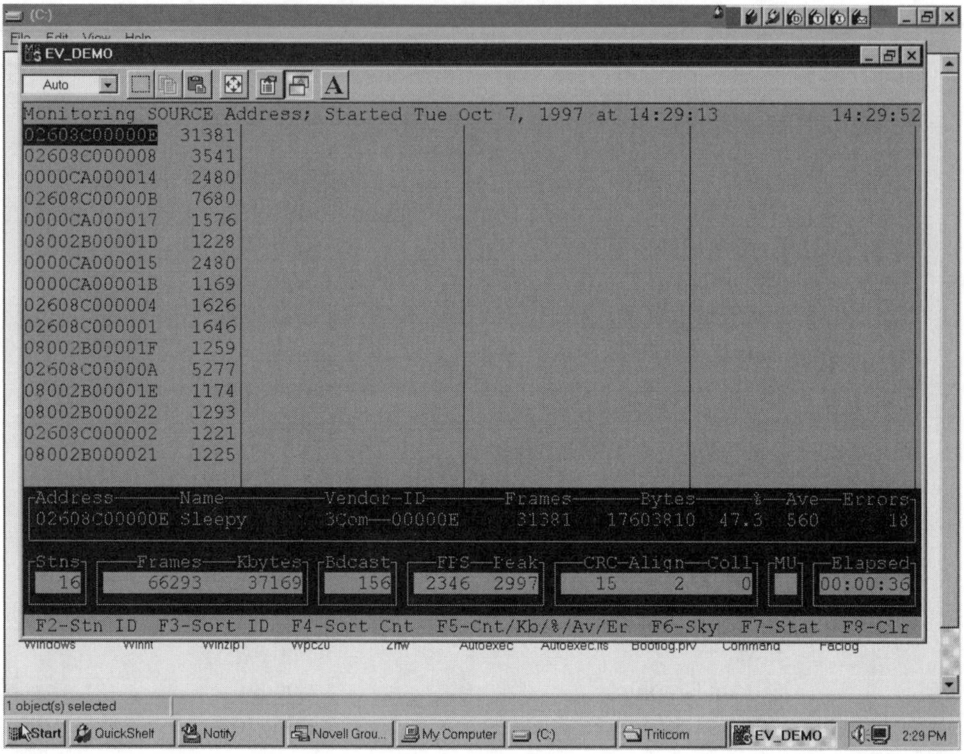

Figure 4.3 The Triticom EtherVision source address monitoring feature discovers the hardware address of each NIC. At the time this screen was captured 16 stations were identified.

the program will display the manufacturer of each NIC encountered and for which statistics are being accumulated. This is indicated in Figure 4.4, which shows the first three bytes of each address replaced by the vendor assigned to the appropriate manufacturer ID. Thus, rows 1, 4, 9, and a few other rows commence with "3Com" to indicate the manufacturer of the NIC.

Organizations can request the assignment of a vendor code by contacting the following:

IEEE Registration Authority

IEEE Standards Department

445 Hoes Lane, POB 1331

Piscataway, NJ 08844

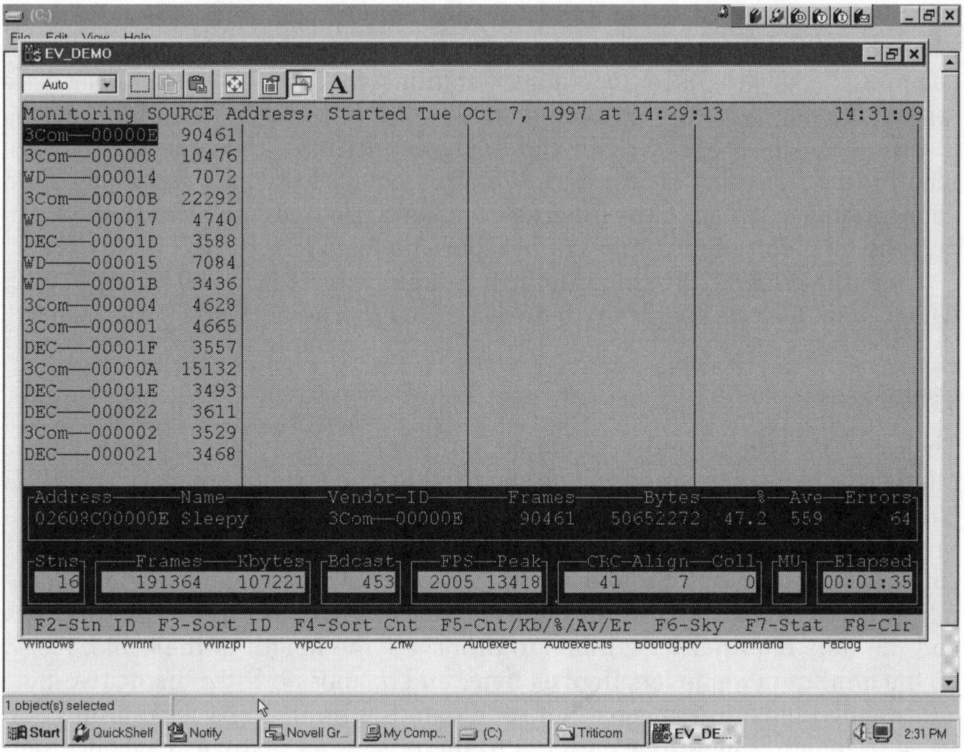

Figure 4.4 By pressing the F2 key, EtherVision will convert the three-byte hex NIC manufacturer ID to the vendor name or an appropriate mnemonic.

A full list of assigned vendor codes is obtainable by FTP at ftp.ieee.org as the file ieee/info/info.stds.oui. Readers should note that the list is limited to those companies that agreed to make their vendor code assignment(s) public.

Type Field

The two-byte type field is applicable only to the Ethernet frame. This field identifies the higher-level protocol contained in the data field. Thus, this field tells the receiving device how to interpret the data field.

Under Ethernet, multiple protocols can exist on the LAN at the same time. Xerox served as the custodian of Ethernet address ranges licensed to NIC manufacturers and defined the protocols supported by the assignment of type field values.

Table 4.2 lists 31 of the more common Ethernet type field assignments. To illustrate the ability of Ethernet to transport multiple protocols, assume a common LAN was used to connect stations to both UNIX and NetWare servers. Frames with the hex value 0800 in the type field would identify the IP protocol, while frames with the hex value 8137 in the type field would identify the transport of IPX and SPX protocols. Thus, the placement of an appropriate hex value in the Ethernet type field provides a mechanism to support the transport of multiple protocols on the local area network.

Under the IEEE 802.3 standard, the type field was replaced by a length field, which precludes compatibility between pure Ethernet and 802.3 frames.

Length Field

The two-byte length field, applicable to the IEEE 802.3 standard, defines the number of bytes contained in the data field. Under both Ethernet and IEEE 802.3 standards, the minimum size frame must be 64 bytes in length from preamble through FCS fields. This minimum size frame ensures that there is sufficient transmission time to enable Ethernet NICs to detect collisions accurately, based on the maximum Ethernet cable length specified for a network and the time required for a frame to propagate the length of the cable. Based on the minimum frame length of 64 bytes and the possibility of using two-byte addressing fields, this means that each data field must be a minimum of 46 bytes in length. The only exception to the preceding involves Gigabit Ethernet. At a 1000-Mbps operating rate the original 802.3 standard would not provide a frame duration long enough to permit a 100-meter cable run. This is because at a 1000-Mbps data rate there is a high probability that a station could be in the middle of transmitting a frame before it becomes aware of any collision that might have occurred at the other end of the segment. Recognizing this problem resulted in the development of a carrier extension, which extends the minimum Ethernet frame to 512 bytes. The carrier extension is discussed in detail in Section 4.6 when we turn our attention to the Gigabit Ethernet carrier extension.

For all versions of Ethernet except Gigabit Ethernet, if data being transported is less than 46 bytes, the data field is padded to obtain 46 bytes. However, the number of PAD characters is not included in the length field value. NICs that support both Ethernet and IEEE 802.3 frame formats use the value in this field to distinguish between the two frames. That is, because the maximum length of the data field is 1,500 bytes, a value that exceeds hex 05DC indicates that instead of a length field (IEEE 802.3), the field is a type field (Ethernet).

TABLE 4.2 Ethernet Type Field Assignments

Protocol	Hex Value Assigned
Experimental	0101-DIFF
Xerox XNS	0600
IP	0800
X.75 Internet	0801
NBS Internet	0802
ECMA Internet	0803
CHAOSmet	0804
X.25 Level 3	0805
Address Resolution Protocol	0806
XNS Compatibility	0807
Banyan Systems	0BAD
BBN Simnet	5208
DEC MOP Dump/Load	6001
DEC MOP Remote Console	6002
DEC DECNET Phase IV Route	6003
DEC LAT	6004
DEC Diagnostic Protocol	6005
3Com Corporation	6010–6014
Proteon	7030
AT&T	8008
Excelan	8010
Tymshare	802E
DEC LANBridge	8038
DEC Ethernet Encryption	803D
AT&T	8046–8047
AppleTalk	809B
IBM SNA Service on Ethernet	80D5
AppleTalk ARP	80F3
Wellfleet	80FF–8103
NetWare IPX/SPX	8137–8138
SNMP	814C

Data Field

As previously discussed, the data field must be a minimum of 46 bytes in length to ensure that the frame is at least 64 bytes in length. This means that the transmission of 1 byte of information must be carried within a 46-byte data field; if the information to be placed in the field is less than 46 bytes, the remainder of the field must be padded. Although some publications subdivide the data field to include a PAD subfield, the latter actually represents optional fill characters that are added to the information in the data field to ensure a length of 46 bytes. The maximum length of the data field is 1500 bytes.

Frame Check Sequence Field

The frame check sequence field, applicable to both Ethernet and the IEEE 802.3 standard, provides a mechanism for error detection. Each transmitter computes a cyclic redundancy check (CRC) that covers both address fields, the type/length field, and the data field. The transmitter then places the computed CRC in the four-byte FCS field.

The CRC treats the previously mentioned fields as one long binary number. The n bits to be covered by the CRC are considered to represent the coefficients of a polynomial $M(X)$ of degree n – 1. Here, the first bit in the destination address field corresponds to the X^{n-1} term, while the last bit in the data field corresponds to the X^0 term. Next, $M(X)$ is multiplied by X^{32}, and the result of that multiplication process is divided by the following polynomial:

$$G(X) = X^{32} + X^{26} + X^{23} + X^{22} + X^{16} + X^{12} + X^{11} + X^{10} + X^8 + X^7 + X^5 + X^4 + X^2 + X + 1$$

Note that the term X^n represents the setting of a bit to a 1 in position n. Thus, part of the generating polynomial $X^5 + X^4 + X^2 + X^1$ represents the binary value 11011.

This division produces a quotient and remainder. The quotient is discarded, and the remainder becomes the CRC value placed in the four-byte FCS field. This 32-bit CRC reduces the probability of an undetected error to 1 bit in every 4.3 billion, or approximately 1 bit in $2^{32} - 1$ bits.

Once a frame reaches its destination, the receiver uses the same polynomial to perform the same operation upon the received data. If the CRC computed by the receiver matches the CRC in the FCS field, the frame is accepted. Otherwise, the receiver discards the received frame, as it is considered to have one or more bits in error. The receiver will also consider a received frame to be invalid and discard it under two additional conditions. Those conditions occur when the frame does not contain an integral number of bytes, or when the length of the data field does not match the value contained in the length field. The latter condition obviously is only applicable to the 802.3 standard, because an Ethernet frame uses a type field instead of a length field.

4.2 Media Access Control

In the first section in this chapter, we examined the frame format by which data is transported on an Ethernet network. Under the IEEE 802 series of 10-Mbps operating standards, the data link layer of the OSI Reference Model is subdivided into two sublayers—logical link control (LLC) and medium access control (MAC). The frame formats examined in Section 4.1 represent the manner in which LLC information is transported. Directly under the LLC sublayer is the MAC sublayer. The MAC sublayer, which is the focus of this section, is responsible for checking the channel and transmitting data if the channel is idle, checking for the occurrence of a collision, and taking a series of predefined steps if a collision is detected. Thus, this layer provides the required logic to control the network.

Figure 4.5 illustrates the relationship between the physical and LLC layers with respect to the MAC layer. The MAC layer is an interface between user data and the physical placement and retrieval of data on the network. To better understand the functions performed by the MAC layer, let us examine the four major functions performed by that layer—transmitting data operations, transmitting medium access management, receiving data operations, and receiving medium access management. Each of those four functions can be viewed as a functional area, because a group of activities is associated with each area. Table 4.3 lists the four MAC functional areas and the activities associated with each area. Although the transmission and reception of data operations activities are self-explanatory, the transmission and reception of media access management require some elaboration. Therefore, let's focus our attention on the activities associated with each of those functional areas.

Transmit Media Access Management

CSMA/CD can be described as a *listen-before-acting* access method. Thus, the first function associated with transmit media access management is to find out whether any data is already being transmitted on the network and, if so, to defer transmission. During the listening process, each station attempts to

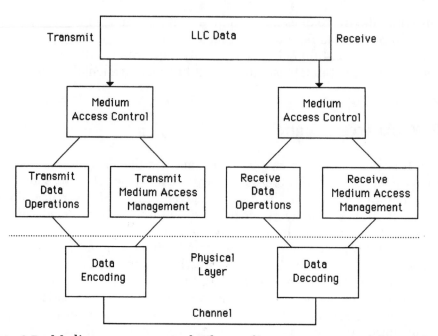

Figure 4.5 Medium access control. The medium access control (MAC) layer can be considered an interface between user data and the physical placement and retrieval of data on the network.

sense the carrier signal of another station, hence the prefix *carrier sense* (CS) for this access method. Although broadband networks use RF modems that generate a carrier signal, a baseband network has no carrier signal in the conventional sense of a carrier as a periodic waveform altered to convey information. Thus, a logical question you may have is how the MAC sublayer on a baseband network can sense a carrier signal if there is no carrier. The answer to this question lies in the use of a digital signaling method, known as *Manchester encoding* on 10-Mbps Ethernet LANs, that a station can monitor to note whether another station is transmitting. Although NRZI encoding is used on broadband networks, the actual data is modulated after it is encoded. Thus, the presence or absence of a carrier is directly indicated by the presence or absence of a carrier signal on a broadband network.

Collision Detection

As discussed in Chapter 3, under Manchester encoding, a transition occurs at the middle of each bit period. This transition serves as both a clocking mecha-

TABLE 4.3 MAC Functional Areas

Transmit data operations	◆ Accept data from the LLC sublayer and construct a frame by appending preamble and start-of-frame delimiter; insert destination and source address, length count; if frame is less than 64 bytes, insert sufficient PAD characters in the data field.
	◆ Calculate the CRC and place in the FCS field.
Transmit media access management	◆ Defer transmission if the medium is busy.
	◆ Delay transmission for a specified interframe gap period.
	◆ Present a serial bit stream to the physical layer for transmission.
	◆ Halt transmission when a collision is detected.
	◆ Transmit a jam signal to ensure that news of a collision propagates throughout the network.
	◆ Reschedule retransmissions after a collision until successful, or until a specified retry limit is reached.
Receive data operations	◆ Discard all frames not addressed to the receiving station.
	◆ Recognize all broadcast frames and frames specifically addressed to station.
	◆ Perform a CRC check.
	◆ Remove preamble, start-of-frame delimiter, destination and source addresses, length count, and FCS; if necessary, remove PAD fill characters.
	◆ Pass data to LLC sublayer.
Receive media access management	◆ Receive a serial bit stream from the physical layer.
	◆ Verify byte boundary and length of frame.
	◆ Discard frames not an even eight bits in length or less than the minimum frame length.

nism, enabling a receiver to clock itself to incoming data, and as a mechanism to represent data. Under Manchester coding, a binary 1 is represented by a high-to-low transition, while a binary 0 is represented by a low-to-high voltage transition. Thus, an examination of the voltage on the medium of a baseband network enables a station to determine whether a carrier signal is present.

If a carrier signal is found, the station with data to transmit will continue to monitor the channel. When the current transmission ends, the station will then transmit its data, while checking the channel for collisions. Because Ethernet and IEEE 802.3 Manchester-encoded signals have a 1-volt average DC voltage level, a collision results at an average DC level of 2 volts. Thus, a transceiver or network interface card can detect collisions by monitoring the voltage level of the Manchester line signal.

Jam Pattern

If a collision is detected during transmission, the transmitting station will cease transmission of data and initiate transmission of a jam pattern. The jam pattern consists of 32 to 48 bits. These bits can have any value other than the CRC value that corresponds to the partial frame transmitted before the jam. The transmission of the jam pattern ensures that the collision lasts long enough to be detected by all stations on the network.

When a repeater is used to connect multiple segments, it must recognize a collision occurring on one port and place a jam signal on all other ports. Doing so results in the occurrence of a collision with signals from stations that may have been in the process of beginning to transmit on one segment when the collision occurred on the other segment. In addition, the jam signal serves as a mechanism to cause nontransmitting stations to wait until the jam signal ends before attempting to transmit, alleviating additional potential collisions from occurring.

Wait Time

Once a collision is detected, the transmitting station waits a random number of slot times before attempting to retransmit. The term *slot* represents 512 bits on a 10-Mbps network, or a minimum frame length of 64 bytes. The actual number of slot times the station waits is selected by a randomization process, formally known as a *truncated binary exponential backoff.* Under this randomization process, a randomly selected integer r defines the number of slot times the station waits before listening to determine whether the channel is clear. If it is, the station begins to retransmit the frame, while listening for another collision.

If the station transmits the complete frame successfully and has additional data to transmit, it will again listen to the channel as it prepares another frame for transmission. If a collision occurs on a retransmission attempt, a slightly different procedure is followed. After a jam signal is transmitted, the station simply doubles the previously generated random number and then waits the prescribed number of slot intervals before attempting a retransmission. Up to 16 retransmission attempts can occur before the station aborts the transmission and declares the occurrence of a multiple collision error condition.

Figure 4.6 illustrates the collision detection process by which a station can determine that a frame was not successfully transmitted. At time t_0 both stations A and B are listening and fail to detect the occurrence of a collision, and

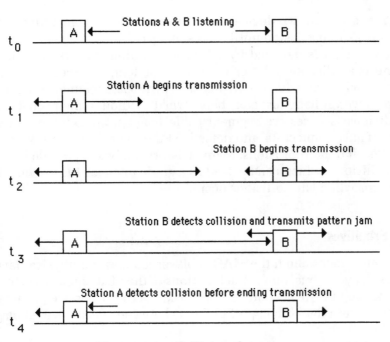

Figure 4.6 Collision detection.

at time t_1 station A commences the transmission of a frame. As station A's frame begins to propagate down the bus in both directions, station B begins the transmission of a frame, since at time t_2 it appears to station B that there is no activity on the network.

Shortly after time t_2 the frames transmitted by stations A and B collide, resulting in a doubling of the Manchester encoded signal level for a very short period of time. This doubling of the Manchester encoded signal's voltage level is detected by station B at time t_3, since station B is closer to the collision than station A. Station B then generates a jam pattern that is detected by station A.

Late Collisions

A late collision is a term used to reference the detection of a collision only after a station places a complete frame on the network. A late collision is normally caused by an excessive network segment cable length, resulting in the time for a signal to propagate from one end of a segment to another part of the segment being longer than the time required to place a full frame on the network. This results in two devices communicating at the same time never seeing the other's transmission until their signals collide.

A late collision is detected by a transmitter after the first slot time of 64 bytes and is applicable only for frames whose lengths exceed 65 bytes. The detection of a late collision occurs in exactly the same manner as a normal collision; however, it happens later than normal. Although the primary cause of late collisions is excessive segment cable lengths, an excessive number of repeaters, faulty connectors, and defective Ethernet transceivers or controllers can also result in late collisions. Many network analyzers provide information on late collisions, which can be used as a guide to check the previously mentioned items when late collisions occur.

Service Primitives

As previously mentioned, the MAC sublayer isolates the physical layer from the LLC sublayer. Thus, one of the functions of the MAC sublayer is to provide services to the LLC. To accomplish this task, a series of service primitives was defined to govern the exchange of LLC data between a local MAC sublayer and its peer LLC sublayer.

The basic MAC service primitives used in all IEEE MAC standards include the medium access data request (MA_DATA.request), medium access data confirm (MA_DATA.confirm), medium access data indicate (MA_DATA.indicate), and medium access data response (MA_DATA.response).

MA_DATA.request

The medium access data request is generated whenever the LLC sublayer has data to be transmitted. This primitive is passed from layer n to layer $n - 1$ to request the initiation of service, and results in the MAC sublayer formatting the request in a MAC frame and passing it to the physical layer for transmission.

MA_DATA.confirm

The medium access data confirm primitive is generated by the MAC sublayer in response to an MA_DATA.request generated by the local LLC sublayer. The confirm primitive is passed from layer $n - 1$ to layer n, and includes a status parameter that indicates the outcome of the request primitive.

MA_DATA.indicate

The medium access data indicate primitive is passed from layer $n - 1$ to layer n to indicate that a valid frame has arrived at the local MAC sublayer. Thus, this service primitive denotes that the frame was received without CRC, length, or frame-alignment error.

MA_DATA.response

The medium access data response primitive is passed from layer n to layer $n - 1$. This primitive acknowledges the MA_DATA.indicate service primitive.

Primitive Operations

To illustrate the use of MAC service primitives, let us assume that station A on a network wants to communicate with station B. As illustrated in Figure 4.7, the LLC sublayer of station A requests transmission of a frame to the MAC sublayer service interface via the issuance of an MA_DATA.request service primitive. In response to the MA_DATA.request, a frame is transmitted to station B. Upon receipt of that frame, the MAC sublayer at that station generates an MA_DATA.indicate to inform the LLC sublayer of the arrival of the frame. The LLC sublayer accepts the frame and generates an MA_DATA.response to inform the MAC sublayer that it has the frame. That response flows across the network to station A, where the MAC sublayer generates an MA_DATA.confirm to inform the LLC sublayer that the frame was received without error.

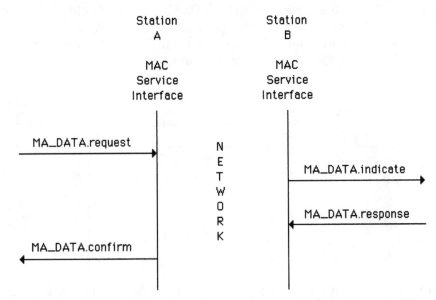

Figure 4.7 Relationship of medium access control service primitives.

4.3 Logical Link Control

As discussed in Chapter 2, the LLC sublayer was defined under the IEEE 802.2 standard to make the method of link control independent of a specific access method. Thus, the 802.2 method of link control spans Ethernet (IEEE 802.3), Token Bus (IEEE 802.4), and Token-Ring (IEEE 802.5) local area networks. Functions performed by the LLC include generating and interpreting commands to control the flow of data, including recovery operations for when a transmission error is detected.

Link control information is carried within the data field of an IEEE 802.3 frame as an LLC protocol data unit (PDU). Figure 4.8 illustrates the relationship between the IEEE 802.3 frame and the LLC PDU.

As discussed in Chapter 2, service access points (SAPs) function much like a mailbox. Because the LLC layer is bounded below the MAC sublayer and bounded above by the network layer, SAPs provide a mechanism for exchanging information between the LLC layer and the MAC and network layers. For example, from the network layer perspective, a SAP represents the place to leave messages about the services requested by an application. There are two broad categories of SAPs, IEEE-administered and manufacturer-implemented. Table 4.4 provides six examples of each type of SAP. In examining the entries in Table 4.4, the hex value AA represents one of the more commonly used SAPs today. When that value is encoded in both DSAP and SSAP fields, it indicates a special type of Ethernet frame referred to as an Ethernet SNAP frame. The SNAP frame, as we will shortly note when we cover it in Section 4.4, unlike the Ethernet 802.3 frame, enables several different protocols to be transported.

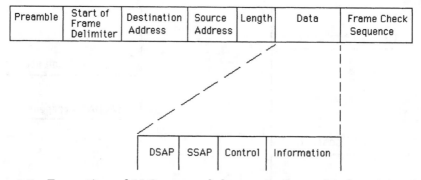

Figure 4.8 Formation of LLC protocol data unit. Control information is carried within a MAC frame.

TABLE 4.4   Examples of SAP Addresses

Address (Hex)	Assignment
IEEE-administered	
00	Null SAP
02	Individual LLC sublayer management functions
06	ARPANET Internet Protocol (IP)
42	IEEE 802.1 Bridge-Spanning Tree Protocol
AA	Sub-Network Access Protocol (SNAP)
FE	ISO Network Layer Protocol
Manufacturer-implemented	
80	Xerox Network Systems
BC	Banyan VINES
EO	Novell NetWare
FO	IBM NetBIOS
F8	IBM Remote Program Load (RPL)
FA	Ungermann-Bass

The destination services access point (DSAP) is one byte in length and is used to specify the receiving network layer process. Because an IEEE 802.3 frame does not include a type field, the DSAP field is used to denote the destination upper-layer protocol carried within the frame. For example, the DSAP hex value E0 indicates that the data field contains NetWare data.

The source service access point (SSAP) is also one byte in length. The SSAP specifies the sending network layer process. Because the destination and source protocols must be the same, the value of the SSAP field will always match the value of the DSAP field. Both DSAP and SSAP addresses are assigned by the IEEE. For example, hex address "FF" represents a DSAP broadcast address.

The control field contains information concerning the type and class of service being used for transporting LLC data. For example, a hex value of 03 when NetWare is being transported indicates that the frame is using an unnumbered format for connectionless services.

Types and Classes of Service

Under the 802.2 standard, there are three types of service available for sending and receiving LLC data. These types are discussed in the next three paragraphs. Figure 4.9 provides a visual summary of the operation of each LLC service type.

Type 1

Type 1 is an unacknowledged connectionless service. The term *connectionless* refers to the fact that transmission does not occur between two devices as if a logical connection were established. Instead, transmission flows on the channel to all stations; however, only the destination address acts upon the data. As the name of this service implies, there is no provision for the acknowledgment of frames. Neither are there provisions for flow control or for error recovery. Therefore, this is an unreliable service.

Type 1 Unacknowledged connectionless service

Type 2 Connection-oriented service

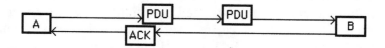

Type 3 Acknowledged connectionless source

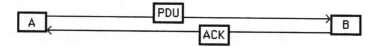

Legend:
PDU = Protocol data unit
ACK = Acknowledgment
A,B = Stations on the network

Figure 4.9 Local link control service types.

Despite those shortcomings, Type 1 is the most commonly used service, because most protocol suites use a reliable transport mechanism at the transport layer, thus eliminating the need for reliability at the link layer. In addition, by eliminating the time needed to establish a virtual link and the overhead of acknowledgments, a Type 1 service can provide a greater throughput than other LLC types of services.

Type 2

The Type 2 connection-oriented service requires that a logical link be established between the sender and the receiver before information transfer. Once the logical connection is established, data will flow between the sender and receiver until either party terminates the connection. During data transfer, a Type 2 LLC service provides all of the functions lacking in a Type 1 service, using a sliding window for flow control. When IBM's SNA data is transported on a LAN, it uses connection-oriented services. Type 2 LLC is also commonly referred to as LLC 2.

Type 3

The Type 3 acknowledged connectionless service contains provision for the setup and disconnection of transmission; it acknowledges individual frames using the stop-and-wait flow control method. Type 3 service is primarily used in an automated factory process-control environment, where one central computer communicates with many remote devices that typically have a limited storage capacity.

Classes of Service

All logical link control stations support Type 1 operations. This level of support is known as Class I service. The classes of service supported by LLC indicate the combinations of the three LLC service types supported by a station. Class I supports Type 1 service, Class II supports both Type 1 and Type 2, Class III supports Type 1 and Type 3 service, and Class IV supports all three service types. Because service Type 1 is supported by all classes, it can be considered a least common denominator, enabling all stations to communicate using a common form of service.

Service Primitives

The LLC sublayer uses service primitives similar to those that govern the exchange of data between the MAC sublayer and its peer LLC sublayer. In doing so, the LLC sublayer supports the Request, Confirm, Indicate, and Response primitives described in Section 4.2 of this chapter. The major difference between the LLC and MAC service primitives is that the LLC sublayer supports three types of services. As previously discussed, the available LLC services are unacknowledged connectionless, connection-oriented, and acknowledged connectionless. Thus, the use of LLC service primitives varies in conjunction with the type of LLC service initiated. For example, a connection-oriented service uses service primitives in the same manner as that illustrated in Figure 4.7. If the service is unacknowledged connectionless, the only service primitives used are the Request and Indicate, because there is no Response nor Confirmation.

4.4 Other Ethernet Frame Types

Two additional frame types that warrant discussion are Ethernet-802.3 and Ethernet-SNAP. In actuality, both types of frames represent a logical variation of the IEEE 802.3 frame, in which the composition of the data field varies from the composition of the LLC protocol data unit previously illustrated in Figure 4.8.

Ethernet-802.3

The Ethernet-802.3 frame represents a proprietary subdivision of the IEEE 802.3 data field to transport NetWare. Ethernet-802.3 is one of several types of frames that can be used to transport NetWare. The actual frame type used is defined at system setup by binding NetWare to a specific type of frame.

Figure 4.10 illustrates the format of the Ethernet-802.3 frame. Due to the absence of LLC fields, this frame is often referred to as *raw 802.3*.

For those using or thinking of using NetWare, a word of caution is in order concerning frame types. Novell uses the term Ethernet-802.2 to refer to the IEEE 802.3 frame. Thus, if you set up NetWare for Ethernet-802.2 frames, in effect, your network is IEEE 802.3–compliant.

Ethernet-SNAP

The Ethernet-SNAP frame, unlike the Ethernet-802.3 frame, can be used to transport several protocols. AppleTalk Phase II, NetWare, and TCP/IP protocols can be transported due to the inclusion of an Ethernet type field in the

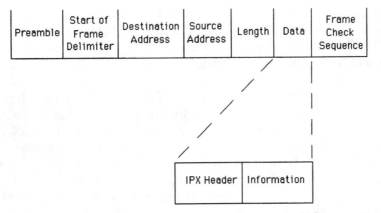

Figure 4.10 Novell's NetWare Ethernet-802.3 frame. An Ethernet-802.3 frame subdivides the data field into an IPX header field and an information field.

Ethernet-SNAP frame. Thus, SNAP can be considered as an extension that permits vendors to create their own Ethernet protocol transports. Ethernet-SNAP was defined by the IEEE 802.1 committee to facilitate interoperability between IEEE 802.3 LANs and Ethernet LANs. This was accomplished, as we will soon note, by the inclusion of a type field in the Ethernet-SNAP frame.

Figure 4.11 illustrates the format of an Ethernet-SNAP frame. Although the format of this frame is based upon the IEEE 802.3 frame format, it does not use DSAP and SSAP mailbox facilities and the control field. Instead, it places specific values in those fields to indicate that the frame is a SNAP frame.

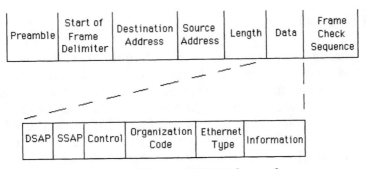

Figure 4.11 Ethernet-SNAP frame format.

The value hex AA is placed into the DSAP and SSAP fields, while hex 03 is placed into the control field to indicate that a SNAP frame is being transported. The hex 03 value in the control field defines the use of an unnumbered format, which is the only format supported by a SNAP frame.

The organization code field references the organizational body that assigned the value placed in the following field, the Ethernet type field. A hex value of 00-00-00 in the organization code field indicates that Xerox assigned the value in the Ethernet type field. Through the use of the Ethernet-SNAP frame, you obtain the ability to transport multiple protocols in a manner similar to the original Ethernet frame that used the type field for this purpose. Here the hex value of 00-00-00 in the organization code field enables the values previously listed in Table 4.2 to represent different protocols carried by the SNAP frame.

Frame Determination

Through software, a receiving station can determine the type of frame and correctly interpret the data carried in the frame. To accomplish this, the value of the two bytes that follow the source address is first examined. If the value is greater than 1500, this indicates the occurrence of an Ethernet frame. If the value is less than or equal to 1500, the frame can be either a pure IEEE 802.3 frame or a variation of that frame. Thus, more bytes must be examined.

If the next two bytes have the hex value FF:FF, the frame is a NetWare Ethernet-802.3 frame. This is because the IPX header has hex FF:FF in the checksum field contained in the first two bytes in the IPX header. If the two bytes contain the hex value AA:AA, this indicates that it is an Ethernet-SNAP frame. Any other value determined to reside in those two bytes then indicates that the frame must be an Ethernet-802.3 frame.

4.5 Fast Ethernet

The frame composition associated with each of the three Fast Ethernet standards is illustrated in Figure 4.12. In comparing the composition of the Fast Ethernet frame with Ethernet and IEEE 802.3 frame formats previously illustrated in Figure 4.1, you will note that other than the addition of starting and ending stream delimiters, the Fast Ethernet frame duplicates the older frames. A third difference between the two is not shown, as it is not actually observable from a comparison of frames, because this difference is associated with the time between frames. Ethernet and IEEE 802.3 frames are Manchester

SSD 1 byte	Preamble 7 bytes	SFD 1 byte	Destination Address 6 bytes	Source Address 6 bytes	L/T 2 bytes	Data 46 to 1500 bytes	FCS 1 byte	ESD 1 byte

Legend:
SSD = Start of Stream Delimiter
SFD = Start of Frame Delimiter
L/T = Length (IEEE 802.3)/Type (Ethernet)
ESD = End of Stream Delimiter

Figure 4.12 Fast Ethernet frame. The 100BASE-TX frame differs from the IEEE 802.3 MAC frame through the addition of a byte at each end to mark the beginning and end of the stream delimiter.

encoded and have an interpacket gap of 9.6 μsec between frames. In comparison, the Fast Ethernet 100BASE-TX frame is transmitted using 4B5B encoding, and IDLE codes (refer to Table 3.6) representing sequences of I (binary 11111) symbols are used to mark a 0.96-μs interpacket gap. Now that we have an overview of the differences between Ethernet/IEEE 802.3 and Fast Ethernet frames, let's focus upon the new fields associated with the Fast Ethernet frame format.

Start-of-Stream Delimiter

The start-of-stream delimiter (SSD) is used to align a received frame for subsequent decoding. The SSD field consists of a sequence of J and K symbols, which defines the unique code 11000 10001. This field replaces the first octet of the preamble in Ethernet and IEEE 802.3 frames whose composition is 10101010.

End-of-Stream Delimiter

The end-of-stream delimiter (ESD) is used as an indicator that data transmission terminated normally, and a properly formed stream was transmitted. This one-byte field is created by the use of T and R codes (see Table 3.6) whose bit composition is 01101 00111. The ESD field lies outside of the Ethernet/IEEE 802.3 frame and for comparison purposes can be considered to fall within the interframe gap of those frames.

4.6 Gigabit Ethernet

Earlier in this chapter it was briefly mentioned that the Ethernet frame was extended for operations at 1 Gbps. In actuality the Gigabit Ethernet standard resulted in two modifications to conventional CSMA/CD operations. The first modification, which is referred to as carrier extension, is only applicable for half-duplex links and was required to maintain an approximate 200-meter topology at Gigabit speeds. Instead of actually extending the fame, as we will shortly note, the time the frame is on the wire is extended. A second modification, referred to as packet burst, enables Gigabit-compatible network devices to transmit bursts of relatively short packets without having to relinquish control of the network. Both carrier extension and packet bursting represent modifications to the CSMA/CD protocol to extend the collision domain and enhance the efficiency of Gigabit Ethernet, respectively. Both topics are covered in detail in this section.

Carrier Extension

In an Ethernet network, the attachment of workstations to a hub creates a segment. That segment or multiple segments interconnected via the use of one or more repeaters forms a collision domain. The latter term is formally defined as a single CSMA/CD network in which a collision will occur if two devices attached to the network transmit at or approximately the same time. The reason we can say approximately the same time is due to the fact that there is a propagation delay time associated with the transmission of signals on a conductor. Thus, if one station is relatively close to another the propagation delay time is relatively short, requiring both stations to transmit data at nearly the same time for a collision to occur. If two stations are at opposite ends of the network the propagation delay for a signal placed on the network by one station to reach the other station is much greater. This means that one station could initiate transmission and actually transmit a portion of a frame while the second station might listen to the network, hear no activity, and begin to transmit, resulting in a collision.

Figure 4.13 illustrates the relationship between a single collision domain and two collision windows. Note that as stations are closer to one another the collision window, which represents the propagation delay time during which one station could transmit and another would assume there is no network activity decreases.

Ethernet requires that a station should be able to hear any resulting collision for the frame it is transmitting before it completes the transmission of the entire frame. This means that the transmission of the next-to-last bit of a frame

Single Collision Domain

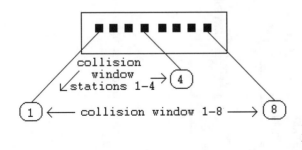

Figure 4.13 Relationship between a collision domain and collision windows.

that results in a collision should allow the transmitting station to hear the collision voltage increase before it transmits the last bit. Thus, the maximum allowable cabling distance is limited by the bit duration associated with the network operating rate and the speed of electrons on the wire.

When Ethernet operates at 1 Gbps, the allowable cabling distance would be reduced to approximately 10 meters or 33 feet. Clearly, this would be a major restriction on the ability of Gigabit Ethernet to be effectively used in a shared media half-duplex environment. To overcome this transmission distance limitation, Sun Microsystems, Inc., suggested the carrier extension scheme, which became part of the Gigabit Ethernet standard for half-duplex operations.

Under the carrier extension scheme, the original Ethernet frame is extended by increasing the time the frame is on the wire. The timing extension occurs after the end of the standard CSMA/CD frame as illustrated in Figure 4.14. The carrier extension extends the frame timing to guarantee at least a 512-byte slot time for half-duplex Ethernet. Note that Ethernet's slot time is considered as the time from the first bit of the destination address field reaching the wire through the last bit of the frame check sequence field. The increase in the minimum length frame does not change the frame size and only alters the time the frame is on the wire. Due to this compatibility it is maintained between the original Ethernet frame and the Gigabit Ethernet frame.

Although the carrier extension scheme enables the cable length of a half-duplex Gigabit network to be extended to a 200-meter diameter, that extension is not without a price. That price is one of overhead, because extension symbols attached to a short frame waste bandwidth. For example, a frame with a 64-byte data field would have 448 bytes of wasted carrier extension symbols attached to it. To further complicate bandwidth utilization, when the data field is less than 46 bytes in length, nulls are added to produce a 64-byte minimum-length data

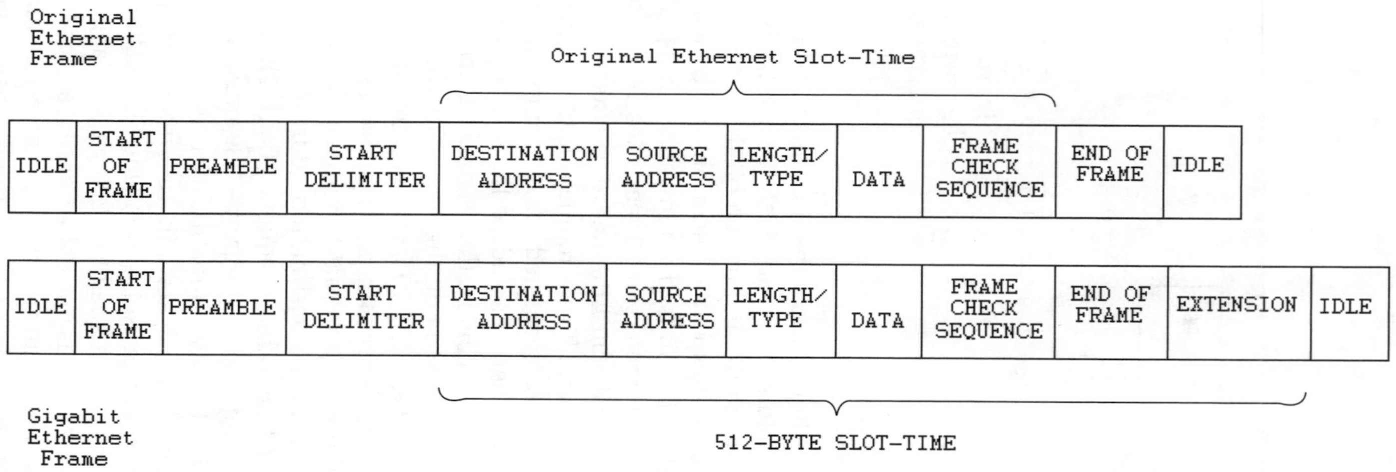

Original
Ethernet
Frame

Original Ethernet Slot-Time

IDLE	START OF FRAME	PREAMBLE	START DELIMITER	DESTINATION ADDRESS	SOURCE ADDRESS	LENGTH/ TYPE	DATA	FRAME CHECK SEQUENCE	END OF FRAME	IDLE

IDLE	START OF FRAME	PREAMBLE	START DELIMITER	DESTINATION ADDRESS	SOURCE ADDRESS	LENGTH/ TYPE	DATA	FRAME CHECK SEQUENCE	END OF FRAME	EXTENSION	IDLE

Gigabit
Ethernet
Frame

512-BYTE SLOT-TIME

Figure 4.14 Half-duplex Gigabit Ethernet uses a carrier extension scheme to extend timing so that the slot time consists of at least 512 bytes.

field. Thus, a simple query to be transported by Ethernet, such as "Enter your age" consisting of 44 data characters, would be padded with 32 null characters when transported by Ethernet to ensure a minimum 72-byte length frame. Under Gigabit Ethernet, the minimum 512-byte time slot would require the use of 448 carrier extension symbols to ensure that the time slot from destination address through any required extension is at least 512 bytes in length.

In examining Figure 4.14, it is important to note that the carrier extension scheme does not extend the Ethernet frame beyond a 512-byte time slot. Thus, Ethernet frames with a time slot equal to or exceeding 512 bytes have no carrier extension. Another important item to note concerning the carrier extension scheme is that it has no relationship to a Jumbo Frames feature that is proprietary to a specific vendor. That feature is supported by a switch manufactured by Alteon Networks and is used to enhance data transfers between servers, permitting a maximum frame size of up to 9 Kbytes to be supported. Because Jumbo Frames are not part of the Gigabit Ethernet standard, you must disable that feature to obtain interoperability between that vendor's 1-Gbps switch and other vendors' Gigabit Ethernet products.

Packet Bursting

Packet bursting represents a scheme added to Gigabit Ethernet to counteract the overhead associated with transmitting relatively short frames. This scheme was proposed by NBase Communications and is included in the Gigabit Ethernet standard as an addition to carrier extension.

Under packet bursting, each time the first frame in a sequence of short frames successfully passes the 512-byte collision window using the carrier extension scheme previously described, subsequent frames are transmitted without including the carrier extension. The effect of packet bursting is to average the wasted time represented by the use of carrier extension symbols over a series of short frames. The limit on the number of frames that can be bursted is a total of 1500 bytes for the series of frames, which represents the longest data field supported by Ethernet. To inhibit other stations from initiating transmission during a burst carrier extension, signals are inserted between frames in the burst.

In addition to enhancing network use and minimizing bandwidth overhead, packet bursting also reduces the probability of collisions occurring. This is because the burst of frames are only susceptible to a collision during the first frame in the sequence. Thereafter, carrier extension symbols between frames followed by additional short frames are recognized by all other stations on the segment, and inhibit those stations from initiating a transmission that would result in the occurrence of a collision.

chapter five

Networking Hardware and Software

Until this chapter, our primary hardware focus was on generic products designed to construct Ethernet-type networks at a single location. Although we discussed the use of electrical fiber-optic repeaters, that discussion was limited to a few network expansion examples. In addition, until now we have essentially avoided discussing the use of bridges, routers, and gateways to extend Ethernet connectivity beyond a single network, and the role of network software and how it relates to your personal computer's operating system. In this chapter, we will focus our attention on those two areas.

First, we will focus our attention on the basic operation of several hardware components that are the building blocks essential to extending the connectivity capability of an Ethernet local area network: repeaters, bridges, routers, brouters, gateways, servers, and wiring hubs. Next, we will discuss the role and operation of three major types of software required for local area network operations: computer operating systems, LAN operating systems, and application programs. This will be followed by a discussion of the software used to route data from one LAN to another using different internet hardware and software products. By examining hardware and software, we will obtain an appreciation for the methods used to link LANs both directly and through wide area networks.

In this chapter and throughout this book, we will use the terms *local area network* and *network* synonymously. We will use the term *internetwork* or just *internet* to refer to the joining of two or more local area networks. Note that we will use the latter term to refer to the combining of networks and not to the specific network called the Internet, whose first letter is capitalized. In Chapter 7 we will examine the connection of Ethernet-based networks to that network, focusing our attention upon the configuration of workstations, servers, and routers to enable an Ethernet network to be connected to the Internet.

5.1 Hardware Components

In this section we will examine hardware products essential to the construction and interconnection of local area networks. These products provide us with the ability to extend the distance of local area network coverage, connect local networks to distant ones, and obtain access to centralized computational facilities.

Repeaters

A repeater is the simplest type of hardware component in terms of design, operation, and functionality. This device operates at the physical layer of the ISO Open Systems Interconnection Reference Model, regenerating a signal received on one cable segment and then retransmitting the signal onto another cable segment. Figure 5.1 illustrates the operation of a repeater with respect to the ISO OSI Reference Model.

Types

There are two basic types of repeaters. An *electrical repeater* simply receives an electrical signal and then regenerates the signal. During the signal regeneration process, a new signal is formed that matches the original characteristics of the received signal. This process is illustrated in the lower portion of Figure 5.1. By transmitting a new signal, the repeater removes any previous distortion and attenuation, enabling an extension in the permissible transmission distance. Although several network segments can be connected by the use of repeaters to extend the coverage of a network, there are constraints that govern the maximum permissible length of a LAN. For example, a 50-ohm coaxial bus-based Ethernet supports a maximum cabling distance of 2.3 km, and that distance cannot be extended through the use of repeaters.

The second type of repeater commonly used is an *electrical-optical device,* such as the FOIRL repeater, the use and general operation of which were discussed in Chapter 3. This type of repeater converts an electrical signal into an optical signal for transmission and performs a reverse function when receiving a light signal. Similar to an electrical repeater, the electrical-optical repeater extends the distance that a signal can be carried on a local area network.

Because a repeater is restricted to operating at the OSI physical layer, it is transparent to data flow. This restricts the use of a repeater to linking identical networks or network segments. For example, you could use repeaters to connect two Ethernet or two Token-Ring network segments, but not to connect an Ethernet network to a Token-Ring network.

a. OSI operation

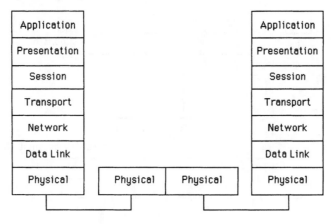

b. Signal regeneration process

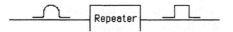

Figure 5.1 Repeater operation. A repeater connects two local area networks or network segments at the OSI physical layer (cable) by regenerating the signal received on one LAN or LAN segment onto the other network or network segment.

Utilization

Figure 5.2 illustrates the use of a repeater to connect two Ethernet bus-based LANs, one serving the accounting department, and the other network serving the data processing department. In this situation, all messages on one local area network are passed to the other, regardless of their intended recipient. The use of repeaters in this manner increases the sum of the traffic on each LAN. If this system is implemented without knowledge of the traffic flow and utilization levels on each network, performance problems may result when separate networks are interconnected through the use of repeaters.

One special type of electrical repeater is a twisted-pair-based hub, such as a 10BASE-T hub. As previously discussed in this book, a hub receives data on one port and regenerates such data bit by bit onto all other ports. Another special type of repeater is a buffered distributor. A buffered distributor represents

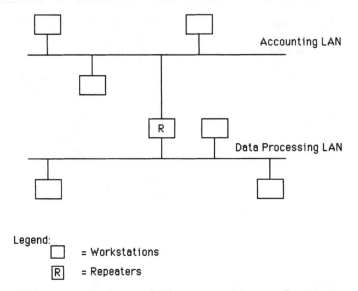

Figure 5.2 Using a repeater to link separate network segments. When a repeater is used to connect separate network segments, traffic on each segment is regenerated onto the other segment.

a relatively new type of IEEE 802.3 hub, which is designed to connect two or more 802.3 links, each operating at 1 Gbps. Similar to other 802.3 repeaters, the buffer distributor is a nonaddressable device, forwarding all inbound frames received on one port onto all other ports. Unlike other repeaters, the buffered distributor, as its name implies, contains an internal memory area that allows one or more incoming frames to be buffered before forwarding those frames. Through the buffering of frames and the ability to use the IEEE 802.3x flow control scheme to manage its internal buffer level of occupancy, the buffered distributor is not subject to the Ethernet collision-domain constraint nor other topology limitations.

Constraints

There are several constraints associated with the use of repeaters. Those constraints include the previously discussed 5-4-3 rule, disabling of the SQE test signal to repeaters to include hub ports, and topology restrictions associated with the use of different types of repeaters. You can use the information presented in this book as well as vendor specification sheets to determine the specific constraints associated with different types of repeaters. Concerning vendor specification sheets, their use is highly recommended, as the constraints associated with the use of different types of repeaters can vary from one manufacturer to another.

Bridges

Unlike repeaters, which lack intelligence and are restricted to linking similar LANs and LAN segments, bridges are intelligent devices that can connect similar and dissimilar local area networks. To obtain an appreciation for the functions performed by bridges, let us examine the use of this type of networking product.

Operation

Figure 5.3 illustrates the operation of a bridge with respect to the OSI Reference Model, as well as its use to connect two separate Ethernet local area networks. Although the use of the bridge in the lower portion of Figure 5.3 looks similar to the use of a repeater previously shown in Figure 5.2, the operation of each device includes a number of key differences.

When a bridge begins to operate, it examines each frame transmitted on connected local area networks at the data link layer—a process beyond the capability of a repeater, which operates transparent to data. By reading the source address included in each frame, the bridge assembles a table of local addresses for each network. In addition to reading each source address, the bridge also reads the destination address contained in the frame. If the destination address is not contained in the local address table that the bridge constructs, this fact indicates that the frame's destination is not on the current network or network segment. In this situation, the bridge transmits the frame onto the other network or network segment. If the destination address is contained in the local address table, this indicates that the frame should remain on the local network. In this situation, the bridge simply repeats the frame without altering its routing.

We can summarize the operation of the bridge illustrated in the lower portion of Figure 5.3 as follows:

- ◆ Bridge reads all frames transmitted on network A.
- ◆ Frames with destination address on network A are discarded by the bridge.
- ◆ Frames with destination address on network B are retransmitted onto network B.
- ◆ The above process is reversed for traffic on network B.

OSI operation

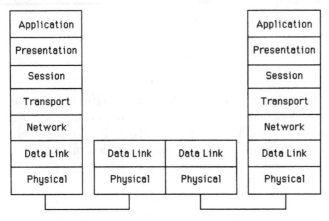

Application Example

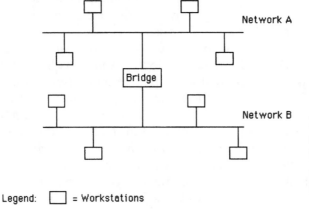

Network A

Bridge

Network B

Legend: ☐ = Workstations

Figure 5.3 Bridge operation. A bridge connects two local area networks or network segments at the data link layer.

To illustrate the method by which bridges operate, let's assume a three-port bridge is used to connect three Ethernet segments together, as illustrated in the top portion of Figure 5.4. In this example, for simplicity, each port address is denoted by a letter of the alphabet while each station address is denoted by a numeric. It should be noted that each bridge port has a MAC address as it is a participant on a LAN. Although the MAC address of bridge ports and stations have the same format and are six hex digits in length, we will use one alphabetic character for each bridge port and one numeric character for each station for simplicity of illustration.

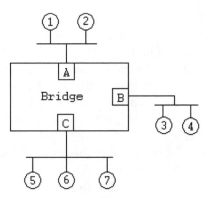

Data Transfer Requirement	Bridge Operation	Address-Port Table
1 transmits to 2	frame flooded	1,A
2 transmits to 1	frame discarded	1,A 2,A
5 transmits to 1	frame forwarded	1,A 2,A 5,C
6 transmits to 3	frame flooded	1,A 2,A 5,C 6,C
3 transmits to 6	frame forwarded	1,A 2,A 3,B 5,C 6,C

Figure 5.4 Bridges are self-learning networking devices that automatically construct address-port table entries used to route data between network segments.

The table in the lower portion of Figure 5.4 provides examples of the three operations a bridge performs—flooding frames, forwarding frames, and discarding frames. In the first entry, station 1 is presumed to transmit data to station 2. Since we will assume the bridge was just powered on and has no entries in its address-port table, it does not know which port station 2 is connected to. Thus, it transmits the frame onto all other ports other than the port it was received on, a technique referred to as flooding. Because station 2 is on the same segment as station 1, the transmission of frames onto the other segments only interferes with traffic on those segments but will not be recognized by a station, because no station connected to port B or C has address 2.

When the frame from station 1 is flooded by the bridge, it enters the source address and port that the frame was received on into its address-port table. Hence the entry "1, A." When the frame reaches station 2, we will assume 2 transmits a response to 1. As the frame propagates down the segment and is read by bridge port A, it notes that address 1 is on port A. Thus, there is no need for the bridge to forward the frame and it simply discards it. However, the bridge notes address 2 is on port A and updates its address-port table.

For the third example, it was assumed that station 5 transmits to station 1. Because the address-port table holds the relationship of address 1 with port A, the bridge forwards the frame onto port A and updates its address-port table. Next, when station 6 transmits to station 3 and the bridge checks its address-port table, it finds no entry for address 3, resulting in the bridge flooding the frame onto ports B and C. Then the bridge notes that station 6 is not in its address-port table and updates that table. In the last example, station 3 transmits a response to station 6. Because an entry for station 6 was just made in the address-port table, the bridge forwards the frame onto port C.

In addition to associating addresses with ports, a bridge also time stamps each entry and updates the time stamp when an address is referenced. As storage is used up and the bridge needs to purge old entries to make room for new entries, it will purge the oldest entries based upon the use of the time stamp.

The previously described method of bridging operation is referred to as *transparent bridging.* Refer to Chapter 6 for detailed information concerning different methods of bridge operations.

Filtering and Forwarding   The process of examining each frame is known as *filtering.* The *filtering rate* of a bridge is directly related to its level of performance. That is, the higher the filtering rate of a bridge, the lower the probability it will become a bottleneck to network performance. A second performance measurement associated with bridges is their *forwarding rate.* The forwarding rate is expressed in frames per second and denotes the maximum capability of a bridge to transmit traffic from one network to another. In Chapter 6, we will expand our examination of bridges to determine their maximum filtering and forwarding rates when used on Ethernet networks.

Types

There are two general types of bridges: transparent and translating. Each type of bridge can be obtained as a local or remote device; a remote device includes a wide area network interface and the ability to convert frames into a WAN transmission protocol.

Transparent Bridge   A transparent bridge provides a connection between two local area networks that employ the same data link protocol. Thus, the bridge shown in the lower portion of Figure 5.3 and the bridge shown in the upper portion of Figure 5.4 are both examples of transparent bridges. At the physical layer, some transparent bridges have multiple ports that support different media. Thus, a transparent bridge does not have to be transparent at the physical level, although the majority of such bridges are.

Although a transparent bridge provides a high level of performance for a small number of network interconnections, its level of performance decreases as the number of interconnected networks increases. The rationale for this loss in performance is based on the method used by transparent bridges to develop a route between LANs. Refer to Chapter 6 for specific information concerning bridge routing and performance issues.

Translating Bridge   A translating bridge provides a connection capability between two local area networks that employ different protocols at the data link layer. Because networks using different data link layer protocols normally use different media, a translating bridge also provides support for different physical layer connections.

Figure 5.5 illustrates the use of a translating bridge to interconnect a Token-Ring and an Ethernet local area network. In this example, the bridge functions as an Ethernet node on the Ethernet and as a Token-Ring node on the Token-Ring. When a frame from one network has a destination on the other network,

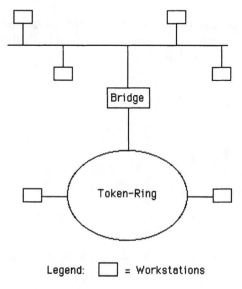

Figure 5.5   Translating bridge operation. A translating bridge connects local area networks that employ different protocols at the data link layer. In this example, the translating bridge is used to connect an Ethernet local area network to a Token-Ring network.

the bridge will perform a series of operations, including frame and transmission rate conversion. For example, consider an Ethernet frame destined to the Token-Ring network. The bridge will strip the frame's preamble and FCS, then it will convert the frame into a Token-Ring frame format. Once the bridge receives a free token, the new frame will be transmitted onto the Token-Ring; however, the transmission rate will be at the Token-Ring network rate and not at the Ethernet rate. For frames going from the Token-Ring to the Ethernet, the process is reversed.

One of the problems associated with the use of a translating bridge is the conversion of frames from their format on one network to the format required for use on another network. As indicated in Chapter 2, the information field of an Ethernet frame can vary from 64 to 1500 bytes. In comparison, a Token-Ring can have a maximum information field size of 4500 bytes when the ring operates at 4 Mbps, or 18,000 bytes when the ring operates at 16 Mbps. If a station on a Token-Ring network has a frame with an information field that exceeds 1500 bytes in length, the bridging of that frame onto an Ethernet network cannot occur. This is because there is no provision within either layer 2 protocol to inform a station that a frame flowing from one network to another was fragmented and requires reassembly. Using a bridge effectively in this situation requires that software on each workstation on each network be configured to use the smallest maximum frame size of any interconnected network. In this example, Token-Ring workstations would not be allowed to transmit information fields greater than 1500 bytes.

Features

The functionality of a bridge is based on the features incorporated into this device. Following is a list of the 11 major bridge features that define both the functionality and the performance level of a bridge.

- Filtering and forwarding rate
- Selective forwarding capability
- Multiple port support
- Wide area network interface support
- Local area network interface support
- Transparent operation at the data link layer
- Translating operation to link dissimilar networks
- Encapsulation operation to support wide area network use
- Stand-alone and adapter-based fabrication

- ◆ Self-learning (transparent) routing
- ◆ Source routing

Filtering and Forwarding The filtering and forwarding rates indicate the ability of the bridge to accept, examine, and regenerate frames on the same network (filtering) and transfer frames onto a different network (forwarding). Higher filtering and forwarding rates indicate better bridge performance.

Selective Forwarding Some bridges have a selective forwarding capability. Bridges with this feature can be configured to forward frames selectively, based on predefined source and destination addresses. With a selective forwarding capability, you can develop predefined routes for frames to take when flowing between networks, and enable or inhibit the transfer of information between predefined workstations.

Figure 5.6 illustrates the use of the selective forwarding capability of two bridges to provide two independent routes for data transfer between an Ether-

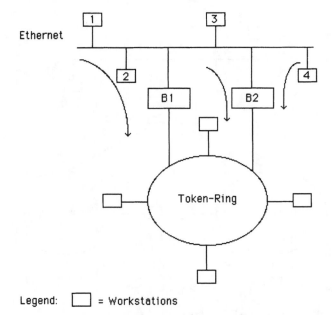

Figure 5.6 Using bridge selective forwarding capability. Using the selective forwarding capability of bridges enables the data flow between networks to be distributed based upon source or destination addresses.

net and a Token-Ring network. In this example, you might enable all work-stations with source address 1 or 2 to have data destined to the Token-Ring flow over bridge 1, while workstations with a source address of 3 or 4 are configured to use bridge 2. Although the bridges illustrated in Figure 5.5 appear to form a closed loop, in effect the previously described method of selective forwarding results in a single logical path for each station on the Ethernet. This ensures there are no closed loops—a condition that would violate the spanning tree bridging algorithm supported by Ethernet bridges. The operation of that algorithm is described in Chapter 6.

Multiple Port Support The multiple port support capability of a bridge is related to its local and wide area network media interface support. Some bridges support additional ports beyond the two that make up a basic bridge. Doing so enables a bridge to provide connectivity between three or more local area networks.

Figure 5.7 illustrates one potential use of a multiple port bridge to link an Ethernet network to two Token-Ring networks.

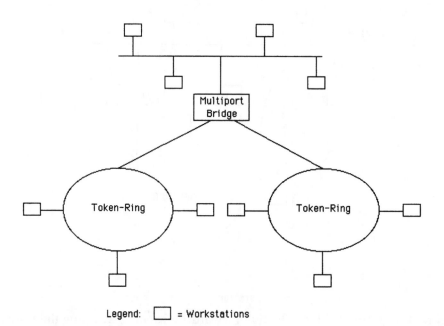

Figure 5.7 Using a multiport bridge. With a multiport bridge, you can interconnect three or more local area networks.

Local and Wide Area Interface Support Local area media interfaces supported by bridges can include thin and thick Ethernet coaxial cable, IEEE 10BASE-T, and other types of twisted-pair cable. Wide area network interfaces are incorporated into remote bridges that are designed to provide an internetworking capability between two or more geographically dispersed LANs linked by a WAN. Common WAN media interfaces can include RS-232 for data rates at or below 19.2 Kbps, ITU X.21 for packet network access at data rates up to 128 Kbps, ITU V.35 for data rates between 48 Kbps and 128 Kbps, and a T1/E1 interface for operations at 1.544 Mbps and 2.048 Mbps, respectively.

Transparent Operation Although bridges are thought of as transparent to data, this is not always true. For interconnecting different networks located in the same geographical area, bridges are normally transparent to data. However, some remote bridges use data compression algorithms to reduce the quantity of data transmitted between bridges connected via a wide area network. Such compression performing bridges are not transparent to data, although they restore data to its original form.

Frame Translation For interconnecting different types of local area networks, bridges must perform a translation of frames. For example, an Ethernet frame must be changed into a Token-Ring frame when the frame is routed from an Ethernet to a Token-Ring network. As previously mentioned, because frames cannot be fragmented at the data link layer, you must set the workstations on the Token-Ring network to the smallest maximum information field of an Ethernet frame, 1500 bytes.

When data is transferred between colocated local area networks, the frame format on one network is suitable for transfer onto the other network; it is modified for transfer when the media access control layers differ. When a bridge is used to connect two local area networks via a wide area network facility, a WAN protocol is employed to control data transfer. The wide area network protocol is better suited for transmission over the WAN, as it is standardized to incorporate error detection and correction, enable a large number of unacknowledged WAN frames to exist to speed information transfer, and support full-duplex data transfers. Examples of such wide area network protocols include IBM's SDLC, Digital Equipment Corporation's DDCMP, and the ITU's HDLC and X.25.

Frame Encapsulation Figure 5.8 illustrates the operation of a pair of remote bridges connecting two local area networks via a wide area network. For transmission from network A to network B, user data from a network A station is

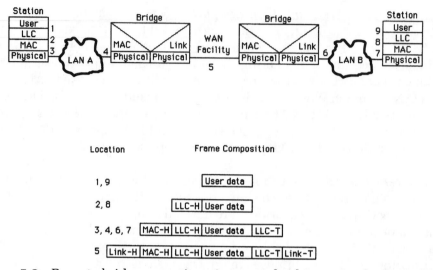

Figure 5.8 Remote bridge operation. A remote bridge wraps the logical link control (LLC) and media access control (MAC) frames in another protocol for transmission over a wide area network.

first converted into logical link control and media access control frames. The bridge then encapsulates one or more LAN frames into the bridging protocol frame used for communications over the wide area network. Because the local area network frame is wrapped in another protocol, we say the LAN frame is *tunneled* within the WAN protocol. At the opposite end of the wide area network, the distant remote bridge performs a reverse operation, removing the WAN protocol header and trailer from each frame.

Fabrication Some bridges are manufactured as stand-alone products. Such devices are called *plug and play,* because you simply connect the bridge ports to the media and turn them on. Other bridges are manufactured as adapter cards for insertion into the system unit of a personal computer, workstation, or reduced instruction set computer (RISC). Through the use of software developed in conjunction with hardware, you may obtain more flexibility with this type of bridge than with a stand-alone device whose software is fixed in ROM.

Routing Method The routing capability of a bridge governs its capability to interconnect local area networks and its level of performance. As previously examined through the use of Figure 5.4, a transparent bridge automatically develops routing tables. Thus, this device is known as a *self-learning bridge* and represents the most elementary type of bridge routing. In the IBM Token-Ring frame, there is an optional routing field that can be used to develop routing information for frames routed through a series of bridges—a technique referred to as *source routing*. Refer to Chapter 6 for an in-depth discussion of bridge routing methods, as well as translating operations that enable a bridge to connect IEEE 802.3 and 802.5 networks.

Routers

A router is a device that operates at the network layer of the ISO OSI Reference Model, as illustrated in Figure 5.9. What this means is that a router examines network addresses and makes decisions about whether data on a local area network should remain on the network or should be transmitted to a different network. Although this level of operation may appear to be insignificant compared with that of a bridge operating at the data link layer, there is actually a considerable difference in the routing capability of bridges and routers.

Operation

A bridge uses 48-bit MAC addresses it associates with ports as a mechanism to determine whether a frame received on one port is ignored, forwarded onto

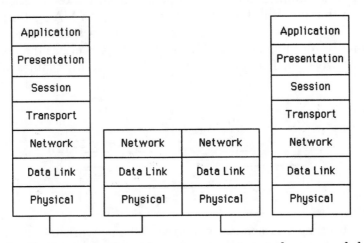

Figure 5.9   Router operation. A router operates at the network layer of the ISO OSI Reference Model. This enables a router to provide network layer services, such as flow control and frame fragmentation.

another port, or flooded onto all ports other than the port it was received on. At the data link layer there is no mechanism to distinguish one network from another. Thus, the delivery of frames between networks requires bridges to learn MAC addresses and base their forwarding decisions on such addresses. Although this is an acceptable technique for linking a few networks together, as the number of networks increase and the number of workstations on interconnected networks increase, bridges would spend a considerable amount of time purging old entries and flooding frames, causing unacceptable performance problems. This resulted in the development of routers that prevent the flooding of frames between networks and operate by using network addresses.

To understand the concept behind routing, consider Figure 5.10, which illustrates two networks connected by a pair of routers. In this example, assume addresses A, B, C, and D represent MAC addresses of workstations, and E and F represent the MAC address of each router connected to each network. Assuming workstation A has data to transmit to workstation C, an application program executing on workstation A assigns network 20 as the destination address in a packet it prepares at the network layer. That packet is transported via one or more MAC frames to MAC address E, which is the data link address of the network adapter card installed in router 1.

In actuality, each device on a network can have a unique network address, with a portion of the address denoting the network and the remainder of the address denoting each host or router interface. This enables the application program on workstation A to transmit a packet destined to workstation C to router 1, with the data link layer passing the packet to MAC address E as a frame or sequence of frames. The router receives the frame or sequence of frames explicitly addressed to it and notes that the packet has the destination address for network 20. The router then searches its routing tables and deter-

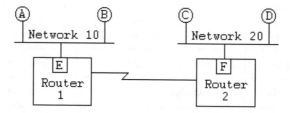

Figure 5.10   Routing between two networks. When a workstation on one network transmits data to a device on another network, an application program provides the destination network address, which is used by routers as a basis for their routing decisions.

mines that it should relay the packet to router 2. When the packet is received at router 2, it recognizes the fact that network 20 is connected to the router via its connection to the LAN by an adapter card using MAC address F. Thus, the router will transport the packet to its destination using one or more frames at the data link layer with a MAC source address of F.

The preceding description represents a simplified description of the routing process. A more detailed description will be presented later in this book after we investigate the TCP/IP protocol suite. We will examine the TCP/IP protocol suite in the second section in this chapter when we turn our attention to networking software and focus our attention upon router operations in Chapter 7.

The ability to operate at the network layer enables a router to extend networking across multiple data links in an orderly and predefined manner. This means that a router can determine the best path through a series of data links from a source network to a destination network. To accomplish this, the router operates under a network protocol, such as the Internet Protocol (IP), Digital Equipment Corporation's DECnet Phase V, or Novell's IPX. This networking protocol must operate on both the source and destination network when protocol-dependent routers are used. If you use protocol-independent routers, you can interconnect networks using different protocols. The protocol-independent router can be considered a sophisticated transparent bridge. Its operation and utilization are described in detail in Chapter 7.

In comparison, because a bridge operates at the data link layer, it can always be used to transfer information between networks operating under different network protocols. This makes a bridge more efficient for linking networks that only have one or a few paths, while a router is more efficient for interconnecting multiple network links via multiple paths.

Network Address Utilization Unlike a bridge, which must monitor all frames at the media access control layer, a router is specifically addressed at the network layer. This means that a router has to examine only frames explicitly addressed to that device. In communications terminology, the monitoring of all frames is referred to as a *promiscuous* mode of operation, while the selective examination of frames is referred to as a *nonpromiscuous* mode of operation.

Another difference between the operation of bridges and routers is the structure of the addresses on which they operate. Bridges operate at the data link layer, which means that they typically examine physical addresses that are contained in ROM on adapter cards and used in the generation of frames. In comparison, routers operate at the network layer, where addresses are normally assigned by a network administrator to a group of stations having a common characteristic, such as being connected on an Ethernet in one area of a building. This type of address is known as a *logical address*, and can be assigned and modified by the network administrator.

Table Operation   Like bridges, routers make forwarding decisions using tables. However, unlike a bridge, which may employ a simple table look-up procedure to determine if a destination address is on a particular network, a router may employ much more sophisticated forwarding decision criteria. For example, a router may be configured to analyze several paths using an algorithm and dynamically select a path based upon the results of the algorithm. Routing algorithms and protocols are discussed in Chapter 7.

Advantages of Use   The use of routers provides a number of significant advantages over the use of bridges. To illustrate these advantages, we will examine the use of routers in Figure 5.11, in which four corporate offices containing seven local area networks are interconnected through the use of four routers. In this example, networks A and B are located in a building in Los Angeles, networks C and D are located in New York, network E is located in Washington, DC, and networks F and G are located in Miami.

Multiple Path Transmission and Routing Control   Suppose a station on network A in Los Angeles requires transmission to a station on network G in Miami. Initially, router R1 might use the path R1-R4 to transmit data between networks. If the path should fail, or if an excessive amount of traffic flows between Los Angeles and Miami using that path, router R1 can seek to establish other paths, such as R1-R3-R4 or even R1-R2-R3-R4. In fact, many routers will consider each packet as a separate entity, routing the packet to its destination over the best available path at the time of transmission. Although this could conceivably result in packets arriving at R4 out of sequence, routers have the capability to resequence packets into their original order before passing data onto the destination network.

Flow Control   As data flows through multiple paths toward its destination, a link can become congested. For example, data from stations on network C and network E routed to network G might build up to the point where the path R3-R4 becomes congested. To eliminate the possibility of packet loss, routers will use flow control. That is, they will inhibit transmission onto a link and notify other routers to inhibit data flow until there is an available level of bandwidth for traffic.

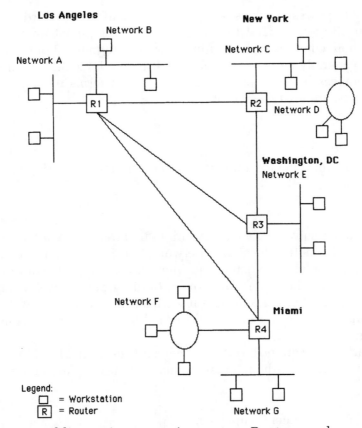

Figure 5.11 Building an internet using routers. Routers can be used to establish complex networks in which traffic is varied over network facilities. This variation is based on the operational status and utilization of different network paths.

Frame Fragmentation   As previously mentioned, bridges cannot break a frame into a series of frames when transmission occurs between networks with different frame sizes. This situation requires workstations to be configured to use the smallest maximum frame size of any of the networks to be connected together. In comparison, most network protocols supported by routers include a provision for fragmentation and reassembly of packets.

The higher level of functionality of routers over bridges is not without a price. That price is in terms of packet processing, software complexity, and cost. Since routers provide a more complex series of functions than bridges, their ability to process packets is typically one-half to two-thirds of the processing capability of bridges. In addition, the development time required to program a more complex series of functions adds to the cost of routers. Thus, routers are generally more expensive than bridges. Table 5.1 summarizes the major differences between bridges and routers in terms of their operation, functionality, complexity, and cost.

Brouters

A brouter is a hybrid device, representing a combination of bridging and routing capabilities.

Operation

When a brouter receives a frame, it examines that frame to determine whether it is destined for another local area network. If it is, the brouter then checks the protocol of the frame to determine whether it is supported at the network layer supported by the router function. If the frame's protocol is supported, the brouter will route the frame as if it were a router. However, if the brouter does not support the protocol, it will instead bridge the frame using layer 2 information.

In comparison to routers, brouters provide an additional level of connectivity between networks, although that connectivity takes place at a lower level

TABLE 5.1   Bridge/Router Comparison

Characteristic	Bridge	Router
Routing based upon an algorithm or protocol	Normally no	Yes
Protocol transparency	Yes	Only protocol-independent router
Uses network addresses	No	Yes
Promiscuous mode of operation	Yes	No
Forwarding decision	Elementary	Can be complex
Multiple path transmission	Limited	High
Routing control	Limited	High
Flow control	No	Yes
Frame fragmentation	No	Yes
Packet processing rate	High	Moderate
Cost	Less expensive	More expensive

in the OSI Reference Model hierarchy. This is because a router would simply ignore a frame for which it does not support the network protocol, while a brouter would bridge the frame.

Utilization

The key advantage of using a brouter is the ability of this device to both bridge and route data. Its ability to perform this dual function enables a brouter to replace the use of separate bridges and routers in some networking applications. For example, consider the use of a separate bridge and router in the top portion of Figure 5.12. In this example, the bridge provides an interconnection capability between two neighboring networks, while the router provides an interconnection capability to distant networks. By replacing the separate bridge and router with a brouter, you can obtain the same level of functional-

Using a separate bridge and router

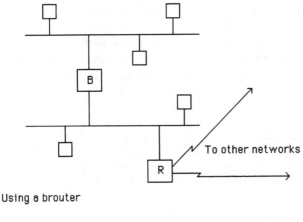

Using a brouter

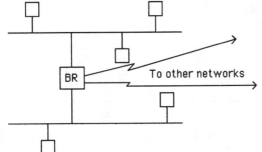

Figure 5.12 Replacing a separate bridge and router with a brouter.

ity, as illustrated in the lower portion of Figure 5.12. Of course, you want to ensure that the filtering and forwarding rates of the brouter are sufficient to be used in the manner illustrated. Otherwise, the replacement of separate bridges and routers by brouters may introduce delays that affect network performance. Refer to Chapters 6 and 7 for information concerning the processing requirements of bridges and routers.

Gateway

The well-known phrase "one person's passion is another's poison" can, in many ways, apply to gateways. The term *gateway* was originally coined to refer to a device providing a communications path between two local area networks, or between a LAN and a mainframe computer, from the physical layer through the application layer. When applied to a device interconnecting networks, the term gateway was originally used and is still commonly used to reference a router. In fact, many programs used to configure workstation and server network operations request the entry of the gateway network address, even though it is more appropriate today to use the term *router*.

Figure 5.13 illustrates the operation of a gateway with respect to the ISO OSI Reference Model. Unfortunately, the term *gateway* has been used loosely to describe a range of products, ranging from bridges and routers that interconnect two or more local area networks to protocol converters that provide

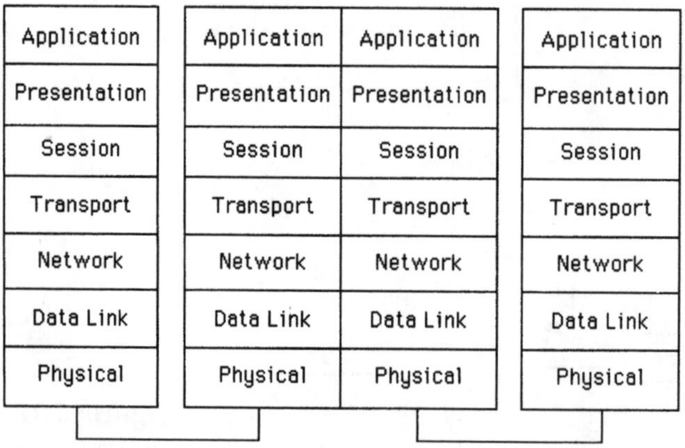

Application	Application	Application	Application
Presentation	Presentation	Presentation	Presentation
Session	Session	Session	Session
Transport	Transport	Transport	Transport
Network	Network	Network	Network
Data Link	Data Link	Data Link	Data Link
Physical	Physical	Physical	Physical

Figure 5.13 Gateway operation. A gateway operates at all seven layers of the ISO OSI Reference Model.

asynchronous dial-up access into an IBM SNA network. Thus, a definition of the term is warranted.

Definition

In this book, we will use the term *gateway* to describe a product that performs protocol conversion through all seven layers of the ISO OSI Reference Model. As such, a gateway performs all of the functions of a router, as well as any protocol conversions required through the application layer.

One of the most common types of gateways is an electronic mail (e-mail) gateway, which converts documents from one e-mail format to another. For example, an internal corporate network might be operating Lotus Development Corporation's CC:MAIL. If they require connectivity with the Internet, the gateway must convert internal CC:MAIL documents so that they can be transported via the Simple Mail Transport Protocol (SMTP), which is a TCP/IP electronic mail application. Similarly, SMTP mail delivered via the Internet to the organization's gateway must be converted by the gateway into the format used by CC:MAIL. A second type of popular gateway enables workstations on a network to communicate with a mainframe as if the workstation was a specific type of terminal device. This type of gateway also operates at all seven layers of the ISO Reference Model.

Operation

Gateways are protocol-specific in function, typically used to provide access to a mainframe computer. Some vendors manufacture multiprotocol gateways. Such products are normally manufactured as adapter cards, containing separate processors that are installed in the system unit of a personal computer or in a specially designed vendor hardware platform. When used in conjunction with appropriate vendor software, this type of gateway is actually an N-in-1 gateway, where N is the number of protocol conversions and separate connections the gateway can perform.

Figure 5.14 shows a multiprotocol gateway used to link LAN stations to an IBM mainframe via an SDLC link and an X.25 connection to a packet switching network. Once connected to the packet switching network, LAN traffic may be further converted by gateway facilities built into that network, or traffic may be routed to a packet network node and transmitted from that node to its final destination in its X.25 packet format.

Gateways are primarily designed and used for LAN-WAN connections and not for inter-LAN communications. Because they perform more sophisticated functions than routers, they are slower in providing network throughput. In

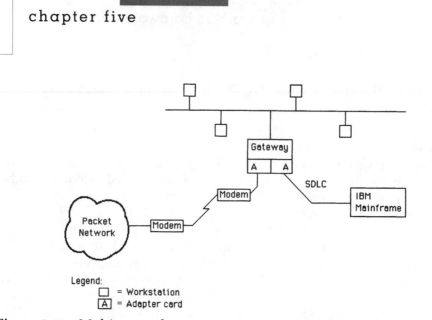

Figure 5.14 Multiprotocol gateway operation. A multiprotocol gateway can be used to provide local area network stations access to different computational facilities, either directly or through the use of a packet network.

addition, because the configuration of a gateway requires the consideration of a large number of protocol options, a gateway installation is considerably more difficult than the setup of a router. Refer to Chapter 8 for specific information concerning the operation and utilization of gateways.

File Servers

The file server is the central repository of information upon which a local area network is normally constructed. The file server is normally a personal computer or workstation that has a very powerful microprocessor, such as an Intel Pentium, Pentium Pro, Pentium II, Digital Alpha, or a RISC chip, and a large amount of fast-access on-line storage. The on-line storage is used to hold the local area network operating system and the application programs that other stations on the network may use. Several software vendors have split application programs, enabling portions of a program to be run on a network station, while other portions, such as the updating of a database, occur on the server. This technique is known as *client–server processing*.

In comparison, the general term *client/server operations* references the access of one computer by another on a network. The computer being accessed, while normally considered to represent a file server, can also be a mainframe or minicomputer. For either situation, the client uses a network to access one or more features of the server. Those features can range in scope from a spread-sheet program stored on a file server to a database query program on a main-frame that provides access to billions of records.

Connectivity Functions

As the heart of a local area network, the server supports every network appli-cation. It is therefore in an ideal position to perform connectivity functions. Some servers are designed to function as asynchronous gateways, providing access to one or more modems that individual network stations can access for communications via the switched telephone network. Here, software on the server considers the group of modems as a pool for access purposes. Hence, the term *modem pooling* is used to refer to a server used to provide this service.

Other servers contain software and hardware to provide access to main-frame computers via a specific protocol, such as SDLC, X.25, or TCP/IP. Depending on the capabilities of the network operating system used on the server, the server may support server-to-server communications on an intra- and inter-LAN basis. When supporting intra-LAN server-to-server communi-cations, you can assign network users to a specific default server for an initial network log-on, distributing the use of servers so that no one server becomes overused. Then, the network operating system would support the transfer of information between servers, such as an electronic mail message created by a network user assigned to one server, who addresses the message to another employee assigned to a different server. If your network operating system supports inter-LAN server-to-server communications, the server in effect functions as a remote bridge.

Types of Servers

The first type of server developed for use with local area networks primarily supported file and printer sharing. Thus, although referred to as a file server, the server also permitted a few printers to be connected to the computer as network-accessible devices. As the concept of local area networking gained acceptance, servers were developed to perform specific functions. Today, popular types of servers include application servers, communications servers, print servers, and remote access servers (RASs). Figure 5.15 illustrates an Ethernet network that contains four distinct types of servers.

The RAS can be considered to represent a hybrid device that consists of a modem pool and router. This type of server permits the support of serial com-munications in the form of analog modems, digital ISDN calls, and the connec-tion of a T1 circuit that contains 24 individual connections grouped together on a common circuit. Incoming communications are prompted for access valida-

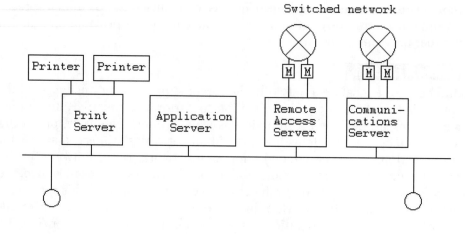

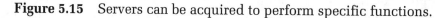

Figure 5.15   Servers can be acquired to perform specific functions.

tion, typically in the form of a user ID and password, to gain access from the RAS onto the network. Once connected to the network, they then obtain access privileges commensurate with the network account they have.

Although a communications server also provides connectivity between a network and a serial communications facility, there are some distinct differences between this server and an RAS. First, a communications server is primarily used for outbound traffic from network users. Thus, it may not support inbound traffic, and if it does, it probably just places the traffic onto the network without checking the validity of the user. Secondly, most communications servers function as replacements for users having individual modems. Thus, another popular name for a limited capability communications server is a modem pooler.

Location Considerations

Figure 5.16 illustrates a file server used both in its traditional role as a repository for application programs and for modem pooling and gateway operations. The transmission of information between workstations and servers far exceeds transmission between workstations. The location of file servers on an Ethernet local area network is therefore critical for ensuring that network performance remains at an acceptable level. In the example shown in Figure 5.16,

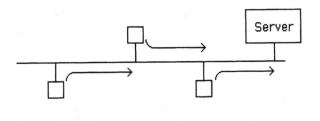

Legend:
☐ = Workstation

Figure 5.16 Server placement. The location of a server on a network is critical for ensuring network performance. In this example, because each workstation requires access to the server, its location requires the greatest transmission distance between individual workstations and the server. This, therefore, is probably a poor server location.

the server is located at a point on an Ethernet bus-based local area network in which the transmission distance between each workstation and the server is maximized. This location results in the greatest propagation delay for the transmission of data between each workstation and the server. This is probably a poor location with respect to network performance if each workstation requires a similar level of access to the server.

The reason for this representing a poor placement is the fact that the longer the distance between two network devices on a CSMA/CD access protocol network, the greater the probability that one station will listen to the network and not hear a signal while another has just began transmitting. This, in turn, results in an increased number of collisions that adversely affects network performance. Because collisions result in the occurrence of a random back-off time interval during which no data can be transferred on the network, the proper location of a server can increase network transmission efficiency.

Wire Hubs

As mentioned in Chapter 3, 10BASE-T Ethernet networks use wiring concentrators, or *hubs*. Hubs are typically located in telephone wiring closets, with stations cabled to the hub in the form of a star. Hubs are then connected to one another to form a bus. Only if the closest workstations to the server require a disproportionate level of server access, in comparison to other workstations, is the server location shown in Figure 5.16 correct. If each workstation has an equal level of server access, the server should be relocated to the middle of the network. This move would minimize propagation delays between the workstations and the server—which, in turn, would minimize the probability of collisions.

Advantages

Ethernet 10BASE-T hubs employ standard wiring between stations and the hub in the form of twisted-pair cable. Because workstations are connected to a single point, administration of a hub-based network is normally simple and economical, because a central point allows network configuration and reconfiguration, monitoring, and management. Due to the value of hubs in local area networking, several vendors have introduced products commonly referred to as *intelligent hubs.* This product provides users with the ability to build local area networks, ranging in scope from a single LAN with a small number of nodes to mixed-protocol LANs with several thousand nodes that can be monitored, modified, and analyzed from a single point.

Intelligent Hubs

An intelligent hub represents a tremendous advance in functionality and capability over conventional wire hubs. The intelligent hub includes its own microprocessor and memory, which not only provide a network management capability, but, in addition, may provide the ability to interconnect separate networks through integrated bridges and routers.

Most intelligent hubs include a multibus backplane, which enables bridges and routers to access and route data originating over multiple types of media. When operating in this manner, the intelligent hub can be viewed as a PBX, providing connectivity between any station on any network connected through the hub, while providing a centralized management and control capability.

Through the use of an intelligent hub, the administrator can enable or disable network ports from a network management workstation, segment a network to balance traffic better and improve performance, and facilitate troubleshooting and maintenance operations. As networks have become more sophisticated, intelligent hubs have evolved to facilitate their operation and management. With the ability of some intelligent hubs to bring together various media flavors of different local area networks, this device also provides a mechanism for the integration of prior piece-by-piece planning, or for the correction of a plan gone astray. Thus, the use of an intelligent hub may provide you with an umbrella mechanism to bring together separate networks and media previously installed in a building.

Switching Hubs

Improvements in the design of intelligent hubs to include faster backplanes, port memory buffers, and one or more mechanisms to control the flow of information resulted in the development of a new series of Ethernet hardware products. Collectively referred to as *switching hubs,* products in this broad category of equipment examine the destination address of each frame as a decision criteria for invoking a switching operation.

A switching hub can be considered to represent a sophisticated bridge that has the ability to support multiple bridging operations at the same time. This is illustrated in Figure 5.17, which shows a 6-port switch with workstations connected to ports 3 and 4 having frames transported to servers connected to ports 5 and 6. If each port operates at 10 Mbps then the two cross-connections provide 20 Mbps of bandwidth. In comparison, a conventional shared media 10BASE-T network only permits one frame at a time to be on the network, limiting bandwidth to 10 Mbps.

Some switching hubs are limited to working with individual workstations connected to each port, while other switching hubs are designed to switch frames from all workstations on a segment connected to the hub. The first type of switching is referred to as port switching, while the second type of switching is referred to as segment-based switching. The development of 100-Mbps high-speed Ethernet technology resulted in several vendors introducing multiple-speed switching hubs during 1994 and 1995, which could be used to significantly improve the performance of many types of networks. This improvement primarily resulted from the connection of 100-Mbps ports to file

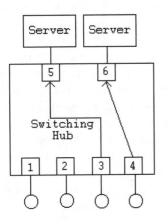

Legend: ◯ = workstations

Figure 5.17 A switching hub supports multiple simultaneous cross-connection operations, which enhance available network bandwidth.

servers, while 10-Mbps ports are connected to 10BASE-T workstations and conventional hubs. Similarly, the first series of Gigabit Ethernet switches, which reached the market during 1997, have 100-Mbps and 1-Gbps ports, with the 100-Mbps ports used to support Fast Ethernet connections. Another technology incorporated into switching hubs is a full-duplex operating capability, permitting the simultaneous transmission and reception of data on a connection. Although many switching hub manufacturers denote this capability for a 10BASE-T connection as a 20-Mbps Ethernet port, in reality you obtain a 20-Mbps transmission rate only when a device is simultaneously transmitting and receiving information. Because file servers benefit more than workstations from a full-duplex transmission capability, most network designers connect their file servers to the full-duplex port on a switching hub that supports this capability, and use the conventional 10BASE-T ports for 10-Mbps connections to workstations with 10BASE-T NICs. Readers are referred to Chapter 9 for an in-depth examination of the operation and utilization of switching hubs.

5.2 Networking Software

The installation of a local area network requires a variety of hardware and software products. At minimum, each workstation on the network normally requires the installation of an interface card into its system unit. This interface card contains a number of ROM modules and specialized circuitry, as well as a microprocessor that implements the access method used to communicate on the common cable.

In some local area networks, one personal computer must be reserved to process the network commands and functions. Because it services these commands and functions, it is normally called the *network server,* although the term *file server* is also commonly used to reference this computer. A combination of specialized software that overlays the operating system on each workstation and software placed on the server governs the operation of the network; this relationship provides a *client–server processing* capability. In comparison, the flow of data from one workstation to another without the use of a server is known as *peer-to-peer processing.* Because the vast majority of Ethernet LANs use servers, we will focus our attention in this section on the software required to support client/server operations. To understand the role of the network server and the functions of LAN software, let us first review how a personal computer operates under a conventional version of the disk operating system (DOS) used in the IBM PC personal computer environment.

DOS

DOS is a single-user operating system designed to provide access to peripherals attached to the system and control of those peripherals, interpretation of commands to perform various functions on the system, and management of disk storage and memory. Under DOS, your keyboard is the standard input device and your display is the standard output device, and control of the personal computer is limited to one user. When you turn on your PC, one of the functions performed by DOS is to load a command processor into a predefined area of your computer's memory. The command processor contains coding that examines your keyboard entries, and coding that performs predefined functions when certain commands are recognized from your keyboard entries. The commands for which the command processor immediately executes code are known as *internal commands.* When other commands are recognized, the command processor loads a predefined file into memory and then executes its contents. These commands are known as *external commands,* because the code used to perform the functions associated with these commands resides on a file external to the command processor's code in memory.

Network Software Components

As soon as a networked personal computer is initialized, its network software routines are added to DOS, permitting the computer to interact with the rest of the network. Before the introduction of DOS Version 3.1, this software was normally an overlay to DOS that served to filter commands, and that translated those commands requiring network access into code to transmit data via the LAN adapter card. Unfortunately, each network operating system vendor developed code to interface the adapter card in a proprietary manner, and software developed to work with one manufacturer's adapter card may not necessarily work with another manufacturer's adapter card.

When a command is issued on the PC, the software overlay permits the command to pass directly to DOS for execution. If a command is issued that refers to the network, the software overlay intercepts or filters the command from reaching DOS and, in conjunction with the adapter board, transmits the command onto the network. If the network is server-based, the nonlocal commands must be sent to a server for additional processing. The left-hand portion of Figure 5.18 illustrates the hardware and software components required when LAN software was originally designed as an overlay to DOS.

Before the introduction of DOS 3.1, most LAN operating system vendors developed proprietary methods to access the LAN adapter card, and either

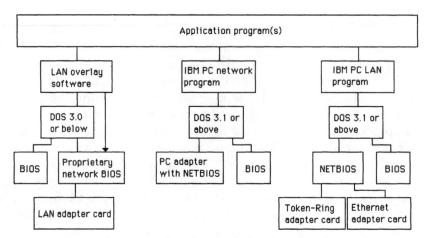

Figure 5.18   Original PC LAN hardware and software relationships in an IBM PC environment.

developed proprietary methods to lock files and records or ignored incorporating such features. In effect, this limited their networks to simple file-swapping and printer-sharing applications. Because there was no Network Basic Input/Output System (NetBIOS), a proprietary network BIOS was developed and accessed via the vendor's LAN overlay software to send and receive data from the LAN adapter card. Here, NetBIOS is the lowest level of software on a local area network, translating commands to send and receive data via the adapter card into the instructions that actually perform the requested functions.

With the introduction of IBM's first local area network, referred to as the PC Network, in August 1984, IBM released all three components required to implement an IBM local area network using IBM equipment: the IBM PC Network Program, PC DOS 3.1, and the IBM PC Network Adapter. The IBM PC Network Program was actually a tailored version of Microsoft Corporation's Microsoft Networks (MS-NET) software, which is essentially a program that overlays DOS and permits workstations on a network to share their disks and peripheral devices. DOS 3.1, also developed by Microsoft, added file- and record-locking capabilities to DOS, permitting multiple users to access and modify data. Without file- and record-locking capabilities in DOS, custom software was required to obtain these functions—without them, the last person saving data onto a file would overwrite changes made to the file by other persons. Thus, DOS 3.1 provided networking and application programmers with a set of standards they could use in developing network software.

Included on the IBM PC Network Adapter card in ROM is an extensive number of programming instructions, known as NetBIOS. The middle portion of Figure 5.18 illustrates the hardware and software components of an IBM PC LAN network.

When the IBM Token-Ring Network was introduced, NetBIOS was removed from the adapter card and incorporated as a separate software program, activated from DOS. The right-hand column of Figure 5.18 illustrates this new relationship between hardware and software. At first, NetBIOS was designed to operate with Token-Ring adapter cards. Later, IBM extended NetBIOS to work with CSMA/CD Ethernet adapter cards.

Due to the standardization of file-and-record locking under DOS 3.1, any multiuser software program written for DOS Version 3.1 or later will run on any LAN that supports this version of DOS. Although DOS 3.1 supports many networking functions, it is not a networking operating system. In fact, a variety of networking operating systems support DOS 3.1 and later versions of DOS, including MS-NET, IBM's PC Network Program, IBM's Token-Ring Program, Microsoft's Windows NT, and Novell's NetWare. You can therefore select a third-party network operating system to use with IBM or non-IBM network hardware, or you can consider obtaining both third-party hardware and software to construct your local area network.

Network Operating Systems

A modern network operating system operates as an overlay to the personal computer's operating system, providing the connectivity that enables personal computers to communicate with one another and share such network resources as hard disks, CD-ROM jukebox drives, and printers, and even obtain access to mainframes and minicomputers. Two of the more popular LAN operating systems are Microsoft Corporation's Windows NT and Novell Corporation's NetWare.

Both Windows NT and NetWare are file server–based network operating systems. This means that most network modules reside on the file server. A shell program loaded into each workstation works in conjunction with the server modules. The shell program workstation filters commands, directing user-entered commands to DOS or to the network modules residing on the server. Communications between the shell and the server modules occur at the OSI Reference Model's Network Layer. Microsoft's Windows NT uses NetBIOS Extended User Interface, commonly referred to as NetBEUI, which is automatically installed when the operating system is installed, while Novell's NetWare uses its Internetwork Packet Exchange (IPX) protocol as the language in which the workstation communicates with the file server. Both Windows NT and NetWare support the concurrent use of multiple protocols. For example, Windows NT includes built-in support for TCP/IP, NWLink, and Data Link control. Until the mid-1980s, it was difficult to support more than one protocol at a time due to the manner by which network software residing on a workstation or server communicated with one or more software modules known as the protocol stack. Once we examine the manner by which a client gains access to a server and obtain an overview of NetWare and Windows NT, we will then turn our attention to the method by which multiple stacks can be employed to support multiple protocols.

Services

The process by which the shell enables a workstation to communicate with a set of services residing on a server is known as a *client/server relationship.* Services provided by network modules on the server can range in scope from file access and transfer, shared printer utilization, and printer queuing to electronic mail. Other features available in most network operating systems include the ability to partition disk storage and allocate such storage to different network users, and the assignment of various types of security levels to individual network users, groups of users, directories, files, and printers. Some network operating systems include a disk mirroring feature and a remote console dial-in capability.

Because file information in the form of updated accounting, payroll, and engineering data can be critical to the health of a company, it is often very important to have duplicate copies of information in case a hard disk should fail. Disk mirroring is a feature that duplicates network information on two or more disks simultaneously. Thus, if one disk fails, network operations can continue.

A remote console dial-in capability enables a network user to gain access to the network from a remote location. This feature can be particularly advantageous for people who travel and wish to transmit and receive messages with people back at the office or obtain access to information residing on the network. Because the administration of a network can be a complex process, a remote dial-in feature may also make life less taxing for a network administrator. Working at home or at another location, the administrator can reassign privileges and perform other network functions that may not be possible in an eight-hour day.

Looking at NetWare

Because the best way to obtain information concerning the relationship of a network operating system to network hardware is to examine the software, we will do so. We will discuss Novell Corporation's NetWare and Microsoft's Windows NT, as those network operating systems (NOS) are by far the most popular of all network operating systems used.

Architecture

The architecture or structure of NetWare can be mapped to the OSI Reference Model. It provides an indication of the method by which this network operating system provides support for different types of hardware, and includes the capability for the routing of packets between networks. Figure 5.19 illustrates the general relationship between NetWare and the OSI Reference Model.

In examining Figure 5.19, note that NetWare supports numerous types of local area networks. This means that you can use NetWare as the network operating system on Ethernet, Token-Ring, ARCnet, and other types of networks. In fact, NetWare also supports different types of personal computer operating systems, such as DOS, OS/2, different versions of Windows, UNIX, and Macintosh's Finder. This means that NetWare is capable of supporting different types of local area networks as well as workstations that use different operating systems.

Using NetWare on a PC requires the loading of two Novell files whenever you turn on your computer or perform a system reset. Those files are IPX and NETx, where x indicates a specific version of the NET file used with a specific version of DOS, such as NET3 used with DOS 3.

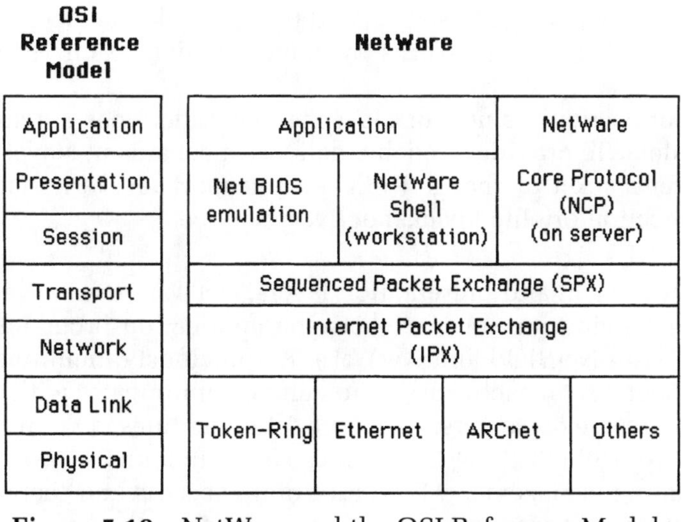

OSI Reference Model	NetWare		
Application	Application		NetWare
Presentation	Net BIOS emulation	NetWare Shell (workstation)	Core Protocol (NCP) (on server)
Session			
Transport	Sequenced Packet Exchange (SPX)		
Network	Internet Packet Exchange (IPX)		
Data Link	Token-Ring	Ethernet	ARCnet	Others
Physical				

Figure 5.19 NetWare and the OSI Reference Model.

The use of IPX and NETx are required through NetWare Release 3.11. In Release 3.12 and in NetWare Version 4.X, NETx was replaced by the use of a virtual loadable module (VLM). Later in this section, we will discuss the use of NetWare's VLM.EXE program.

Both IPX and NET are workstation shell programs that interpret and filter commands entered from the keyboard and provide a mechanism for communications between the workstation and the server. Before NetWare Version 2.1, the shell was known as ANET3.COM, and was combined with IPX and NETx into one file. Later versions of NetWare separated IPX from NETx.

To automate the loading of NetWare on your workstation to establish a network connection, you would normally insert appropriate commands into your computer's AUTO-EXEC.BAT file. Those commands would include:

```
IPX
NETx
F:
LOGIN <servername/username>
```

IPX   The command IPX would cause Novell's IPX.COM file to be loaded and executed. This file is a driver that establishes communications with the network interface board, and it is responsible for providing communications with servers and other stations on the network using a network protocol known as IPX. At the network layer, Novell's IPX protocol performs addressing and internet routing functions. To accomplish this, an IPX packet contains both the source and destination network addresses. Those addresses are assigned by a network administrator, and they provide the mechanism for the routing of data between networks by routers which examine the network layer.

IPX is a connectionless network layer protocol that does not guarantee the delivery of data. To provide a reliable delivery mechanism, Novell developed its Sequenced Packet eXchange (SPX)—a transport level interface that provides a connection-oriented packet delivery service.

NCP   At the session and presentation layers, NetWare uses a NetBIOS emulator, which provides an interface between application programs written in compliance with NetBIOS and NetWare. As previously mentioned, the NetWare shell operates on each workstation and communicates with a core set of modules that reside on servers. That core set of modules is known as the NetWare Core Protocol (NCP). NCP provides such functions as workstation and network naming management, file partitioning, access and locking capabilities, accounting, and security.

NET   The command NETx loads NETx.COM, which is the true workstation shell, because it interprets and filters commands entered from the keyboard. In addition, NETx supports a large number of NetWare commands, which, when entered, are converted into IPX packets and transmitted to the server for processing. The NetWare Core Protocol decodes the command request, processes the request, and then transmits a response to the workstation using one or more IPX packets. The workstation's NET module then processes and displays the response. For example, typing the NetWare command CHKVOL at the workstation transmits a request to the server to obtain statistics concerning the logical driver (volume) assigned to the workstation user. The results of that request are transmitted back to the workstation and displayed on its screen the same way a DOS CHKDSK command is displayed.

When the shell (NETx) is loaded, it normally establishes a connection to a network server by sending a request to IPX to broadcast a Get Nearest Server command. The first server that responds to the request then establishes a connection to the workstation and displays the message "Attached to server <servername>" on your computer's console. You can also specify a preferred server by adding the PS= parameter to the NETx command; this provides you with the ability to distribute workstation server usage over a number of servers.

Once a connection to a NetWare server occurs, the command F: in the AUTOEXEC.BAT file moves the workstation user to the server's SYS:LOGIN directory. That directory is designated or mapped to drive F: on your DOS-operated workstation. Once this is accomplished, the command LOGIN initiates the LOGIN module on the server. If you include the servername and username, LOGIN will then request only your password to obtain access to the server.

Versions   Several versions of NetWare have been marketed during the past ten years. NetWare 286, which was renamed NetWare 2.2, is designed to operate on Intel 286–based servers. This operating system supports up to 100 users. A more modern version of NetWare, NetWare 386 (renamed NetWare 3.1), operates on Intel 386–based servers. This network operating system supports up to 250 users.

The introduction of NetWare 4.0 and the release of NetWare 4.1 extended Novell's NetWare support to local area networks consisting of up to several thousand workstations. As previously discussed, NetWare 3.12 as well as all versions of NetWare 4.X resulted in the replacement of NETx by the virtual loadable module VLM.EXE. By including the command VLM.EXE in your AUTOEXEC.BAT file, you would cause the executable virtual loadable module to be loaded. This executable file will automatically load a number of files with the .VLM extension, tailoring NetWare to your workstation.

A second change to NetWare is the fact that in November 1991 Novell ceased supporting its dedicated IPX driver. IPX was specific to the network interface card and version of NetWare being used on a workstation, and required you to create a new version each time you installed a new network card. A second problem associated with IPX is the fact that once used with an adapter card, you cannot use another protocol with that card. For example, if you want to communicate using TCP/IP to a UNIX server with the same card, you would have to change your AUTOEXEC.BAT file, remove or *comment out* via REM statements your invocation of IPX and NETx, add your TCP/IP commands, and reboot your computer. Obviously this was not a pleasant situation.

Recognizing the preceding problems, Novell released a new architecture known as the Open Data-Link Interface (ODI) in 1989. By 1991, ODI became the only IPX standard interface supported by Novell. Through the use of ODI, you can support multiple protocols through a common adapter without requiring the rearrangement of statements in your AUTOEXEC.BAT file and rebooting your computer. To do so, you must obtain the following special files—LSL, IPXODI, and an interface driver. LSL is a link support layer program that you must obtain from Novell. The interface driver is provided by the manufacturer of the adapter card, while IPXODI is furnished by both Novell and the adapter card manufacturer.

Figure 5.20 illustrates the relationship of the three previously mentioned programs when a multiprotocol or dual stack operation is desired. The interface driver provides low-level I/O operations to and from the adapter card, and passes information received from the LAN to the Link Support Program. That program examines incoming data to determine if it is NetWare (IPX) or IP

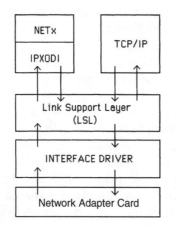

Figure 5.20 Multiprotocol support using Novell's ODI.

(TCP/IP) in the example illustrated in Figure 5.20. LSL then passes received data to the appropriate stack. Thus, IPXODI represents a modification to IPX, which permits it to interface Novell's LSL program.

Although LSL resides on top of the interface driver, you must load it before loading that driver. Thus, your AUTOEXEC.BAT file would have the following generic entries to support ODI on your workstation:

```
LSL
HRDRIVER
IPXODI
NETX
F:
LOGIN
```

In examining the preceding entries, note that *HRDRIVER* would be replaced by the actual name of your adapter card's interface driver. In addition, under NetWare 3.12 and 4.X, you would replace NETx with VLM.

To add the TCP/IP protocol stack under DOS you would add the appropriate statements to your AUTOEXEC.BAT file. Those statements must follow the execution of LSL.COM but can either precede or succeed the statements used to invoke the NetWare protocol stack. For example, assume NetWare files are located in the NetWare directory and the appropriate packet driver is contained in the file ODIPKT and the TCP/IP program is contained in the file TCPIP, while both the ODIPKT and TCP/IP files are located in the directory TCP. Then, the AUTOEXEC.BAT file would contain the following statements with the REM(ark) statements optionally added for clarity.

```
REM *Install NetWare*
C:\NETWARE\LSL.COM
C:\NETWARE\LANDRIVER
C:\NETWARE\IPXODI.COM
C:\NETWARE\NETx.EXE
F:
LOGIN GHELD
REM *Install TCP/IP*
C:\TCP\ODIPKT
C:\TCP\TCPIP
```

NET.CFG One important file not shown in Figure 5.20 and until now not discussed is NET.CFG. This file describes the network adapter card configuration to the ODI driver and should be located in the same directory as the IPX-ODI and NETx files. However, through the use of an appropriate PATH statement you can actually locate NET.CFG anywhere you desire.

NET.CFG is an ASCII text file that can contain up to four main areas of information, which describe the environment of a workstation. Those areas include a link support area, protocol area, link driver area, and parameter area.

Link Support Area   The link support area is used to define the number of communications buffers and memory set aside for those buffers. This area is required to be defined when running TCP/IP, however, because IPX does not use buffers or memory pools maintained by LSL you can skip this section if you are only using a NetWare protocol stack. The following illustration represents an example of the coding of the link support area in the NET.CFG file to support TCP/IP. The actual coding you would enter depends upon the network adapter card to be used and you would obtain the appropriate information from the manual accompanying the adapter card.

```
LINK SUPPORT
BUFFERS 8 1144
MemPool 4096
MaxStacks 8
```

Protocol Area   The protocol area is used to bind one or more protocols to specific network adapter cards. By default, IPXODI binds to the network adapter in the lowest system expansion slot as it scans slots in their numeric order. If you have two or more network adapter cards in a workstation, you can use the protocol area to specify which protocols you want to bind to each card. You can also accomplish this at the link driver area by specifying *Slot n,* where *n* is the slot number of the network adapter card you are configuring. Assuming you wish to bind IPX to an adapter card whose address is h123, you would add the following statements to the NET.CFG file.

```
Protocol
    PROTOCOL IPX
    BIND h123
```

Because each computer using TCP/IP requires an IP address, the IP address information must be included in the NET.CFG file if you intend to use the TCP/IP protocol stack. For example, if the network administrator assigned your computer the IP address 133.49.108.05, the IP address information would be entered as follows:

```
PROTOCOL TCP/IP
ip_address 133.49.108.05
```

When using TCP/IP, each workstation on the network is assigned the address of a default router (commonly referred to as a gateway) by the network administrator. Thus, another statement commonly added to the NET.CFG file includes the address of the router that the workstation will use. For example, if the router's address is 133.49.108.17, then you would add the following statement to the NET.CFG file in its protocol area.

```
ip_router 133.49.108.17
```

The ip_address and ip_router statements can be avoided if the network administrator sets up a Reverse Address Resolution Protocol (RARP) server configured with IP and hardware addresses for workstations on the network. Then, when the workstation is powered on it will broadcast an RARP packet that will contain its hardware address. The RARP server will respond with the workstation's IP address associated with the hardware address.

Link Driver Area The link driver area is used to set the hardware configuration of the network adapter card so it is recognized by LAN drivers. If you are only using Novell's IPX, the first line of your NET.CFG file is a LINK DRIVER statement which tells NETX the type of LAN card installed in the workstation, such as

```
Link Driver 3C5X9
```

The reason this statement becomes the first statement is because the link support area is omitted and, if you only have one adapter card, you do not require a protocol area.

If you're using an NE 2000 Ethernet card, your link driver area would appear as follows:

```
Link Driver NE2000
    INT 5
    PORT 300
    Frame Ethernet_802.3
    Frame Ethernet_II
    Protocol IPX 0 Ethernet_802.3
    Protocol IP 8137 Ethernet_II
```

In this example the frame statements define the types of frames that will be supported by the adapter cards. Although most adapter cards include software that automatically construct or modify the NET.CFG file, upon occasion you may have to customize the contents of that file. To do so you can use the manual accompanying the network adapter card, which will normally indicate the statements required to be placed in the file.

Virtual Loadable Modules   The introduction of NetWare 4.0 resulted in the replacement of NETX by VLMs that sit behind DOS. In comparison, NETX sat in front of DOS and acted as a filter to identify and act upon network requests entered from the keyboard. VLMs are referred to as the NetWare DOS Requester as they use DOS redirection to satisfy file and print service requests. Because VLMs replace NETX.EXE, you would load VLM.EXE in the position previously used for NETX.EXE. That is, the sequence of commands placed in your AUTOEXEC.BAT file to initialize the NetWare protocol stack would appear as follows:

```
C:\NETWARE\LSL
C:\NETWARE\LANDRIVER
C:\NETWARE\IPXODI
C:\NETWARE\VLM.EXE
F:
LOGIN GHELD
```

To modify the AUTOEXEC.BAT file to support dual-stack operations you could add the appropriate commands either after invoking LSL or after the "Login" statement.

Looking at Windows NT

Windows NT, to include workstation and server, represents both a computer operating system and network operating system that can function together or independently. The basic networking protocol used by Windows NT is NetBEUI, which provides a network user interface for local workstations and servers.

NetBIOS   The NetBIOS Extended User Interface (NetBEUI) represents an extension of PC BIOS to the network. NetBIOS was originally developed by IBM as a simple network protocol for interconnecting PCs on a common network. The naming structure of the protocol results in names assigned to devices being translated into network adapter card (that is, MAC) addresses. This results in NetBIOS operating at the data link layer. In addition, because the NetBIOS naming structure is nonhierarchical, there is no provision for specifying network addresses. Due to this, NetBIOS is considered to be nonroutable. Thus, the initial method used to join two or more NetBIOS networks together was restricted to bridging.

NetBEUI Recognizing the routability problem of NetBIOS, NetBEUI allows data to be transported by a transport protocol to obtain the ability to interconnect separate networks. In fact, NetBEUI can be transported by TCP/IP and even IPX/SPX. To accomplish this, NetBEUI maintains a table of NAMES that are associated with TCP/IP addresses when TCP/IP is used as a transport protocol, and a similar table matched to NetWare network addresses and station MAC addresses when NetBEUI is transported via IPX/SPX.

To illustrate the operation of a few of the capabilities of Windows NT networking, we will briefly use a Windows NT workstation and a Windows NT server to illustrate the installation of network software and adapter cards. In addition, we will use a Windows NT workstation to display the servers on a network where both NT and NetWare servers reside, transferring a file from an NT workstation to a Novell file server. Both NetWare and Windows NT can communicate on a common network, because NT supports the NWLink protocol that provides communications compatibility with NetWare's IPX/SPX protocol.

Adapter and Software Support Windows NT workstation and server products use common methods to add support for network software and adapter cards. Although the screen display for configuring network software and adapter cards varies between versions of Windows NT, the basic methods remain the same. Thus, although Figure 5.21 illustrates the network settings screen for Version 3.51 of NT, the basic methods we will describe are also applicable to other versions of NT.

In examining Figure 5.21, note that five network software modules are shown in the upper box labeled Installed Network Software, and one adapter card is shown as being installed in the lower box labeled Installed Adapter Card. Windows NT supports the binding of multiple protocols to a common adapter via the use of the network driver interface specification (NDIS), which will be described at the end of this section. You can add network software, such as TCP/IP, by clicking on the Add Software button shown in Figure 5.21. This action will result in the display of a list of networking software directly supported by Windows NT. Similarly, if you want to add another adapter you would click on the Add Adapter button. If the adapter you wish to add is not directly supported by Windows NT, you can select the option "Other—have disk" at the end of the list of supported adapters. This will allow you to add support for a wide range of NICs that are commonly shipped with Windows NT drivers, but which are not directly supported by NT.

Network Operation Figure 5.22 illustrates the use of File Manager on a Windows NT workstation to view the names of devices on both a Windows net-

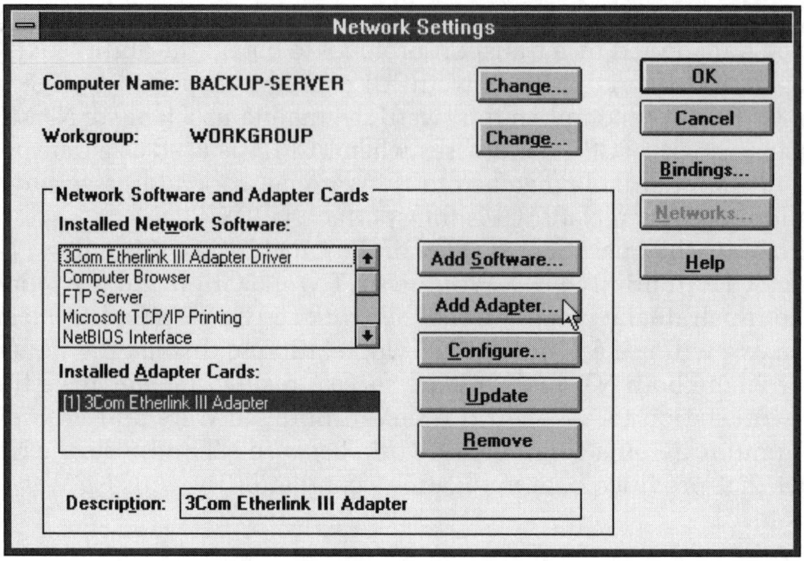

Figure 5.21 Using the Windows NT dialog box to review, add, or change network software and adapter card support.

work and a NetWare network. Figure 5.23 illustrates the result obtained by first selecting an appropriate NetWare server and then selecting a directory on that server that we wish to access. This action will result in the mapping of drive E on the local workstation to the path shown in Figure 5.23. Once we enter the appropriate connection information, drive E on the local Windows NT workstation will be mapped to the directory FRED located under the directory SYS on the server MDPC-1.

After we correctly log onto the server, we can run network applications or transfer data to or from the server. Figure 5.24 illustrates how you could select "Move" from the File menu and enter the command c:\funds*.* to move all files under the subdirectory FUNDS on the local workstation to the network server.

NDIS Operation Considerations Similar to the manner by which Novell developed an architecture for supporting multiple protocols via a common adapter, Microsoft developed a competing standard referred to as NDIS. In this section we will focus our attention upon obtaining an overview of the structure of NDIS, even though it is well-hidden from view when you use a

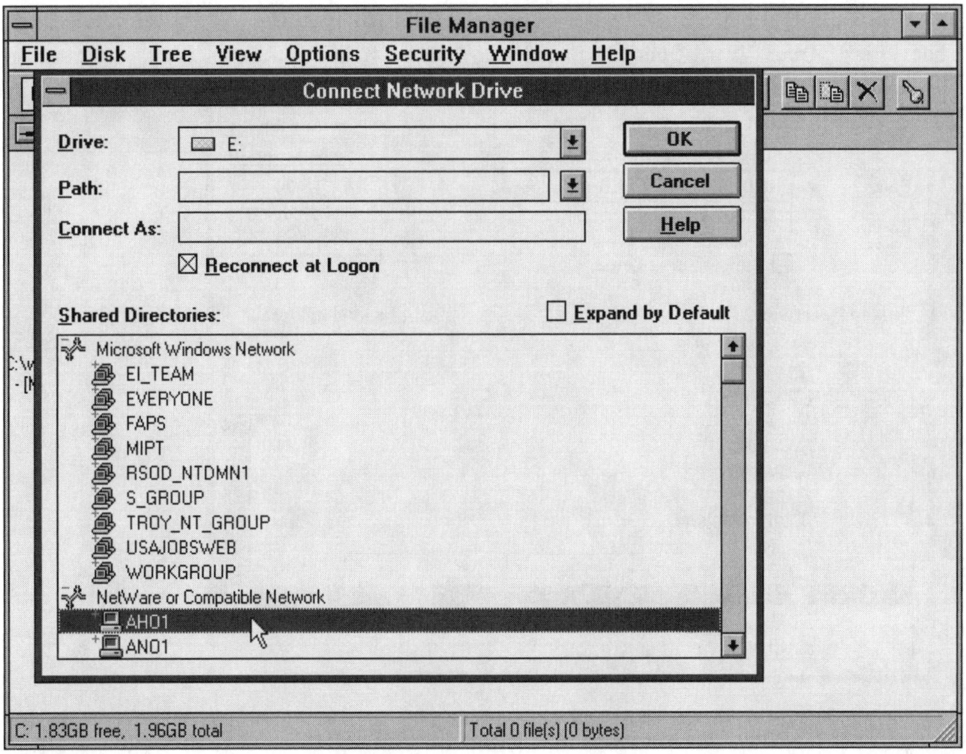

Figure 5.22 Viewing devices on both a Windows and a Novell network through the Windows NT File Manager.

Windows operating environment. Although NDIS provides a dual-stack capability similar to that provided by ODI, its setup for operation varies considerably from the previously discussed dual-stack mechanism. Figure 5.25 illustrates the relationship between NDIS software modules, upper-layer protocol stacks, and the network adapter card.

CONFIG.SYS Usage   Unlike ODI, which represents a series of files loaded from an AUTOEXEC.BAT file, NDIS was designed as a series of device drivers that are loaded through the CONFIG.SYS file. In a DOS environment the first statement in the CONFIG.SYS file required for NDIS is:

```
DEVICE=drive:\path\PROTMAN.DOS
```

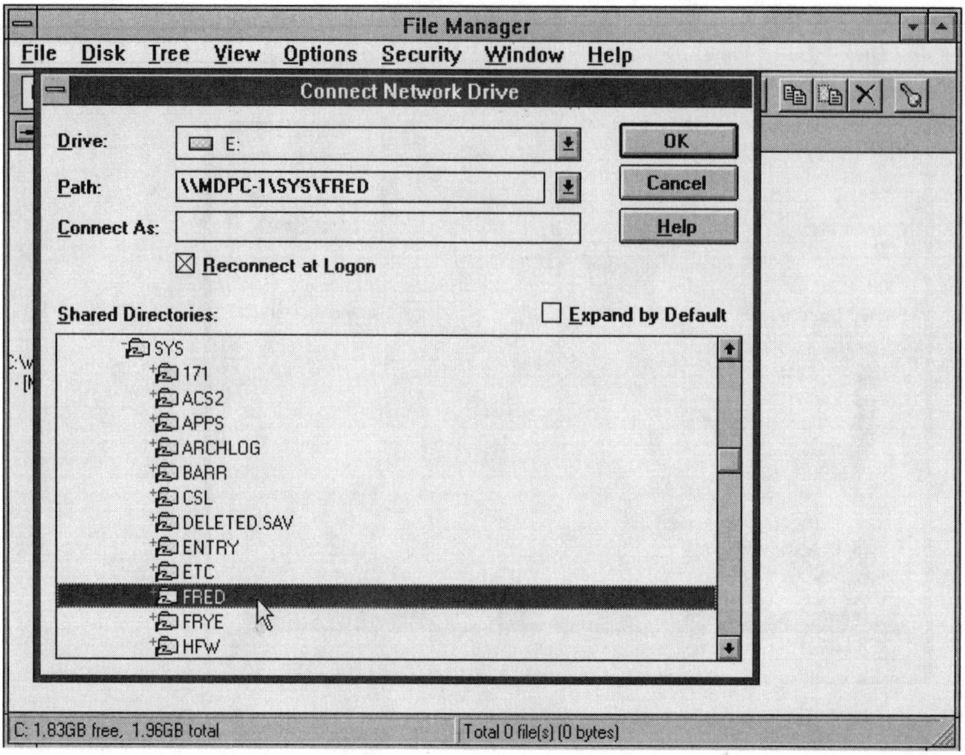

Figure 5.23 Selecting a path to a directory on a Novell server that will be mapped to drive E on a local workstation.

For OS/2, the file becomes PROTMAN.OS2. Both PROTMAN.DOS and PROT-MAN.OS2 are the NDIS Protocol Manager for each workstation operating DOS or OS/2. The Protocol Manager reads the file PROTOCOL.INI, which contains initialization parameters and stores the contents of that file in memory for use by other NDIS drivers. Thus, a short discussion of PROTOCOL.INI file is in order.

PROTOCOL.INI Overview The PROTOCOL.INI file can be considered to represent the NDIS equivalent of the NET.CFG file associated with ODI. Although most network products to include Windows NT will automatically create or modify the PROTOCOL.INI file, some products require users to create or modify that file. In addition, you may be able to enhance network performance by modifying an existing parameter set by a network program that does not consider your total user environment.

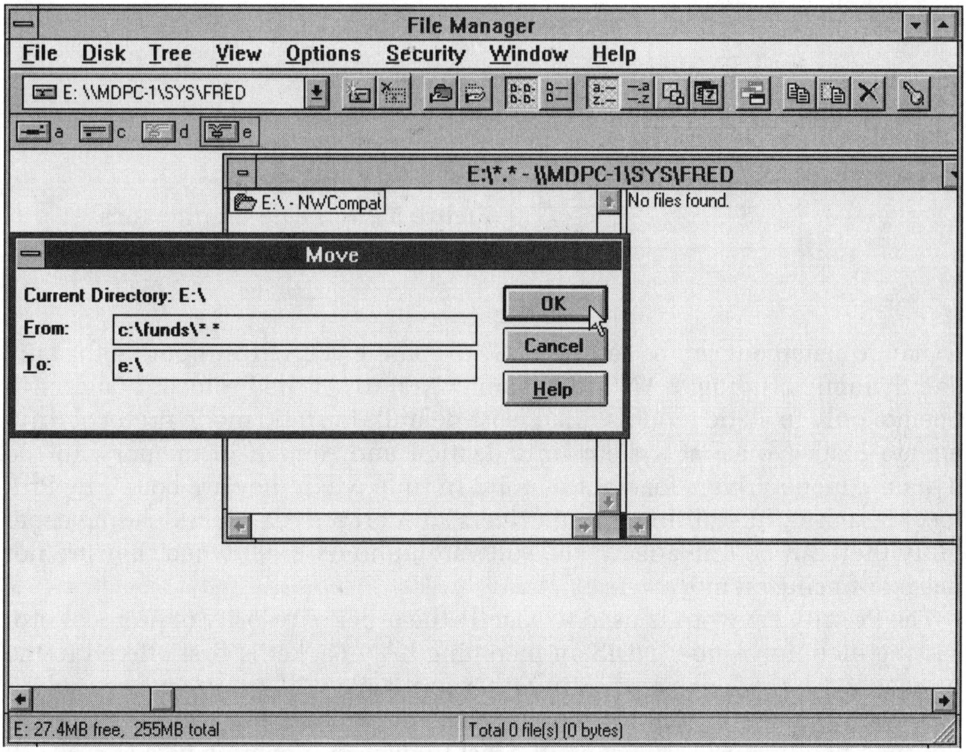

Figure 5.24 Using File Manager to move all files in the directory FUNDS on the local workstation to the directory FRED on the file server.

Entries in PROTOCOL.INI occur in sections, with each section name surrounded in brackets ([]). Under each section name are one or more named configuration entries, which appear in the format "name=value". Although configuration entries can appear anywhere in a line under the section name, normal practice is to indent each entry three character positions to enhance readability.

The first section in the PROTOCOL.INI file has the heading [PROTMAN_MOD]. The first configuration entry for both DOS and OS/2 is the device name PROTMAN$. Thus, the first section entry becomes:

```
[PROTMAN_MOD]
    DriverName=PROTMAN$
```

Other entries in the [PROTMAN_MOD] section are optional and can include keywords Dynamic, Priority, and Bindstatus in assignment statements. The

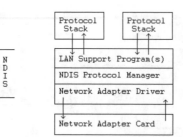

Figure 5.25   NDIS architecture.

Dynamic statement can be set to "YES" (Dynamic=YES) to support both static and dynamic binding or "NO" (Dynamic=NO) to set the Protocol Manager to operate only in static mode, which is its default. In static mode protocol drivers are loaded once at system initialization and remain in memory. In the dynamic mode drivers load at the point in time when they are bound by Protocol Manager. In addition, if the drivers support a dynamic unloading capability they can be unloaded if the software unbinds them when they are not needed, freeing memory.

The Priority keyword is used to specify the order of priority of protocol processing modules. Under NDIS an incoming LAN packet is first offered to the protocol with the highest priority. Other protocols will see the packet only if a higher protocol does not first recognize and process the packet. Protocols not specified in a priority list are the last to inspect incoming packets.

The Bindstatus keyword is used to specify whether Protocol Manager can optimize memory and can be set to "YES" or "NO". If the keyword is not used, a default of "NO" is assumed.

The second communications statement included in a CONFIG.SYS file for NDIS operations invokes the network adapter card driver. For example, if you were using the NE2000 adapter, you would include the following statement in the CONFIG.SYS file.

```
DEVICE=[drive:]\path\NE2000.DOS
```

NDIS Adapter Support   The adapter driver, which is compatible with the NDIS Protocol Manager, is referred to as an NDIS MAC driver. The NDIS MAC driver is normally contained on a diskette that is included in a box in which your NDIS-compatible network adapter is packaged. When using Windows NT the operating system includes built-in NDIS support for approximately 30 adapter cards. As previously explained, if the adapter you are using is not directly supported by Windows NT, you would select the Other option from the install adapter card entry from the network configuration display obtained from the Windows Control Panel. Then you would use the diskette that accompanies your adapter card to install the required driver.

Once you install your adapter card and appropriate communications protocols under Windows NT, the operating system will automatically connect the software layers as required to form appropriate protocol stacks. Microsoft refers to this as network bindings, and Figure 5.26 illustrates an example of the NT Network Bindings display after a large number of protocols were installed.

Application Software

The third major component of software required for productive work to occur on a local area network is application software. These application programs support electronic mail, multiple access to database records, or the use of spreadsheet programs; they operate at the top layer of the OSI Reference Model.

Until the mid-1980s, most application programs used on LANs were not tailored to operate correctly in a multiuser environment. A large part of their inability to work correctly was due to the absence of file- and record-locking capabilities on PC operating systems—a situation that was corrected with the introduction of DOS 3.1. A second problem associated with application programs occurred when the program was written to bypass the personal computer's BIOS. Although this action in many instances would speed up screen

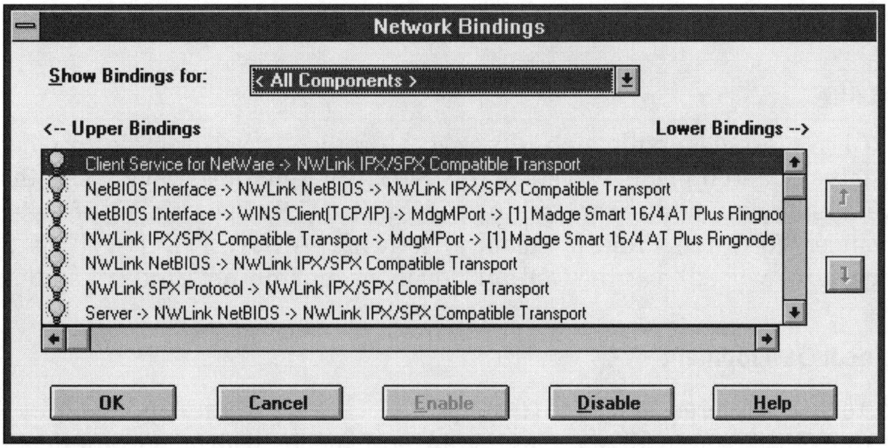

Figure 5.26   Viewing an example of the Windows NT Network Bindings display.

displays, disk access, and other operations, in this case it resulted in nonstandardized program actions. This made it difficult, if not impossible, for some network operating systems to support ill-defined programs, because an interrupt clash could bring the entire network to a rapid halt.

Today, most application programs use BIOS calls and are well defined. Such programs are easily supported by network operating systems. A few programs that bypass BIOS may also be supported, because the application program that caused operating system vendors to tailor their software to support such applications was so popular.

5.3 The TCP/IP Protocol Suite

No discussion of networking hardware and software related to Ethernet would be complete without covering the TCP/IP protocol suite. Although the development of TCP/IP occurred at the Advanced Research Projects Agency (ARPA), which was funded by the U.S. Department of Defense, while Ethernet traces its origin to the Xerox Palo Alto Research Center, within a short period of time the two were linked together. Ethernet frames provide the data link (layer 2) transportation mechanism for the delivery of network layer (layer 3) IP and transport layer (layer 4) TCP packets that transport such application data as file transfer, remote access, and Web server information on an intra-LAN basis. In comparison, TCP/IP provides the mechanism to route data between LANs and convert IP addresses used by the protocol suite to MAC addresses used by Ethernet so that TCP/IP packets can be delivered by Ethernet frames.

Overview

TCP/IP represents a collection of network protocols that provide services at the network and transport layers of the ISO's OSI Reference Model. Originally developed based upon work performed by the U.S. Department of Defense Advanced Research Projects Agency Network (ARPANET), TCP/IP is also commonly referred to as the DOD protocols or the Internet protocol suite.

Protocol Development

In actuality, a reference to the TCP/IP protocol suite includes applications that use the TCP/IP protocol stack as a transport mechanism. Such applications range in scope from a remote terminal access program known as Telnet to a file transfer program appropriately referred to as FTP, as well as the Web browser transport mechanism referred to as the HyperText Transport Protocol (HTTP).

The effort behind the development of the TCP/IP protocol suite has its roots in the establishment of ARPANET. The research performed by ARPANET resulted in the development of three specific protocols for the transmission of information—the Transmission Control Protocol (TCP), the Internet Protocol (IP), and the User Datagram Protocol (UDP). Both TCP and UDP represent transport layer protocols. Transmission Control Protocol provides end-to-end reliable transmission while UDP represents a connectionless layer 4 transport protocol. Thus, UDP operates on a best-effort basis and depends upon higher layers of the protocol stack for error detection and correction and other functions associated with end-to-end reliable transmission. Transmission Control Protocol includes such functions as flow control, error control, and the exchange of status information, and is based upon a connection being established between source and destination before the exchange of information occurs. Thus, TCP provides an orderly and error-free mechanism for the exchange of information.

At the network layer, the IP protocol was developed as a mechanism to route messages between networks. To accomplish this task, IP was developed as a connectionless mode network layer protocol and includes the capability to segment or fragment and reassemble messages that must be routed between networks that support different packet sizes than the size supported by the source and/or destination networks.

The TCP/IP Structure

TCP/IP represents one of the earliest developed layered communications protocols, grouping functions into defined network layers. Figure 5.27 illustrates the relationship of the TCP/IP protocol suite and the services they provide with respect to the OSI Reference Model. In examining Figure 5.27 note that only seven of literally hundreds of TCP/IP application services are shown. Because TCP/IP preceded the development of the OSI Reference Model, its developers grouped what are now session, presentation, and application layers that correspond to layers 5 through 7 of the OSI Reference Model into one higher layer. Thus, TCP/IP applications, when compared with the OSI Reference Model, are normally illustrated as corresponding to the upper three layers of that model. Continuing our examination of Figure 5.27, you will note that the subdivision of the transport layer indicates which applications are carried via TCP and those that are transported by UDP. Thus, FTP, Telnet, HTTP, and SMTP represent applications transported by TCP.

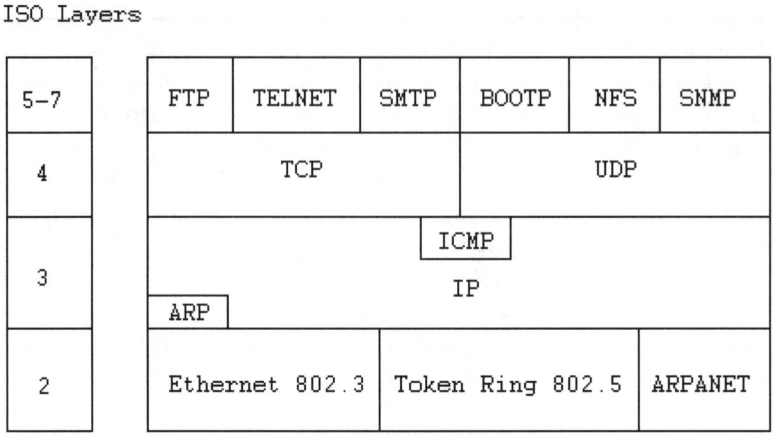

ISO Layers

5-7	FTP	TELNET	SMTP	BOOTP	NFS	SNMP
4	TCP			UDP		
3	ARP / IP / ICMP					
2	Ethernet 802.3		Token Ring 802.5		ARPANET	

Legend:

```
ARP  =Address Resolution Protocol
BOOTP=Bootstrap Protocol
FTP  =File Transfer Protocol
NSF  =Network File System
SMTP =Simple Mail Transfer Protocol
SNMP =Simple Network Management Protocol
```

Figure 5.27   TCP/IP protocols and services.

Although many persons equate Web browsing with TCP/IP, that application is but one of many commonly supported by that protocol suite. In fact, many Web browsers support plug-in modules to provide file transfer, remote terminal access, and support for other applications, while other vendors market stand-alone TCP/IP applications as part of an application suite.

Figures 5.28 and 5.29 illustrate the use of the FTP and TN3270 applications from the NetManage Chameleon TCP/IP application suite. Figure 5.28 illustrates FTP access to an FTP server with the file g-d13.pdf being prepared for copying from the server to the local computer. Figure 5.29 illustrates the use of the NetManage TN3270 program, which is a Telnet derivative developed to provide remote terminal access to IBM mainframes. In this example the TN3270 program was used to enable a PC to obtain a connection as if it were a 3270 terminal device to an IBM OfficeVision application running on a S/390 mainframe which provides electronic mail, calendars, and even access to the Internet.

Returning to our examination of Figure 5.27, note that TCP/IP can be transported at the data link layer by a number of popular LANs, to include Ethernet,

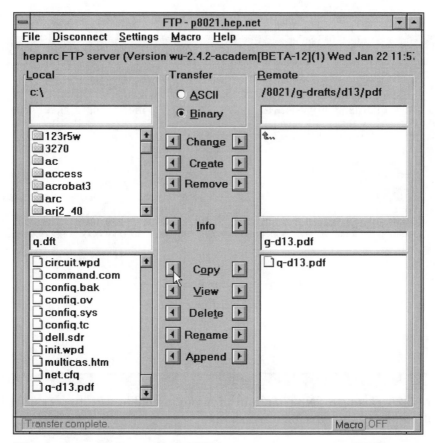

Figure 5.28 Using a client FTP program to access an FTP server.

Fast Ethernet, Gigabit Ethernet, Token-Ring, and FDDI frames. Due to the considerable effort expended in the development of LAN adapter cards to support the bus structures used in Apple MacIntosh, IBM PCs and compatible computers, DEC Alphas and SUN Microsystem's workstations, and even IBM mainframes, the development of software-based protocol stacks to facilitate the transmission of TCP/IP on LANs provides the capability to interconnect LAN-based computers to one another whether they are on the same network and only require the transmission of frames on a common cable, or if they are located on networks separated thousands of miles from one another. Thus, TCP/IP represents both a local and wide area network transmission capability. In the remainder of this section I will review IP and TCP packet headers, as well as discuss

```
─  ┌─────────────── 3270 Terminal - 198.78.46.1 [Session A] ───────────────┐ ▼ ▲
  File  Edit  Disconnect  Script  Settings  Help
  ┌──────────────────────────────────────────────────────────────────────┐
                          OfficeVision/VM Main Menu                        A00
   Press one of the following PF keys.
   PF1   Process calendars                            Time:     3:25 PM
   PF2   Open the mail                                                      |
   PF3   Work with DW/370 Documents              1997      OCTOBER      1997
   PF4   Process notes and messages              S   M   T   W   T   F   S
   PF5   INTERNET Menu                                           1   2   3   4
                                                   5   6   7   8   9  10  11
                                                  12  13  14  15  16  17  18
                                                  19  20  21  22  23  24  25
                                                  26  27  28  29  30  31
                                                           Day of Year: 288

   PF11  Functional Menus
         5684-084 (C) Copyright IBM Corp. 1983, 1992     PF9 Help    PF12 End
   xxxxxxxxxxxxxxxxxxxxxxxxxxxxxxx BUSH '96 xxxxxxxxxxxxxxxxxxxxxxxxxxxxx




   ===>


 Ready                                                         NUM 23, 6
```

Figure 5.29   Using a TN3270 client program to enable a PC to access an IBM mainframe as if it were a 3270 terminal.

the use of several related network and transport layer protocols and higher-level protocols implemented over TCP and its related protocol suite.

Datagrams versus Virtual Circuits

In examining Figure 5.27 you will note that IP provides a common layer 3 transport for TCP and UDP. As briefly noted earlier in this section, TCP is a connection-oriented protocol that requires the acknowledgment of the existence of the connection and for packets transmitted once the connection is established. In comparison, UDP is a connectionless mode service that provides a parallel service to TCP. Here *datagram* represents a term used to identify the basic unit of information that represents a portion of a message and that is transported across a TCP/IP network.

A datagram can be transported either via an acknowledged connection-oriented service or via an unacknowledged, connectionless service, where each information element is addressed to its destination and its transmission is at the mercy of network nodes. IP represents an unacknowledged connectionless service; however, although it is an unreliable transmission method, you should view the term in the context that delivery is not guaranteed instead of having second thoughts concerning its use. As a nonguaranteed delivery mechanism IP is susceptible to queuing delays and other problems that can result in the loss of data. However, higher layers in the protocol suite, such as TCP, can provide error detection and correction, which results in the retransmission of IP datagrams.

Datagrams are routed via the best path available to the destination as the datagram is placed onto the network. An alternative to datagram transmission is the use of a virtual circuit, where network nodes establish a fixed path when a connection is initiated and subsequent data exchanges occur on that path. TCP implements transmission via the use of a virtual circuit, while IP provides a datagram-oriented gateway transmission service between networks.

The routing of datagrams through a network can occur over different paths, with some datagrams arriving out of sequence from the order in which they were transmitted. In addition, as datagrams flow between networks they encounter physical limitations imposed upon the amount of data that can be transported based upon the transport mechanism used to move data on the network. For example, the information field in an Ethernet frame is limited to 1500 bytes, while a 4-Mbps Token-Ring can transport 4500 bytes in its information field. Thus, as datagrams flow between networks, they may have to be fragmented into two or more datagrams to be transported through different networks to their ultimate destination. For example, consider the transfer of a 20,000-byte file from a file server connected to a Token-Ring network to a workstation connected to an Ethernet LAN via a pair of routers providing a connection between the two local area networks. The 4-Mbps Token-Ring network supports a maximum information field of 4500 bytes in each frame transmitted on that network, while the maximum size of the information field in an Ethernet frame is 1500 bytes. In addition, depending upon the protocol used on the wide area network connection between routers, the WAN protocol's information field could be limited to 512 or 1024 bytes. Thus, the IP protocol must break up the file transfer into a series of datagrams whose size is acceptable for transmission between networks. As an alternative, IP can transmit data using a small maximum datagram size, commonly 576 bytes, to prevent fragmentation. If fragmentation is necessary, the source host can transmit using the maximum datagram size available on its network. When the datagram arrives at the router,

IP operating on that communications device will then fragment each datagram into a series of smaller datagrams. Upon receipt at the destination, each datagram must then be put back into its correct sequence so that the file can be correctly reformed, a responsibility of IP residing on the destination host.

Figure 5.30 illustrates the routing of two datagrams from workstation 1 on a Token-Ring network to server 2 connected to an Ethernet LAN. As the routing of datagrams is a connectionless service, no call setup is required, which enhances transmission efficiency. In comparison, when TCP is used, it provides a connection-oriented service regardless of the lower-layer delivery system (for example, IP).

TCP requires the establishment of a virtual circuit in which a temporary path is developed between source and destination. This path is fixed and the flow of datagrams is restricted to the established path. When UDP, a different layer 4 protocol in the TCP/IP protocol suite, is used in place of TCP, the flow of data at the transport layer continues to be connectionless and results in the transport of datagrams over available paths rather than a fixed path resulting from the establishment of a virtual circuit.

The actual division of a message into datagrams is the responsibility of the layer 4 protocol, either TCP or UDP, while fragmentation is the responsibility of IP. In addition, when the TCP protocol is used, that protocol is responsible for reassembling datagrams at their destination as well as for requesting the retransmission of lost datagrams. In comparison, IP is responsible for routing of individual datagrams from source to destination. When UDP is used as the layer 4 protocol, there is no provision for the retransmission of lost or garbled datagrams. As previously noted by our discussion of IP, this is not necessarily

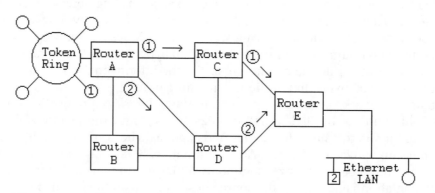

Figure 5.30   Routing of datagrams can occur over different paths.

a bad situation, as applications that use UDP then become responsible for managing communications.

Figure 5.31 illustrates the relationship of an IP datagram, UDP datagram, and TCP segment to a LAN frame. The headers shown in Figure 5.31 represent a group of bytes added to the beginning of a datagram to allow a degree of control over the datagram. For example, the TCP header will contain information that allows this layer 4 protocol to track the sequence of the delivery of datagrams so they can be placed into their correct order if they arrive out of sequence. Before focusing our attention on TCP and IP, let's briefly discuss the role of ICMP and ARP, two additional network layer protocols in the TCP/IP suite.

ICMP and ARP

The Internet Control Message Protocol (ICMP) provides a mechanism for communicating control message and error reports. Both gateways and hosts use ICMP to transmit problem reports about datagrams back to the datagram originator. In addition, ICMP includes an echo request/reply that can be used to determine if a destination is reachable and if so, is responding. The Address Resolution Protocol (ARP) maps the high-level IP address configured via software to a low-level physical hardware address, typically the NIC's ROM

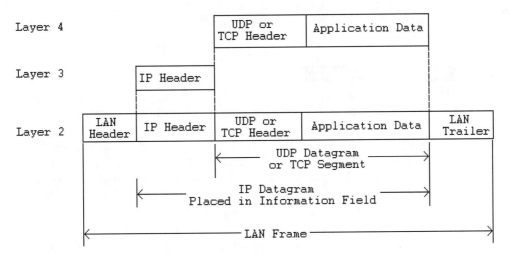

Figure 5.31   Forming a LAN frame.

address. The high-level IP address is currently 32 bits in length (IP version 4) and is commonly represented by four decimal numbers, ranging from 0 to 255 per number, separated from one another by decimals. Thus, another term used to reference an IP address is the *dotted decimal address*. The physical hardware address represents the MAC address. Thus, ARP provides an IP to MAC address resolution, which enables an IP packet to be transported in a LAN frame to its appropriate MAC address. Later in this section we will examine IP addresses in detail.

TCP

The Transmission Control Protocol (TCP) represents a layer 4 connection-oriented reliable protocol. TCP provides a virtual circuit connection mode service for applications that require connection setup, error detection, and automatic retransmission. In addition, TCP is structured to support multiple application programs on one host to communicate concurrently with processes on other hosts, as well as for a host to demultiplex and service incoming traffic among different applications or processes running on the host.

Each unit of data carried by TCP is referred to as a segment. Segments are created by TCP subdividing the stream of data passed down by application layer protocols that use its services, with each segment identified by the use of a sequence number. This segment identification process enables a receiver, if required, to reassemble data segments into their correct order.

Figure 5.32 illustrates the format of the TCP protocol header. To obtain an appreciation for the functionality and capability of TCP, let's examine the fields in its header.

Source and Destination Port Fields

The source and destination ports are each 16 bits in length and identify a process or service at the host receiver. The source port field entry is optional and when not used is padded with zeros. Both source and destination port values are commonly referred to as "well-known ports," as they typically identify an application layer protocol or process. Table 5.2 lists the well-known port numbers associated with eight popular TCP/IP application layer protocols. In examining the entries in the previously referenced table, note that some protocols, such as FTP, use two port addresses or logical connections. In the case of FTP, one address (21) is used for the transmission of commands, responses, and functions as a control path. In comparison, the second port address (20) is used for the actual file transfer.

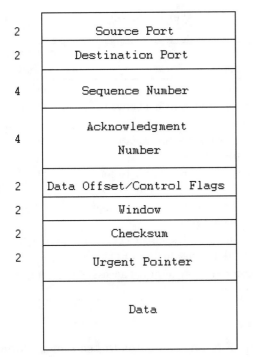

2	Source Port
2	Destination Port
4	Sequence Number
4	Acknowledgment Number
2	Data Offset/Control Flags
2	Window
2	Checksum
2	Urgent Pointer
	Data

Figure 5.32   TCP protocol header.

Sequence Fields

The sequence number is used to identify the data segment transported. The acknowledgment number interpretation depends upon the setting of the ACK control flag which is not directly shown in Figure 5.32. If the ACK control flag bit position is set, the acknowledgment field will contain the next sequence number the sender expects to receive. Otherwise the field is ignored.

Control Field Flags

There are six control field flags that are used to establish, maintain, and terminate connections. Those flags include URG (urgent), SYN, ACK, RST (reset), PSH (push), and FIN (finish).

Setting URG=1 indicates to the receiver urgent data is arriving. The SYN flag is set to 1 as a connection request and thus serves to establish a connection. As previously discussed, the ACK flag, when set, indicates that the acknowledgment flag is relevant. The RST flag, when set, means the connection should be reset, while the PSH flag tells the receiver to immediately deliver the data in

TABLE 5.2 Examples of TCP/IP Application Layer Protocol Use of Well-Known Ports

Name	Acronym	Description	Well-Known Port
Domain Name Protocol	DOMAIN	Defines the DNS	53
File Transfer Protocol	FTP	Supports file transfers between hosts	20,21
Finger Protocol	FINGER	Provides information about a specified user	79
HyperText Transmission Protocol	HTTP	Transmits information between a Web browser and a Web server	80
Post Office Protocol	POP	Enables host users to access mail from a mail server	110
Simple Mail Transfer Protocol	SMTP	Provides for the exchange of network management information	161,162
TELENET Protocol	Telnet	Provides remote terminal access to a host.	23

the segment. Finally, the setting of the FIN flag indicates the sender is done and the connection should be terminated.

Window Field

The window field is used to convey the number of bytes the sender can accept and functions as a flow control mechanism. This 16-bit field indicates the number of octets, beginning with the one in the acknowledgment field, that the originator of the segment can control. Since TCP is a full-duplex protocol, each host can use the window field to control the quantity of data that can be sent to the computer. This enables the recipient to, in effect, control its destiny. For example, if a receiving host becomes overloaded with processing or another reason results in the inability of the device to receive large chunks of data, it can use the window field as a flow control mechanism to reduce the size of data chunks sent to it. At the end of our review of TCP header fields, we will examine a TCP transmission sequence to note the interrelated role of the sequence, acknowledgment, and window fields.

Checksum Field

The checksum provides error detection for the TCP header and data carried in the segment. Thus, this field provides the mechanism for the detection of errors in each segment.

Urgent Pointer Field

The urgent pointer field is used in conjunction with the URG flag as a mechanism to identify the position of urgent data within a TCP segment. When the URG flag is set the value in the urgent pointer field represents the last byte of urgent data.

When an application uses TCP, TCP breaks the stream of data provided by the application into segments and adds an appropriate TCP header. Next, an IP header is prefixed to the TCP header to transport the segment via the network layer. As data arrives at its destination network, it's converted into a data link layer transport mechanism. For example, on an Ethernet network TCP data would be transported within Ethernet frames.

TCP Transmission Sequence Example

To illustrate the interrelationship between the sequence, acknowledgment, and window fields, let's examine the transmission of a sequence of TCP segments between two hosts. Figure 5.33 illustrates via the use of a time chart the transmission of a sequence of TCP segments.

At the top of Figure 5.33 it was assumed that a window size of 16 segments is in use. Although TCP supports full-duplex transmission, for simplicity of illustration we will use a half-duplex model in the time chart.

Assuming the host, whose address is ftp.fbi.gov, is transmitting a program or performing a similar lengthy file transfer operation, the first series of segments will have sequence numbers 64 through 79, assuming sequence number 63 was just acknowledged. The ACK value of 28 acknowledges that segments through number 27 were received by the host ftp.opm.gov and that it next expects to receive segment 28.

Assuming segments 64 through 79 arrive error-free, the host with the address ftp.opm.gov returns an ACK value of 80 to indicate the next segment it expects to receive. At this point in time, let's assume host ftp.opm.gov is running out of buffer space and halves the window size to 8. Thus, host ftp.opm.gov sets the window field value in the TCP header it transmits to host ftp.fbi.gov to 8. Upon receipt of the TCP segment, host ftp.fbi.gov reduces the number of segments it will transmit to 8 and uses an initial SEQ value of 80, increasing that value by 1 each time it transmits a new segment until 8 new segments are transmitted. Assuming all 8 segments were received error-free, host ftp.opm.gov then returns an ACK value of 88, which acknowledges the receipt of segments with sequence field numbers through 87.

Next, host ftp.fbi.gov transmits to host ftp.opm.gov another sequence of 8 segments using sequence field values of 88 to 95. However, let's assume a transmission impairment occurs that results in the segments being incorrectly

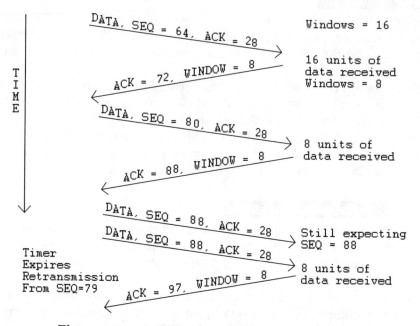

Host ftp.fbi.gov

Host ftp.opm.gov

T
I
M
E

DATA, SEQ = 64, ACK = 28

Windows = 16

ACK = 72, WINDOW = 8

16 units of
data received
Windows = 8

DATA, SEQ = 80, ACK = 28

8 units of
data received

ACK = 88, WINDOW = 8

DATA, SEQ = 88, ACK = 28

Still expecting
SEQ = 88

DATA, SEQ = 88, ACK = 28

Timer
Expires
Retransmission
From SEQ=79

8 units of
data received

ACK = 97, WINDOW = 8

Figure 5.33   A TCP transmission sequence.

received or perhaps not even received at all at their intended destination. If host ftp.opm.gov does not receive anything, it does not transmit anything back to host ftp.fbi.gov. Instead of waiting forever for a response, the TCP/IP protocol stack includes an internal timer that clicks down to zero while host ftp.fbi.gov waits for a response. When that value is reached, the timer expires and the transmitting station retransmits its sequence of 8 segments. On the second time around, the sequence of 8 segments are shown acknowledged at the bottom of Figure 5.33. If the impairment continued, the transmitting station would attempt a predefined number of retransmissions after which it would terminate the session if no response was received.

The altering of window field values provides a sliding window that can be used to control the flow of information. That is, by adjusting the value of the window field, a receiving host can inform a transmitting station whether or not an adjustment in the number of segments transmitted is required. In doing so there are two special window field values that can be used to further control the flow of information. A window field value of 0 means a host has shut down communications, while a window field value of 1 requires an acknowledgment for each unit of data transmitted, limiting transmission to a segment-by-segment basis.

UDP

The User Datagram Protocol (UDP) is the second layer 4 transport service supported by the TCP/IP protocol suite. UDP is a connectionless service, which means that the higher-layer application is responsible for the reliable delivery of the transported message. Figure 5.34 illustrates the composition of the UDP header.

Source and Destination Port Fields

The source and destination port fields are each 16 bits in length and, as previously described for TCP, identify the port number of the sending and receiving process, respectively. Here each port number process identifies an application running at the corresponding IP address in the IP header prefixed for the UDP header. The use of a port number provides a mechanism for identifying network services as they denote communications points where particular services can be accessed. For example, a value of 161 in a port field is used in UDP to identify SNMP.

Length Fields

The length field indicates the length of the UDP packets in octets to include the header and user data. The checksum, which is one's complement arithmetic sum, is computed over a pseudoheader and the entire UDP packet. The pseudoheader is created by the conceptual prefix of 12 octets to the header previously illustrated in Figure 5.34. The first 8 octets are used by source and

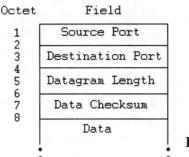

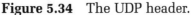

Figure 5.34   The UDP header.

destination IP addresses obtained from the IP packet. This is followed by a zero-filled octet and an octet that identifies the protocol. The last 2 octets in the pseudoheader denote the length of the UDP packet. By computing the UDP checksum over the pseudoheader and user data, a degree of additional data integrity is obtained.

IP

As previously mentioned, IP provides a datagram-oriented gateway service for transmission between subnetworks. This provides a mechanism for hosts to access other hosts on a best-effort basis but does not enhance reliability as it relies on upper-layer protocols for error detection and correction. As a layer 3 protocol, IP is responsible for the routing and delivery of datagrams. To accomplish this task IP performs a number of communications functions to include addressing, status information, management, fragmentation, and re-assembly of datagrams when necessary.

IP Header Format

Figure 5.35 illustrates the IP header format while Table 5.3 provides a brief description of the fields in the IP header.

Version Field

The four-bit version field identifies the version of the IP protocol used to create the datagram. The current version of the IP protocol is 4 and is encoded as 0100 in binary. The next-generation IP protocol is version 6, which is encoded as 0110 in binary. In our discussion of IP we will focus on IPv4 in this section.

Header Length and Total Length Fields

The header length field follows the version field and is also 4 bits in length. This field indicates the length of the header in 32-bit words. In comparison, the total length field indicates the total length of the datagram to include its header and higher-layer information. The use of 16 bits for the total length field enables an IP datagram to be up to 2^{16} or 65,535 octets in length.

Type of Service Field

The type of service field identifies how the datagram is handled. Three of the eight bits in this field are used to denote the precedence or level of importance assigned by the originator. Thus, this field provides a priority mechanism for routing IP datagrams.

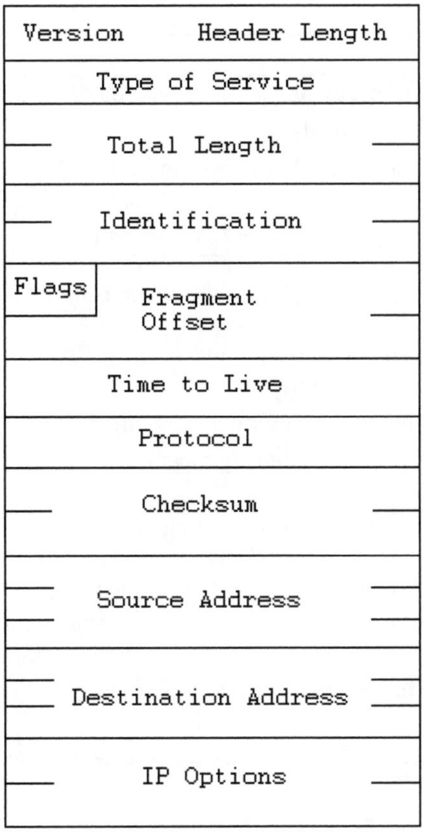

Version	Header Length
Type of Service	
Total Length	
Identification	
Flags	Fragment Offset
Time to Live	
Protocol	
Checksum	
Source Address	
Destination Address	
IP Options	

Figure 5.35 IP header format.

Identification and Fragment Offset Fields

The identification field enables each datagram or fragmented datagram to be identified. If a datagram was previously fragmented, the fragment offset field specifies the offset in the original datagram of the data being carried. In effect, this field indicates where the fragment belongs in the complete message. The actual value in this field is an integer that corresponds to a unit of eight octets, providing an offset in 64-bit units.

Time to Live Field

The time to live (TTL) field specifies the maximum time that a datagram can live. Because an exact time is difficult to measure, almost all routers decrement this field by one as a datagram flows between networks, with the

TABLE 5.3 IP Header Fields

Field	Description
Version	The version of the IP protocol used to create the datagram.
Header length	Header length in 32-bit words.
Type of service	Specifies how the datagram should be handled.

```
 0   1   2  3 4 5  6   7
|PRECEDENCE|D|T|R|UNUSED|
```

PRECEDENCE   indicates importance of the datagram
D   When set requests low delay
T   When set requests high throughput
R   When set requests high reliability

Field	Description
Total length	Specifies the total length to include header and data.
Identification	Used with source address to identify fragments belonging to specific datagrams.
Flags	Middle bit when set disables possible fragmentation. Low-order bit specifies whether the fragment contains data from the middle of the original datagram or the end.
Fragment offset	Specifies the offset in the original datagram of data being carried in a fragment.
Time to live	Specifies the time in seconds a datagram is allowed to remain in the internet.
Protocol	Specifies the higher-level protocol used to create the message carried in the data field.
Header checksum	Protects the integrity of the header.
Source IP address	The 32-bit IP address of the datagram's sender.
Destination IP address	The 32-bit IP address of the datagram's intended recipient.
IP options	Primarily used for network testing or debugging.

```
  0   1    2    3  4    5    6   7
|COPY|OPTION CLASS | OPTION NUMBER|
```

When copy bit set it tells gateways that the option should be copied into all fragments.
When set to 0 the option is copied into the first fragment.

Option Class	Meaning
0	Datagram or network control
1	Reserved for future use
2	Debugging
3	Reserved for future use

The option number defines a specific option within a class.

datagram being discarded when the field value reaches zero. Thus, this field more accurately represents a hop count field. You can consider this field to represent a fail-safe mechanism, as it prevents misaddressed datagrams from continuously flowing on the Internet.

Flags Field

The flags field contains two bits that indicate how fragmentation occurs while a third bit is currently unassigned. The setting of one bit can be viewed as a direct fragment control mechanism as a value of zero indicates the datagram can be fragmented, while a value of one denotes don't fragment. The second bit is set to zero to indicate that a fragment in a datagram is the last fragment and set to a value of one to indicate more fragments follow the current protocol.

Protocol Field

The protocol field specifies the higher-level protocol used to create the message carried in the datagram. For example, a value of decimal 6 would indicate TCP, while a value of decimal 17 would indicate UDP.

Source and Destination Address Fields

The source and destination address fields are both 32 bits in length. As previously discussed, each address represents both a network and a host computer on the network.

In examining the IP header a common network problem relates to the IP address carried in the source and destination address fields. Thus, a description of IP addressing is warranted as it forms the basis for network addressing as well as the domain name service translation of English-type mnemonics into what is known as dotted decimal IP addresses.

IP Addressing

The IP addressing scheme uses a 32-bit address, which is divided into an assigned network number and a host number. The latter can be further segmented into a subnet number and a host number. Through subnetting you can construct multiple networks while localizing the traffic of hosts to specific subnets, a technique I will shortly illustrate.

IP addressing numbers are assigned by the InterNIC network information center and can fall into one of five unique network classes, referenced as Classes A through E. Figure 5.36 illustrates the IP address formats for Class A, B, and C networks. Class D addresses are reserved for multicast groups, while Class E addresses are reserved for future use.

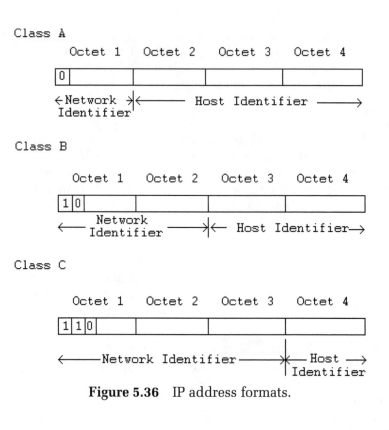

Figure 5.36 IP address formats.

In examining Figure 5.36, note that by examining the first bit in the IP address you can distinguish a Class A address from Class B and C addresses. Thereafter, examining the composition of the second bit position enables a Class B address to be distinguished from a Class C address.

An IP 32-bit address is expressed as four decimal numbers, with each number ranging in value from 0 to 255 and separated from another number by a dot (decimal point). This explains why an IP address is commonly referred to as a dotted decimal address.

Class A In examining Figure 5.36, note that a Class A address has three bytes available for identifying hosts on one network or on subnets, which provide support for more hosts than other address classes. Thus, Class A addresses are only assigned to large organizations or countries. Since the first bit in a Class A address must be 0, the first byte ranges in value from 1 to 127 instead of to 255. Through the use of 7 bits for the network portion and 24 bits for the host portion of the address, 128 networks can be defined with approximately 16.78 million hosts capable of being addressed on each Class A network.

Class B A Class B address uses two bytes for the network identifier and two for the host or subnet identifier. This permits up to 65,636 hosts and/or subnets to be assigned; however, since the first 2 bits of the network portion of the address are used to identify a Class B address, the network portion is reduced to a width of 14 bits. Thus, up to 16,384 Class B networks can be assigned. Due to the manner by which Class B network addresses are subdivided into network and host portions, such addresses are normally assigned to relatively large organizations with tens of thousands of employees.

Class C In a Class C address three octets are used to identify the network, leaving one octet to identify hosts and/or subnets. The use of 21 bits for a network address enables approximately two million distinct networks to be supported by the Class C address class. Because one octet only permits 256 hosts or subnets to be identified, many small organizations with a requirement to provide more than 256 hosts with access to the Internet must obtain multiple Class C addresses.

Host Restrictions In actuality the host portion of an IP address has two restrictions, which reduces the number of hosts that can be assigned to a network. First, the host portion cannot be set to all-zero bits, as an all-zeros host number is used to identify a base network. Secondly, an all-ones host number represents the broadcast address for a network or subnetwork. Thus, the maximum number of hosts on a network must be reduced by two. For a Class C network, a maximum of 254 hosts can then be configured for operation.

Subnetting Through the use of subnetting you can use a single IP address as a mechanism for connecting multiple physical networks. To accomplish subnetting you logically divide the host portion of an IP address into a network address and a host address.

Figure 5.37 illustrates an example of the IP subnet addressing format for a Class B address. In this example, all traffic routed to the address XY, where X and Y represent the value of the first two Class B address octets, flows to a common location connected to the Internet, typically a router. The router in turn connects two or more Class B subnets, each with a distinct address formed by the third decimal digit, which represents the subnet identifier. Figure 5.38 illustrates a Class B network address location with two physical networks using subnet addressing.

Class B Address Format

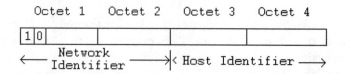

Class B Subnet Address Format

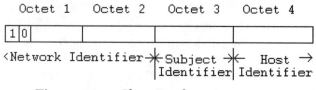

Figure 5.37 Class B subnetting.

Subnet Masks The implementation of a subnet addressing scheme is accomplished by the partitioning of the host identifier portion of an IP address. To accomplish this a 32-bit subnet mask must be created for each network, with bits set to 1 in the subnet mask to indicate the network portion of the IP address, while bits are set to 0 to indicate the host identifier portion. Thus, the Class B subnet address format illustrated in the lower portion of Figure 5.37 would require the following 32-bit subnet mask:

11111111   11111111   00000000   00000000

The prior mask would then be entered as 255.255.0.0 in dotted decimal representation into a router configuration screen as well as in software configuration screens on TCP/IP program stacks operating on each subnet. Concerning the latter, you must then configure each station to indicate its subnet and host identifier so that each station obtains a full 4-digit dotted decimal address.

Although the prior example used octet boundaries for creating the subnet mask, this is not an addressing requirement. For example, you could assign the following mask to a network:

11111111   11111111   00001110   00001100

The only submask restriction is to assign 1s to at least all the network identifier positions, resulting in the ability to extend masking into the host identifier

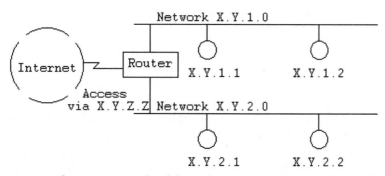

Figure 5.38 A Class B network address location with two physical networks using subnet addressing. IP datagrams with the destination address X.Y.Z.Z, where Z can be any decimal value representing a Class B network address that can consist of 256 subnets, with 256 hosts on each subnet.

field if you desire to arrange the specific assignment of addresses to computers. However, doing so can make it more difficult to verify the correct assignment of addresses in routers and workstations. Due to this, it is highly recommended that you should implement subnet masking on integral octet boundaries.

Domain Name Service

Addressing on a TCP/IP network occurs through the use of four decimal numbers ranging from 0 to 255, which are separated from one another by a dot. This dotted decimal notation represents a 32-bit address, which consists of an assigned network number and a host number as previously described during our examination of IP addressing. Because numeric addresses are difficult to work with, TCP/IP also supports a naming convention based upon English words or mnemonics that are both easier to work with and remember. The translation of English words or mnemonics to 32-bit IP addresses is performed by a domain name server. Each network normally has at least one domain name server, and the communications established between such servers on TCP/IP networks connected to the Internet are referred to as a domain name service (DNS).

The DNS is the naming protocol used in the TCP/IP protocol suite, which enables IP routing to occur indirectly through the use of names instead of IP addresses. To accomplish this, DNS provides a domain name to IP address translation service.

A domain is a subdivision of a wide area network. When applied to the Internet where the capitalized *I* references the collection of networks interconnected to one another, there are six top-level and server-pending domain names, which were specified by the Internet Network Information Center (InterNIC) at the time this book was prepared. Those top-level domains are listed in Table 5.4.

Under each top-level domain the InterNIC will register subdomains, which are assigned an IP network address. An organization receiving an IP network address can further subdivide their domain into two or more subdomains. In addition, instead of using dotted decimal notation to describe the location of each host, they can assign names to hosts as long as they follow certain rules and install a name server that provides IP address translation between named hosts and their IP addresses.

To illustrate the operation of a name server, consider the network domain illustrated in Figure 5.39. In this example we will assume that a well-known government agency has a local area network with several computers that will be connected to the Internet. Each host address will contain the specific name of the host plus the names of all of the subdomains and domains to which it belongs. Thus, the computer *warrants* would have the official address:

telnet.warrants.fbi.gov

TABLE 5.4 Internet Top-Level Domain Names

Domain Name	Assignment
Existing	
.COM	Commercial organization
.EDU	Educational organization
.GOV	Government agency
.MIL	Department of Defense
.NET	Networking organization
.ORG	Not-for-profit organization
Pending	
.firm	Business/commercial firms
.store	Goods for purchase
.web	World Wide Web–related activities
.arts	Culture/entertainment organizations
.rec	Recreation/entertainment organizations
.info	Information/services
.nom	Individual/personal nomenclature

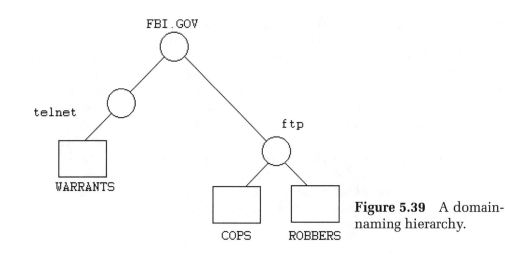

Figure 5.39 A domain-naming hierarchy.

Similarly, the computer *cops* would have the address:

ftp.cops.fbi.gov

In examining the domain-naming structure illustrated in Figure 5.39 note that computers were placed in subdomains using common Internet application names, such as telnet and ftp. This is a common technique that organizations use to make it easier for network users within and outside of the organization to remember mnemonics that represent specific hosts on their network.

Although domain names provide a mechanism for identifying objects connected to wide area networks, hosts in a domain require network addresses to transfer information. Thus, another host functioning as a name server is required to provide a name-to-address translation service.

Name Server

The name server plays an important role in TCP/IP networks. In addition to providing a name-to-IP address translation service, it must recognize that an address is outside its administrative zone of authority. For example, assume a host located on the domain illustrated in Figure 5.39 will use the address fred.microwear.com to transmit a message. The name server must recognize that that address does not reside in the current domain and must forward the address to another name server for translation into an appropriate IP address. Because most domains are connected to the Internet via an Internet service provider, the name server on the domain illustrated in Figure 5.39 would have a pointer to the name server of the Internet service provider (ISP) and forward the query to that name server. The ISP's name server will either have an entry in its table-in-cache memory or forward the query to another higher-level name server. Eventually, a name server will be reached that has administrative authority over the domain containing the host name to resolve and will return an IP address through a reversed hierarchy to provide the originating name server with a response to its query. Most name servers cache the results of previous name queries, which can considerably reduce off-domain or Internet DNS queries. In the event a response is not received, possibly due to an incorrect name or the entry of a name no longer used, the local name server will generate a "failure to resolve" message after a period of time that will be displayed on the requesting host's display.

TCP/IP Configuration

The configuration of a station on a TCP/IP network normally requires the specification of four IP addresses as well as the station's host and domain names. To

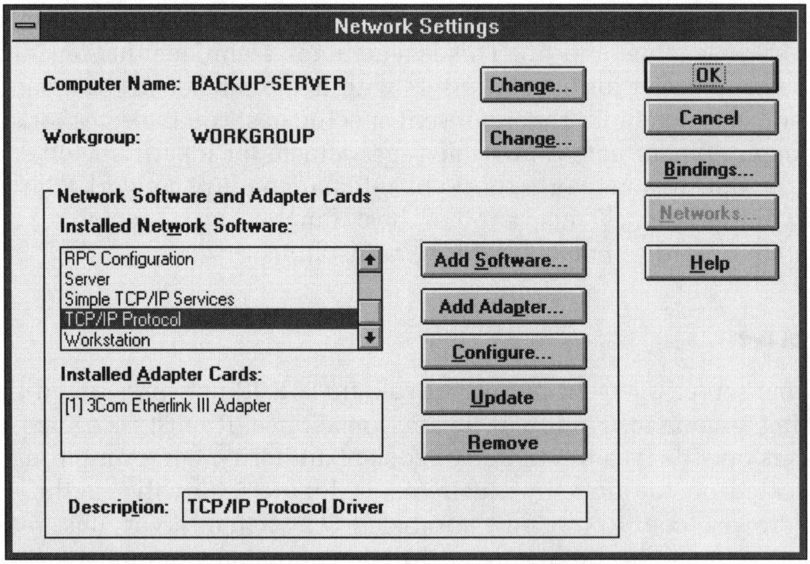

Figure 5.40 Using the Windows NT Network Settings dialog box to configure the use of the TCP/IP protocol.

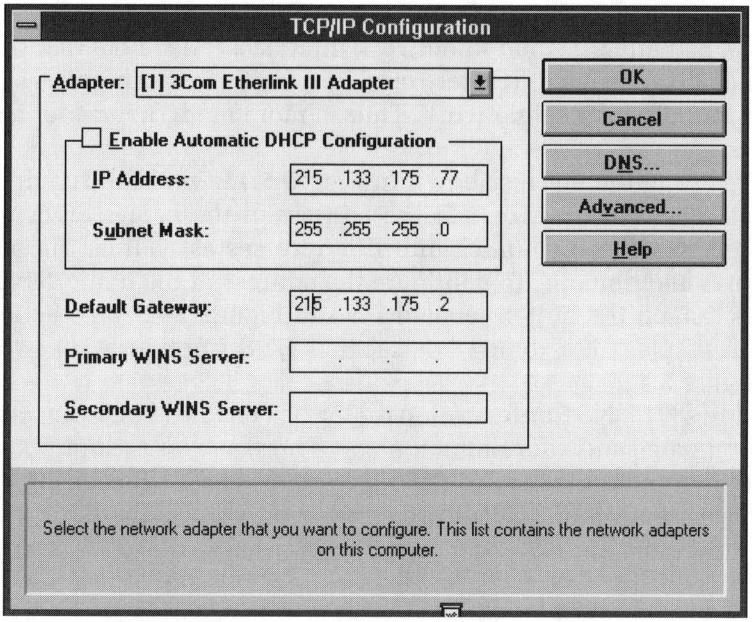

Figure 5.41 The Windows NT TCP/IP configuration dialog box with entries for the IP address of the network interface, subnet mask, and default gateway.

illustrate the configuration of a TCP/IP station, Figures 5.40 through 5.42 show the screen settings on a Microsoft Windows NT server used to configure the station as a participant on a TCP/IP network.

Figure 5.40 illustrates the Windows NT Network Settings dialog box with the TCP/IP protocol selected in the installed network software box. Note that at the top of that box the entry NWLink IPX/SPX Compatible Transport is shown. Windows NT has the ability to operate multiple protocol stacks to include NWLink, which is Microsoft's implementation of the Novell IPX and SPX protocols. Also note that we previously configured the server to use a 3 Com Etherlink III Adapter as indicated in the box labeled Installed Adapter Cards in the lower left portion of the screen display.

Clicking on the button labeled Configure in Figure 5.40 results in the display of another dialog box, this one labeled TCP/IP Configuration. Figure 5.41 illustrates the TCP/IP Configuration dialog box with three address entries shown. Those address entries indicate the IP address of the interface assigned to the selected adapter card, the subnet mask, and the IP address of the default gateway. Note that a computer can have multiple adapter cards, thus IP addresses are actually assigned to network interfaces. Also note that the term gateway dates to when such devices routed packets to other networks if their address was not on the local network. Thus, a more modern term for gateway is router.

After configuring the entries shown in Figure 5.41, you will require a few more entries. Those entries include the address of the name server used to translate near-English mnemonics into IP addresses as well as the name of your computer and domain. To configure the address of the name server, you would first click on the button labeled DNS in Figure 5.41. This action will result in the display of a dialog box labeled DNS Configuration, which is shown in Figure 5.42.

The Windows NT DNS Configuration dialog box enables you to specify your host computer name and your domain name. Those entries are optional; however, if you do not include those entries and your local DNS uses this configuration information, other TCP/IP users either on your network or a distant

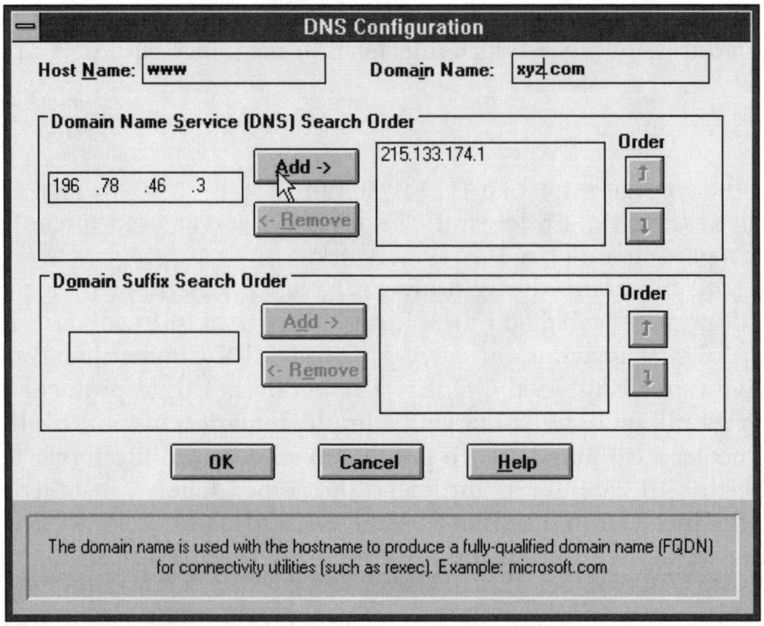

Figure 5.42   Using the Windows NT DNS Configuration dialog box to specify the station's name and domain name as well as two name server addresses.

network will not be able to access your computer by entering your computer's near-English address name, which in Figure 5.42 would be www.xyz.com. Instead, users would have to know your numeric IP address.

The DNS entry area in Figure 5.42 allows you to specify up to three name servers in the order they should be searched. Many organizations operate two name servers, so the ability to enter three should suffice for most organizations.

Operating Multiple Stacks

In concluding this chapter we will use three Windows NT screens to expand upon illustrating the flexibility you can obtain from operating multiple protocol stacks. In the example we will shortly view, we will use Microsoft's Windows NT to show how to access both Windows NT and NetWare networks as well as operate a Netscape browser to run a TCP/IP application.

Figure 5.43 illustrates the use of the Windows NT Connect Network Drive dialog box to view both Microsoft Windows and Novell NetWare network

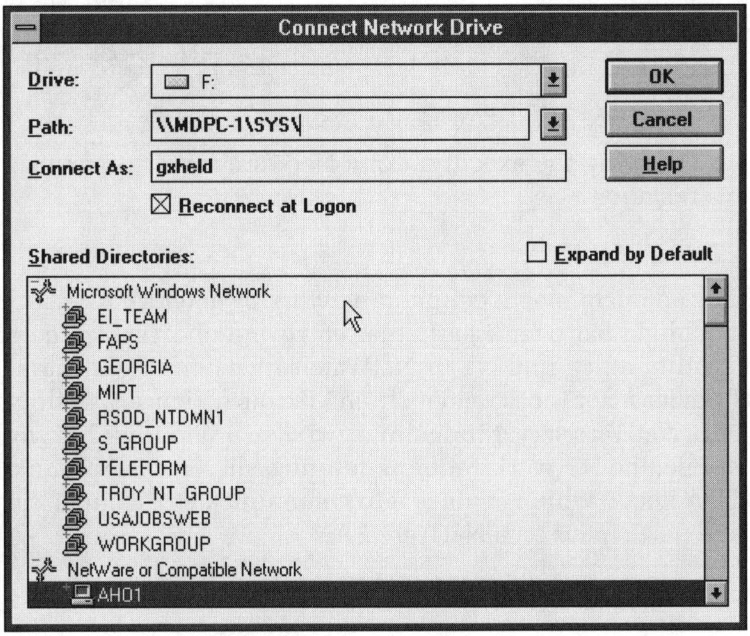

Figure 5.43 Using the Windows NT Connect Network Drive dialog box to view Windows and NetWare network devices.

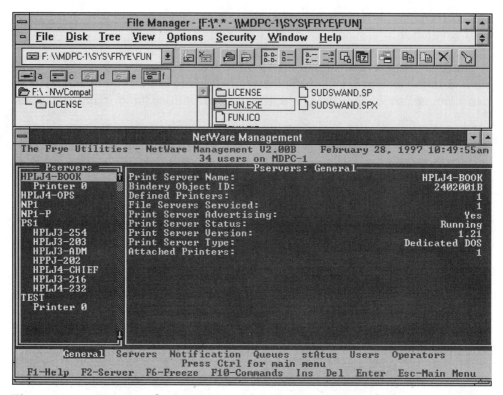

Figure 5.44 Viewing the execution of a NetWare server program on a Windows NT workstation.

devices that can operate on a common network or network infrastructure. By moving a highlight bar over a particular entry and clicking on the entry, you obtain the ability to log into NT or NetWare servers or access-shared directories on NT devices. For those readers from Missouri, Figure 5.44 illustrates the execution of a NetWare server program viewed on a Windows NT workstation. In this example, the NT workstation is running Microsoft's NWLink IPX/SPX compatible protocol, which enables it to communicate in a client/server environment as a participant on a NetWare LAN.

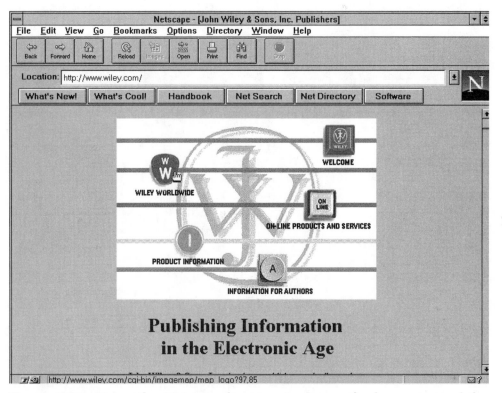

Figure 5.45   Using the Netscape browser to access the home page of the author's publisher.

For our last stack example, since we previously configured TCP/IP we should be able to operate a TCP/IP application. Figure 5.45 illustrates the use of the Netscape browser to access the home page of this author's publisher. Thus, this short section illustrates the worth of operating multiple protocol stacks to access NT and NetWare servers as well as a Web server.

chapter six

Bridging Methods and Performance Issues

In Chapter 5, an overview of bridge operations was presented, along with information concerning the functionality of other local area network hardware and software components. That chapter deferred until now a detailed examination of bridging methods, to include their network use and performance issues. In this chapter, we will focus our attention on those issues, examining different methods that bridges use for routing frames, performance issues that govern their ability to examine and forward frames without introducing network bottlenecks, and their typical employment for interconnecting LANs.

6.1 Bridging Methods

Bridges operate by examining MAC layer addresses, using the destination and source addresses within a frame as a decision criterion to make their forwarding decisions. Operating at the MAC layer, bridges are not addressed, and must therefore examine all frames that flow on a network.

Address Issues

Since bridges connect networks, it is important to ensure that duplicate MAC addresses do not occur on joined networks—a topology we will refer to as an *internet.* While duplicate addresses will not occur when universally administered addressing is used, when locally administered addressing is used duplicate addresses become possible. Thus, the addresses assigned to stations on separate networks joined to form an internet should be reviewed before using bridges to connect two or more separate networks.

Two primary routing methods are used by bridges for connecting local area networks: transparent or self-learning and source routing. Transparent bridges were originally developed to support the connection of Ethernet networks, as briefly described in Chapter 5.

Transparent Bridging

A transparent bridge examines MAC frames to learn the addresses of stations on the network, storing information in internal memory in the form of an address table. Thus, this type of bridge is also known as a *self-learning bridge*. To understand the operation of a transparent bridge in more detail and realize some of the limitations associated with the use of this device, consider the simple internet illustrated in Figure 6.1. This internet consists of three Ethernet local area network segments connected through the use of two self-learning bridges. For simplicity of illustration, only two workstations are shown and labeled on each local area network. Those labels represent the 48-bit MAC address of each station.

As previously mentioned, transparent bridges were originally developed to interconnect Ethernet local area networks. This type of bridge can also be used to connect Ethernet and Token-Ring networks; however, for this purpose, the bridge must at least be capable of performing frame conversion.

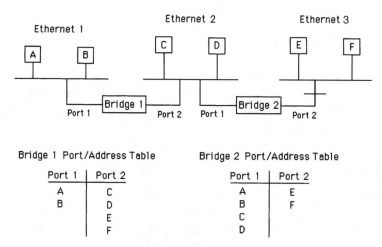

Figure 6.1 Transparent bridge operation. A transparent or self-learning bridge examines the source and destination addresses to form port/address or routing tables in memory.

Port/Address Table Construction

In examining the construction of bridge port/address tables for the network shown in Figure 6.1, we will assume that each bridge operates as a transparent bridge. As frames flow on the Ethernet, bridge 1 examines the source address of each frame. Eventually, after both stations A and B have become active, the bridge associates their address as being on port 1 of that device. Any frames with a destination address other than stations A or B are considered to be on another network. Thus, bridge 1 would eventually associate addresses C, D, E, and F with port 2, once it receives frames with those addresses in their destination address fields. Similarly, bridge 2 constructs its own port/address table. Since frames from Ethernet 1 and 1 Ethernet 2 can have source addresses of A, B, C, or D, eventually the port/address table of bridge 2 associates those addresses with port 1 of that device. Since frames from Ethernet 1 or Ethernet 2 with a destination address of E or F are not on those local area networks, bridge 2 then associates those addresses with port 2 of that device.

The port/address tables previously shown in Figure 6.1 are normally stored in bridge memory sorted by MAC address. In addition, the time the entry occurred is also added to the table, resulting in a three-column table. The time of occurrence is used by bridges to periodically purge old entries. Entry purging is important because inactive entries both use finite memory and extend the search time associated with the reading of each frame received on a bridge port and its comparison to entries in the port/address table. This searching is required to determine if the frame is to be forwarded along with the port onto which the frame should be placed.

To illustrate the necessity for time stamping, bridge port/address table entries assume the interconnected Ethernet segments shown in Figure 6.1 are expanded by the addition of two additional segments to the right of segment 3, with each new segment containing 50 workstations. Without the use of time stamping and the purging of aged table entries, the port/address table of bridge 2 would eventually grow to 102 entries, even if each station powered on at 8:00 A.M., connected to their local server, and thereafter did not use the network for the rest of the day. Then, each time a frame arrived at port 2 of bridge 2 the destination address of the frame would have to be compared against a table with 100 inactive entries, consuming valuable time.

Advantages

One of the key advantages of a transparent bridge is that it operates independently of the contents of the information field and is protocol-independent.

Because this type of bridge is self-learning, it requires no manual configuration and is essentially a "plug and play" device. Thus, this type of bridge is attractive for connecting a few local area networks together, and is usually sufficient for most small and medium-sized businesses. Unfortunately, its use limits the development of certain interconnection topologies, as we will soon see.

Disadvantages

To see the disadvantages associated with transparent bridges, consider Figure 6.2, in which the three Ethernet local area networks are interconnected through the use of three bridges. In this example, the interconnected networks form a *circular* or *loop topology*. Because a transparent bridge views stations as being connected to either port 1 or port 2, a circular or loop topology will create problems. Those problems can result in an unnecessary duplication of frames, which not only degrades the overall level of performance of the interconnected networks, but will quite possibly confuse the end stations. For example, consider a frame whose source address is A and whose destination

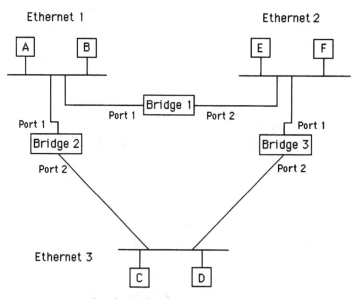

Figure 6.2 Transparent bridges do not support network loops. The construction of a circular or loop topology with transparent bridges can result in an unnecessary duplication of frames, and may confuse end stations. To avoid these problems, the Spanning Tree Protocol (STP) opens a loop by placing one bridge in a standby mode of operation.

address is F. Both bridge 1 and bridge 2 will forward the frame. Although bridge 1 will forward the frame to its appropriate network using the most direct route, the frame will also be forwarded by bridge 3 to Ethernet 2, resulting in a duplicate frame arriving at workstation F. At station F, a mechanism would be required to reject duplicate frames. Even if such a mechanism is available, the additional traffic flowing across multiple internet paths would result in an increase in network usage approaching 100 percent. This, in turn, would saturate some networks, while significantly reducing the level of performance of other networks. For these reasons, transparent bridging is prohibited from creating a loop or circular topology. However, transparent bridging supports concurrently active multiple bridges, using an algorithm known as the *spanning tree* to determine which bridges should forward and which bridges should only filter frames.

Spanning Tree Protocol

The problem of active loops was addressed by the IEEE Committee 802 in the 802.1D standard with an intelligent algorithm known as the Spanning Tree Protocol (STP). The STP, based on graph theory, converts a loop into a tree topology by disabling a link. This action ensures there is a unique path from any node in an internet to every other node. Disabled nodes are then kept in a standby mode of operation until a network failure occurs. At that time, the STP will attempt to construct a new tree using any of the previously disabled links.

Operation

To illustrate the operation of the STP, we must first become familiar with the difference between the physical and active topology of bridged networks. In addition, there are a number of terms associated with the spanning tree algorithm, as defined by the protocol, that we should become familiar with. Thus, we will also review those terms before discussing the operation of the algorithm.

Physical versus Active Topology

In transparent bridging, a distinction is made between the physical and active topology resulting from bridged local area networks. This distinction enables the construction of a network topology in which inactive but physically constructed routes can be placed into operation if a primary route should fail, and in which the inactive and active routes would form an illegal circular path violating the spanning tree algorithm if both routes were active at the same time.

The top of Figure 6.3 illustrates one possible physical topology of bridged networks. The cost (C) assigned to each bridge will be discussed later in this chapter. The lower portion of Figure 6.3 illustrates a possible active topology for the physical configuration shown at the top of that illustration.

When a bridge is used to construct an active path, it will forward frames through those ports used to form active paths. The ports through which frames are forwarded are said to be in a *forwarding state of operation.* Ports

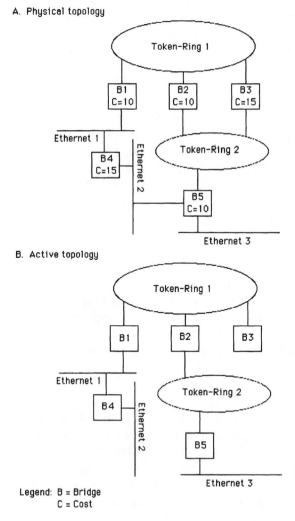

A. Physical topology

B. Active topology

Legend: B = Bridge
        C = Cost

Figure 6.3 Physical versus active topology. When transparent bridges are used, the active topology cannot form a closed loop in the internet.

that cannot forward frames because their operation forms a loop are said to be in a *blocking state of operation.*

Under the spanning tree algorithm, a port in a blocking state can be placed into a forwarding state to provide a path that becomes part of the active network topology. This new path usually occurs because of the failure of another path, bridge component, or the reconfiguration of interconnected networks, and must not form a closed loop.

Spanning Tree Algorithm

The basis for the spanning tree algorithm is a tree structure, since a tree forms a pattern of connections that has no loops. The term *spanning* is used because the branches of a tree structure span or connect subnetworks.

As a review for readers unfamiliar with graph theory, let's examine the concept behind spanning trees. To appropriately do so we need a point of reference, so let's begin with the graph structure shown at the top of Figure 6.4. A

a. Network graph

b. Possible spanning trees

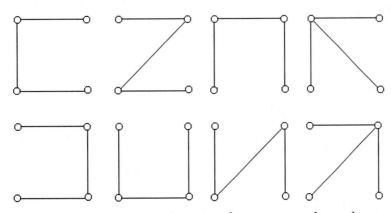

Figure 6.4 Forming spanning trees from a network graph.

spanning tree of a graph is a subgraph that connects all nodes and represents a tree. The graph shown at the top of Figure 6.4 has eight distinct spanning trees. The lower portion of Figure 6.4 illustrates the spanning trees associated with the graph structure illustrated at the top of the previously referenced figure.

Minimum Spanning Tree

Suppose the links connecting each node are assigned a length or weight. Then, the weight of a tree represents the sum of its links or edges. If the weight or length of the links or tree edges differ, then different tree structures will have different weights. Thus, the identification of the minimum spanning tree requires us to examine each of the spanning trees supported by a graph and identify the structure that has the minimum length or weight.

The identification of the minimum spanning tree can be accomplished by listing all spanning trees and finding the minimum weight or length associated with the list. This is a brute force method that always works but is not exactly efficient, especially when a graph becomes complex and can contain a significant number of trees. A far better method is obtained by the use of an appropriate algorithm.

Kruskal's Algorithm

There are several popular algorithms developed for solving the minimum spanning tree of a graph. One of those algorithms is the Kruskal algorithm which is relatively easy to understand and will be used to illustrate the computation of a minimum spanning tree. Because we need weights or lengths assigned to each edge or link in a graph, let's revise the network graph previously shown in Figure 6.4 and add some weights. Figure 6.5 illustrates the weighted graph.

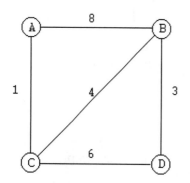

Figure 6.5   A weighted network graph.

Kruskal's algorithm can be expressed as follows:

1. Sort the edges of the graph (G) in their increasing order by weight or length.
2. Construct a subgraph (S) of G and initially set it to the empty state.
3. For each edge (e) in sorted order:
   If the endpoints of the edges (e) are disconnected in S, add them to S.

Using the graph shown in Figure 6.5, let's apply Kruskal's algorithm as follows:

1. The sorted edges of the graph in their increasing order by weight or length produces the following table:

Edge	Weight/Length
A-C	1
B-D	3
C-B	4
C-D	6
A-B	8

2. Set the subgraph of G to the empty state. Thus, S = null.
3. For each edge add to S as long as the endpoints are disconnected. Thus, the first operation produces:

$$S = A,C \quad \text{or}$$

The next operation produces:

$$S = (A,C) + (B,D) \quad \text{or}$$

The third operation produces:

$$S = (A,B) + (B,D) + (C,B) \quad \text{or}$$

Note that we cannot continue as the endpoints in S are now all connected. Thus, the minimum spanning tree consists of the edges or links (A,B) + (B,D) + (C,B) and has the weight 1 + 4 + 3, or 7. Now that we have an appreciation for the method by which a minimum spanning tree is formed, let's turn our attention to its applicability in transparent bridge-based networks.

Similar to the root of a tree, one bridge in a spanning tree network will be assigned to a unique position in the network. Known as the *root bridge,* this bridge is assigned as the top of the spanning tree, and because of this position, it has the potential to carry the largest amount of internet traffic due to its position.

Because bridges and bridge ports can be active or inactive, a mechanism is required to identify bridges and bridge ports. Each bridge in a spanning tree network is assigned a unique bridge identifier. This identifier is the MAC address on the bridge's lowest port number and a two-byte bridge priority level. The priority level is defined when a bridge is installed and functions as a bridge number. Similar to the bridge priority level, each adapter on a bridge that functions as a port has a two-byte port identifier. Thus, the unique bridge identifier and port identifier enable each port on a bridge to be uniquely identified.

Path Cost

Under the spanning tree algorithm, the difference in physical routes between bridges is recognized, and a mechanism is provided to indicate the preference for one route over another. That mechanism is accomplished by the ability to assign a path cost to each path. Thus, you could assign a low cost to a preferred route and a high cost to a route you only want to be used in a backup situation.

Once path costs are assigned to each path in an internet, each bridge will have one or more costs associated with different paths to the root bridge. One of those costs is lower than all other path costs. That cost is known as the bridge's *root path cost,* and the port used to provide the least path cost toward the root bridge is known as the *root port.*

Designated Bridge

As previously discussed, the spanning tree algorithm does not permit active loops in an interconnected network. To prevent this situation from occurring, only one bridge linking two networks can be in a forwarding state at any particular time. That bridge is known as the designated bridge, while all other bridges linking two networks will not forward frames and will be in a blocking state of operation.

Constructing the Spanning Tree

The spanning tree algorithm employs a three-step process to develop an active topology. First, the root bridge is identified. In Figure 6.3B we will assume bridge 1 was selected as the root bridge. Next, the path cost from each bridge to the root bridge is determined, and the minimum cost from each bridge becomes the root path cost. The port in the direction of the least path cost to the root bridge, known as the root port, is then determined for each bridge. If the root path cost is the same for two or more bridges linking LANs, then the bridge with the highest priority will be selected to furnish the minimum path cost. Once the paths are selected, the designated ports are activated.

In examining Figure 6.3A, let us now use the cost entries assigned to each bridge. Let us assume that bridge 1 was selected as the root bridge, since we expect a large amount of traffic to flow between Token-Ring 1 and Ethernet 1 networks. Therefore, bridge 1 will become the designated bridge between Token-Ring 1 and Ethernet 1 networks.

In examining the path costs to the root bridge, note that the path through bridge 2 was assigned a cost of 10, while the path through bridge 3 was assigned a cost of 15. Thus, the path from Token-Ring 2 via bridge 2 to Token-Ring 1 becomes the designated bridge between those two networks. Hence, Figure 6.3B shows bridge 3 inactive by the omission of a connection to the Token-Ring 2 network. Similarly, the path cost for connecting the Ethernet 3 network to the root bridge is lower by routing through the Token-Ring 2 and Token-Ring 1 networks. Thus, bridge 5 becomes the designated bridge for the Ethernet 3 and Token-Ring 2 networks.

Bridge Protocol Data Unit

One question that is probably in your mind by now is how each bridge knows whether to participate in a spanned tree topology. Bridges obtain topology information by the use of bridge protocol data unit (BPDU) frames.

The root bridge is responsible for periodically transmitting a "HELLO" BPDU frame to all networks to which it is connected. According to the spanning tree protocol, HELLO frames must be transmitted every 1 to 10 seconds. The BPDU has the group MAC address 800143000000, which is recognized by each bridge. A designated bridge will then update the path cost and timing information and forward the frame. A standby bridge will monitor the BPDUs, but will not update nor forward them.

When a standby bridge is required to assume the role of the root or designated bridge, the HELLO BPDU will indicate that a standby bridge should become a designated bridge. The process by which bridges determine their role in a spanning tree network is iterative. As new bridges enter a network, they assume a listening state to determine their role in the network. Similarly, when a bridge is removed, another iterative process occurs to reconfigure the remaining bridges.

Although the STP algorithm procedure eliminates duplicate frame and degraded internet performance, it can be a hindrance for situations where multiple active paths between networks are desired. Another disadvantage of STP occurs when it is used in remote bridges connecting geographically dispersed networks. For example, returning to Figure 6.2, suppose Ethernet 1 were located in Los Angeles, Ethernet 2 in New York, and Ethernet 3 in Atlanta. If the link between Los Angeles and New York were placed in a standby mode of operation, all frames from Ethernet 2 routed to Ethernet 1 would be routed through Atlanta. Depending on the traffic between networks, this situation might require an upgrade in the bandwidth of the links connecting each network to accommodate the extra traffic flowing through Atlanta. Since the yearly cost of upgrading a 56- or 64-Kbps circuit to a 128-Kbps fractional T1 link can easily exceed the cost of a bridge or router, you might wish to consider the use of routers to accommodate this networking situation. In comparison, when using local bridges, the higher operating rate of local bridges in interconnecting local area networks normally allows an acceptable level of performance when LAN traffic is routed through an intermediate bridge.

Protocol Dependency

Another problem associated with the use of transparent bridges concerns the differences between Ethernet and IEEE 802.3 frame field compositions. As noted in Chapter 4, the Ethernet frame contains a type field that indicates the higher-layer protocol in use. Under the IEEE 802.3 frame format, the type field is replaced by a length field, and the data field is subdivided to include logical link control (LLC) information in the form of destination (DSAP) and source (SSAP) service access points. Here, the DSAP and SSAP are similar to the type field in an Ethernet frame: they also point to a higher-level process. Unfortunately, this small difference can create problems when you are using a transparent bridge to interconnect Ethernet and IEEE 802.3 networks.

The top portion of Figure 6.6 shows the use of a bridge to connect an AppleTalk network supporting several Macintosh computers to an Ethernet network on which a Digital Equipment Corporation VAX computer is located. Although the VAX may be capable of supporting DecNet Phase IV, which is true Ethernet, and AppleTalk if both modules are resident, a pointer is required to direct the IEEE 802.3 frames generated by the Macintosh to the right protocol on the VAX. Unfortunately, the Ethernet connection used by the VAX will not provide the required pointer. This explains why you should avoid connecting Ethernet and IEEE 802.3 networks via transparent bridges. Fortunately, almost all Ethernet NICs manufactured today are IEEE 802.3–compatible to alleviate this problem; however, older NICs may operate as true Ethernets and result in the previously mentioned problem.

Source Routing

Source routing is a bridging technique developed by IBM for connecting Token-Ring networks. The key to the implementation of source routing is the use of a portion of the information field in the Token-Ring frame to carry rout-

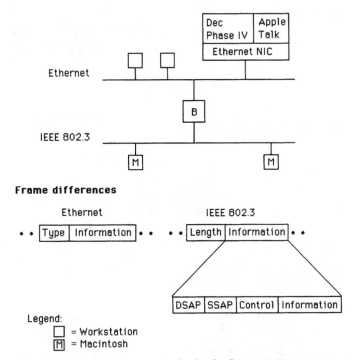

Figure 6.6 Protocol differences preclude linking IEEE 802.3 and Ethernet networks using transparent bridges. A Macintosh computer connected on an IEEE 802.3 network using AppleTalk will not have its frame pointed to the right process on a VAX on an Ethernet. Thus, the differences between Ethernet and IEEE 802.3 networks require transparent bridges for interconnecting similar networks.

ing information and the transmission of *discovery* packets to determine the best route between two networks.

The presence of source routing is indicated by the setting of the first bit position in the source address field of a Token-Ring frame to a binary 1. When set, this indicates that the information field is preceded by a route information field (RIF), which contains both control and routing information.

The RIF Field

Figure 6.7 illustrates the composition of a Token-Ring RIF. This field is variable in length and is developed during a discovery process, described later in this section.

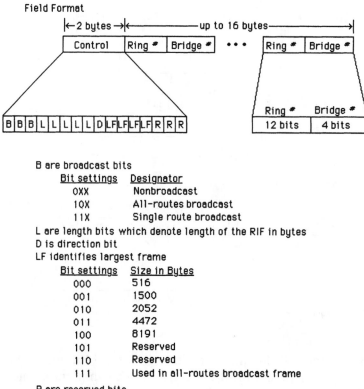

Figure 6.7 Token-Ring route information field. The Token-Ring RIF is variable in length.

The control field contains information that defines how information will be transferred and interpreted and what size the remainder of the RIF will be. The three broadcast bit positions indicate a nonbroadcast, all-routes broadcast, or single-route broadcast situation. A nonbroadcast designator indicates a local or specific route frame. An all-routes broadcast designator indicates that a frame will be transmitted along every route to the destination station. A single-route broadcast designator is used only by designated bridges to relay a frame from one network to another. In examining the broadcast bit settings shown in Figure 6.7, note that the letter X indicates an unspecified bit setting that can be either a 1 or 0.

The length bits identify the length of the RIF in bytes, while the D bit indicates how the field is scanned, left to right or right to left. Since vendors have incorporated different memory in bridges which may limit frame sizes, the LF bits enable different devices to negotiate the size of the frame. Normally, a default setting indicates a frame size of 512 bytes. Each bridge can select a number, and if it is supported by other bridges, that number is then used to represent the negotiated frame size. Otherwise, a smaller number used to represent a smaller frame size is selected, and the negotiation process is repeated. Note that a 1500-byte frame is the largest frame size supported by Ethernet IEEE 802.3 networks. Thus, a bridge used to connect Ethernet and Token-Ring networks cannot support the use of Token-Ring frames exceeding 1500 bytes.

Up to eight route number subfields, each consisting of a 12-bit ring number and a 4-bit bridge number, can be contained in the routing information field. This permits two to eight route designators, enabling frames to traverse up to eight rings across seven bridges in a given direction. Both ring numbers and bridge numbers are expressed as hexadecimal characters, with three hex characters used to denote the ring number and one hex character used to identify the bridge number.

Operation Example

To illustrate the concept behind source routing, consider the internet illustrated in Figure 6.8. In this example, let us assume that two Token-Ring networks are located in Atlanta and one network is located in New York.

Each Token-Ring and bridge is assigned a ring or bridge number. For simplicity, ring numbers R1, R2, and R3 are used here, although as previously explained, those numbers are actually represented in hexadecimal. Similarly, bridge numbers are shown here as B1, B2, B3, B4, and B5 instead of hexadecimal characters.

When a station wants to originate communications, it is responsible for finding the destination by transmitting a discovery packet to network bridges and

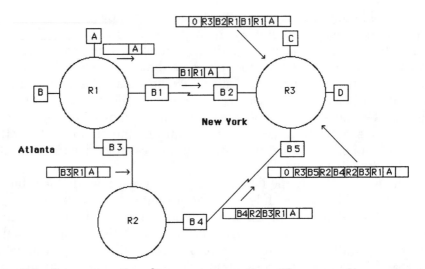

Figure 6.8 Source routing discovery operation. The route discovery process results in each bridge entering the originating ring number and its bridge number into the RIF.

other network stations whenever it has a message to transmit to a new destination address. If station A wishes to transmit to station C, it sends a route discovery packet containing an empty RIF and its source address, as indicated in the upper left portion of Figure 6.8. This packet is recognized by each source routing bridge in the network. When a source routing bridge receives the packet, it enters the packet's ring number and its own bridge identifier in the packet's routing information field. The bridge then transmits the packet to all of its connections except the connection on which the packet was received, a process known as *flooding.* Depending on the topology of the interconnected networks, it is more than likely that multiple copies of the discovery packet will reach the recipient. This is illustrated in the upper right corner of Figure 6.8, in which two discovery packets reach station C. Here, one packet contains the sequence R1B1R1B2R30—the zero indicates that there is no bridging in the last ring. The second packet contains the route sequence R1B3R2B4R2B5R30. Station C then picks the best route, based on either the most direct path or the earliest arriving packet, and transmits a response to the discover packet originator. The response indicates the specific route to use, and station A then enters that route into memory for the duration of the transmission session.

Under source routing, bridges do not keep routing tables like transparent bridges. Instead, tables are maintained at each station throughout the network.

Thus, each station must check its routing table to determine what route frames must traverse to reach their destination station. This routing method results in source routing using distributed routing tables instead of the centralized routing tables used by transparent bridges.

Advantages

There are several advantages associated with source routing. One advantage is the ability to construct mesh networks with loops for a fault-tolerant design; this cannot be accomplished with the use of transparent bridges. Another advantage is the inclusion of routing information in the information frames. Several vendors have developed network management software products that use that information to provide statistical information concerning internet activity. Those products may assist you in determining how heavily your wide area network links are being used, and whether you need to modify the capacity of those links; they may also inform you if one or more workstations are hogging communications between networks.

Disadvantages

Although the preceding advantages are considerable, they are not without a price. That price includes a requirement to identify bridges and links specifically, higher bursts of network activity, and an incompatibility between Token-Ring and Ethernet networks. In addition, because the structure of the Token-Ring RIF supports a maximum of seven entries, routing of frames is restricted to crossing a maximum of seven bridges.

When using source routing bridges to connect Token-Ring networks, you must configure each bridge with a unique bridge/ring number. In addition, unless you wish to accept the default method by which stations select a frame during the route discovery process, you will have to reconfigure your LAN software. Thus, source routing creates an administrative burden not incurred by transparent bridges.

Due to the route discovery process, the flooding of discovery frames occurs in bursts when stations are turned on or after a power outage. Depending upon the complexity of an internet, the discovery process can degrade network performance. This is perhaps the most problematic for organizations that require the interconnection of Ethernet and Token-Ring networks.

A source routing bridge can be used only to interconnect Token-Ring networks, since it operates on RIF data not included in an Ethernet frame. Although transparent bridges can operate in Ethernet, Token-Ring, and mixed environments, their use precludes the ability to construct loop or mesh topologies, and inhibits the ability to establish operational redundant paths for load sharing. Another problem associated with bridging Ethernet and

Token-Ring networks involves the RIF in a Token-Ring frame. Unfortunately, different LAN operating systems use the RIF data in different ways. Thus, the use of a transparent bridge to interconnect Ethernet and Token-Ring networks may require the same local area network operating system on each network. To alleviate these problems, several vendors introduced source routing transparent (SRT) bridges, which function in accordance with the IEEE 802.1D standard approved during 1992.

Source Routing Transparent Bridges

A source routing transparent bridge supports both IBM's source routing and the IEEE transparent STP operations. This type of bridge can be considered two bridges in one; it has been standardized by the IEEE 802.1 committee as the IEEE 802.1D standard.

Operation

Under source routing, the MAC packets contain a status bit in the source field that identifies whether source routing is to be used for a message. If source routing is indicated, the bridge forwards the frame as a source routing frame. If source routing is not indicated, the bridge determines the destination address and processes the packet using a transparent mode of operation, using routing tables generated by a spanning tree algorithm.

Advantages

There are several advantages associated with source routing transparent bridges. First and perhaps foremost, they enable different networks to use different local area network operating systems and protocols. This capability enables you to interconnect networks developed independently of one another, and allows organization departments and branches to use LAN operating systems without restriction. Secondly, also a very important consideration, source routing transparent bridges can connect Ethernet and Token-Ring networks while preserving the ability to mesh or loop Token-Ring networks. Thus, their use provides an additional level of flexibility for network construction.

Translating Operations

When interconnecting Ethernet/IEEE 802.3 and Token-Ring networks, the difference between frame formats requires the conversion of frames. A bridge that performs this conversion is referred to as a *translating bridge*.

As previously noted in Chapter 4, there are several types of Ethernet frames, such as Ethernet, IEEE 802.3, Novell's Ethernet-802.3, and Ethernet-SNAP. The latter two frames represent variations of the physical IEEE 802.3 frame format. Ethernet and Ethernet-802.3 do not use logical link control, while IEEE 802.3 CSMA/CD LANs specify the use of IEEE 802.2 logical link control. In comparison, all IEEE 802.5 Token-Ring networks either directly or indirectly use the IEEE 802.2 specification for logical link control.

The conversion from IEEE 802.3 to IEEE 802.5 can be accomplished by discarding portions of the IEEE 802.3 frame not applicable to a Token-Ring frame, copying the 802.2 LLC protocol data unit (PDU) from one frame to another, and inserting fields applicable to the Token-Ring frame. Figure 6.9 illustrates the conversion process performed by a translating bridge linking an IEEE 802.3 network to an IEEE 802.5 network. Note that fields unique to the IEEE 802.3 frame are discarded, while fields common to both frames are copied. Fields unique to the IEEE 802.5 frame are inserted by the bridge.

Since an Ethernet frame, as well as Novell's Ethernet-802.3 frame, does not support logical link control, the conversion process to IEEE 802.5 requires more

IEEE 802.3

Legend:

DA	= Destination Address
SA	= Source Address
AC	= Access Control
FC	= Frame Control
RIF	= Routing Information Field
DSAP	= Destination Service Access Point
SSAP	= Source Service Access Point
ED	= End Delimiter
FS	= Frame Status Field

Figure 6.9   IEEE 802.3 to 802.5 frame conversion.

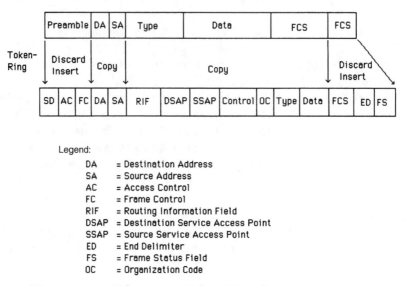

Legend:

DA	= Destination Address
SA	= Source Address
AC	= Access Control
FC	= Frame Control
RIF	= Routing Information Field
DSAP	= Destination Service Access Point
SSAP	= Source Service Access Point
ED	= End Delimiter
FS	= Frame Status Field
OC	= Organization Code

Figure 6.10   Ethernet to Token-Ring frame conversion.

processing. In addition, each conversion is more specific and may or may not be supported by a specific translating bridge. For example, consider the conversion of Ethernet frames to Token-Ring frames. Since Ethernet does not support LLC PDUs, the translation process results in the generation of a Token-Ring-SNAP frame. This conversion or translation process is illustrated in Figure 6.10.

6.2 Network Utilization

In this section, we will examine the use of bridges to interconnect separate local area networks and to subdivide networks to improve performance. In addition, we will focus our attention on how we can increase network availability by employing bridges to provide alternate communications paths between networks.

Serial and Sequential Bridging

The top of Figure 6.11 illustrates the basic use of a bridge to interconnect two networks serially. Suppose that monitoring of each network indicates a high level of intranetwork use. One possible configuration to reduce intra-LAN traffic on each network can be obtained by moving some stations off each of the two existing networks to form a third network. The three networks would then be interconnected through the use of an additional bridge, as illustrated in the middle portion of Figure 6.11. This extension results in *sequential* or *cascaded bridging,* and is appropriate when intra-LAN traffic is necessary but minimal. This internet topology is also extremely useful when the length of an Ethernet must be extended beyond the physical cabling of a single network. By locating servers appropriately within each network segment, you may be able to minimize inter-LAN transmission. For example, the first network segment could be used to connect marketing personnel, while the second and third segments could be used to connect engineering and personnel depart-

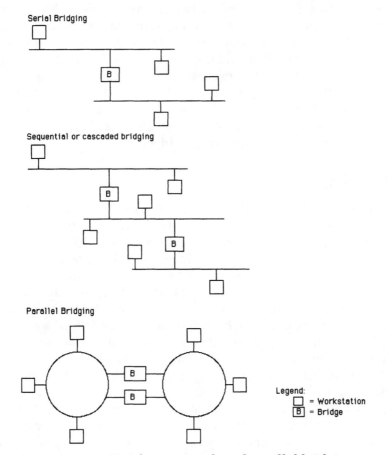

Figure 6.11   Serial, sequential, and parallel bridging.

ments. This might minimize the use of a server on one network by persons connected to another network segment.

A word of caution is in order concerning the use of bridges. Bridging forms what is referred to as a *flat* network topology, because it makes its forwarding decisions using layer 2 MAC addresses, which cannot distinguish one network from another. This means that broadcast traffic generated on one segment will be bridged onto other segments which, depending upon the amount of broadcast traffic, can adversely affect the performance on other segments.

The only way to reduce broadcast traffic between segments is to use a filtering feature included with some bridges or install routers to link segments. Concerning the latter, routers operate at the network layer and forward packets explicitly addressed to a different network. Through the use of network addresses for forwarding decisions, routers form hierarchical structured networks, eliminating the so-called broadcast storm effect that occurs when broadcast traffic generated from different types of servers on different segments are automatically forwarded by bridges onto other segments.

Both serial and sequential bridging are applicable to transparent, source routing, and source routing transparent bridges that do not provide redundancy nor the ability to balance traffic flowing between networks. Each of these deficiencies can be alleviated through the use of parallel bridging. However, this bridging technique creates a loop and is only applicable to source routing and source routing transparent bridges.

Parallel Bridging

The lower portion of Figure 6.11 illustrates the use of parallel bridges to interconnect two Token-Ring networks. This bridging configuration permits one bridge to back up the other, providing a level of redundancy for linking the two networks as well as a significant increase in the availability of one network to communicate with another. For example, assume the availability of each bridge used at the top of Figure 6.11 (serial bridging) and bottom of Figure 6.11 (parallel bridging) is 90 percent. The availability through two serially connected bridges would be 0.9×0.9 (unavailability of bridge 1 × unavailability of bridge 2), or 81 percent. In comparison, the availability through parallel bridges would be $1-(0.1 \times 0.1)$, which is 99 percent.

The dual paths between networks also improve inter-LAN communications performance, because communications between stations on each network can be load balanced. The use of parallel bridges can thus be expected to provide a higher level of inter-LAN communications than the use of serial or sequential bridges. However, as previously noted, this topology is not supported by transparent bridging.

Star Bridging

With a multiport bridge, you can connect three or more networks to form a star internet topology. The top portion of Figure 6.12 shows the use of one bridge to form a star topology by interconnecting four separate networks. This topology, or a variation on this topology, could be used to interconnect networks on separate floors within a building. For example, the top network could be on floor N + 1, while the bottom network could be on floor N − 1 in a building. The bridge and the two networks to the left and right of the bridge might then be located on floor N.

Although star bridging permits several networks located on separate floors within a building to be interconnected, all internet data must flow through

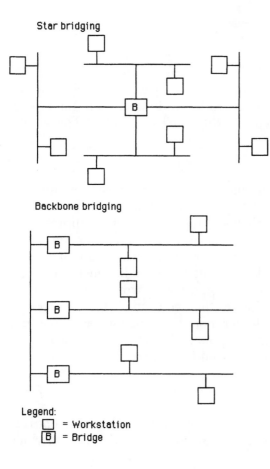

Figure 6.12 Star and backbone bridging.

one bridge. This can result in both performance and reliability constraints to traffic flow. Thus, to internet separate networks on more than a few floors in a building, you should consider using backbone bridging.

Backbone Bridging

The lower portion of Figure 6.12 illustrates the use of backbone bridging. In this example, one network runs vertically through a building with Ethernet *ribs* extending from the backbone onto each floor. Depending upon the amount of internet traffic and the vertical length required for the backbone network, the backbone can be either a conventional Ethernet bus-based network or a fiber-optic backbone. For the latter, you might consider using a 100-Mbps FDDI network that could serve as a *super highway* to transport data among many individual Ethernet networks installed on separate floors within a building.

6.3 Performance Issues

The key to obtaining an appropriate level of performance when interconnecting networks is planning. The actual planning process will depend upon several factors, such as whether separate networks are in operation, the type of networks to be connected, and the type of bridges to be used—local or remote.

Traffic Flow

If separate networks are in operation and you have appropriate monitoring equipment, you can determine the traffic flow on each of the networks to be interconnected. Once this is accomplished, you can expect an approximate 10- to 20-percent increase in network traffic. This additional traffic represents the flow of information between networks after an interconnection links previously separated local area networks. Although this traffic increase represents an average encountered by the author, your network traffic may not represent the typical average. To explore further, you can examine the potential for internet communications in the form of electronic messages that may be transmitted to users on other networks, potential file transfers of word processing files, and other types of data that would flow between networks.

Network Types

The types of networks to be connected will govern the rate at which frames are presented to bridges. This rate, in turn, will govern the filtering rate at which bridges should operate so that they do not become bottlenecks on a network. For example, the maximum number of frames per second will vary between different types of Ethernet and Token-Ring networks, as well as between different types of the same network. The operating rate of a bridge may thus be appropriate for connecting some networks while inappropriate for connecting other types of networks.

Type of Bridge

Last but not least, the type of bridge—local or remote—will have a considerable bearing upon performance issues. Local bridges pass data between networks at their operating rates. In comparison, remote bridges pass data between networks using wide area network transmission facilities, which typically provide a transmission rate that is only a fraction of a local area network operating rate. Now that we have discussed some of the aspects governing bridge and internet performance using bridges, let's probe deeper by estimating network traffic.

Estimating Network Traffic

If we do not have access to monitoring equipment to analyze an existing network, or if we are planning to install a new network, we can spend some time developing a reasonable estimate of network traffic. To do so, we should attempt to classify stations into groups based on the type of general activity performed, and then estimate the network activity for one station per group. This will enable us to multiply the number of stations in the group by the station activity to determine the group network traffic. Adding up the activity of all groups will then provide us with an estimate of the traffic activity for the network.

As an example of local area network traffic estimation, let us assume that our network will support 20 engineers, 5 managers, and 3 secretaries. Table 6.1 shows how we would estimate the network traffic in terms of the bit rate for each station group and the total activity per group, and then sum up the network traffic for the three groups that will use the network. In this example, which for the sake of simplicity does not include the transmission of data to a workstation printer, the total network traffic was estimated to be slightly below 50,000 bps.

To plan for the interconnection of two or more networks through the use of bridges, our next step should be to perform a similar traffic analysis for each of the remaining networks. After this is accomplished, we can use the network traffic to estimate inter-LAN traffic, using 10 to 20 percent of total intranet-

TABLE 6.1 Estimating Network Traffic

Activity	Message Size (Bytes)	Frequency	Bit Rate*
Engineering workstations			
Request program	1,500	1/hour	4
Load program	480,000	1/hour	1,067
Save files	120,000	2/hour	533
Send/receive e-mail	2,000	2/hour	9
Total engineering activity			
= 1,613 × 20 = 32,260 bps			1,613
Managerial workstations			
Request program	1,500	2/hour	7
Load program	320,000	2/hour	1,422
Save files	30,000	2/hour	134
Send/receive e-mail	3,000	4/hour	27
Total managerial activity			
= 1,590 × 5 = 7,950 bps			1,590
Secretarial workstations			
Request program	1,500	4/hour	14
Load program	640,000	2/hour	2,844
Save files	12,000	8/hour	214
Send/receive e-mail	3,000	6/hour	40
Total secretarial activity			
= 3,112 × 3 = 9,336 bps			3,112
Total estimated network activity			
= 49,546 bps			

*Note: Bit rate is computed by multiplying message rate by frequency by 8 bits/byte and dividing by 3,600 seconds/hour.

work traffic as an estimate of the internet traffic that will result from the connection of separate networks.

Internet Traffic

To illustrate the traffic estimation process for the interconnection of separate LANs, let us assume that network A's traffic was determined to be 50,000 bps, while network B's traffic was estimated to be approximately 100,000 bps. Figure 6.13 illustrates the flow of data between networks connected by a local bridge. Note that the data flow in each direction is expressed as a range, based on the use of an industry average of 10 to 20 percent of network traffic routed between interconnected networks.

Network Types

Our next area of concern is to examine the types of networks to be interconnected. In doing so, we should focus our attention on the operating rate of each LAN. If network A's traffic was estimated to be approximately 50,000 bps, then the addition of 10,000 to 20,000 bps from network B onto network A will raise network A's traffic level to between 60,000 and 70,000 bps. Similarly, the addition of traffic from network A onto network B will raise network B's traffic level to between 105,000 and 110,000 bps. In this example, the resulting traffic on each network is well below the operating rate of all types of local area networks, and will not present a capacity problem for either network.

Bridge Type

As previously mentioned, local bridges transmit data between networks at the data rate of the destination network. This means that a local bridge will have a lower probability of being an internet bottleneck than a remote bridge, since the latter provides a connection between networks using a wide area transmission facility, which typically operates at a fraction of the operating rate of a LAN.

In examining the bridge operating rate required to connect networks, we will use a bottom-up and a top-down approach. That is, we will first determine the operating rate in frames per second for the specific example previously discussed. This will be followed by computing the maximum frame rate supported by an Ethernet network.

For the bridge illustrated in Figure 6.13, we previously computed that its maximum transfer rate would be 20,000 bps from network B onto network A. This is equivalent to 2500 bytes per second. If we assume that data is transported in 512-byte frames, this would be equivalent to 6 frames per second—a minimal transfer rate supported by every bridge manufacturer. However, when remote bridges are used, the frame forwarding rate of the bridge will more than likely be constrained by the operating rate of the wide area network transmission facility.

Bridge Operational Considerations

A remote bridge wraps a LAN frame into a higher-level protocol packet for transmission over a wide area network communications facility. This operation requires the addition of a header, protocol control, error detection, and trailer fields, and results in a degree of overhead. A 20,000-bps data flow from

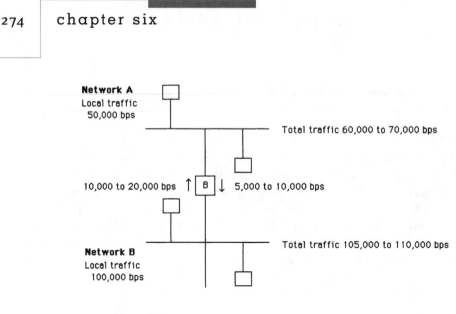

Figure 6.13 Considering internet data flow. To determine the traffic flow on separate networks after they are interconnected, you must consider the flow of data onto each network from the other network.

network B to network A, therefore, could not be accommodated by a transmission facility operating at that data rate.

In converting LAN traffic onto a wide area network transmission facility, you can expect a protocol overhead of approximately 20 percent. Thus, your actual operating rate must be at least 24,000 bps before the wide area network communications link becomes a bottleneck and degrades internet communication. Now that we have examined the bridging performance requirements for two relatively small networks, let us focus our attention on determining the maximum frame rates of an Ethernet network. This will provide us with the ability to determine the rate at which the frame processing rate of a bridge becomes irrelevant, since any processing rate above the maximum network rate will not be useful. In addition, we can use the maximum network frame rate when estimating traffic, because if we approach that rate, network performance will begin to degrade significantly when use exceeds between 60 to 70 percent of that rate.

Ethernet Traffic Estimation

An Ethernet frame can vary between a minimum of 72 bytes and a maximum of 1526 bytes. Thus, the maximum frame rate on an Ethernet will vary with the frame size.

Ethernet operations require a dead time between frames of 9.6 μsec. The bit time for a 10-Mbps Ethernet is $1/10^7$ or 100 nsec. Based upon the preceding, we can compute the maximum number of frames/second for 1526-byte frames. Here, the time per frame becomes:

$$9.6 \text{ μsec} + 1526 \text{ bytes} \times 8 \text{ bits/byte}$$

or
$$9.6 \text{ μsec} + 12,208 \text{ bits} \times 100 \text{ nsec/bit}$$

or
$$1.23 \text{ msec}$$

Thus, in one second there can be a maximum of 1/1.23 msec or 812 maximum-size frames. For a minimum frame size of 72 bytes, the time per frame is:

$$9.6 \text{ μsec} + 72 \text{ bytes} \times 8 \text{ bits/byte} \times 100 \text{ nsec/bit}$$

or
$$67.2 \times 10^{-6} \text{ sec.}$$

Thus, in one second there can be a maximum of $1/67.2 \times 10^{-6}$ or 14,880 minimum-size 72-byte frames. Since 100BASE-T Fast Ethernet uses the same frame composition as Ethernet, the maximum frame rate for maximum- and minimum-length frames are ten times that of Ethernet. That is, Fast Ethernet supports a maximum of 8120 maximum-size 1526-byte frames per second and a maximum of 148,800 minimum-size 72-byte frames per second. Similarly, Gigabit Ethernet uses the same frame composition as Ethernet but is 100 times faster. This means that Gigabit Ethernet is capable of supporting a maximum of 81,200 maximum-length 1526-byte frames per second and a maximum of 1,488,000 minimum-length 72-byte frames per second. Table 6.2 summarizes the frame processing requirements for a 10-Mbps Ethernet, Fast Ethernet, and Gigabit Ethernet under 50 percent and 100 percent load conditions, based on minimum and maximum frame lengths. Note that those frame processing requirements define the frame examination (filtering) operating rate of a bridge connected to different types of Ethernet networks. That rate indicates the number of frames per second a bridge connected to different types of Ethernet local area networks must be capable of examining under heavy (50-percent load) and full (100-percent load) traffic conditions.

In examining the different Ethernet network frame processing requirements indicated in Table 6.2, it is important to note that the frame processing requirements associated with Fast Ethernet and Gigabit Ethernet commonly preclude the ability to upgrade a bridge by simply changing its adapter cards. Due to the much greater frame processing requirements associated with Fast Ethernet and Gigabit Ethernet, bridges are commonly designed to support those technologies from the ground up to include adapters and a central processor to support the additional frame processing associated with their higher operating rate.

TABLE 6.2   Ethernet Frame Processing Requirements
(Frames per Second)

Average Frame Size (Bytes)	Frame Processing Requirements	
	50% Load	100% Load
Ethernet		
1526	406	812
72	7440	14,880
Fast Ethernet		
1526	4050	8120
72	74,400	148,800
Gigabit Ethernet		
1526	40,600	81,200
72	744,000	1,488,000

We can extend our analysis of Ethernet frames by considering the frame rate supported by different link speeds. For example, let us consider a pair of remote bridges connected by a 9.6-Kbps line. The time per frame for a 72-byte frame at 9.6 Kbps is:

$$9.6 \times 10^{-6} + 72 \times 8 \times 0.0001041 \text{ s/bit} \quad \text{or} \quad 0.0599712 \text{ seconds per frame}$$

Thus, in one second the number of frames is 1/.0599712, or 16.67 frames per second. Table 6.3 compares the frame-per-second rate supported by different link speeds for minimum- and maximum-size Ethernet frames. As expected, the frame transmission rate supported by a 10-Mbps link for minimum- and maximum-size frames is exactly the same as the frame processing requirements under 100 percent loading for a 10-Mbps Ethernet LAN, as indicated in Table 6.2.

In examining Table 6.3, note that the entries in this table do not consider the effect of the overhead of a protocol used to transport frames between two networks. You should therefore decrease the frame-per-second rate by approximately 20 percent for all link speeds through 1.536 Mbps. The reason the 10-Mbps rate should not be adjusted is that it represents a local 10-Mbps Ethernet bridge connection that does not require the use of a wide area network protocol to transport frames. Also note that the link speed of 1.536 Mbps represents a T1 transmission facility that operates at 1.544 Mbps. However, since the framing bits on a T1 circuit use 8 Kbps, the effective line speed available for the transmission of data is 1.536 Mbps.

TABLE 6.3 Link Speed versus Frame Rate

	Frames per Second	
Link Speed	Minimum	Maximum
9.6 Kbps	16.67	0.79
19.2 Kbps	33.38	1.58
56.0 Kbps	97.44	4.60
64.0 Kbps	111.17	5.25
1.536 Mbps	2815.31	136.34
10.0 Mbps	14,880.00	812.00

Predicting Throughput

Until now, we have assumed that the operating rate of each LAN linked by a bridge is the same. However, in many organizations this may not be true, because LANs are implemented at different times using different technologies. Thus, accounting may be using a 10-Mbps LAN, while the personnel department might be using a 100-Mbps LAN.

Suppose we wanted to interconnect the two LANs via the use of a multimedia bridge. To predict throughput between LANs, let us use the network configuration illustrated in Figure 6.14. Here, the operating rate of LAN A is assumed to be R_1 bps, while the operating rate of LAN B is assumed to be R_2 bps.

In one second, R_1 bits can be transferred on LAN A and R_2 bits can be transferred on LAN B. Similarly, it takes $1/R_1$ seconds to transfer one bit on LAN A and $1/R_2$ seconds to transfer one bit on LAN B. So, to transfer one bit across the bridge from LAN A to LAN B, ignoring the transfer time at the bridge:

$$\frac{1}{R_T} = \frac{1}{R_1} + \frac{1}{R_2}$$

or

$$R_T = \frac{1}{(1/R_1) + (1/R_2)}$$

We computed that a 10-Mbps Ethernet would support a maximum transfer of 812 maximum-sized frames per second. If we assume that the second LAN operating at 100 Mbps is also an Ethernet, we would compute its transfer rate to be approximately 8120 maximum-sized frames per second. The throughput in frames per second would then become:

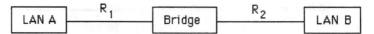

Figure 6.14 Linking LANs with different operating rates. When LANs with different operating rates (R_1 and R_2) are connected via a bridge, access of files across the bridge may result in an unacceptable level of performance.

$$R_T = \frac{1}{(1/812) + (1/8120)} = 738 \text{ frames per second}$$

Knowing the transfer rate between LANs can help us answer many common questions. It can also provide us with a mechanism for determining whether we should alter the location of application programs on different servers. For example, suppose that a program located on a server on LAN B suddenly became popular for use by workstations on LAN A. If the program required 1024 K of storage, we could estimate the minimum transfer time required to load that program and, depending on the results of our calculation, we might want to move the program onto a server on LAN A. For this example, the data transfer rate would be 738 frames/second × 1500 bytes/frame or 1,107,000 bytes per second. Dividing the data to be transferred by the data transfer rate, we obtain:

$$\frac{1024 \text{ Kbytes} \times 1024 \text{ bytes/K}}{1,107,000 \text{ bytes/seconds}} = .95 \text{ seconds}$$

The preceding computation represents a best-case scenario, in which the use of each network is limited to the user on LAN A loading a program from a server on LAN B. In reality, the average number of users using the resources of each network must be used to adjust the values of R_1 and R_2. For example, suppose that through monitoring you determined that the average number of active users on LAN A was 5 and on LAN B was 10. In that case, you would adjust the value of R_1 by dividing 812 by 5 to obtain 162.4 and adjust the value of R_2 by dividing 8120 by 10 to obtain 812. You would then use the new values of R_1 and R_2 to obtain the average value of R_T, based on the fact that the program loading operation would be performed concurrently with other operations on each network. Thus, you would compute R_T as follows:

$$R_T = \frac{1}{(1/162.5) + (1/812)} = 135.4 \text{ frames per second}$$

Once you compute the average frame transfer rate, you would divide that value into the quantity of data to be transferred to obtain the average expected transfer time. For our adjusted computation, in which there was an average of five users on LAN A, and ten on LAN B, we now obtain:

$$\frac{1024 \text{ Kbytes} \times 1024 \text{ bytes/K}}{135.4 \text{ frames/sec} \times 1500 \text{ bytes/frame}} = 5.16 \text{ seconds}$$

Note that for the preceding example the time required to transfer a 1024 K-byte file increases from 0.95 to 5.16 seconds when you consider the effect of other users on each network.

chapter seven

Routers

In Chapter 5, we examined the basic operation and use of a variety of local area networking components, including routers. Information presented in that chapter will serve as a foundation for the more detailed discussion of the operation and use of routers presented in this chapter.

7.1 Router Operation

By operating at the ISO Reference Model network layer, a router becomes capable of making intelligent decisions concerning the flow of information in a network. To accomplish this, routers perform a variety of functions that are significantly different from those performed by bridges. Unlike bridges, routers are addressable. Routers examine frames that are directly addressed to them by looking at the network address within each frame to make their forwarding decisions.

IP Support Overview

The most popular network layer protocol supported by routers is the Internet Protocol (IP), whose packet format was described in Chapter 5. Each IP network has a distinct network address, and each interface on the network has a unique host address that represents the host portion of a 32-bit address. Since the IP address occurs at the network layer while frames that move data on a LAN use MAC addresses associated with the data link layer, a translation process is required to enable IP-compatible devices to use the transport services of a local area network. Thus, any discussion of how routers support IP requires an overview of the manner by which hosts use the services of a router.

When a host has a packet to transmit, it will first determine if the destination IP address is on the local network or a distant network, with the latter requiring the services of a router. To accomplish this, the host will use the subnet mask bits set in its configuration to determine if the destination is on the local network. For example, assume the subnet mask is 255.255.255.128. This means the mask extends the network portion of an IP address to 11111111.11111111.11111111.1, or 25 bit positions, resulting in 7 (32–25) bit positions being available for the host address. This also means you can have two subnets, with subnet 0 containing host addresses 0 to 127 and subnet 1 having host addresses 128 to 255, with the subnet defined by the value of the 25th bit position in the IP address.

If we assume the base network IP address is 193.56.45.0, then the base network, two subnets, and the subnet mask are as follows:

```
Base network:   11000001.00111000.00101101.00000000 = 193.56.45.0
Subnet 0:       11000001.00111000.00101101.00000000 = 193.56.45.0
Subnet 1:       11000001.00111000.00101101.10000000 = 193.56.45.128
Subnet mask:    11111111.11111111.11111111.10000000 = 193.56.45.128
```

Now suppose a host with the IP address 193.56.45.21 needs to send a packet to the host whose address is 193.56.45.131. By using the subnet mask, the transmitting host notes that the destination, while on the same network, is on a different subnet. Thus, the transmitting host will require the use of a router in the same manner as if the destination host was on a completely separate network.

Figure 7.1 illustrates the internal and external network view of the subnetted network. Note that from locations exterior to the network, routers forward packets to the router connecting the two subnets as if no subnetting existed. The corporate router is configured via the use of subnet masks to differentiate hosts on one subnet from those on the other subnet. From an interior view, packets originating on one subnet must use the resources of the router to reach hosts on the other subnet as well as hosts on other networks.

Once the transmitting host notes that the destination IP address is either on a different network or different subnet, it must use the services of a router. Although each host will be configured with the IP address of the router, the host will transport packets via the data link layer, which requires knowledge of the 48-bit MAC address of the router port connected to the segment the transmitting host resides on.

The translation between IP and MAC addresses is accomplished by the use of the Address Resolution Protocol (ARP). To obtain the MAC address of the

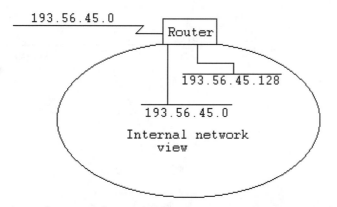

Figure 7.1 Using subnet masks to subdivide a common IP network address.

router's LAN interface the host will broadcast an ARP request. This request will be received by all stations on the segment, with the router recognizing its IP address and responding by transmitting an ARP response.

Because a continuous use of ARP would rapidly consume network bandwidth, hosts normally maintain the results of ARP requests in cache memory. Thus, once the relationship between an IP address and MAC address is learned, subsequent requests to transmit additional packets to the same destination can be accomplished by the host checking its cache memory.

When packets arrive at the router destined for a host on one of the subnets, a similar process occurs. That is, the router must obtain the MAC addresses associated with the IP address to enable the packet to be transported by data link layer frames to its appropriate destination. Thus, in addition to being able to correctly support the transmission of packets from one interface to another, an IP-compatible router must also support the ARP protocol. Later in this chapter we will discuss and describe additional protocols routers can support.

Basic Operation and Use of Routing Tables

To see the basic operation of routers, consider the simple mesh structure formed by the use of three routers labeled R1, R2, and R3 in Figure 7.2A. In this illustration, three Ethernet networks are interconnected through the use of three routers.

The initial construction of three routing tables is shown in Figure 7.2B. Unlike bridges, which learn MAC addresses, most routers are initially config-

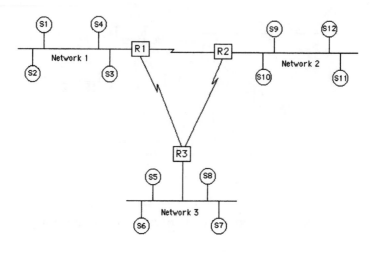

A. Simple mesh structure

B. Routing tables

C. Packet composition

Legend: [R]=Router (S)=Network station

Figure 7.2 Basic router operation.

ured, and routing tables are established at the time of equipment installation. Thereafter, periodic communication between routers updates routing tables to take into consideration any changes in internet topology and traffic.

In examining Figure 7.2B, note that the routing table for router R1 indicates which routers it must communicate with to access each interconnected Ethernet network. Router R1 would communicate with router R2 to reach Token-Ring network 2, and with router R3 to reach Token-Ring network 3.

Figure 7.2C illustrates the composition of a packet originated by station S2 on Ethernet 1 that is to be transmitted to station S12 on Ethernet 2. Router R1 first examines the destination network address and notes that it is on another network. The router searches its routing table and finds that the frame should be transmitted to router R2 to reach Ethernet network 2. Router R1 forwards the frame to router R2. Router R2 then places the frame onto Ethernet network 2 for delivery to station S12 on that network.

Since routers use the network addresses instead of MAC addresses for making their forwarding decisions, it is possible to have duplicate locally administered MAC addresses on each network interconnected by a router. The use of bridges, on the other hand, requires you to review and then eliminate any duplicate locally administered addresses. This process can be time-consuming when large networks are connected.

Another difference between bridges and routers is that a router can support the transmission of data on multiple paths between local area networks. Although a multiport bridge with a filtering capability can perform intelligent routing decisions, the result of a bridge operation is normally valid for only one point-to-point link within a wide area network. In comparison, a router may be able to acquire information about the status of a large number of paths and select an end-to-end path consisting of a series of point-to-point links. In addition, most routers can fragment and reassemble data. This permits packets to flow over different paths and to be reassembled at their final destination. With this capability, a router can route each packet to its destination over the best possible path at a particular instant in time, and change paths dynamically to correspond to changes in network link status on traffic activity.

For example, each of the routing tables illustrated in Figure 7.2B can be expanded to indicate a secondary path to each network. While router R1 would continue to use the entry of R2 as its primary mechanism to reach network 2, a secondary entry of R3 could be established to provide an alternative path to network 2 via routers R3 and R2, rather than directly via router R2.

Networking Capability

For an illustration of the networking capability of routers, see Figure 7.3. It shows three geographically dispersed locations that have a total of four Ethernet and three Token-Ring networks, interconnected through the use of four routers and four wide area network transmission circuits or links. For simplicity, modems and DSUs on the wide area network are not shown. This figure will be referred to several times in this chapter to illustrate different types of router operations.

In addition to supporting a mesh structure that is not obtainable from the use of transparent bridges, routers offer other advantages in the form of

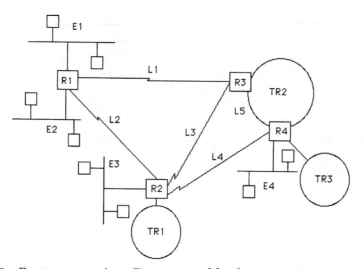

Figure 7.3 Router operation. Routers enable the transmission of data over multiple paths, alternate path routing, and the use of a mesh topology that transparent bridges cannot support.

addressing, message processing, link utilization, and priority of service. A router is known to stations that use its service. Packets can thus be addressed directly to a router. This eliminates the necessity for the device to examine in detail every packet flowing on a network, and results in the router having to process only messages that are addressed to it by other devices.

Assume that a station on E1 transmits to a station on TR3. Depending on the status and traffic on network links, packets could be routed via L1 and use TR2 to provide a transport mechanism to R4, from which the packets are delivered to TR3. Alternatively, links L2 and L4 could be used to provide a path from R1 to R4. Although link availability and link traffic usually determine routing, routers can support prioritized traffic, and may store low-priority traffic for a small period of time to allow higher-priority traffic to gain access to the wide area transmission facility. Because of these features, which are essentially unavailable with bridges, the router is a more complex and more expensive device.

7.2 Communication, Transport, and Routing Protocols

For routers to be able to operate in a network, they must normally be able to speak the same language at both the data link and network layers. The key to accomplishing this is the ability to support common communication, transport, and routing protocols.

Communication Protocol

Communication protocols support the transfer of data from a station on one network to a station on another network; they occur at the OSI network layer. In examining Figure 7.4, which illustrates several common protocol implementations with respect to the OSI Reference Model, you will note that Novell's NetWare uses IPX as its network communications protocol, while IBM LANs use the PC LAN Support Program, and Microsoft's LAN Manager uses the Internet Protocol (IP). Also note that when a TCP/IP stack is used, certain applications are transported by TCP while others are transported using UDP; however, both TCP and UDP obtain their routing via the use of IP. This means that a router linking networks based on Novell, IBM, and Microsoft LAN operating systems must support those three communication protocols.

OSI Layer	Common Protocol Implementation				
Application	Application Programs			TCP/IP Applications	
	Application Protocols				
Presentation	Novell Network File Server Protocol (NFSP)	IBM Server Message Block (SMB)	Microsoft LAN Manager		
Session	Xerox Networking System (XNS)	NetBIOS	NetBIOS Advanced Peer-to-Peer Communications		
Transport	Sequenced Packet Exchange (SPX)	PC LAN Support Program	Transmission Control Protocol (TCP) Transport Protocol Class 4 (TCP4)	TCP	UDP
Network	Internetwork Packet Exchange (IPX)		Internet Protocol (IP)	Internet Protocol (IP)	
Data Link	Logical Link Control 802.2				
	Media Access Control				
Physical	Transmission Media: Twisted pair, coax, fiber optic				

(NetBIOS appears vertically spanning the Session and Transport rows between the Novell/Xerox column and the IBM column.)

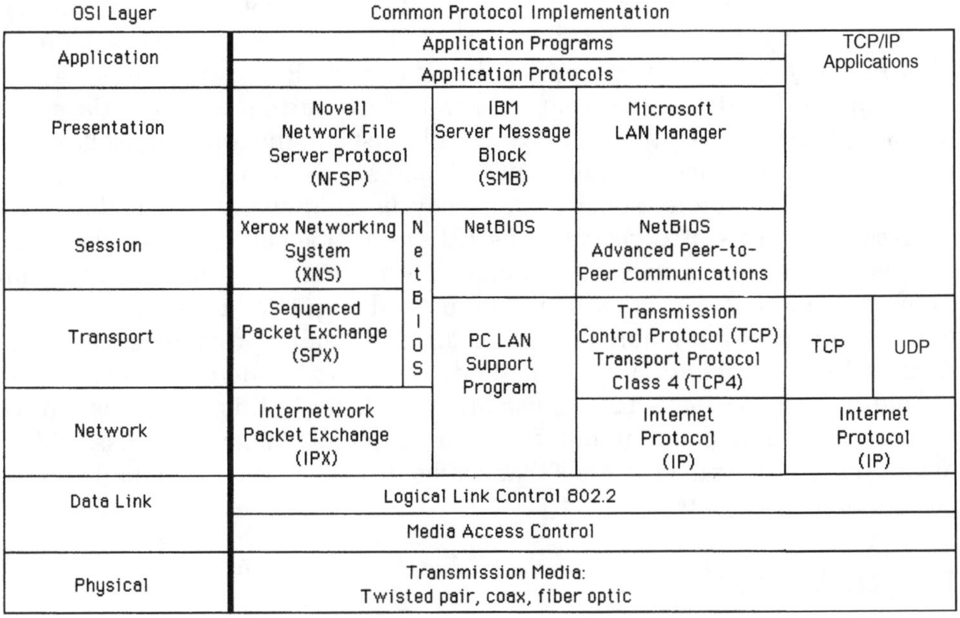

Figure 7.4 Common protocol implementations. Although Novell, IBM, and Microsoft LAN operating system software support standardized physical and data link operations, they differ considerably in their use of communication and routing protocols.

Thus, router communication protocol support is a very important criterion in determining whether a particular product is capable of supporting your networking requirements.

Routing Protocol

The routing protocol is the method used by routers to exchange routing information; it forms the basis for providing a connection across an internet. In evaluating routers, it is important to determine the efficiency of the routing protocol, its effect upon the transmission of information, the method used and memory required to construct routing tables, and the time required to adjust those tables. Examples of router-to-router protocols include Xerox Network Systems' (XNS) Routing Information Protocol (RIP), TCP/IP's RIP, Open Shortest Path First (OSPF), and Hello routing protocols.

Handling Nonroutable Protocols

Although many mainframe users consider IBM's System Network Architecture (SNA) as a router protocol, in actuality it is nonroutable in the traditional sense of having network addresses. This means that for a router to support SNA or another nonroutable protocol, such as NetBIOS, the router cannot compare a destination network address against the current network address as there are no network addresses to work with. Instead, the router must be capable of performing one or more special operations to handle nonroutable protocols. For example, some routers may be configurable such that SNA addresses in terms of physical units (PUs) and logical units (LUs) can be associated with pseudonetwork numbers, enabling the router to route an unroutable protocol. Another common method employed by some routers is to incorporate a nonroutable protocol within a routable protocol, a technique referred to as *tunneling*. A third method, and one considered by many to be the old reliable mechanism, is to use bridging. Later in this chapter when we cover protocol-independent routers and in Chapter 9 when we discuss SNA in detail, we will describe methods that can be used to route nonroutable protocols, to include SNA traffic.

Transport Protocol

The transport protocol guarantees the delivery of information between two points. Here, the transport protocol represents the fourth layer illustrated in Figure 7.4. Examples of transport protocols include SPX, TCP, UDP, X.25, and Frame Relay.

There is a wide variety of communication and transport protocols in use today. Some of these protocols, such as Apple Computer's AppleTalk, were designed specifically to operate on local area networks. Other protocols, such as X.25 and Frame Relay, were developed as wide area network protocols.

Sixteen popular communication and transport protocols are listed below. Many routers support only a subset of these protocols.

- AppleTalk
- Apple Domain
- Banyan VINES
- CHAOSnet
- DECnet Phase IV
- DECnet Phase V
- DDN X.25
- Frame Relay
- ISO CLNS
- HDLC
- Novell IPX
- SDLC
- TCP/IP
- Xerox XNS
- X.25
- Ungermann-Bass Net/One

7.3 Router Classifications

Depending upon their support of communication and transport protocols, routers can be classified into two groups: protocol-dependent and protocol-independent.

Protocol-Dependent Routers

To understand the characteristics of a protocol-dependent router, consider the internet illustrated in Figure 7.3. If a station on network E1 wishes to transmit data to a second station on network E3, router R1 must know that the second station resides on network E3, and it must know the best path to use to reach that network. The method used to determine the destination station's network also determines the protocol dependency of the router.

If the station on network E1 tells router R1 the destination location, it must supply a network address in every LAN packet it transmits. This means that all routers in the internet must support the protocol used on network E1. Otherwise, stations on network E1 could not communicate with stations residing on other networks, and vice versa.

NetWare IPX Example

To illustrate the operation of a protocol-dependent router, let us assume that networks E1 and E3 use Novell's NetWare as their LAN operating system. The routing protocol used at the network layer between a station and server on a Novell network is known as IPX. This protocol can also be used between servers.

Under NetWare's IPX, a packet addressed to a router will contain the destination address in the form of network and host addresses, and the origination address in the form of the source network and source host addresses. Here, the IPX term *host* is actually the physical address of a network adapter card.

Figure 7.5a illustrates in simplified format the IPX packet composition for workstation A on network E1, transmitting data to workstation B on network E3, under Novell's NetWare IPX protocol.

After router R1 receives and examines the packet, it notes that the destination address E3 requires the routing of the packet to router R2. It converts the

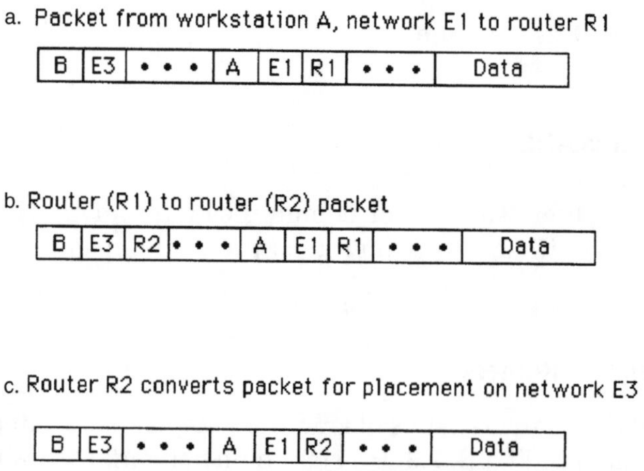

a. Packet from workstation A, network E1 to router R1

| B | E3 | • • • | A | E1 | R1 | • • • | Data |

b. Router (R1) to router (R2) packet

| B | E3 | R2 | • • • | A | E1 | R1 | • • • | Data |

c. Router R2 converts packet for placement on network E3

| B | E3 | • • • | A | E1 | R2 | • • • | Data |

Figure 7.5　NetWare IPX routing.

first packet into a router (R1) to router (R2) packet, as illustrated in Figure 7.5b. At router R2, the packet is again examined. Router R2 notes that the destination network address (E3) is connected to that router, so it reconverts the packet for delivery onto network E3. It does this by converting the destination router address to a source router address and transmitting the packet onto network E3. This is illustrated in Figure 7.5c.

Addressing Differences

In the preceding example, note that each router uses the destination workstation and network addresses to transfer packets. If all protocols used the same format and addressing structure, routers would be protocol-insensitive at the network layer. Unfortunately, this is not true. For example, TCP/IP addressing conventions are very different from those used by NetWare. This means that networks using different operating systems require the use of multiprotocol routers configured to perform address translation. Each multiprotocol router must maintain separate routing tables for each supported protocol, requiring additional memory and time.

Other Problems

Two additional problems associated with protocol-dependent routers are the time required for packet examination and the fact that not all LAN protocols are routable. If a packet must traverse a large network, the time required by a series of routers to modify the packet and assure its delivery to the next router can significantly degrade router performance. To overcome this problem, organizations should consider the use of a frame relay service.

In addition to providing an enhanced data delivery service by eliminating error detection and correction within the network, the use of a frame relay service can significantly reduce the cost of routers. Consider, for example, the network in Figure 7.3, in which four routers are interconnected through the use of five links. To support transmission on five links, the routers require ten ports. Normally, each router port is obtained as an adapter card installed in a high-performance computer. If a frame relay service is used, the packet network providing that service also provides the routing paths to interconnect routers, as illustrated in Figure 7.6. This reduces the number of required router ports to four. This reduction can result in a considerable hardware savings.

A second problem associated with protocol-dependent routers is the fact that some LAN protocols cannot be routed using that type of device. This is because some LAN protocols, such as NetBIOS and IBM's LAN Server—and unlike NetWare, DECnet, and TCP/IP—do not include routing information within a

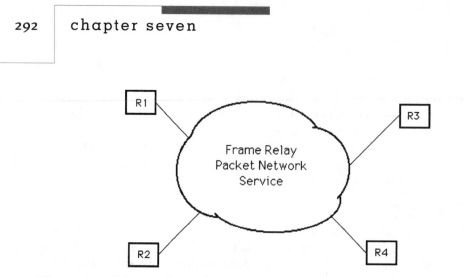

Figure 7.6 Using a frame relay service. If a frame relay service is used, the packet network provides the capability for interconnecting each network access port to other network access ports. Thus, only one router port is required to obtain an interconnection capability to numerous routers connected to the network.

packet. Instead, those protocols employ a user-friendly device-naming convention instead of using network and device addresses. This convention permits such names as "Gil's PC" and "Accounting Printer" to be used. For example, IBM's NetBIOS was designed to facilitate program-to-program communication by hiding the complexities of network addressing from the user. Thus, NetBIOS uses names up to 16 alphanumeric characters long to define clients and servers on a network. Unfortunately, NetBIOS does not include a facility to distinguish one network from another, since it lacks a network addressing capability. Such protocols are restricted to using the physical addresses of adapter cards, such as Token-Ring source and destination addresses. Since a protocol-dependent router must know the network on which a destination address is located, it cannot in a conventional sense route such protocols. A logical question, then, is how a router interconnects networks using an IBM LAN protocol or a similar nonroutable protocol. The answer to this question will depend upon the method used by the router manufacturer to support nonroutable protocols. As previously discussed, such methods can include bridging, tunneling, or the configuration of a router that enables pseudonetwork addresses to be assigned to each device.

Protocol-Independent Routers

A protocol-independent router functions as a sophisticated transparent bridge. That is, it addresses the problem of network protocols that do not have network addresses. It does this by examining the source addresses on connected networks to learn automatically what devices are on each network. The protocol-independent router assigns network identifiers to each network whose operating system does not include network addresses in its network protocol. This activity enables both routable and nonroutable protocols to be serviced by a protocol-dependent router.

In addition to building address tables automatically like a transparent bridge, a protocol-independent router exchanges information concerning its routing directions with other internet routers. This enables each router to build a map of the interconnected networks. The method used to build the network map falls under the category of a link state routing protocol, which is described later in this chapter.

Advantages

There are two key advantages to using protocol-independent routers. Those advantages are the abilities of routers to learn network topology automatically and to service nonroutable protocols. The ability to learn network topology automatically can considerably simplify the administration of an internet. For example, in a TCP/IP network, each workstation has an IP address and must know the IP addresses of other LAN devices it wants to communicate with.

IP addresses are commonly assigned by a network administrator, and they must be changed if a station is moved to a different network, or if a network is segmented because of a high level of traffic or other reason. In such situations, LAN users must be notified about the new IP address, or they will not be able to locate the moved station. Obviously, the movement of stations within a building between different LANs could become a considerable administrative burden. The ability of a protocol-independent router to learn addresses automatically removes the administrative burden of notifying users of changes in network addresses.

An exception to the preceding occurs through the use of the Dynamic Host Configuration Protocol (DHCP). Through the use of a DHCP server and appropriate client software, stations are dynamically assigned IP addresses for a relatively short period of time. Once they complete an application the server can reassign the address to a new station. Although the use of the DHCP can ease the administrative burden of configuring and reconfiguring IP workstations, it requires the use of a server and client software. Thus, there continues to be no free lunch in networking.

The ability to route nonroutable protocols can be of considerable assistance in integrating IBM SNAs into an enterprise network. Otherwise, without the use of protocol-independent routers, organizations may have to maintain separate transmission facilities for SNA and LAN traffic.

Supporting SNA Traffic

Figure 7.7 illustrates an example of the use of protocol-independent routers to support both inter-LAN and SNA traffic. In this example, an IBM SNA network, a 3174 control unit with a Token-Ring adapter (TRA) at a remote site provides communications connectivity to an IBM 3745 communications controller at a central site. Routers must be capable of routing both SNA and LAN traffic to enable the use of a common transmission facility between the central and remote site.

Methods to Consider

There are essentially three methods by which SNA and LAN traffic can be combined for routing over a common network: encapsulation, conversion, and protocol-independent routing. Under the encapsulation method, SNA packets are modified so that another protocol's header, addressing, and trailer fields surround each SNA packet. For example, a TCP/IP protocol–dependent router would encapsulate SNA into TCP/IP packets for routing through a TCP/IP network. Since a TCP/IP packet has over 60 bytes of overhead, and the average SNA packet is 30 bytes in length, encapsulation can reduce performance considerably when transmission occurs over low-speed WAN links. A second disadvantage of encapsulation is that it requires the existence of a corporate network using the encapsulation protocol. Otherwise, you would have to build this network to obtain an encapsulation capability.

The second method used for integrating SNA traffic with LAN traffic occurs through the use of protocol conversion. This technique eliminates the need

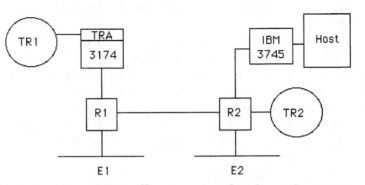

Figure 7.7 Supporting SNA traffic. A protocol-independent router can support SNA traffic and other LAN traffic over a common transmission facility.

for adding network headers and enhances the efficiency of the protocol integration efforts.

The third method by which an SNA network can be integrated with LAN traffic is through protocol-independent routing. Protocol-independent routers assign a LAN device address to each SNA control unit and communications controller. Then, SNA packets are prefixed with source and destination addresses to permit their routing through the internet. At the destination router, the addressing information is removed, and the SNA packets are delivered to their destination in their original form. Since the addition of source and destination addresses adds a significantly lower number of bytes than an encapsulation process, overhead is reduced. This, in turn, enables you to consider using lower-speed circuits to interconnect locations. Readers are referred to Chapter 8 for additional information concerning the use of gateways to integrate SNA and other protocols into a common network infrastructure.

Another advantage of protocol-independent routing over encapsulation relates directly to the operation of SNA networks. Although such networks are discussed in detail in Chapter 8, several SNA operational characteristics now warrant attention. They will help us appreciate the advantages of protocol-independent routing, and they will explain the rationale for such routers' requiring a traffic priority mechanism to support SNA traffic efficiently.

Need for Priority Mechanism

In its original incarnation, SNA represents a hierarchically structured network, as shown in Figure 7.8. Here, the communications controller communicates with control units, which in turn communicate with attached terminal devices. The communications controller periodically polls each control unit, and the control unit periodically polls each terminal device. If there is no data to transmit in response to a poll, each polled device indicates this fact to the higher-level device by responding negatively to the poll. Thus, the communications controller expects to receive a response to each poll it generates. In fact, if it does not receive a response within a predefined period of time (typically less than five seconds), the communications controller will assume that the control unit has malfunctioned, terminate any active sessions to devices attached to the control unit, and then attempt to reestablish communications by sending an initialization message to the control unit.

When SNA and LAN traffic is integrated into a common router-based network, the operation of routers can adversely affect SNA traffic because of the time delays associated with routing and encapsulation. For example, routers may alter the path used to transmit data, depending on internet traffic and cir-

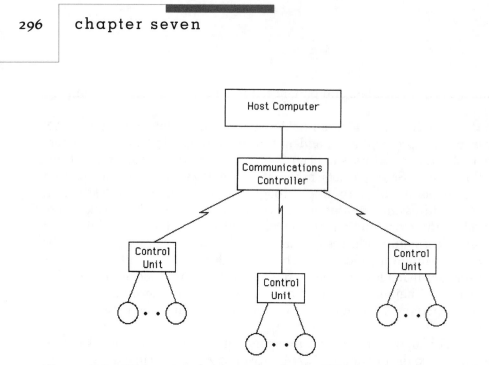

Figure 7.8 SNA network hierarchy. In an SNA network, communications controllers poll control units, which in turn poll attached devices.

cuit availability. If path switching makes the SNA traffic exceed its timeout threshold, the communications controller will terminate sessions and reinitialize control units that fail to respond to its poll within the predefined time period. Similarly, delays caused by encapsulation can also result in unintended timeouts.

To prevent unintended timeouts caused by path switching, some vendors have added a traffic priority mechanism to their protocol-independent routing capability. This priority mechanism enables users to assign a higher priority to SNA traffic than to LAN traffic, thus enabling SNA data to be forwarded across wide area networks ahead of other inter-LAN traffic. This can considerably reduce or even eliminate the potential for LAN traffic to obstruct the flow of SNA data; it may also result in unintended timeouts, inadvertently causing session terminations.

7.4 Routing Protocols

The routing protocol is the key element to transferring information across an internet in an orderly manner. The protocol is responsible for developing paths between routers, using a predefined mechanism.

Types of Routing Protocols

There are two types of routing protocols: interior and exterior domain. Here, we use the term *domain* to refer to the connection of a group of networks to form a common entity, such as a corporate or university enterprise network.

Interior Domain Routing Protocols

An *interior domain routing protocol* is used to control the flow of information within a series of separate networks that are interconnected to form an internet. Thus, interior domain routing protocols provide a mechanism for the flow of information within a domain and are also known as *intradomain* routing protocols. Such protocols create routing tables for each autonomous system within the domain, using such metrics as the hop count or time delay to develop routes from one network to another within the domain. Examples of interior domain routing protocols include RIP, OSPF, and Hello.

Exterior Domain Routing Protocols

Exterior domain routing protocols are used to connect separate domains together. Thus, they are also referred to as *interdomain* routing protocols. Currently, interdomain routing protocols are defined only for OSI and TCP/IP. Example of interdomain routing protocols include the Exterior Gateway Protocol (EGP), the Border Gateway Protocol (BGP), and the Inter-Domain Routing Protocol (IDRP). Unlike interior domain routing protocols, which are focused on the construction of routing tables for data flow within a domain, interdomain routing protocols specify the method by which routers exchange information concerning what networks they can reach on each domain.

Figure 7.9 illustrates the use of interior and exterior domain routing protocols. In this example, OSPF is the intradomain protocol used in Domain A, while RIP is the intradomain protocol used in Domain B. Routers in Domains A and B use the interdomain routing protocols EGP and/or BGP to determine what networks on other domains they can reach.

Exterior Gateway Protocol

There are four basic functions performed by the Exterior Gateway Protocol. First, the EGP performs an acquisition function, which enables a router in one domain to request information exchange with a router on another domain. Since routers also serve as gateways to the domain, they are sometimes referred to as *gateways*. A second function performed by the router gateway is to test periodically whether its EGP neighbors are responding. The third and

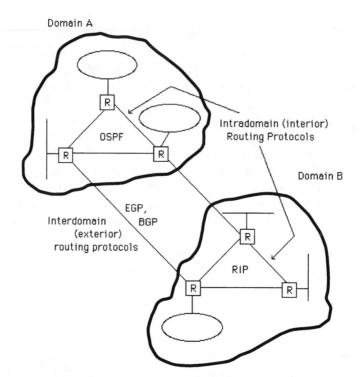

Figure 7.9 Interior and exterior routing protocols. An interior routing protocol controls the flow of information within a collection of interconnected networks known as a *domain*. An exterior routing protocol provides routers with the ability to determine what networks on other domains they can reach.

most important function performed by the EGP is to enable router gateways to exchange information concerning the networks in each domain by transmitting routing update messages. The fourth function involves terminating an established neighbor relationship between gateways on two domains.

To accomplish its basic functions, EGP defines nine message types. Figure 7.10 illustrates EGP message types associated with each of the three basic features performed by the protocol.

Under the EGP, once a neighbor is acquired, Hello messages must be transmitted at a minimum of 30-second intervals. In addition, routing updates must be exchanged at a minimum of two-minute intervals. This exchange of information at two-minute intervals can result in the use of a considerable amount of the bandwidth linking domains when the number of networks on each domain is large, or when the circuits linking domains consist of low-

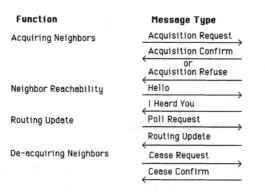

Function	Message Type
Acquiring Neighbors	Acquisition Request →
	← Acquisition Confirm or Acquisition Refuse ←
Neighbor Reachability	Hello →
	← I Heard You
Routing Update	Poll Request →
	← Routing Update
De-acquiring Neighbors	Cease Request →
	← Cease Confirm

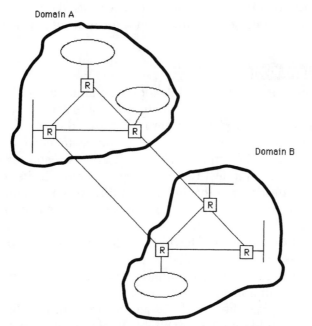

Figure 7.10   Exterior gateway protocol message types.

speed lines. The Border Gateway Protocol was developed to alleviate those potential problems.

Border Gateway Protocol

The Border Gateway Protocol represents a follow-on to the EGP. Unlike the EGP, in which all network information is exchanged at two-minute or shorter intervals, the BGP transmits incremental updates as changes occur. This can significantly reduce the quantity of data exchanged between router gateways, thus freeing up a considerable amount of circuit bandwidth for the transmission of data. Both the EGP and the BGP run over TCP/IP and are standardized by Internet documents RFC904 and RFC1105, respectively.

Types of Interior Domain Routing Protocols

As previously discussed, interior domain routing protocols govern the flow of information between networks. This is the type of routing protocol that is of primary interest to most organizations. Interior domain routing protocols can be further subdivided into two broad categories, based on the method they use for building and updating the contents of their routing tables: vector distance and link state.

Vector Distance Protocol

A vector distance protocol constructs a routing table in each router, and periodically broadcasts the contents of the routing table across the internet. When the routing table is received at another router, that device examines the set of reported network destinations and the distance to each destination. The receiving router then determines whether it knows a shorter route to a network destination, finds a destination it does not have in its routing table, or finds a route to a destination through the sending router where the distance to the destination changed. If any one of these situations occurs, the receiving router will change its routing tables.

The term *vector distance* relates to the information transmitted by routers. Each router message contains a list of pairs, known as vector and distance. The *vector* identifies a network destination, while the *distance* is the distance in hops from the router to that destination.

Figure 7.11 illustrates the initial distance vector routing table for the routers R1 and R2 shown in Figure 7.3. Each table contains an entry for each directly connected network and is broadcast periodically throughout the internet. The distance column indicates the distance in hops to each network from the router.

At the same time router R1 is constructing its initial distance vector table, other routers are performing a similar operation. The lower portion of Figure 7.11 illustrates the composition of the initial distance vector table for router R2. As previously mentioned, under a distance vector protocol, the contents of each router's routing table are periodically broadcast. When routers R1 and R2 broadcast their initial distance vector routing tables, each router uses the

a. Router R1

Destination	Distance
E1	0
E2	0

b. Router R2

Destination	Distance
E3	0
TR1	0

Figure 7.11 Initial distance vector routing tables.

received routing table to update its initial routing table. Figure 7.12 illustrates the result of this initial routing table update process for routers R1 and R2.

As additional routing tables are exchanged, the routing table in each router will converge with respect to the internet topology. However, to ensure that each router knows the state of all links, routing tables are periodically broadcast by each router. Although this process has a minimal effect upon small networks, its use with large networks can significantly reduce available bandwidth for actual data transfer. This is because the transmission of lengthy router tables will require additional transmission time in which data cannot flow between routers.

Popular vector distance routing protocols include the TCP/IP Routing Information Protocol (RIP), the AppleTalk Routing Table Management Protocol (RTMP), and Cisco's Interior Gateway Routing Protocol (IGRP).

a. Router R1

Destination	Distance	Route
E1	0	direct
E2	0	direct
E3	1	R2
TR1	1	R2

b. Router R2

Destination	Distance	Route
E1	1	R1
E2	1	R1
E3	0	direct
TR1	0	direct

Figure 7.12 Initial routing table update.

Routing Information Protocol

Under RIP, participants are either active or passive. *Active* participants are normally routers that transmit their routing tables, while *passive* machines listen and update their routing tables based upon information supplied by other devices. Normally, host computers are passive participants, while routers are active participants.

Operation

Under RIP, an active router broadcasts its routing table every 30 seconds. Each routing table entry contains a network address and the hop count to the network. To illustrate an example of the operation of RIP, let's redraw the network previously shown in Figure 7.2 in terms of its links and nodes, replacing the four routers by the letters A, B, C, and D for simplicity of illustration. Figure 7.13 contains the revised network consisting of four nodes and five links.

When the routers are powered up they only have knowledge of their local conditions. Thus, each routing table would contain a single entry. For example, the table of router n would have the following value:

From n to	Link	Hop Count
n	local	0

For the router represented by node A, its table would then become:

From A to	Link	Hop Count
A	local	0

Thirty seconds after being turned on, node A will broadcast its distance vector (A = 0) to all its neighbors, which, in Figure 7.13 are nodes B and C. Node

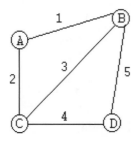

Figure 7.13 Redrawing the network in Figure 7.2 in terms of its links and nodes.

B receives on link 1 the assistance vector A = 0. Upon receipt of this message, it updates its routing table as follows, adding one to the hop count associated with the distance vector supplied by node 1:

From B to	Link	Hop Count
B	Local	0
A	1	1

Node B can now prepare its own distance vector (B = 0, A = 1) and transmit that information on its connections (links 1, 3, and 5).

During the preceding period node C would have received the initial distance vector transmission from node A. Thus, node C would have updated its routing table as follows:

From C to	Link	Hop Count
C	Local	0
A	2	1

Once it updates its routing table, node C will then transmit its distance vector (C = 0, A = 1) on links 2, 3, and 4.

Assuming the distance vector from node B is now received at nodes A and C, each will update their routing tables. Thus, their routing tables would appear as follows:

From A to	Link	Hop Count
A	Local	0
B	1	1

From C to	Link	Hop Count
C	Local	0
A	2	1
B	3	1

At node D, its initial state is first modified when it receives the distance vector (B = 0, A = 1) from node B. Since D received that information on link 5, it updates its routing table as follows, adding one to each received hop count:

From D to	Link	Hop Count
D	Local	0
B	5	1
A	5	2

Now, let's assume node D receives the update of node C's recent update (C = 0, A = 1, B = 1) on link 4. As it does not have an entry for node C, it will add it to its routing table by entering C = 1 for link 4. When it adds 1 to the hop count for A received on link 4, it notes that the value is equal to the current hop count for A in its routing table. Thus, it discards the information about node A received from node C. The exception to this would be if the router maintained alternate routing entries to use in the event of a link failure. Next, node D would operate upon the vector B = 1 received on link 4, adding one to the hop count to obtain B = 2. Since that is more hops than the current entry, it would discard the received distance vector. Thus, D's routing table would appear as follows:

From D to	Link	Hop Count
D	Local	0
C	4	1
B	5	1
A	5	2

The preceding example provides a general indication of how RIP enables nodes to learn the topology of a network. In addition, if a link should fail, the condition can be easily compensated for as similar to bridge table entries, those of routers are also time stamped and the periodic transmission of distance vector information would result in a new route replacing the previously computed one.

One key limitation of RIP is the maximum hop distance it supports. This distance is 16 hops, which means that an alternative protocol must be used for large networks.

Routing Table Maintenance Protocol

The Routing Table Maintenance Protocol (RTMP) was developed by Apple Computer for use with that vendor's AppleTalk network. Under RTMP, each router transmits messages to establish routing tables and update them periodically. The update process, during which information on an internet is exchanged between routers, also serves as a mechanism for implementing alternate routing. This is because the absence of update information for a greater than expected period of time converts the status of an entry in other router routing tables from "good" to "suspect" and then to "bad."

RTMP is delivered by AppleTalk's Data Delivery Protocol (DDP), which is a network layer connectionless service operating between two upper-layer processes referred to as *sockets*. Four types of packets are specified by RTMP: data, request, route data request, and response. Routing updates are transmitted as data packets. End nodes transmit request packets to acquire information about the identity of the internet routers (IRs) to which they can transmit nonlocal packets. Internet routers respond to route request packets with response packets, while end nodes that want to receive an RTMP data packet indicate this by sending a route data request packet. The latter packet type is also used by nodes that require routing information from IRs not directly connected to their network.

Routing Process

In the AppleTalk routing process, the source node first examines the destination network number. If the packet has a local network address, it is passed to the data link layer for delivery. Otherwise, the packet is passed to any of the IRs that reside on a network segment. The IR will examine the destination address of the packet and then check its routing tables to determine the next hop, routing the packet on a specific port that enables it to flow toward the next hop. Thus, a packet will travel through the internet on a hop-by-hop basis. When the packet reaches an IR connected to the destination network, the data link layer is used to deliver the packet to its local destination.

Figure 7.14 illustrates a sample AppleTalk network and the routing table for one router. Each AppleTalk routing table has five entries, as indicated. The *network range* defines the range of network numbers assigned to a particular network segment. The *distance* entry specifies the number of routers that must be traversed prior to the destination being reached, and *port* defines the router port used to provide access to a destination location. The *next IR* entry indicates the identifier of the next IR on the internet, and *entry state* defines the status of receiving routing updates. An entry state can go from "good" to "suspect" to "bad" if routing updates are not received within predefined time intervals.

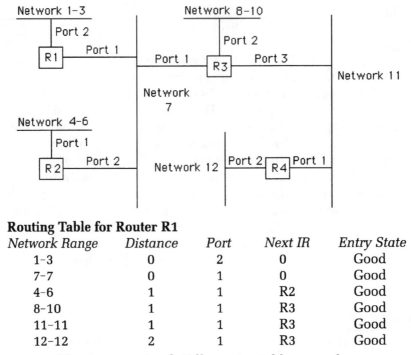

Routing Table for Router R1

Network Range	Distance	Port	Next IR	Entry State
1–3	0	2	0	Good
7–7	0	1	0	Good
4–6	1	1	R2	Good
8–10	1	1	R3	Good
11–11	1	1	R3	Good
12–12	2	1	R3	Good

Figure 7.14 AppleTalk routing table example.

Interior Gateway Routing Protocol

Cisco's proprietary Interior Gateway Routing Protocol is a distance vector protocol in which updates are transmitted at 90-second intervals. Each IGRP gateway operates on a local basis to determine the best route for forwarding data packets. Unlike protocols that require each router to have a complete routing table, each IGRP router computes only a portion of the routing table, based on its perspective of the internet. This enables the IGRP to support distributed routing without requiring each router to have a complete view of the internet.

Other features of the IGRP include the ability to establish routes automatically, perform load balancing dynamically over redundant links, and detect and remove bad circuits from the internet routing tables it develops. Routes are declared inaccessible if an update is not received within three update periods (270 seconds). After five update periods (450 seconds), the route is removed from the routing table.

Link State Protocols

A link state routing protocol addresses the traffic problem associated with any large networks that use a vector distance routing protocol. It does this by transmitting routing information only when there is a change in one of its links. A second difference between vector difference and link state protocols concerns the manner in which a route is selected when multiple routes are available between destinations. For a vector distance protocol, the best path is the one that has the fewest intermediate routers on hops between destinations. A link state protocol, however, can use multiple paths to provide traffic balancing between locations. In addition, a link state protocol permits routing to occur based on link delay, capacity, and reliability. This provides the network manager with the ability to specify a variety of route development situations.

SPF Algorithms

Link state routing protocols are implemented by a class of algorithms known as Shortest Path First (SPF). Unfortunately, this is a misnomer, since routing is not based on the shortest path.

The use of SPF algorithms requires each participating router to have complete knowledge of the internet topology. Each router participating in an SPF algorithm then performs two tasks: status testing of neighboring routers and periodic transmission of link status information to other routers.

To test neighboring routers, a short message is periodically transmitted. If the neighbor replies, the link is considered to be up. Otherwise, the absence of a reply after a predefined period of time indicates that the link is down.

To provide link status information, each router will periodically broadcast a message indicating the status of each of its links. Unlike the vector distance protocol, in which routes are specified, an SPF link status message simply indicates whether communications are possible between pairs of routers. Using information in the link status message, routers are able to update their network maps.

Unlike vector distance protocols, in which tables are required to be exchanged, link state protocols such as SPF algorithms exchange a much lower volume of information in the form of link status queries and replies. Then, SPF participating routers simply broadcast the status of each of their links, and other routers use this information to update their internet maps. This routing technique permits each router to compute routes independently of other routers, and eliminates the potential for the table flooding that can occur when a vector state protocol is used to interconnect a large number of networks.

Destination	Distance	Route	Status
E1	0	direct	up
E2	0	direct	up
E3	1	R2	up
E3	2	R3,R2	up
E3	3	R3,R4,R2	up
E4	2	R2,R4	up
E4	2	R3,R4	up
E4	3	R3,R2,R4	up
TR1	1	R2	up
TR1	2	R3,R2	up
TR1	3	R3,R4,R2	up
TR2	1	R3	up
TR2	2	R2,R3	up
TR2	2	R2,R4	up
TR3	2	R3,R4	up
TR3	2	R2,R4	up
TR3	3	R3,R2,R4	up

Figure 7.15   Router R1 initial network map.

To illustrate the operation of a link state routing protocol, let us return to the internet configuration previously illustrated in Figure 7.14. Figure 7.15 indicates the initial network map for router R1. This map lists the destination of all networks on the internet from router R1, with their distances and routes. Note that if multiple routes exist to a destination, each route is listed. This defines a complete network topology, and allows alternate routes to be selected if link status information indicates that one or more routes cannot be used.

Let us suppose that at a particular point in time, the link status messages generated by the routers in the internet are as indicated in Figure 7.16. Note that both routers R2 and R3 have determined that link L3 is down. Using this information, router R1 would then update the status column for its network map. Since link L3 is down, all routes that require a data flow between R2 and R3 would have their status changed to "down." For example, for destination E3 via route R3, R2 would have its status changed to "down." Since the minimum distance to E3 is 1 hop via router R2, the failure of link L3 would not affect data flow from router R1 to network E3. Now consider the effect of link L2 becoming inoperative. This would affect route R2, which has the minimum distance to network E3. It would still leave route R3 = R4 = R2, although this

R1 link status

Link	Status
L1	Up
L2	Up

R2 link status

Link	Status
L2	Up
L3	Down
L4	Up

R3 link status

Link	Status
L1	Up
L3	Down

R4 link status

Link	Status
L4	Up
L5	Up

Figure 7.16   Link status messages.

route would have a distance of three hops. Of course, when a new link status message indicates that a previously declared down link is up, each router's network map is updated accordingly.

Examples of link state protocols include Open Shortest Path First (OSPF), OSI Intermediate System to Intermediate System (IS-IS), DECnet Phase V, and IBM's Advanced Peer-to-Peer Networking (APPN). Due to space limitations, we will review briefly the operational features of only the first of these link state protocols.

Open Shortest Path First Protocol

The OSPF protocol is an interior domain routing protocol that uses the SPF algorithm. Like the EGP, the OSPF protocol consists of a small core of different types of messages. Under the OSPF protocol, five message types are defined.

A Hello message is used to test the reachability of other devices. A database description message passes the topology. The remaining message types include a link status request, a link status update, and a link status acknowledgement message.

Initially, OSPF generates database description messages to initialize its network topology database. These messages are flooded through the domain. However, once a topological database is formed, routing table updates are transmitted at 30-minute intervals unless there is a change in the network, in which case there is an immediate update.

Like the EGP, OSPF routers use a Hello message to discover their neighbors. One of the key features of the OSPF protocol is its ability to authenticate messages. This means that you can't entice routers to transmit packets to a specific computer for examination or interception by generating low-cost routes. Another key feature of the OSPF protocol is its ability to support multiple active paths of equal weight: it selects each path in a round-robin manner. Table 7.1 provides a summary of 16 common routing protocol abbreviations, their meanings, and a short description of each protocol.

7.5 Filtering

The filtering capability of routers is primarily thought of as a mechanism to implement security. Although filtering does indeed provide a mechanism to implement network security, it also provides a mechanism to regulate network traffic. Through the regulation of network traffic you may be able to predefine routes for particular types of packets, protocols, and addresses, as well as different combinations of the preceding.

The filtering capability of routers is highly dependent upon the functionality of a router as well as the ingenuity of the router manager or administrator. To illustrate the latter, we will define a few generic router filtering functions to illustrate how those functions can be applied to achieve a variety of filtering results that could satisfy different organizational requirements. Although the router filtering functions we will define are not applicable to a specific router, most routers will support the functions we will cover. Thus, the filtering examples presented in this section represent practical examples that illustrate how you can control network traffic.

The key to the functionality of a router's filtering capability is the router's ability to *look* inside the composition of packets. Most routers, at a minimum, provide filtering based upon the examination of the contents of the destination and source addresses transported by a packet. Other routers provide a filtering capability based upon the Ethernet protocol value carried in the type/length field, and the DSAP and SSAP values carried in the data field. This additional capability provides you with the ability, for example, to enable or disable Novell IPX traffic between certain router ports, enable or dis-

TABLE 7.1 Common Routing Protocols

AURP	AppleTalk Update Routing Protocol. This routing protocol is implemented in Apple networks and sends changes to routing tables via updates.
BGP	Border Gateway Protocol. This is a TCP/IP interdomain routing protocol.
CLNP	Connectionless Network Protocol. This is the OSI version of the IP routing protocol.
DDP	Datagram Delivery Protocol. This routing protocol is used in Apple's AppleTalk network.
EGP	Exterior Gateway Protocol. This TCP/IP protocol is used to locate networks on another domain.
IDRP	Inter-Domain Routing Protocol. This is the OSI interdomain routing protocol.
IGP	Interior Gateway Protocol. This TCP/IP protocol is used by routers to move information within a domain.
IGRP	Interior Gateway Routing Protocol. This is a proprietary routing protocol developed by Cisco Systems.
IP	Internet Protocol. This is the network layer protocol of the TCP/IP (Transmission Control Protocol/Internet Protocol) suite of protocols.
IPX	Internet Packet Exchange. This routing protocol is based on Xerox's XNS, was developed by Novell, and is implemented in Novell's NetWare.
IS-IS	Intermediate-Station-to-Intermediate-Station. This is an OSI link-state routing protocol that routes both OSI and RIP traffic.
NCP	NetWare Core Protocol. This is Novell's NetWare specific routing protocol.
OSPF	Open Shortest Path First. This is a TCP/IP link-state routing protocol that provides an alternative to RIP.
RIP	Routing Information Protocol. This routing protocol is used in TCP/IP, XNS, and IPX. Under RIP, a message is broadcast to find the shortest route to a destination based on a hop count.
RTMP	Routing Table Maintenance Protocol. This is Apple's distance-vector protocol.
SPF	Shortest Path First. This link-state routing protocol uses a set of user-defined parameters to find the best route between two points.

able TCP/IP traffic between the same or different router ports, and regulate other protocols that may be carried to and from an Ethernet LAN.

Another common filtering capability associated with routers that support the TCP/IP protocol stack is the ability to filter based upon TCP and UDP well-known ports. For example, by blocking outbound packets with a TCP port address of 80 an organization could bar HTTP traffic, in effect prohibiting employees from surfing the World Wide Web.

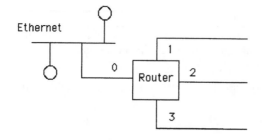

Figure 7.17 Through filtering you can implement security as well as regulate network traffic.

Figure 7.17 illustrates the connection of an Ethernet network to a four-port router. In this example, ports 1, 2, and 3 can represent connections to other routers via wide area network transmission facilities or to other LANs a short distance away. Since we are primarily interested in how we can use filtering as a mechanism to regulate traffic, it is more important to focus upon the flow of data between router ports than the devices connected to each hub. However, since we need a point of reference, we will discuss traffic routed to and from the Ethernet network connected to port 0 in Figure 7.17.

Filtering Expressions

Most routers perform filtering based upon specified patterns linked by logical operators. Thus, you would first specify one or more patterns to be filtered, and then link multiple patterns or prefix a single pattern with an appropriate logical operator. Before actually creating a filter pattern, it is important to note how the manufacturer of the router implements filtering. Some vendors enable everything, requiring you to preclude certain data flows by filtering. Other vendors inhibit everything, only permitting data flow based upon positive filters. For our examples, we will presume the manufacturer of our router permits or enables all data flow unless it is specifically precluded.

Filtering Examples

For our first example, let's assume you have a UNIX server connected to the Ethernet LAN and do not want IP traffic from port 2 to flow to the server. Assuming P1 (pattern 1) = IP, originating port is PORT2, and destination port is PORT0, you would set up the filter as follows:

Originate	Destination
P1 AND PORT2	PORT0

Thus, any IP frames received on port 2 and destined for port 0 would be filtered or blocked.

Now let's assume you do not want to transfer Ethernet broadcast packets beyond that network. To do so you would set the pattern (P1) to recognize a destination address of FF-FF-FF-FF-FF-FF, which is the Ethernet broadcast address. Then, you would set up the filter as follows:

Originate	Destination
P1 AND PORT0	PORT1 OR PORT2 OR PORT3

For another example, let's assume router filtering patterns and ports support the use of the logical NOT operator. Then, you could set up the filter for the preceding example as follows:

Originate	Destination
P1 AND PORT0	NOT PORT0

Router Access Lists

To illustrate the use of filtering for protecting stations on an internal corporate network from potential hackers lurking on the Internet, consider Figure 7.18. In that illustration several workstations and a server are shown connected to an Ethernet LAN, which in turn is shown connected via a router to an ISP, which in turn is connected to the Internet. Assuming the corporate Ethernet is assigned the IP network address 206.172.31.0, let's assume the workstations and server have host addresses of .2, .3, and .4, as indicated in the lower portion of Figure 7.18.

Many routers use what are referred to as access lists to enable filtering operations on an inbound and outbound basis. To illustrate the potential use of an access list, let's assume we are using that list with the TCP/IP protocol and each list entry has the following format:

Operation direction from IP address/port to IP address/port

Here "operation" is either *enable* or *disable,* while "direction" is either *inbound* or *outbound.*

Let's further assume that you can use the global asterisk character (*) to reference *all.* Then, assuming you want to restrict inbound traffic to the server to Telnet operations from any IP address, you would code the following access list entry:

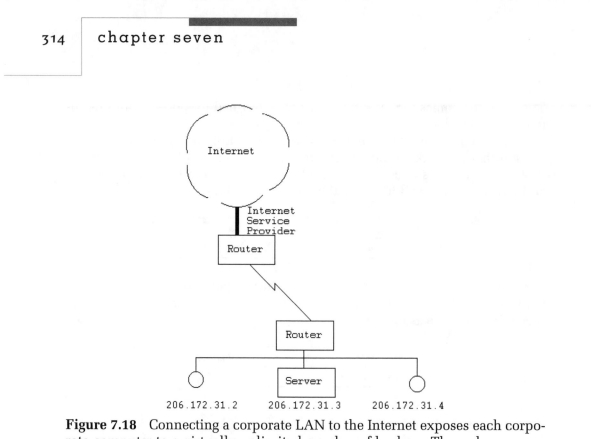

Figure 7.18 Connecting a corporate LAN to the Internet exposes each corporate computer to a virtually unlimited number of hackers. Through programming router access lists this exposure can be minimized.

ENABLE INBOUND */23 206.172.31.3/23

The preceding entry allows Telnet (port 23) from any IP address to the server running Telnet at address 206.172.31.3 to its Telnet port. The reason a port address is required at the destination results from the fact that both workstations and servers can support multiple simultaneous TCP/IP applications. For example, a Web server can also support FTP as well as ping, finger, and other TCP/IP applications.

For a second example of the use of an access list, let's assume you wish to bar all employees on your local LAN from sending Internet mail. Since SMTP uses port 25, your access list entry would appear as follows:

DISABLE OUTBOUND 206.172.31*/25 */25

In this example we used the global character (*) to replace the last digit in the 206 network dotted decimal position, in effect barring all stations (1 to 254) on the network from sending data on port 25 to any IP address.

Although the preceding examples illustrate but a fraction of router filtering capability, they illustrate several important concepts. First, by filtering on source and/or destination addresses and protocols, it becomes possible to enable or disable traffic. Secondly, by reaching into the frame router, filtering permits you to enable or disable the flow of specific protocols. The latter is an important consideration when connecting a LAN to the Internet, since many organizations do not wish to provide access to their computer systems connected to the LAN by anyone that has Internet access.

By carefully using the filtering capability of a router, you can construct a *firewall* to protect your LAN from unwanted access. Although many trade publications rightly refer to a firewall as a stand-alone computer system located between an organization's LAN and router, in actuality the filtering capability of a router may be sufficient to perform firewall functions. The key difference between a firewall and a router's access list filtering capability is in the areas of encryption, IP address hiding, and authentication. A firewall may support those additional functions as well as perform filtering based upon IP addresses and TCP and UDP ports. In comparison, a router's security capability is limited to its filtering capability.

7.6 Performance Considerations

Regardless of the type of router and its protocol support and routing algorithm, the processing required for its operation is considerably more than that required for a bridge. This means that you can expect the packet processing capability of routers to be considerably less than that of bridges.

High-capacity bridges marketed during 1998 can be expected to provide a forwarding rate between 100,000 and 200,000 packets per second. In comparison, most routers have a forwarding capacity rated under 100,000 packets per second. Although this may appear to indicate a poor level of performance in comparison to bridges, note that only when functioning as a local bridge will a high-capacity bridge actually use its full capacity. Otherwise, when used to interconnect remote networks via a wide area transmission facility, a remote bridge will be able to use only a fraction of its packet-processing capability for the forwarding of packets over a relatively slow-speed WAN transmission facility. Similarly, when routers are connected to a T1 or E1 line or to a frame relay service, they may not be able to use their full packet forwarding capability. To see this, refer to Table 7.2, which indicates the maximum packets-per-second transfer capability of a router connected to five types of transmission lines, based on five packet sizes. Note that a T1 line operating at 1.544 Mbps

TABLE 7.2 Maximum Packet Transfer Rates (Packets per Second)

Packet Size (bytes)	Wide Area Network Transmission Facility				
	56 Kbps	128 Kbps	256 Kbps	512 Kbps	1.544 Mbps
64	109	250	500	1000	3015
128	54	125	250	500	1508
500	14	32	64	128	386
1000	7	16	32	64	193
1518	5	10	20	40	127

supports a maximum transfer of 3015 64-byte packets per second. In actuality, since the wide area network transmission facility results in the use of a WAN protocol to wrap LAN packets, the actual PPS rate obtainable is normally 15 to 20 percent less than that indicated in Table 7.2. Thus, the forward rate of most routers greatly exceeds the capacity of a single WAN connection. This means that only a requirement for the use of multiple router ports should make the forwarding rate of the router into a key equipment acquisition issue. Otherwise, the communication, transport, and routing protocols supported are more important criteria for determining whether a vendor's product can support the requirements of an organization.

One key exception to the preceding involves the use of routers connected to very high-speed transmission facilities, such as a T3 line operating at approximately 45 Mbps or a synchronous optical network (SONET) connection operating at 155 Mbps. In such situations, the forwarding rate of the router would be an extremely important consideration.

chapter eight

Gateway Methods

In Chapter 5, we discussed the basic operation of gateways and the ways in which they enable networks with different protocols to communicate. In that chapter, we discussed how a gateway operates through the highest layer of the OSI Reference Model, the application layer, and how gateways essentially perform protocol conversion. We also briefly described several methods by which an Ethernet network could be connected to an IBM mainframe computer system. Although those methods involved different types of gateways, our primary focus of attention until now was simply on concepts and the use of different types of hardware, without considering the relationship of network architecture to gateway operations.

Since the protocol conversion performed by a gateway is directly related to such architectures as IBM's SNA and Digital Equipment's DECnet, we must obtain a basic understanding of the architecture developed to support access to conventional mainframe computers. This will enable us to obtain an appreciation for the different access methods supported by gateways, along with their functions and applications. These are the focus of this chapter. We will first discuss SNA and IBM's 3270 Information Display System to obtain an understanding of the basic functions of hardware and software used to establish a wide area networking capability, providing local and remote terminal users with access to IBM mainframe computers in an SNA environment. In doing so we will cover both SNA and the more modern Advanced Peer-to-Peer Networking (APPN) evolution of IBM's networking strategy. This information will provide the foundation for discussing the use of gateways to exchange information between local area networks and mainframes connected to the dominant computer company network architecture. The latter, with plug-compatible computers, represents approximately 70 percent of all large computer installations.

Although the preceding information is primarily focused upon gateways that provide end stations on LANs with the ability to access SNA- and APPN-based information, there are other types of gateways that warrant discussion.

Thus, in the remainder of this chapter, we will turn our attention to several other types of gateways to include SNA-to-TCP/IP gateways, electronic mail gateways, and application gateways.

8.1 Network Architecture

To satisfy customers' requirements for remote computing capability, mainframe computer manufacturers developed a variety of network architectures. Such architectures defined the relationship of a particular vendor's hardware and software products that is necessary to permit communications to flow through a network to the manufacturer's mainframe computer.

IBM's SNA is a very complex and sophisticated network architecture that defines the rules, procedures, and structure of communications from the input/output statements of an application program to the screen display on a user's personal computer or terminal. SNA consists of protocols, formats, and operational sequences governing the flow of information within a data-communications network. Such a network may link IBM mainframe computers, minicomputers, terminal controllers, communications controllers, personal computers, and terminals.

Since approximately 70 percent of the mainframe computer market belongs to IBM and plug-compatible systems manufactured by Amdehl and other vendors, SNA can be expected to remain a common connectivity platform for the foreseeable future. This means that a large majority of the connections of local area networks to mainframe computers will require the use of gateways that support SNA operations.

As we will shortly note when examining SNA, it is a mainframe-centric, hierarchical structured networking architecture. While appropriate for most computer communications requirements of the 1980s, the growth in distributed processing and peer-to-peer communications represented a significant problem for network managers and LAN administrators that required access to mainframes in an SNA environment as well as the ability to support peer-to-peer communications. Recognizing this problem, IBM significantly revised SNA in the form of developing a new network architecture known as APPN. After becoming familiar with SNA, we will then turn our attention to APPN in this section.

SNA Concepts

An SNA network consists of one or more domains, where *domain* refers to all of the logical and physical components that are connected to and controlled by one common point in the network. This common point of control is called the *system services control point* or *SSCP*. The SSCP can be considered the highest location in an SNA network whose structure is based on a rigidly defined hierarchy of devices. Within an SNA network, there are three types of network-addressable units: SSCPs, physical units, and logical units.

The SSCP

The SSCP resides in the communications access method operating in an IBM mainframe computer. For example, it may be a virtual telecommunications access method (VTAM) operating in a System/360, System/370, System/390, 4300 series or 308X, 309X, or an Enterprise series computer. It may also be in the system control program of an IBM minicomputer, such as a System/3X or AS/400. The SSCP contains the network's address tables, routing tables, and translation tables, which it uses to establish connections between nodes in the network and to control the flow of information in an SNA network.

Figure 8.1 illustrates single and multiple domain SNA networks. Each network domain includes one or more nodes; an SNA network node consists of a unique grouping of networking components. Examples of SNA nodes include cluster controllers (also referred to as control units), communications controllers, and terminal devices. The address of each device in the network is unique.

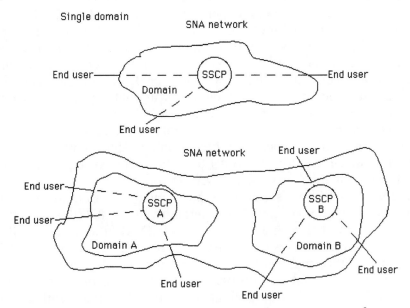

Figure 8.1   Single and multiple domain SNA networks.

The PU

Each node in an SNA network contains a *physical unit* (*PU*) that controls the node's other resources. The PU is not a physical device, as its name suggests, but rather a set of SNA components that provide services for controlling terminals, controllers, processors, and data links in the network. In programmable devices, such as mainframe computers and communications controllers, the PU is normally implemented in software. In less intelligent devices, such as older cluster controllers and display terminals, the PU is typically implemented in ROM. In an SNA network, each PU operates under the control of an SSCP. The PU functions as an entry point between the network and one or more logical units.

The LU

The third type of network-addressable unit in an SNA network is the *logical unit,* known by its abbreviation as the *LU*. The LU is the interface or point of access between the end user and an SNA network. Through the LU, an end user gains access to network resources and transmits and receives data over the network. Each PU can have one or more LUs; each LU has a distinct address.

SNA Network Structure

The structure of an SNA network is a hierarchy in which each device controls a specific part of the network and operates under the control of a device at the next higher level. The highest level in an SNA network is a host or mainframe computer, which executes a software module known as a *communications access method.* At the next lower level are one or more communications controllers—IBM's term for a front-end processor. Each communications controller executes a network control program (NCP) that defines the operation of devices connected to the controllers, along with their PUs and LUs, operating rate, data code, and other communications-related functions, such as the maximum packet size that can be transmitted. Connected to communications controllers are cluster controllers, IBM's term for a control unit. These cluster controllers are the third level in an SNA network.

The cluster controllers support the attachment of terminals and printers, which are the lowest level of an SNA hierarchy. Figure 8.2 illustrates the SNA hierarchy and the network addressable units (NAUs) associated with each hardware component used to construct an SNA network. Note that NAUs include lines connecting mainframes to communications controllers and cluster controllers, and cluster controllers to terminals and printers. In addition, NAUs also define application programs that reside in the mainframe. NAUs

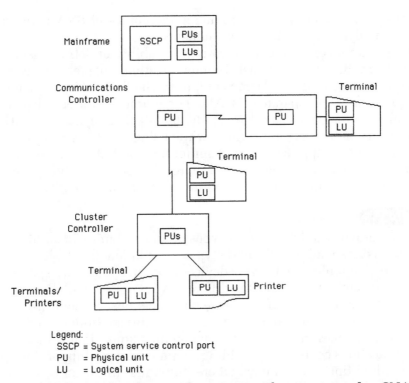

Figure 8.2   SNA hierarchical network structure. The structure of an SNA network is built upon a hierarchy of equipment, with mainframes connected to communications controllers and communications controllers connected to cluster controllers.

provide the mechanism for terminals to access specific programs via a routing through explicitly identified hardware and transmission facilities.

An SNA network is a relatively static network in which the addition and removal of terminal devices requires specific entries in address tables. Changing address table entries requires the creation and modification of macroinstruction in the communications controller's NCP and in the mainframe computer's VTAM. Since NCP and VTAM program changes require a recompilation of each program, and this temporarily places the network in never-never land while the resulting compiled programs are loaded, such program changes are typically accomplished on weekends or very early in the morning during weekdays. In addition, many organizations batch NCP and VTAM changes and then perform those changes only once a week or perhaps once a month, further reducing the ability of SNA networks to be adjusted to dynamic working environments.

As an example of the communications capability of SNA, consider an end user with an IBM PC and an SDLC communications adapter who establishes a connection to an IBM mainframe computer. The IBM PC is a PU, and its display and printer are separate LUs. After communication is established, the PC user can direct a file to his or her printer by establishing an LU-to-LU session between the mainframe and printer, while using the PC as an interactive terminal running an application program for a second LU-to-LU session. Thus, the transfer of data between PUs can represent a series of multiplexed LU-to-LU sessions, enabling multiple activities to occur concurrently.

Types of PUs

Table 8.1 provides a list of the six types of physical units in an SNA network and their corresponding SNA node types. In addition, this table contains representative examples of hardware devices that can operate as a specific type of PU. As indicated in Table 8.1, the different types of PUs, with the exception of PU 2.1, form a hierarchy of hardware classifications. At the lowest level, PU Type 1 is a single terminal. PU Type 2 is a cluster controller, used to connect many SNA devices into a common communications circuit. PU Type 4 is a communications controller, providing communications support for up to several hundred line terminations, where individual lines can be connected in turn to cluster controllers. At the top of the hardware hierarchy, PU Type 5 is a mainframe computer.

PU2.1 is a special type of node that supports IBM's APPN. Unlike SNA, which is based on a hierarchical, master–slave control structure, APPN permits cooperative program-to-program communications in which each computer on the network is considered as just another peer node. A session can thus be established between two type 2.1 nodes without requiring a data flow through an SSCP.

TABLE 8.1   SNA PU Summary

PU Type	Node Type	Representative Hardware
PU Type 5	Mainframe	S/370, 43XX, 308X
PU Type 4	Communications controller	3705, 3725, 3745
PU Type 3	Not currently defined	N/A
PU Type 2.1	APPN	Any computer
PU Type 2	Cluster controller	3174, 3274, 3276
PU Type 1	Terminal	3180, PC with SNA adapter

Multiple Domains

Figure 8.3 illustrates a two-domain SNA network. By establishing a physical connection between the communications controller in each domain and coding appropriate software for operation on each controller, cross-domain data flow becomes possible. When cross-domain data flow is established, terminal

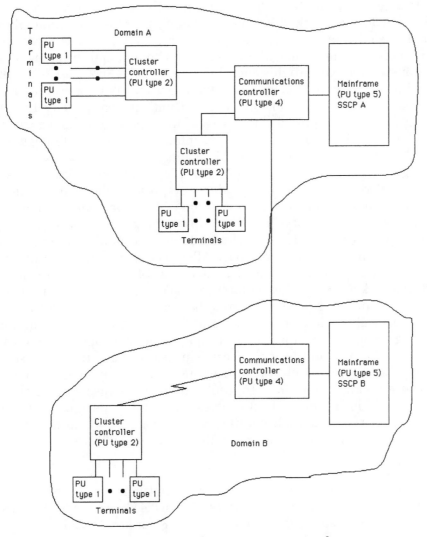

Figure 8.3   Two-domain SNA network.

devices connected to one mainframe can access applications operating on the other mainframe.

SNA was originally implemented as a networking architecture in which users established sessions with application programs operating on a mainframe computer within the network. Once a session was established, a NCP operating on an IBM communications controller, which in turn was connected to the IBM mainframe, controlled the information flow between the user and the applications program. With the growth in personal computing, many users no longer require access to a mainframe to obtain connectivity to another personal computer. Therefore, IBM modified SNA to permit peer-to-peer communications capability, so that two devices on the network with appropriate hardware and software can communicate with one another without requiring access through a mainframe computer. To this end, IBM introduced a PU2.1 node in 1987, in recognition of the growing requirement of its customers for a peer-to-peer networking capability. Unfortunately, it wasn't until the early 1990s that APPN became available and provided this networking capability, enabling communications between PU2.1 nodes without mainframe intervention through the use of LU6.2 sessions described later in this chapter.

The PU2.1 node—in conjunction with LU6.2 and new releases of VTAM and associated communications products—represents the evolving networking concept known as APPN. Although the PU2.1-type node was announced in 1987, many portions of APPN were still evolving or were being developed. For example, VTAM Version 4.1, which allows IBM mainframes to participate actively within APPN as peer-to-peer APPN nodes, was released during the latter part of 1992. Other products, such as 3174 microcode to support an APPN network node function for both coaxial cable–connected terminals and workstations on a Token-Ring network, became available during 1993. Since many organizations have a large base of SNA communications equipment, replacing or upgrading that base of equipment to support APPN can be expected to be an evolutionary process. This is especially true because of the current lack of APPN software applications. Since many organizations have invested a literal fortune in SNA applications, the expected availability of APPN applications over the next few years will not by itself cause a massive migration to APPN. Instead, we can expect organizations to obtain APPN-compliant equipment and then gradually migrate to APPN.

SNA Layers

IBM's SNA is a layered protocol that provides seven layers of control for every message that flows through the network. Figure 8.4 shows the SNA layers and provides a comparison to the seven-layer OSI Reference Model.

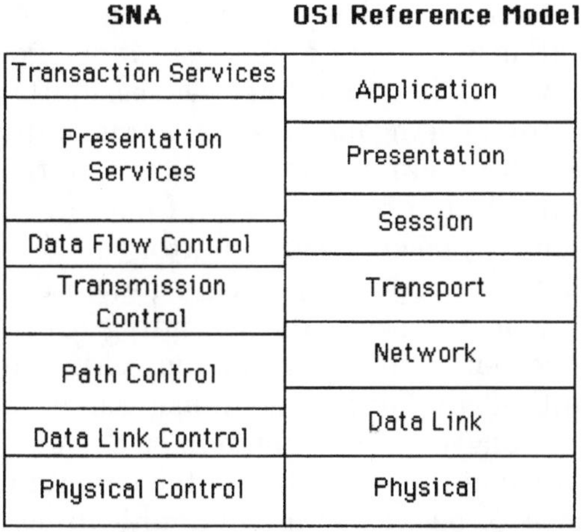

SNA   OSI Reference Model

SNA	OSI Reference Model
Transaction Services	Application
Presentation Services	Presentation
Data Flow Control	Session
Transmission Control	Transport
Path Control	Network
Data Link Control	Data Link
Physical Control	Physical

Figure 8.4   SNA and the OSI Reference Model.

Like the OSI physical layer, SNA's physical control layer is concerned with the electrical, mechanical, and procedural characteristics of the physical media and interfaces to the physical media. SNA's data link control layer is also quite similar to OSI's data link layer. Protocols defined by SNA include SDLC, System/370 channel, Token-Ring, and X.25; however, only SDLC is used on a communications link in which primary stations communicate with secondary stations. Some implementations of SNA using special software modules can also support the still widely used IBM pre-SNA protocol, bisynchronous communications (BSC), as well as asynchronous communications.

Two of the major functions of the path control layer are routing and flow control. Since there can be many data links connected to a node, path control is responsible for ensuring that data is passed correctly through intermediate nodes as it flows from source to destination. At the beginning of an SNA session, the sending and receiving nodes, along with all nodes between those nodes, cooperate to select the most efficient route for the session. Since this route is established only for the duration of the session, it is known as a *virtual route*. To increase the efficiency of transmission in an SNA network, the path control layer at each node through which the virtual route is established has the ability to divide long messages into shorter segments for transmission by the data link layer. Similarly, path control may join short messages into larger data blocks for transmission by the data link layer. This enables the efficiency of SNA's transmission facility to be independent of the length of messages flowing on the network.

The SNA transmission control layer provides a reliable end-to-end connection service, similar to the OSI Reference Model transport layer. Other transmission control layer functions include session level pacing and encryption and decryption. Pacing ensures that a transmitting device does not send more data than a receiving device can accept during a given period of time. Pacing is similar to the flow control of data in a network; however, unlike flow control, NAUs negotiate and control pacing. To accomplish this, the two NAUs at the session's end points negotiate the largest number of messages, known as a *pacing group,* that a sending NAU can transmit before receiving a pacing response from a receiving NAU. The pacing response enables the transmitting NAU to resume transmission. Session level pacing occurs in two stages along a session's route in an SNA network. One stage of pacing is between the mainframe NAU and the communications controller, and the second stage is between the communications controller and an attached terminal NAU.

The data flow control services layer handles the order of communications within a session for error control and flow control. The order of communications is set by the layer controlling the transmission mode. Transmission modes available include *full-duplex,* which permits each device to transmit at any time; *half-duplex flip-flop,* in which devices can only transmit alternately; and *half-duplex contention,* in which one device is considered a master device and the slave cannot transmit until the master completes its transmission.

The SNA presentation services layer is responsible for the translation of data from one format to another. This layer also performs the connection and disconnection of sessions, updates the network configuration, and performs network management functions. At this layer, the NAU services manager is responsible for formatting of data from an application to match the display or printer that is communicating with the application. Other functions performed at this layer include the compression and decompression of data to increase the efficiency of transmission on an SNA network.

The highest layer in SNA is the transaction services layer. This layer is responsible for application programs that implement distributed processing and management services, such as distributed databases, document interchange, and the control of LU-to-LU session limits.

SNA Developments

The most significant development to SNA, prior to the formal introduction of APPN, can be considered to be the addition of new LU and PU subtypes to support what is known as Advanced Peer-to-Peer Communications (APPC), which represents the communications protocol of an APPN network. Previously, LU types used to define an LU-to-LU session were restricted to application-to-device and program-to-program sessions. LU1-LU4 and LU7 are application-to-device sessions, as indicated in Table 8.2, whereas LU5 and LU6 are program-to-program sessions.

The addition of LU6.2, which operates in conjunction with PU2.1 to support LU6.2 connections, permits devices to transfer data to any other device that also supports this LU without first sending the data through a mainframe computer. The introduction of new software products to support LU6.2 permits a more dynamic flow of data through SNA networks, and many data links to mainframes that were previously heavily used can gain capacity.

Under APPN, multiple LU-to-LU sessions per LU6.2 become possible, since LU6.2 supports parallel sessions with no restrictions on the session originator. In comparison, under SNA, peripheral nodes (such as LUs) in a control unit can participate in only one LU-to-LU session at any one time, and the host resident LU must function as the master. Other differences between SNA and APPN include the maximum number of LUs supported by a peripheral node and the manner in which resources and routes are defined.

Under SNA, the maximum number of LUs in a peripheral node is limited to 255. Under APPN, there is a theoretical limit of 64 K LUs per link; however, in operation there will probably be only one LU6.2 per node, since LU6.2 provides the ability to support multiple users. SNA is a relatively static networking environment in which tables must be coded manually to define resources and routes. Under APPN, most routes and resources are discovered by the equipment; this minimizes the necessity for extensive manual definitions.

TABLE 8.2 SNA LU Session Types

LU Type	Session Type
LU1	Host application and a remote batch terminal
LU2	Host application and a 3270 display terminal
LU3	Host application and a 3270 printer
LU4	Host application and an SNA word processor, or two terminals connected by a mainframe
LU5	Currently undefined
LU6	Two applications programs typically residing on different mainframe computers
LU6.2	Peer-to-peer
LU7	Host application and a 5250 terminal

SNA Sessions

All communications in SNA occur within sessions between NAUs. A *session* can be defined as a logical connection established between two NAUs over a specific route for a specific period of time, where the connection and disconnection of a session are controlled by the SSCP. SNA defines four types of sessions: SSCP-to-PU, SSCP-to-LU, SSCP-to-SSCP, and LU-to-LU. The first two types of sessions are used to request or exchange diagnostic and status information. The third type of session enables SSCPs in the same or different domains to exchange information. The LU-to-LU session is the core type of SNA session, since all end-user communications take place over LU-to-LU sessions.

LU-to-LU Sessions

In an LU-to-LU session, one logical unit, known as the *primary LU* (*PLU*), becomes responsible for error recovery. The other LU, which normally has less processing power, becomes the *secondary LU* (*SLU*).

An LU-to-LU session is initiated by the transmission of a message from the PLU to the SLU. That message is known as a *bind,* and contains information stored in the communications access method (VTAM) tables on the mainframe. It identifies the hardware devices by screen size, printer type, and so forth, as configured in the VTAM table. This information enables a session to occur with supported hardware. Otherwise, the SLU will reject the bind and the session will not start.

Addressing Previously, we discussed the concept of a domain consisting of an SSCP and the network resources it controls. Within a domain exists a set of smaller network units known as *subareas.* In SNA terminology, each host is a subarea, along with each communications controller and its peripheral nodes. The identification of an NAU in an SNA network consists of a subarea address and an element address within the subarea having the format: subarea: element. The subarea is like an area code: it identifies a portion of the network. Figure 8.5 illustrates the relationship between a domain and three subareas residing in that particular domain.

In SNA, a subarea address is 8 bits in length, while the element address within a subarea is also 8 bits in length. This limits the number of subareas within a domain to 255, and restricts the number of PUs and LUs within a subarea to 255.

Each subarea address is shared by an SSCP and all of its LUs and PUs and represents a unique address within a domain. In comparison, element addresses are only unique within a subarea and can be duplicated. A third component of

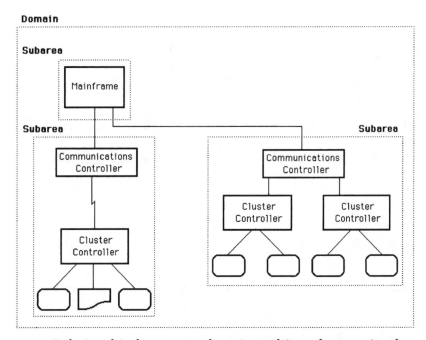

Figure 8.5 Relationship between a domain and its subareas. A subarea is a host or a communications controller and its peripheral nodes.

SNA addressing is a character-coded network name that is assigned to each component. Each name must be unique within a domain and SSCPs maintain tables which map names to addresses.

The routing of packets between SNA subarea nodes occurs through the use of a sequence of message units created at different layers in the protocol stack. An application on an SNA node generates a request header (RH) which pre-fixes user data to form a basic transmission unit (BTU) as shown at the top of Figure 8.6. At the path control layer, a transmission header (TH) is added as a prefix to the BTU to form a basic information unit (BIU). The TH contains source and destination addresses that represent the sender and receiver of the packet, with subarea nodes examining the destination address within the TH of the BIU to make forwarding decisions.

Once a packet arrives at its destination subarea, routing must occur between the subarea and peripheral nodes in the destination subarea. That routing is based upon the data link header (DLC) added to the BIU to form a basic link unit (BLU), shown at the bottom of Figure 8.6. Now that we have a basic understanding of SNA, let's turn our attention to APPN.

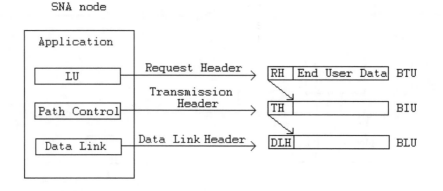

SNA node

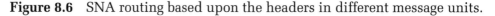

Legend:

    BTU = Basic Transmission Unit
    BIU = Basic Information Unit
    BLU = Basic Link Unit

Figure 8.6 SNA routing based upon the headers in different message units.

Advanced Peer-to-Peer Networking

Although SNA represents one of the most successful networking strategies developed by a vendor, its centralized structure based upon mainframe-centric computing became dated in an evolving era of client/server distributive computing. Recognizing the requirements of organizations to obtain peer-to-peer transmission capability instead of routing data through mainframes, IBM developed its APPN architecture during 1992 as a mechanism for computers, ranging from PCs to mainframes to communicate as peers across local and wide area networks. The actual ability of programs on different computers to communicate with one another is obtained from special software known as Advanced Program-to-Program Communication (APPC), which represents a more marketable name for LU6.2 software. Since APPC enables the operation of APPN, we will first focus our attention upon APPC before examining the architecture associated with APPN.

APPC Concepts APPC represents a software interface between programs requiring communications with other programs and the network computers running those programs. APPC represents an open communications protocol that is available on a range of platforms to include PCs, mainframes, Macintosh, and UNIX-based systems, as well as IBM 3174 control units and its 6611 NWay router series.

In its most basic structure, APPC can be considered to represent a stack existing above a network adapter but below the application using the adapter. Figure 8.7 illustrates the general relationship of APPC to the software stack on two computers communicating with one another on a peer-to-peer basis. In this example, program A on computer 1 is shown communicating with program B on computer 2.

Under APPC terminology communications between two programs is referred to as a conversation, which occurs according to a set of rules defined by the APPC protocol. Those rules specify how a conversation is established, how data is transmitted, and how the conversation is broken or deallocated.

Similar to most modern programming concepts, APPC supports a series of verbs that provide an application programming interface (API) between transaction programs and APPC software residing on a host. For example, the APPC verb ALLOCATE is used to initiate a conversation with another transaction program, the verb SEND_DATA enables the program to initiate the data transfer to its partner program, and the verb DEALLOCATE would be used to inform APPC to terminate the conversation previously established. Now that we have a general appreciation for the software that enables program-to-program communications, let's turn our attention to the architecture of APPN.

APPN Architecture   APPN is a platform-independent network architecture which consists of three types of computers—low-entry networking (LEN) nodes, end nodes (ENs), and network nodes (NNs). Similar to SNA, APPN applications use network resources via LU software. LUs reside on each type of APPN node, and application-to-application sessions occur between LUs,

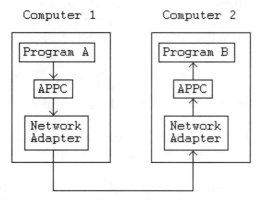

Figure 8.7   APPC software profiles an interface between application programs and the network used.

which in the case of APPN are LU6.2 LUs. APPN nodes can support a nearly unlimited number of LUs in comparison to the 255 SNA supports. In addition, APPN LUs can support multiple users, significantly increasing its flexibility over SNA.

When an application program on one host requires communications with an application on another host, the first host tells its local LU to find a partner LU. The location of the partner LU is accomplished by a process in which several types of searches occur through an APPN network. Since those searches depend upon knowledge of the characteristics of the three types of APPN nodes, let's first turn our attention to the features and functions of those nodes.

LEN Nodes   Low-entry networking (LEN) nodes date to the early 1980s when they were introduced as SNA Type 2.1 nodes. LEN nodes can be considered to represent the most basic subset of APPN functionality and have the ability to communicate with applications on other LEN nodes, ENs, or NNs.

APPN includes a distributed directory mechanism which enables routes to be dynamically established through an APPN network. However, unlike IP networks that use 32-bit addresses, APPN uses alphanumeric names.

LEN nodes are manually configured with a limited set of LUs. Thus, to use APPN directory services a LEN node requires the assistance of an adjacent APPN node, where adjacency is obtained through a LAN connection or a direct point-to-point link.

End Nodes   End nodes (ENs) can be viewed as a more sophisticated type of LEN. In addition to supporting all of the functions of LEN nodes, ENs know how to use APPN services, such as its directory services. To learn how to use such services, an EN identifies itself to the network when it is initially brought up. This identification process is accomplished by the EN registering its LUs with an NN server. Here the NN represents the third type of APPN node and is discussed in the next section. In comparison, LEN nodes do not perform this activity.

Network Nodes   Network nodes (NNs) are the third component of an APPN network. NNs provide all of the functions associated with ENs as well as routing and partner LU location services. Concerning routing, NNs work together to route information between such nodes, in effect providing a backbone transmission capability.

The partner LU location service depends upon NN searches when the partner is not registered by the NN serving the requestor. In such situations, the NN server will broadcast a search request to adjacent NNs, requesting the location of the partner LU. This broadcasting will continue until the partner LU is located and a path or route is returned. Since broadcast searches are bandwidth intensive, NNs place directory entries they locate into cache memory, which serves to limit broadcasts being propagated through an APPN network.

Operation To illustrate the operation of an APPN network, let's examine a small network in which two ENs are connected by an NN. Figure 8.8 illustrates an example of this network structure.

When the links between EN1 and NN1 and EN2 and NN1 are activated, the computers on each link automatically inform each other of their capabilities to include whether they are an EN or an NN, and ENs will register their capabilities with NNs. Thus, the NN will know the location and capability of both EN1 and EN2. When an application on EN1 needs to locate an LU in the network, such as LUX, it sends a request to its NN server, in this case NN1. Since NN1 is the server for EN1, both nodes establish a pair of control-point sessions to exchange APPN control information and EN1 registers its APPC LUs with NN1. Similarly, EN2 and NN1 establish a pair of control-point sessions when the link between those two nodes is brought up. Thus, NN1 knows how to get to EN1 and EN2 and what LUs are located at each node.

When EN1 asks NN1 to find LUX and determine a path through the network, NN1 checks its cache memory and notes that the only path available is *EN1 to NN1 to EN2*. NN1 passes this path information back to EN1, which enables the application operating on EN1 to establish an APPN session to LUX and initiate the exchange of information.

Now that we have an appreciation for basic APPN routing, let's examine a more complex example in which originating and destination LUs reside on ENs separated from one another by multiple NNs. Figure 8.9 illustrates this more complex APPN network consisting of four ENs and three NNs grouped together in a topology that allows multiple path routing between certain nodes.

```
Legend:
   EN = End Node
   NN = Network Node
   LU = Logical Unit
```

Figure 8.8   An APPN network consisting of two end nodes and a network node.

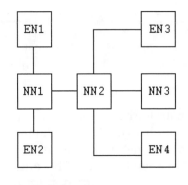

Legend:
  EN = End Node
  NN = Network Node

Figure 8.9 A more complex APPN network with multiple paths to some nodes.

Let's assume an APPN application on EN1 wants to initiate a conversation with an application on EN4. EN1 first requests NN1 to locate EN4 and determine which path through the network should be used. Since NN1 is not EN4's NN server, it will initially have no knowledge of EN4's location. Thus, NN1 will transmit a request to each adjacent NN in its quest to locate EN4. Since NN2 is the only NN adjacent to NN1, it passes the request to its adjacent nodes. Based upon the configuration shown in Figure 8.9, there is only one adjacent NN, NN3. Although EN4 is connected to both NN2 and NN3, an EN can only have one NN server. Thus, if we assume NN3 is the server for EN4, then NN2 has no knowledge of EN4 and does not respond on its behalf.

Next, upon locating EN4, NN3 queries EN4 to determine its existing communications links. Upon receipt of information from EN4 that has links to both NN2 and NN3, NN2 passes the information about EN4 to NN2, which passes the information back to NN1. NN1 uses the information received to determine which route to EN4 is best, selects an appropriate route, and passes the selected route back to EN1, allowing that EN to establish an APPC session to EN4.

Route Selection Under APPN, routing is based upon NNs maintaining a *route addition resistance* value set up by network administrators and a *class of service* of data to be routed. Class-of-service routing enables different types of data to be routed via paths optimized for batch, interactive, batch-secure, and interactive-secure. APPN uses eight values that are defined for each network link that are used in conjunction with the class of service to select an appropriate route. Values defined for each link include propagation delay, cost per byte, cost for connect time, effective capacity, and security. Using values defined for the links, a batch session might be routed on a path with high capacity and low cost, while an interactive session would probably be placed on a terrestrial link instead of a satellite link to minimize propagation delay.

APPN can be considered to represent a considerable enhancement to SNA as it provides efficient routing services that bypass the requirement of SNA data to flow in a hierarchical manner. However, APPN is similar to SNA in the fact that such networks do not have true network addresses, making pure routing between different networks difficult. In addition, the structure of APPN is similar to SNA with respect to its basic network layer operations which are illustrated in Figure 8.10. In examining Figure 8.10 note that APPN's network layer can be considered to represent APPC, which converts LU service requests into frames for transport at the data link layer. Although SNA was originally limited to LLC Type 2 (LLC2) and SDLC transmission via a variety of physical layer interfaces, a number of conversion devices have been developed that extend both SNA and APPN transmission to Frame Relay.

In addition, other products enable SNA and APPN data to be transported under a different network layer, a technique referred to as encapsulation or tunneling. Once we review the composition of the IBM 3270 Information Display System to obtain an appreciation for conventional gateway methods used to connect to SNA and APPN networks, we will then turn our attention to more modern gateway solutions, such as techniques to encapsulate SNA and APPN such that they can be routed over an IP network, a technique referred to as data link switching (DLSw).

Application	Application Program		
	LU Services		
Network Layer	APPC Path Control		
Data Link Layer	LLC2 SNAP Ethernet 2	LLC2 SNAP	Frame Relay, SDLC
Physical Layer	Ethernet/ 802.5	Token-Ring	FDDI	V.24, V.35, RS232, T1, E1, HSSI

Figure 8.10   The general structure of APPN.

8.2 The 3270 Information Display System

The IBM 3270 Information Display System describes a collection of products, ranging from display stations with keyboards and printers that communicate with mainframe computers to several types of cluster controllers.

First introduced in 1971, the IBM 3270 Information Display System was designed to extend the processing power of the mainframe computer to locations remote from the computer room. Controllers, more commonly known as *control units,* were made available to economize on the number of lines required to link display stations to mainframe computers. Typically, a number of display stations are connected to a control unit on individual cables; the control unit, in turn, is connected to the mainframe via a single cable. Both local and remote control units are offered. The key differences between the two pertain to the method of attachment to the mainframe computer and the use of intermediate devices between the control unit and the mainframe.

Local control units are usually attached to a channel on the mainframe, whereas remote control units are connected to the mainframe's communications controller. Since a local control unit is within a limited distance of the mainframe, no intermediate communications devices, such as modems or data service units, are required to connect a local control unit to the mainframe. In comparison, a remote control unit can be located in another building or even in a different city, and normally requires the use of intermediate communications devices, such as a pair of modems or a pair of DSUs, for communications between the control unit and the communications controller. The relationship of local and control units to display stations, mainframes, and a communications controller is illustrated in Figure 8.11. Note that this hardware relationship represents the hierarchy of equipment supported by SNA and explains the original hierarchical data flow associated with SNA networks.

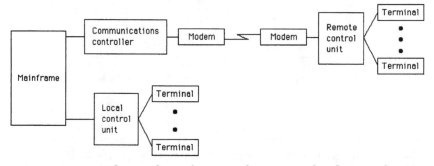

Figure 8.11 Relationship of 3270 information display products.

Data Flow

The control unit polls each connected display station to ascertain whether the station has data stored in its transmit buffer. If the station has data in its buffer, it will transmit that data to the control unit when it is polled. The control unit then formats the data with the display station's address, adds the control unit's address and other pertinent information, and transmits it in a synchronous data format to the communications controller or to the I/O channel on the mainframe, depending on the method used to connect the control unit to the mainframe.

Addressing information flowing to the mainframe begins with a terminal address. The control unit formats each data block received from a terminal device and adds its control unit identifier. If the control unit is connected to a communications controller, the latter device adds a line identifier address to the data block, indicating the port on the controller where the information was received. After operating on the data block, the mainframe responds by generating a screen of data that will be routed to a specific terminal. To ensure that the response is routed correctly, the mainframe includes the line, control unit, and terminal address. The communications controller strips off the line identifier and forwards the data to the appropriate line. Since an SNA network supports multidrop circuits, in which two or more control units can share the use of a common transmission line, the control unit address defines the control unit. That control unit removes the control unit address. Next, it examines the terminal identifier, and removes it from the data block once it knows the line to transmit the block.

3270 Protocols

IBM supports two different protocols to connect 3270 devices to a mainframe. The original protocol used with 3270 devices, still in limited use today, is the *byte-oriented bisynchronous protocol,* often referred to as *3270 bisyn* or *BSC.* In the late 1970s, when IBM introduced its SNA, it also introduced a bit-oriented protocol for data transmission known as *Synchronous Data Link Control,* or *SDLC.* Thus, communications between an IBM mainframe and the control units attached to the communications controller are either BSC or SDLC, depending on the type of control units obtained and the configuration of the communications controller. Today, almost all BSC control units have been replaced by more modern SDLC devices.

Types of Control Units

Control units marketed by IBM support up to 8, 16, 32, or 64 attached devices, depending on the model. The IBM 3276 control unit, which can be considered a very obsolete device, supports up to 8 devices, while the IBM 3274 control unit can support 16 or 32 attached devices. Older control units, such as the 3271, 3272, and 3275, have essentially been replaced by the 3274 and operate only bisynchronously. Certain models of the 3274 are soft devices that can be programmed with a diskette to operate either with the originally developed bisynchronous protocol or with the newer SDLC protocol.

Devices to include display stations and printers are normally attached to each control unit with coaxial cable. Under this design philosophy, every display station must be connected to a control unit before it can access a mainframe application written for a 3270-type terminal. This method of connection prevented dial-up terminals from accessing 3270-type applications, and resulted in numerous third-party vendors marketing devices to permit lower-cost ASCII terminals to be attached to 3270 networks. In late 1986, IBM introduced a new controller known as the 3174 Subsystem Control Unit. This controller, which has now replaced older models, can be used to connect terminals via standard coaxial cable, shielded twisted-pair wire, or twisted-pair wire. Other key features of the controller include an optional protocol converter that can support up to 24 asynchronous ports and the ability to be attached to Token-Ring or Ethernet local area networks. The latter is accomplished through the use of a Token-Ring or Ethernet adapter card installed in a 3174 slot, converting the 3174 into an active participant on a Token-Ring or Ethernet network.

The 3174 can support 8, 16, 32, or 64 ports. A 64-port 3174 supports a maximum of 254 LUs, while a 32-port control unit supports a maximum of 128 LUs. All other 3174 control units normally provide an LU support capability equal to four times the number of ports on the device; however, there are some exceptions, and you should examine IBM equipment specifications to determine the LU support for different 3174 models. For example, the 64-port model varies slightly from this scheme, because LU0 and LU1 are reserved on that device and unavailable for general use.

When used with a Token-Ring adapter (TRA), the 3174 was originally limited to supporting up to 140 downstream PUs (DSPUs). In 1992, new microcode extended DSPU support to 250 for a local 3174. A DSPU can be considered a gateway PC; the software on each gateway determines the number of LUs supported on the Token-Ring. For example, Novell NetWare gateway software can be obtained to provide support for 16, 32, or 97 LUs. In this type of networking configuration, shown in Figure 8.12, the communications controller polls the control unit, the control unit polls individual PU gateways, and each gateway is responsible for polling the LUs it services. In this example, the gateway PC is a downstream PU that polls downstream LUs. Although Figure 8.12 shows the connection of a 3174 to a Token-Ring network, a similar connection can be

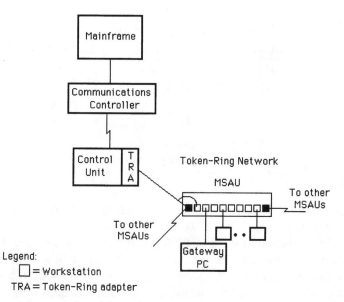

Figure 8.12 Using a control unit TRA to interconnect a Token-Ring network. Through the installation of a TRA, both local and remote control units provide a connection capability to a Token-Ring network.

established to an Ethernet network. To do so, you would substitute an Ethernet adapter card for the TRA in the 3174 and cable the adapter to an Ethernet hub port.

Since SNA's architecture is a polling structure, it is wise to limit the number of LUs on a gateway. Otherwise, the polling time from the gateway PC to the LUs—different sessions on each LAN station or the screen and printer of a workstation—can result in excessive delays. A good rule of thumb is to add another downstream PU in the form of an additional gateway for every 32 stations on a local area network.

Terminal Displays

IBM 3270 terminals fall into three display classes: monochrome, color, and gas plasma. Members of the monochrome display class include the 3278-, 3178-, 3180-, 3191-, and 3193-type terminals. The 3278 is a large, bulky terminal that covers a significant portion of one's desk. It was replaced by the 3178, 3180, 3191, and 3193 display stations, which are lighter, more compact, and less expensive versions of the 3278. The 3279 color display station was similarly replaced by the 3179 and the 3194, which are lower cost and more

TABLE 8.3 IBM Display Stations

Model Number	Display Type	Screen (Inches)
3178	Monochrome	12
3179	Color	14
3180	Monochrome	15
3191	Monochrome	12
3193	Monochrome	15
3194	Color	14

compact color display terminals. The last class of display stations, the gas plasma display, consists of the 3270 flat panel display.

The physical dimensions of a 3270-type screen may vary by class and model within the class. For example, the 3178 and 3278 Model 2 display stations have a screen size of 24 rows by 80 columns, the 3278 Model 3 has a screen size of 32 rows by 80 columns, and the 3278 Model 4 has a screen size of 43 rows by 80 columns.

Table 8.3 lists a portion of the family of terminals marketed for use with the IBM 3270 Information Display System. Note that the 3170 and 3180 display stations can also be used with IBM System/3X minicomputers. In addition, the 3193 and 3194 terminals can support the display of up to four host sessions when connected to the 3174 controller.

Each 3270 screen consists of fields that are defined by the application program connected to the display station. Attributes sent by the application program further define the characteristics of each field, as indicated in Table 8.4.

TABLE 8.4 3270 Terminal Field Characteristics

Field Characteristic	Result
Highlighted	Field is displayed at a brighter intensity than normal-intensity field.
Nondisplay	Field does not display any data typed into it.
Protected	Field does not accept any input.
Unprotected	Field accepts any data typed into it.
Numeric-only	Field accepts only numbers as input.
Autoskip	Field sends the cursor to the next unprotected field after it is filled with data.
Underscoring	Field causes characters to be underlined.
Blinking	Field causes characters to blink.

Any technique used to enable a personal computer to function as a 3270 display station requires the PC to obtain at least the field attributes listed in Table 8.4.

3270 Keyboard Functions

In comparison to the keyboard of most personal computers, a 3270 display station contains approximately 40 additional keys, which, when pressed, perform functions unique to the 3270 terminal environment. Table 8.5 contains a list of the more common of these new 3270 keys.

Since most, if not all, of the 3270 keyboard functions may be required for the successful use of a 3270 application program, the codes generated from pressing keys on a personal computer keyboard must be converted into appropriate codes representing 3270 keyboard functions if a PC is to be used as a

TABLE 8.5   Common 3270 Keys Differing from Most Personal Computer Keyboards

Key(s)	Function
CLEAR	Erases screen except for characters in message area, repositioning cursor to row 1, column 1.
PA1	Transmits a code to the application program that is interpreted as a break signal. In TSO or CMS, the PA1 key terminates the current command.
PA2	Transmits a code to the application program that is often interpreted as a request to redisplay the screen, or to clear the screen and display additional information.
PFnn	The 24 program function keys on a 3270 terminal are defined by the application program in use.
TAB	Moves the cursor to the next unprotected field.
BACKTAB	Moves the cursor to the previous unprotected field.
RESET	Disables the insert mode.
ERASEEOF	Deletes everything from the cursor to the end of the input field.
NEWLINE	Advances the cursor to the first unprotected field on the new line.
FASTRIGHT	Moves the cursor to the right two characters at a time.
FASTLEFT	Moves the cursor to the left two characters at a time.
ERASE INPUT	Clears all the input fields on the screen.
HOME	Moves the cursor to the first unprotected field on the screen.

3270 terminal. Due to the lesser number of keys on a personal computer keyboard, a common approach to most emulation techniques is to use two- or three-key sequences on the PC keyboard to represent many of the keys unique to a 3270 keyboard.

Emulation Considerations

In addition to converting keys on a personal computer keyboard to 3270 keyboard functions, 3270 emulation requires the PC's screen to function as a 3270 display screen. The 3270 display terminal operates by displaying an entire screen of data in one operation and then waiting for the operator to signal that he or she is ready to proceed with the next screen of information. This operation mode is known as full-screen operation. It is exactly the opposite of TTY emulation, where a terminal operates on a line-by-line basis. A key advantage of full-screen editing is the ability of the operator to move the cursor to any position on the screen to edit or change data.

To use a personal computer workstation located on a local area network as a 3270 display station, you must convert the transmission codes used to position the 3270 screen and effect field attributes to equivalent codes recognizable by the PC. This means that individual workstations on the local area network must operate a terminal emulation program. This program works in tandem with the application program and communications controller, through the 3174 control unit and gateway, to enable the workstation to be recognized as a supported 3270-type terminal. In addition to gateway software, each workstation on the local area network that requires access to the mainframe must operate a terminal emulation program.

8.3 SNA and APPN Gateway Options

Now that we have a basic understanding of the architecture of SNA and APPN and the components and operations of the 3270 Information Display System, let us turn our attention to linking local area networks to IBM and IBM-compatible host computers. First, we will expand on our knowledge of how the 3174 control unit works, and how it differs as a gateway from a PC on a Token-Ring network connected to a 3174. Next, we will examine several enhancements to 3174 control units that extend this device's capability to function as a gateway supporting different organizational networking requirements.

3174 Control Unit

As shown in Figure 8.12, the IBM 3174 control unit provides a basic mechanism for connecting a Token-Ring or Ethernet network to an SNA network. Although Figure 8.12 shows a gateway PC, in reality the gateway is optional, and is used primarily for resource management and message switching. Without a gateway, all LAN station definitions and definition changes must be performed on the mainframe. If a new user is added to the LAN, new definitions must be added to VTAM on the mainframe. Normally, such changes require a new compilation to source code macrochanges and are typically performed late at night or on weekends. New users may therefore experience a delay in obtaining access to a mainframe.

Such changes are performed more readily with a gateway PC, since mainframe sessions can be allocated to LU and PU pools. The gateway then provides a mechanism to assign new users to the pool so they can obtain immediate access to the mainframe. Unfortunately, there is no free lunch. The gateway adds a degree of processing delay that may be noticeable when an extended process, such as a large file transfer, occurs.

Enhancements

During 1992, IBM introduced several enhancements for their 3174 control unit that extend its capability for gateway operations. These enhancements include a multihost support capability, extended support for up to 250 downstream physical units, APPN support, the ability of the 3174 to serve as an Ethernet gateway, and the introduction of a group polling feature.

Multihost Support

The introduction of a concurrent communications adapter capable of supporting multiple SDLC, BSC, or X.25 protocols for the 3174 formed the basis for permitting the 3174 to serve as a multihost gateway. Figure 8.13 illustrates the use of a 3174 as a multihost Ethernet network gateway. In this example, the 3174 provides access to a local mainframe via a high-speed direct channel connection, and access to a remote mainframe via a communications circuit. The multihost Ethernet gateway supports one direct channel and two communications circuit connections when implemented on a local control unit, and up to three communications circuit connections when implemented on a remote control unit. Regardless of the control unit used, all connections are restricted to IBM SNA mainframes.

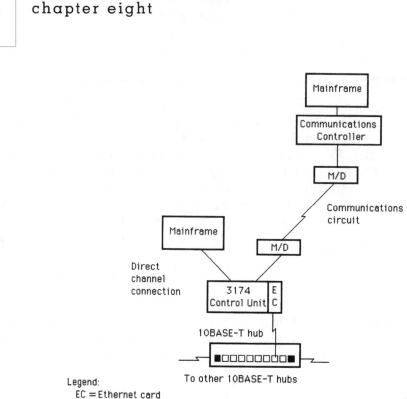

Figure 8.13 Multihost Token-Ring gateway. With a concurrent communications adapter, a 3174 control unit can connect LAN stations to multiple mainframe computers.

Extended PU Support

The first 3174 introduced with a Token-Ring adapter supported a maximum of 140 downstream physical units. Newer 3174 control units are now capable of supporting up to 250 downstream physical units. However, not all 3174s are equal. For example, a low-cost 3174 Model 90R control unit, designed to provide a remote gateway connection to a communications controller at a data rate up to 64 Kbps, provides support for no more than 40 downstream physical units.

Group Polling

Understanding the performance enhancement obtainable by the support of group polling by a 3174 gateway requires a review of the method by which terminals and workstations access a host via a gateway control unit. Before group polling was available, the gateway would poll each PU on the LAN in response to polls generated by the communications controller.

To see the problem with this method of polling, picture a 3174 supporting both workstations and a group of conventional 3270 display terminals and printers via an Ethernet adapter. One PU would be assigned to the control unit to serve as a general address for the display terminals and printers that are cabled directly to the 3174. A second PU would be assigned to the Ethernet adapter. The communications controller would alternately poll each PU, and the control unit would alternately poll each group of LUs assigned to each PU.

Since a station on the Ethernet can transmit only in response to a poll, a relatively large amount of time can occur until the 3174 polls the appropriate LU with data to transmit. In the interim, the 3174 may be polling many PUs that have no data to send. Figure 8.14 shows how the NCP operating on an IBM communications controller would poll the two PUs associated with the 3174 control unit under our scenario.

Under group polling, PU addresses are assigned to each workstation downstream from the control unit, and are then referred to as *downstream physical units (DSPUs)*. The DSPUs are defined in the NCP, and the NCP issues a group poll to the control unit's PU address. For the example shown in Figure 8.14, this would be to address PU B. When the group poll to PU B occurs, the 3174 responds by transmitting any LU data it has in storage. This enables the control unit to retrieve LU data from each DSPU and respond to the group poll by transmitting any LU data it has stored, rather than having to wait for a specific

a. Conventional polling

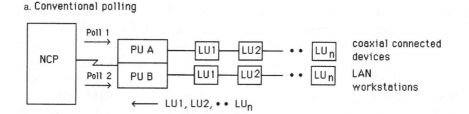

b. Group polling

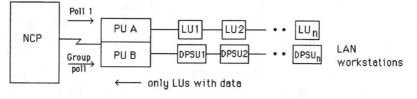

Figure 8.14 Conventional versus group polling.

LU poll. Group polling thus reduces the nonproductive polling cycles associated with conventional LU polling. This reduction causes an increase in the capacity of a communications line to support data transfer, and typically reduces LAN workstation response times by 10 to 20 percent.

Ethernet Connectivity

Until 1992, 3174 control units supported only the use of Token-Ring adapter cards, limiting direct connectivity of the 3174 to a Token-Ring network. Although IBM now provides an Ethernet adapter card for its 3174 control unit, there are alternative methods for using a 3174 to provide gateway support for Ethernet networks. These are worth examining, since we can then note some of the numerous vendor gateway construction options available for connecting different types of LANs into an SNA network.

In Figure 8.12, we saw how a Token-Ring network could be connected to an SNA network through a 3174 control unit Token-Ring adapter. A similar mixture of hardware and software can be used to connect an Ethernet/IEEE 802.3 network to an SNA network, as illustrated in Figure 8.13, in which an Ethernet card inserted into a 3174 control unit provides connectivity to an Ethernet LAN.

Figure 8.15 demonstrates the use of a gateway PC to connect an Ethernet 10BASE-T network to an SNA network. In this example, the gateway PC contains a Token-Ring adapter card for connection to a MAU and an Ethernet card for connection to a 10BASE-T wire hub. Although it may appear that the gateway functions as a bridge, it operates at a much higher level—although it does transfer information between the Token-Ring and the Ethernet network. If the Ethernet is operating Novell NetWare, the gateway PC translates LUs into IPX addresses and vice versa. This address conversion is based on configuring the gateway PC software when the gateway is installed. Since LU assignments are defined in the NCP in the communications controller, this means that the gateway installation process must occur in close coordination with NCP programmers, who encode the NCP to recognize the gateway as a downstream PU with LUs assigned to that PU. In addition, to enable stations on the Ethernet to gain full-screen access to mainframe applications, each station desiring such access must execute an appropriate terminal emulation program similar to that described for the previous Token-Ring network.

In the example illustrated in Figure 8.10, one vendor markets a gateway that can be configured to operate as one to eight separate PUs, with each PU capable of supporting up to 32 LUs. Since two LUs on one PU are reserved, that vendor's product provides the ability to support up to 254 LUs. This provides the servicing of up to 127 workstations that use separate LUs for screen and printer, or a lesser number of workstations that require the ability to execute

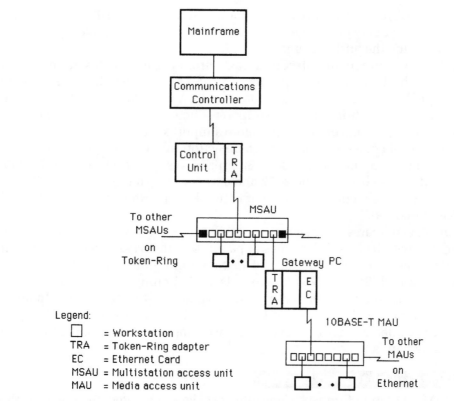

Figure 8.15 Using a control unit TRA to interconnect an Ethernet network. Through the installation of a Token-Ring adapter and an Ethernet card and appropriate software, the gateway PC provides a connection from a 10BASE-T network to the mainframe via a Token-Ring network.

multiple SNA sessions in the form of additional LUs. Although Figure 8.15 presumes the use of a gateway PC to provide connectivity to a 10BASE-T network, the previously described network structure would also be applicable for a Fast Ethernet connection. To do so, a 100BASE-T NIC would be installed in the gateway PC and connected to a Fast Ethernet hub.

3172 InterConnect Controller

A relatively recent addition to the family of IBM networking products is that vendor's 3172 InterConnect Controller. The 3172 can be viewed as a sophisticated local 3174 control unit gateway, because it provides access to a channel-attached host for workstations on Ethernet, Token-Ring, FDDI, and PC Network local area networks. The latter is a broadband LAN developed by Sitec for IBM during the mid-1980s.

Under the control of an InterConnect Control Program, LAN stations obtain access to a host subsystem operating TCP/IP. This enables the mainframe to provide TCP/IP functions to each connected LAN, including both static and RIP routing. In addition, the 3172 supports concurrent access to SNA and OSI subsystems. This controller can therefore support separate local area network connections via one common direct connection to the high-speed channel of a mainframe computer, such as an Enterprise system or an older S370/390. Other differences between the 3172 and a 3174 concern the number of Token-Ring network connections, the type of networks supported, and the number of DSPUs supported.

Table 8.6 compares the major features of a local 3174 with a 3172. In comparing the two devices, it becomes apparent that the 3172 is better suited for organizations that have a number of LANs within a building where a mainframe is located. Since the 3172 supports a maximum of four LAN adapters, its use permits the replacement of four separate 3174 control units. In addition, by supporting four different types of local area networks, the 3172 provides a considerably greater level of networking gateway support than that obtainable with a 3174.

Using the 3172 InterConnect Controller

The IBM 3172 InterConnect Controller can be considered to represent the Swiss Army knife equivalent of gateway computers. The 3172 can be directly channel attached to S/370 and S/390 computers either via a parallel or ESCON

TABLE 8.6 Comparison of 3172 and 3174 General Features

Feature	3172	Local 3174
Parallel channel support	2	1
Token-Ring network support	4*	1
Ethernet support	4*	1
FDDI	1*	0
PC network support	4*	0
DSPU support	1020**	250

*Maximum total of 4 LAN adapters.

**Maximum of 255 per adapter.

channel, and supports the connection of a variety of LAN and WAN connections as well as a mixture of protocols that can run over those connections.

Although we previously discussed the general networking capability of the 3172 InterConnect Controller, we will now look at a specific example of its flexibility. Figure 8.16 illustrates how a 3172 InterConnect Controller can be used as a gateway between an IBM host and the Internet. In this example, the 3172 InterConnect Controller enables TCP/IP communications to flow on the Token-Ring and Ethernet networks shown connected to the 3172. This in turn enables the router-based connection to the Internet to reach the mainframe via the 3172. As a word of caution, this schematic relies upon the filtering capability of the router for security. Many organizations will prefer an additional level of protection in the form of a firewall that can add authentication and encryption to the use of access lists.

Software Considerations

Although the 3172 and other gateway products provide users with the ability to route data between devices that communicate using different protocols, you must also consider the software on the end station accessing the host to obtain a full gateway capability. As previously noted in this chapter, IBM's 3270 Information Display system uses special codes to enable and disable a variety of terminal features associated with that vendor's original series of

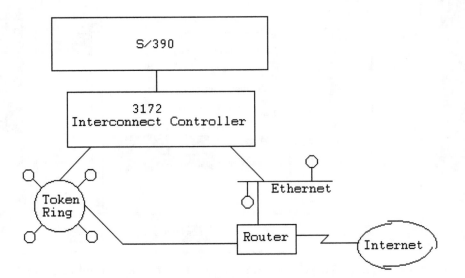

Figure 8.16 Using the 3172 InterConnect Controller.

fixed-logic terminal devices. As PCs began to replace dumb terminals, emulation programs were required to enable PC-based LAN workstations to obtain keyboard and screen operation compatibility with IBM hosts. One of the most popular IBM 3270 display station emulation programs is IBM's PCOM/3270, an acronym for IBM's Personal Communications/3270 series of emulation programs.

If the 3172 can be considered as the Swiss Army knife of gateways, the PCOM/3270 can be considered to represent the Swiss Army knife of emulation programs. PCOM/3270 supports a variety of mainframe attachment methods, ranging from LAN adapters and coaxial cable to asynchronous and synchronous serial communications. Figure 8.17 illustrates the PCOM/3270 Customize Communications display screen, which shows four options for communicating from a coaxial-based PC to a S/390 host. In examining Figure 8.17, note that the entry Coax in the column labeled Adapter is shown selected, which results in the display of four attachment methods shown in

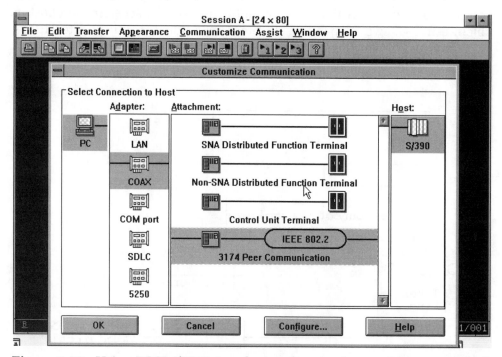

Figure 8.17 Using PCOM/3270 to select an appropriate attachment method when using a coaxial cable adapter for host communications.

the middle of the illustration. In comparison, the use of a LAN adapter card provides a terminal emulation capability for a larger number of attachment options. Figure 8.18 illustrates the PCOM/3270 configuration display after the LAN option was selected for the adapter card. In this example, the highlighted bar is shown placed over the IEEE 802.2 attachment method. Thus, if we were configuring a LAN station or an Ethernet or Token-Ring network connected to an S/390 via a TIC or a similar gateway method, we would select that attachment method.

Once you select your attachment method, you can customize your workstation's session parameters. Figure 8.19 illustrates the customization screen for an SDLC connection from a PC to an S/390 host. Although the default screen display of 24 lines by 80 columns is shown, PCOM/3270 supports a number of screen-size options that work relatively well with SVGA-based workstations. For example, if your requirements include a 132-column display, you can easily adjust the screen size by a simple point and click operation.

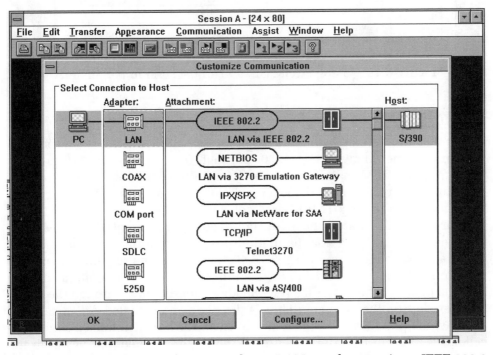

Figure 8.18   Using PCOM/3270 to select a LAN attachment via an IEEE 802.2 network.

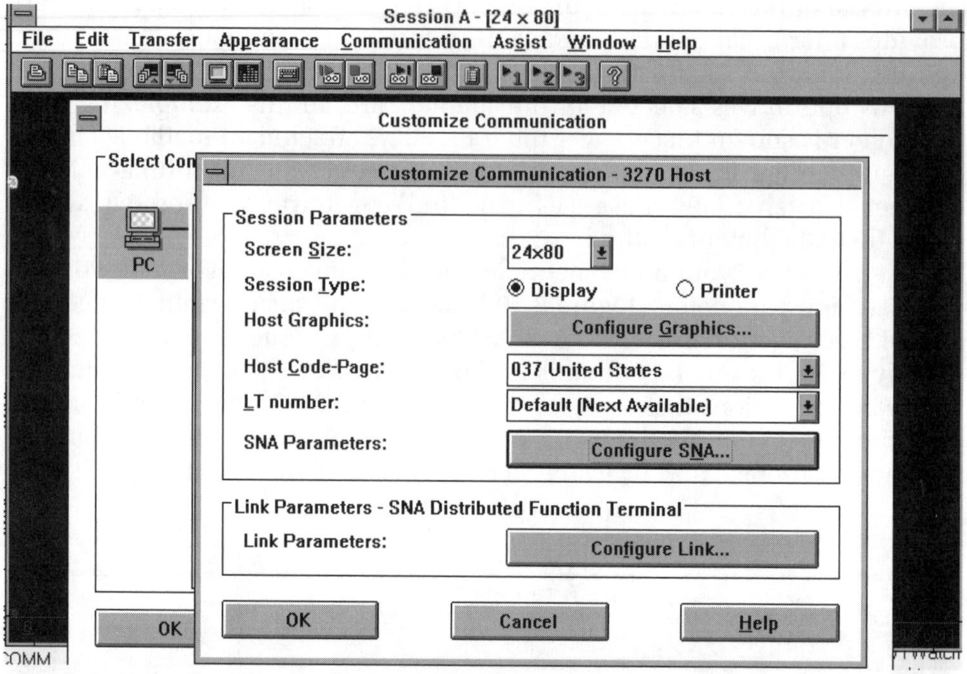

Figure 8.19 Using PCOM/3270 to adjust session parameters.

TN3270 Operations

One of the more interesting methods for accessing S/390 hosts is via a special version of Telnet known as TN3270. Through the use of a TN3270 program you can access IBM mainframes connected to the Internet via the Internet. This capability results from the fact that TN3270 represents a TCP/IP program that operates on top of a TCP/IP protocol stack.

Figure 8.20 illustrates the connection configuration of the NetManage Chameleon TN3270 terminal emulation program to initiate a session with a mainframe whose IP address is 192.76.46.1. Note that the session request will occur on TCP port 23, and the PC running TN3270 will operate as a 3270 model 2 display which uses a 24- by 80-character display. Through the use of the More button the program displays the dialog box labeled Advanced Settings, which provides users with the ability to further customize a communications session. In fact, the selection of the button labeled Settings from the Advanced Settings dialog box generates the box labeled Graphics located in the lower portion of Figure 8.20. Note that clicking the Program Symbols

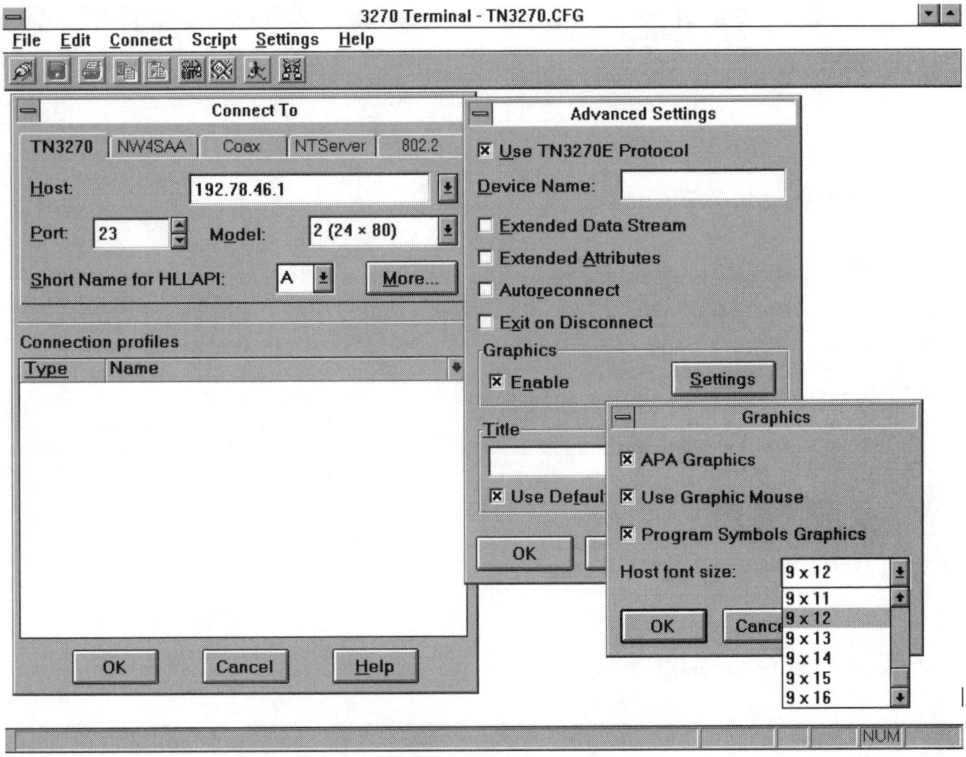

Figure 8.20 Using the NetManage Chameleon TN3270 terminal emulation program to obtain TCP/IP access to an IBM SNA host.

Graphics box enables a user to change the host font size whose default value is shown highlighted as 9 by 12 pixels. Thus, the NetManage TN3270 terminal emulation program provides users with the ability to tailor their screen display to a particular requirement as well as to set specific parameters to access a mainframe. Figure 8.21 illustrates a TCP/IP connection to a S/390 using TN3270 via an Internet connection to a 3172, which in turn is connected to a S/390 mainframe. Although the TN3270 program used by the author uses a GUI interface, the actual display generated by the S/390 host is text based. This is illustrated in Figure 8.21, which shows the use of TN3270 to access a calendar stored on a mainframe calendar system. Now that we have an appreciation for APPN and SNA gateways and the use of emulation software, we can turn our attention to the integration of APPN and SNA traffic into a TCP/IP network. Since this capability can be considered to represent an

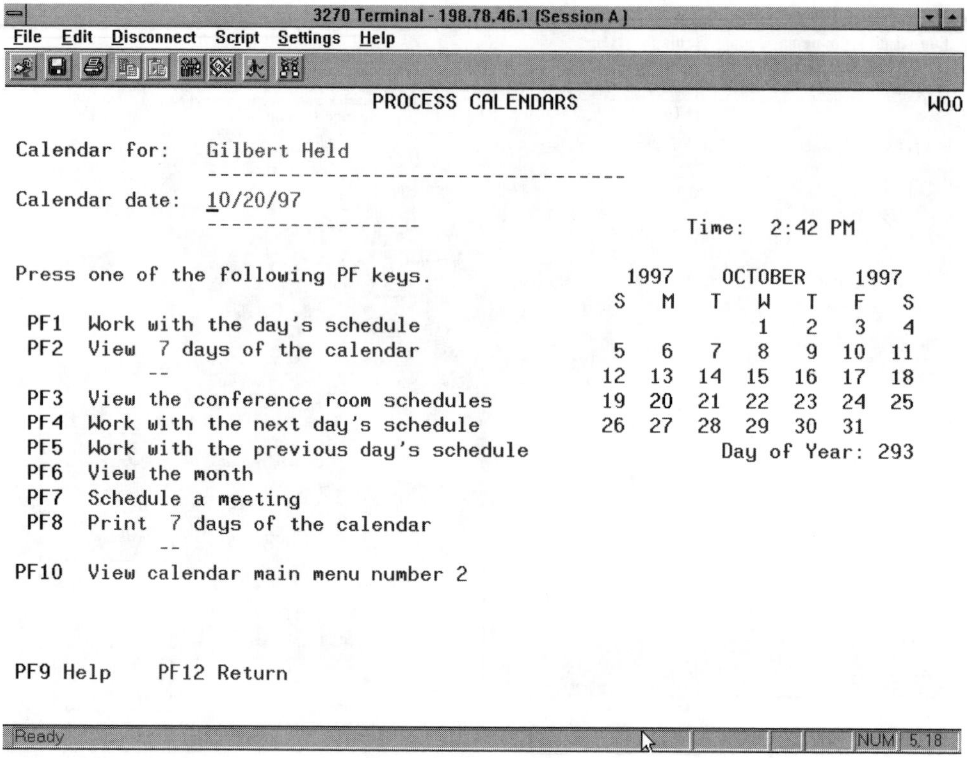

```
—|                    3270 Terminal - 198.78.46.1 (Session A )              |▼|▲|
 File  Edit  Disconnect  Script  Settings  Help
 ┌──┬──┬──┬──┬──┬──┬──┬──┐
 │  │  │  │  │  │  │  │  │
 └──┴──┴──┴──┴──┴──┴──┴──┘
                         PROCESS CALENDARS                              WOO

   Calendar for:   Gilbert Held
                   ------------------------------------
   Calendar date:  10/20/97
                   ------------------             Time:   2:42 PM

   Press one of the following PF keys.        1997    OCTOBER    1997
                                              S   M   T   W   T   F   S
     PF1  Work with the day's schedule                    1   2   3   4
     PF2  View  7 days of the calendar        5   6   7   8   9  10  11
          --                                 12  13  14  15  16  17  18
     PF3  View the conference room schedules 19  20  21  22  23  24  25
     PF4  Work with the next day's schedule  26  27  28  29  30  31
     PF5  Work with the previous day's schedule       Day of Year: 293
     PF6  View the month
     PF7  Schedule a meeting
     PF8  Print  7 days of the calendar
          --
     PF10 View calendar main menu number 2



     PF9 Help    PF12 Return

 |Ready                                                ▷|    |    |   |NUM| 5,18|
```

Figure 8.21 Using a TN3270 session to access a mainframe-based calendar system.

SNA to TCP/IP gateway performed by data link switching, we will next focus our attention upon this gateway technique.

Alternative Gateway Methods

The previous gateways used the services of a TRA or Ethernet card on a control unit, or an InterConnect Controller requiring the physical presence of a 3172 or a 3174 to connect to an SNA network. Several vendors, including IBM and third-party vendors like Eicon Technology of Montreal, Canada, recognize that the additional cost of a control unit or InterConnect Controller can limit the effectiveness of that gateway method. They therefore market alternative solutions that enable different types of local area networks to access SNA networks over wide area network facilities. Thus, let's examine a few of these alternative solutions.

SDLC Connectivity

An SDLC gateway consists of a pair of adapter cards installed in a personal computer and appropriate software to perform the required conversion from the local area network's packet format to an SNA data stream. One card is an SDLC adapter, which provides the framing for the bit-oriented protocol used by SNA. Most vendor SDLC gateways include SNA functions in ROM on the adapter card, which makes the card function as if it were a series of 3274 control units (multiple PUs), with each PU associated with a group of LUs. This second adapter is typically a Token-Ring or Ethernet adapter, used to connect the gateway to either a Token-Ring or Ethernet local area network.

Figure 8.22 shows the use of an SDLC gateway to obtain access to a communications controller via a wide area network or an extended distance cable.

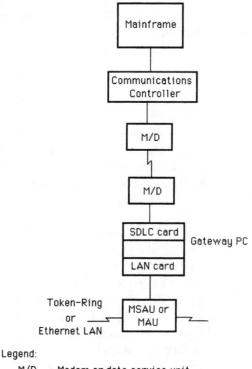

Legend:
    M/D   = Modem or data service unit
    MSAU = Multistation access unit
    MAU   = Media access unit

Figure 8.22   Using an SDLC gateway. An SDLC gateway provides access to an SNA network by providing communications between a LAN and a communications controller.

For the latter, the use of an SDLC gateway may permit the connection of a LAN to a communications controller via a lengthy cable within a building. This may be more attractive than using the gateway via a control unit LAN adapter whose cable distance is limited by LAN cabling restrictions.

Both RS-232 and V.35 connectors can be obtained with most SDLC adapters. Using an RS-232 connector limits the SDLC transmission rate to 19.2 Kbps, while using a V.35 connector enables digital transmission facilities at 56 or 64 Kbps to connect the gateway to the communications controller.

Some SDLC gateways are limited to support of one PU and 32 LUs. Other SDLC gateways expand considerably on that basic level of support. For example, an Eicon SNA gateway product that uses SDLC connectivity to a communications controller supports 32 PUs and up to 254 sessions. In addition, an Eicon gateway can be configured using up to four cards, and can then support a total of 128 PUs and 1016 sessions. Of course, limiting the transmission to either 19.2 Kbps or 56/64 Kbps per card may severely restrict LAN performance during mainframe access.

Gateway Software

As previously discussed, one of the more commonly used gateway software programs is IBM's Personal Communications/3270 (PC/3270) program, which is a replacement for that vendor's earlier PC 3270 Emulation Program (EP). PC/3270 supports communications with LAN workstations using PC/3270 or OS/2 Extended Edition, PC 3270 Emulation Program, or IBM's 3270 Workstation Program. The gateway can be configured to communicate with an IBM SNA host via an Ethernet, Token-Ring, or SDLC, or as an SNA distributed functional terminal (DFT). Later in this chapter, we will discuss the concept behind DFT access to a mainframe.

Unlike the PC 3270 Emulation Program, which limits support to 32 concurrent sessions, a gateway using IBM's PC/3270 program can support up to 253 host sessions; it permits up to 256 stations to be configured per gateway, although only 64 can be active at any one time. The gateway appears to the host as a single PU Type 2.0 node with up to 253 attached LUs. To attached stations, the gateway appears as an SNA primary communications device, emulating the PU and LU activation and deactivation functions that are required to establish and maintain SSCP-PU and SSCP-LU sessions between the host and the downstream workstations.

Another IBM software product worth mentioning is the OS/2 Extended Edition SNA Gateway (EE gateway). Although this program works very much like IBM's PC/3270 gateway, it adds LU pooling, which makes LU assignments considerably more efficient.

Under LU pooling, a group of LUs is allocated on a first-come-first-served basis. Since it is quite common for only a subset of users to require the simultaneous use of LU sessions—for example, by directing output to a printer—the pool of LUs can be smaller than when LUs are assigned on an individual basis. LU pooling can thus reduce the number of LUs required in the network and enable those resources, such as memory buffer areas, to be used more efficiently. This typically improves the response of a gateway to an LU request. In addition, to avoid any possible LU pool contention, OS/2 EE permits specific sessions to be dedicated and bypass LU pool contention. Another advantage of LU pooling is its ability to support more than 64 concurrently active stations: the OS/2 EE gateway places some or all of its available LUs into an LU pool and allocates those LUs when individual users request access to the mainframe.

Gateway Configuration

The configuration of an SDLC gateway is similar to that of most other gateways. That is, it requires the installer to make a large number of configuration decisions, and demands a prior knowledge of the SNA network to which the gateway will provide a connection. Some of the configuration parameters are related to the SDLC connection to a communications controller, while other configuration parameters govern the manner in which workstation users gain access to the SNA network through the gateway.

Examples of SDLC configuration parameters include defining the type of line connection (switched or nonswitched), transmission mode (full- or half-duplex), circuit type (point-to-point or multipoint), clocking provider (modem/DSU or adapter card), the maximum information frame size, number of PUs and LUs, and the maximum window size for transmission. For an SDLC leased line connection, you would normally specify a nonswitched, multipoint line. The maximum information frame size should be set to equal the MAXDATA macrodefinition, as defined in the NCP, plus three bytes. The maximum window size is the number of frames that can be received before an acknowledgment is required; this, to a degree, governs the efficiency of the SDLC communications circuit. Conventional SDLC supports up to seven unacknowledged frames, while extended control field SDLC supports a maximum of 127 unacknowledged frames before requiring an acknowledgement. Normally, large window sizes are preferred for use on circuits that have a significant propagation delay, such as circuits established by a satellite transmission or a relatively long international circuit. Extending the window size reduces delays associated with acknowledgments that propagate in the reverse direction to transmission. This significantly increases the transmission efficiency of the line.

A second set of configuration parameters governs the manner in which the gateway functions as a control unit. Configuration parameters include the number of PUs and LUs and the manner in which LUs are allocated. Under dynamic LU allocation, the SNA gateway software maintains a list of all free LUs. When the gateway receives a request to function as an LU, one is assigned from the pool. In comparison, the direct allocation of LUs requires each station user to specify an LU number to be used. If the LU is not free, the user must then specify another LU.

X.25 Connectivity

As previously mentioned in this chapter, SNA networks support the ITU X.25 protocol. This support is not a standard part of an SNA network—it requires that an IBM software program known as NCP Packet Switching Interface (NPSI) be obtained and loaded as an NCP module in a communications controller. Through the use of NPSI, an IBM communications controller, such as the 3745, can be directly connected to a packet switching network. This, in turn, enables any terminal device capable of supporting the X.25 protocol to communicate with the communications controller via a packet network's transmission facilities.

To take advantage of NPSI and the use of a packet switching network as a data transport mechanism, several vendors introduced X.25 gateways. This type of gateway is also constructed through the use of adapter cards installed in the system unit of a personal computer. Typically, two or three adapter cards may be required, although the actual number is dependent on a vendor's use of ROM versus loadable software. One adapter card provides the connection to the local area network, and a second adapter card packages data into packets for transmission on the packet network. Either a third card or loadable software will make the gateway PC function as a downstream PU with LUs—in effect, as a control unit. Data from the local area network is converted into a 3270 format and encapsulated into an X.25 data stream by the gateway personal computer. That data is routed through the packet network to the IBM communications controller, where the NPSI port converts the datastream back into the 3270 format created by the gateway PC. Figure 8.23 shows the operation of an X.25 gateway.

One of the major advantages of an X.25 gateway is its ability, through the use of packet switching, to support multiple logical connections inherently over a single physical connection. This means that one SNA X.25 gateway can be used to provide a connection to multiple IBM host computers connected to a packet network. Since each host computer requires a PU definition, this also

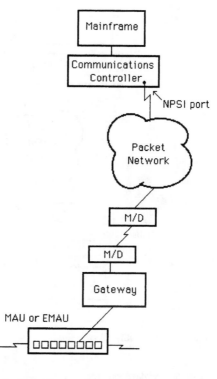

Figure 8.23 X.25 gateway operation. An X.25 gateway converts LAN packets into a 3270 data stream and encapsulates the data into X.25 packets for transmission through a packet network.

means that there is a practical limit of 32 concurrent connections that are obtainable through the use of an X.25 gateway.

Figure 8.24 shows a single SNA X.25 gateway used to support multiple logical connections via a single physical link—in this example, to two SNA host computers. Software used for the support of multiple logical connections is referred to as *X.25 Qualified Logical Link Control* (*QLLC*), and must operate on the gateway as well as on each IBM communications controller.

As with an SDLC gateway, the major constraints of an X.25 gateway are its operating rate, throughput, and PU and LU support. The operating rate of an X.25 card is limited to 64 Kbps; however, its throughput may be consider-

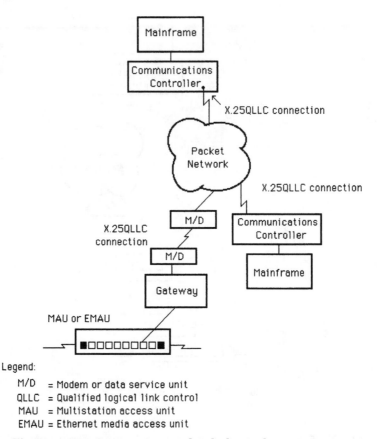

Legend:

M/D = Modem or data service unit
QLLC = Qualified logical link control
MAU = Multistation access unit
EMAU = Ethernet media access unit

Figure 8.24 Supporting multiple logical connections.

ably less than that of an SDLC gateway operating at the same data rate. This is because the X.25 gateway not only packets data, adding additional overhead, but also has its data checked as it flows through the packet network. The additional delays due to the error checking performed at packet switches can add between 0.25 and 0.5 seconds to the response time of network users. However, one NPSI port can provide support for more than one X.25 gateway connected via a packet network to the mainframe location. In comparison, each SDLC gateway requires the use of a separate SDLC port on the communications controller. Therefore, the decision to use SDLC or X.25 gateways must consider the cost of using a public network versus building a network. There is also a trade-off between performance and hardware cost in the form of additional communications controller ports. Since an X.25 gateway encapsulates the functions of an SDLC gateway into X.25 packets, it should come as no surprise that their PU and LU support should be the same. This appears to be true for all vendor products examined by the author.

The TIC Connection

Using a token interface coupler (TIC) installed in a communications controller provides a gateway access method very similar to that of a control unit with a TRA. That is, the TIC is cabled to an MAU port, and one or more gateway PCs are also cabled to an MAU port. However, as the name of the TIC implies, it supports only the direct attachment of a Token-Ring network. Through the addition of an Ethernet adapter and translating bridging software, the gateway can support an Ethernet network. At the time this book was written, there was no such hardware as an Ethernet interface coupler.

Figure 8.25 illustrates the use of a TIC to provide mainframe access from both Token-Ring and Ethernet network users to a mainframe via a translation gateway. Here the gateway must perform as a translating bridge converting Ethernet frames to Token-Ring frames and vice versa as well as supporting conventional gateway operations. This network structure is best suited for organizations that already use a TIC to support a Token-Ring network and wish to add Ethernet access to the mainframe via the addition of a translating gateway with Token-Ring and Ethernet network adapters so it becomes a participant on both networks.

The primary differences between the use of a communications controller TIC and a control unit TRA are in the areas of connection method, cost, network interconnection distance, operating rate, and PU and LU support.

Although a TIC provides a direct connection for a Token-Ring network, it cannot be used similarly to provide connectivity for an Ethernet network. Instead, you would have to connect an Ethernet network via a Gateway PC to a Token-Ring MSAU, with the MSAU in turn cabled to a TIC.

A TIC can cost well over $5,000. In comparison, a TRA costs under $500. The use of a TIC restricts access to the LAN cabling distance, since the communications controller must be cabled to an MAU under lobe length distance restrictions. A local control unit, on the other hand, can be connected via coaxial cable to a communications controller. This enables the gateway distance to be extended. If a remote control unit is used, that device functions similarly to a remote communications controller, since both the TRA and the TIC cabling distances to an MAU are governed by lobe distance restrictions.

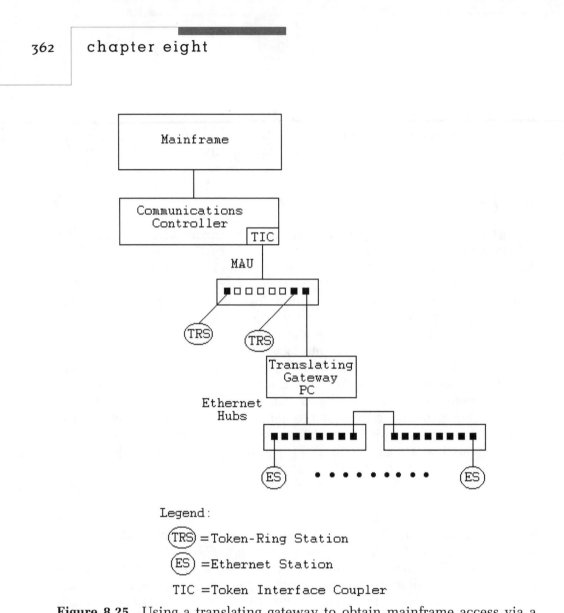

Figure 8.25 Using a translating gateway to obtain mainframe access via a Token-Ring interface coupler.

In a local environment, the communications controller and control unit are both channel-attached to a host computer, and their data transfer capabilities are similar. In a remote environment, the transmission rate of a control unit is restricted to a maximum of 56 Kbps. A remote communications controller can operate at T1/E1 data rates, providing over 20 times the data transfer capability of a control unit. Thus, the TIC can provide a higher level of throughput when used at a remote location.

The biggest difference between using a TRA or Ethernet card and using a TIC is in the area of PU and LU support. The NCP on a communications controller can support up to 9999 PUs for a TIC. Each gateway PC functioning as a PU will support a grouping of LUs based on the gateway software used. Another key difference between using a TRA or Ethernet card and using a TIC concerns the method of gateway communications.

When a control unit LAN adapter provides a connection to the Token-Ring or Ethernet network, the communications controller polls the control unit, the control unit polls each downstream PU, and each gateway polls its LUs. When a TIC is used, each downstream PU requests service from the TIC by using a dial-up service. This can considerably reduce the polls flowing on an attached local area network. As a result, the TIC can theoretically support up to 9999 PUs.

3278/9 Coaxial Connection

A rather outdated and limited-function gateway is based on the use of a 3278/9 coaxial adapter card. Instead of emulating a 3X74 control unit like SDLC and X.25 gateways, the coaxial adapter permits a gateway PC to be connected to a port on a 3X74 control unit. That port can be configured as a distributed function terminal (DFT) port. When used in this manner, the DFT port provides access to five sessions, because it represents five LUs. Gateway software then divides the five SNA mainframe sessions among contending workstations on the local area network. This means that a coaxial adapter–based gateway is limited to providing a maximum of five simultaneous host sessions. As with the other gateways described in this section, a Token-Ring or Ethernet adapter card would be installed in the gateway to provide a connection to the local area network. Figure 8.26 shows the hardware used to provide a 3278/9 coaxial cable gateway.

Although a coaxially connected gateway is limited in its session support, it operates at coaxial cable data transfer rates to the control unit. If a local control unit is used, the operating rate of a coaxially connected gateway can approach 2 Mbps. In comparison, SDLC- and X.25-type gateways are limited to a 56-Kbps data transfer rate. Coaxially connected gateways can provide a high level of SNA access performance for small local area networks when such networks are at the mainframe location. In addition, this method eliminates the necessity of obtaining a TIC, TRA, or Ethernet card, and can be used with older 3274 control units that cannot support the installation of a LAN adapter. Thus, the coaxially connected gateway also represents the lowest cost gateway.

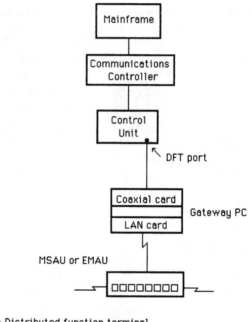

Legend:

DFT = Distributed function terminal
MSAU = Multistation access unit
EMAU = Ethernet media access unit

Figure 8.26 3278/9 coaxial connectivity. Through the use of a 3278/9 coaxial adapter card, LAN card, and a DFT port on a control unit, up to five LAN workstations can access an SNA network simultaneously.

8.4 Data Link Switching

One of the major problems associated with SNA- and APPN-based networks is the fact that both are essentially proprietary. As the use of TCP/IP expanded for interconnecting LANs on private intranets as well as for communications with the Internet, many organizations were forced to maintain two separate networks, one for SNA and one for a second network protocol, which is commonly TCP/IP.

In an effort to better support customer requirements for improving connectivity and lowering the cost associated with multiprotocol networking, IBM developed a tunneling mechanism referred to as data link switching (DLSw). DLSw was first introduced by IBM in 1992 as a feature of its 6611 bridge-router series of products referred to as the NWay 6611 Network Processor. IBM submitted its effort to the Internet Engineering Task Force (IETF), which resulted in DLSw being standardized as RFC 1434. It was also standardized by an IBM-sponsored, multivendor forum known as the APPN Implementors' Workshop.

Overview

Data link switching was developed as a mechanism to support SNA and Net-BIOS data traffic via both bridged and router-based networks in a multiprotocol environment. Although DLSw is primarily used to tunnel SNA and NetBIOS under IP, it can also be used to tunnel other protocols. Since DLSw enables organizations to merge their SNA and APPN networks with their IP-based networks, many redundant communications links become candidates for removal, enabling organizations to operate a more efficient and less costly network infrastructure.

Operation

Under DLSw the connection-oriented protocols of SNA and NetBIOS in the form of Logical Link Control Type 2 (LLC2) and SDLC packets are encapsulated into IP packets. Figure 8.27 illustrates an example of the manner by which

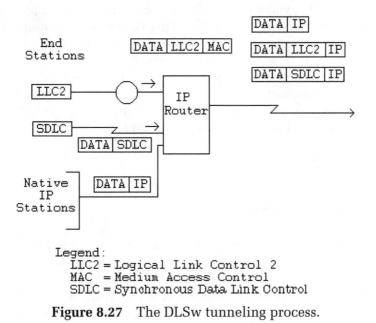

Figure 8.27 The DLSw tunneling process.

point-to-point SDLC traffic and LAN-based LLC2 traffic are integrated into an IP router-based network. In examining Figure 8.27, note that the tunneling effort involves wrapping the IP header around SDLC or LLC2 data. Since such data then becomes encapsulated, as you might expect, another term used to reference the transport of SDLC and LLC2 data in IP packets is encapsulation.

Although the actual tunneling or encapsulation process appears to be relatively simple to accomplish, in actuality it is a complicated process. The complication results from the fact that SNA uses connection-oriented protocols, LLC2 and SDLC, which are based upon positive acknowledgment with retransmission (PAR). As such, if an ACK is not received within a period of time after a sequence of frames are transmitted, a timer will expire, resulting in the sending station retransmitting the data. If due to network congestion a circuit failure or other impairments repeat, after a predefined number of repeats the connection will be terminated, resulting in the loss of any in-progress SNA and NetBIOS sessions. Since IP is a connectionless protocol, the transport of SDLC and LLC2 data within IP would very likely result in periodic session time-outs as traffic density varies during the day. To prevent this situation from occurring, DLSw relies on spoofing, with the sending router acknowledging frames as they are received. The routers then use a reliable transport protocol, such as TCP, to ensure that data arrives at its intended destination. A slightly different procedure is used for SDLC, which relies on the constant polling between primary and secondary SDLC stations. DLSw-capable routers perform proxy polling. That is, the sending router intercepts polls from the SDLC primary station while another router polls the SDLC secondary station as if it were the SDLC primary station. Since polls are not passed onto the IP network, transmission efficiency is enhanced.

Although any encapsulation or tunneling method adds overhead in the form of an additional header, the use of spoofing and proxy polling can be considered as a significant counterbalance. Thus, in most cases the overhead associated with the use of additional headers will have a negligible effect upon the overall performance of DLSw.

8.5 Communications Servers

A communications server is a relatively new term being used for a multifunction protocol gateway. The idea behind the communications server is to provide network managers and LAN administrators with protocol independence, enabling network design and restructuring decisions to be made independent of existing network topology constraints associated with network protocols currently being used.

Although DLSw can be considered to represent a mechanism that provides a multiprotocol gateway capability, it is based upon the use of tunneling of LLC2 and SDLC in IP. Thus, it is restricted to enabling specific protocols to be transported under IP which, while an acceptable solution for the networking requirements of many organizations, may not be sufficient for use by other organizations. Another problem associated with the use of tunneling or encapsulation is the fact that application data must first be structured through one protocol stack before being encapsulated and processed through a second protocol stack. This means that in addition to an additional load being placed on the network in the form of dual headers, there is also an additional processing time at each device that performs the encapsulation function.

MPTN

Recognizing the previously described problems, IBM developed a protocol conversion facility which works on several types of hardware platforms operating its AIX and OS/2 operating systems as well as under Microsoft's Windows NT. This protocol conversion facility is called Multiprotocol Transport Networking (MPTN) and employs protocol conversion instead of encapsulation whenever possible.

MPTN operates at the application programming interface (API) layer. Operating at the lower portion of the application layer in the protocol stack, MPTN would, for example, convert the sockets interface to use SNA protocols instead of TCP/IP or the APPC interface to use TCP/IP protocols instead of SNA. Through the use of MPTN, an application invokes its preferred API without knowledge of the actual network protocol that will be used. MPTN then converts the API calls to use the protocol of the desired transport network. Figure 8.28 provides a comparison between protocol encapsulation and MPTN's protocol conversion.

Through the use of protocol conversion the transport of information is not tied to a specific protocol. This means that from a theoretical basis a communications server could be developed to provide a large number of protocol conversions that could provide organizations with a protocol-independent capability. However, from a practical standpoint the development of conversion software is a time-consuming effort and most communications servers are limited to providing a gateway between SNA and TCP/IP networks, although certain IBM products also provide a conversion capability for Novell IPX as well as IBM's LAN Manager's NetBIOS.

Figure 8.29 illustrates the use of two communications servers to integrate IPX- and TCP/IP-based LANs with an SNA network. In this example one com-

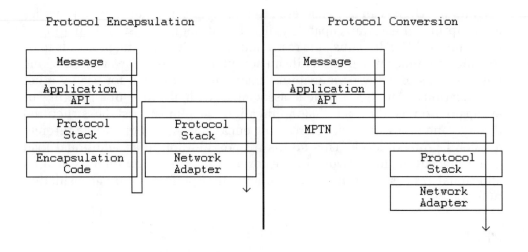

Protocol Encapsulation   Protocol Conversion

Legend:
 API = Application Program Interface
 MPTN = Multiprotocol Transport Networking

Figure 8.28   Comparing protocol encapsulation and conversion.

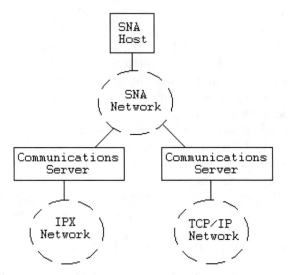

Figure 8.29   Using communications servers.

munications server provides conversion from the TCP/IP-based networks to SNA while the second server performs a similar function for an IPX network.

Other Gateways

Since any conversion device can be considered to represent a gateway, there are numerous gateway products network managers and administrators can consider when linking LANs and WANs. Some of those products include electronic mail gateways, which provide you with the ability to interconnect different e-mail systems, application gateways, and trusted gateways. An application gateway is another name for a proxy server and represents a more secure type of firewall. The proxy, which functions at one layer of the protocol stack, services all requests from clients, and, if allowed, forwards them to the other side of the network to their intended destination. In comparison, a trusted gateway represents a firewall whose software operates on a very secure operating system.

chapter nine

Intelligent and Switching Hubs

This chapter focuses upon two of the most rapidly evolving areas of communications technology—intelligent and switching hubs. The intelligent hub resulted from the incorporation of a microprocessor into a conventional hub as well as a redesign of the hub's backplane, enabling the collection of statistical information along with the ability to alter network configurations through a management port. Building upon the functionality of the intelligent hub, the switching hub uses the power of the microprocessor to examine the destination address of frames for use as a decision criterion concerning the routing of data through the switch. By adding a matrix switching fabric to the switch, data input on one port can then be routed to a different port on a dynamic basis. In addition, since an n port switch enables up to n/2 possible concurrent simultaneous cross-connections to be supported, the use of a switching hub can significantly enhance available bandwidth in comparison to the use of a shared media network.

Since switching hubs can be considered as an evolution in the development of intelligent hubs, we will first examine the operation and use of intelligent hubs in this chapter. Once this is accomplished, we will focus our attention upon switching hubs. In doing so, we will first note how both conventional and nonswitching intelligent hubs can become a network bottleneck, providing us with an appreciation of how the operation of switching hubs can overcome many network bottleneck situations.

In our examination of switching hubs we will note the use of both layer 2 and layer 3 switches. Although the vast majority of switching hubs currently operates at the media access control layer, during 1997 several types of switches were introduced that operate at the network layer. As we examine switching features, we will also review the operation of several types of layer 3 switches to obtain an appreciation for their potential use.

After examining different switching methods supported by switching hubs and their features, we will turn our attention to the use of this product in constructing different types of networks. Since no product, to include a switching hub, is without one or more limitations, we will conclude this chapter by examining a key problem associated with this device, and methods used by some manufacturers to overcome this key switching hub limitation.

9.1 Intelligent Hubs

As we noted earlier in this book, every Ethernet 10BASE-T network contains a minimum of one hub. The hub operates as a multiport repeater, receiving signals from any device connected to it and repeating the signal at its full strength.

As the number of stations on an Ethernet 10BASE-T network expands, a hub will eventually run out of ports. Expanding the network successfully requires the use of another hub, with one hub connected to another to form a bus structure. The process by which hubs are connected to one another is commonly referred to as *cascading*. Figure 9.1 shows the cascading of three hubs, each capable of supporting 8 devices, resulting in the support of a total of 24 devices.

Although most hubs are capable of being rack mounted, most 10BASE-T hubs consist of an individual chassis. In addition, the installation of two or more hubs into a rack requires the cabling of one hub to another in a cascading manner to form a bus structure. To facilitate the installation of multiple hubs, vendors developed a device commonly referred to as a *concentrator*.

Concentrators and Hubs

An Ethernet 10BASE-T concentrator is a special type of hub: it has a built-in expansion capability that eliminates the need to install cascaded hubs as your network grows, if you desire that such growth be controlled from a centrally located wiring closet. A concentrator consists of a chassis to which you add module boards. Depending on the manufacturer, module boards may contain one or more ports. Some of the more common concentrators support up to 100

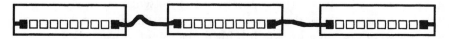

Figure 9.1   Cascading hubs. The process by which hubs are connected to one another to form a bus is commonly referred to as *cascading*.

Ethernet 10BASE-T connections, with two additional connections reserved for special use. One connection is typically reserved to connect a personal computer or workstation running network management software, while the other reserved port connection allows diagnostic test equipment to be attached to the network without requiring a port serving an existing device. The backplane of the concentrator serves as a cascaded cable, and the insertion of module boards makes it relatively easy to expand the number of ports to accommodate a growing network.

A hub or conventional concentrator treats all network devices as equals. That is, each device is cabled to a port to obtain access to the network.

Hub Cards

Hub cards provide an alternative architecture to stand-alone hubs and concentrators. First brought to market by Novell, hub cards are designed to turn a personal computer into a network hub. Using a Novell hub, you can integrate a hub function into a NetWare server, enabling the Novell software operating on the server to provide a network management capability. In comparison, stand-alone concentrators and other types of hubs that provide network management support typically require the use of a separate personal computer to initiate network management operations.

Advantages of Use

In our introductory discussion of hubs, we alluded to a few of the advantages of their use. Now, let us focus in some detail on the advantages of using hubs by examining the capabilities of different hub configurations. In our discussion of the use of different hub configurations, we will actually refer to the use of intelligent hubs. Thus, we should first differentiate between intelligent and nonintelligent hubs.

Intelligent versus Nonintelligent Hubs

An intelligent hub is a hub with a built-in microprocessor designed to perform certain predefined functions. Those functions may include recognizing commands to turn ports on and off, obtaining statistics concerning the usage level of different ports, displaying those statistics and the status of defined ports or groups of ports, permitting network traffic to be viewed from a control console, and facilitating diagnostic testing. In addition, certain types of intelligent hubs provide you with the ability to integrate different types of local area networks because they support the use of bridge and router modules. The modern intelligent hub is thus a building block for the construction of an enterprise network. However, since the hub simply repeats data received on one port onto all other ports, it maintains the shared media bandwidth constraint. Thus, although intelligent hubs provide a significantly enhanced network management capability, they do not alter the basic shared media bandwidth constraint associated with the use of an Ethernet network. This is true whether the intelligent hub supports 10 Mbps, 100 Mbps, or Gigabit Ethernet operations.

Single Hub/Single LAN

A single hub used to support the connectivity requirements of users on a single LAN is one of the most common types of hub applications. Note that in using the term *hub,* we are now excluding the conventional Ethernet hub from consideration. For the remainder of this section, we will restrict our use of the term hub to refer to an intelligent device with a built-in microprocessor capable of responding to predefined commands. For simplicity, we will refer to the intelligent hub as a hub; however, our discussion is also applicable to an intelligent concentrator.

   The top portion of Figure 9.2 shows, from a physical perspective, the use of a ten-module hub to establish a four-station Ethernet network. Here, the remaining six modules can be used to expand the network, provide spare connections, and connect test equipment or a network management console to the network. The lower portion of Figure 9.2 illustrates a logical view of the Ether-

Physical view

Logical view

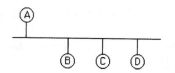

Figure 9.2   Single hub/single LAN configuration.

net network established through the use of the hub. So far, this is no different from the results obtained from a dumb hub, so you may be wondering what advantages there are to using intelligent hubs.

With most intelligent hubs, you can turn port traffic on and off with the simple click of a mouse, drag icons representing stations to reposition devices on a ring, or remove a station from the ring for testing without disrupting traffic from stations remaining on the ring.

Figure 9.3 shows the physical and logical view of using an intelligent hub to isolate station D from the Ethernet network and then test the adapter board in that station without disrupting traffic on the network. Note that in comparing Figure 9.3 with Figure 9.2, the use of an intelligent hub enables test equipment to be cabled to any available port module on the hub. Then, the intelligent hub enables the user to create a test logical bus–based network, which is used to connect test equipment to the station to be tested. This capability to separate one network into two or more logical segments derives from the ability of the backplane of the hub to transfer data at a rate significantly beyond that of a LAN. This enables the creation of two or more separate LANs within the hub by the multiplexing of separate LAN transmissions over time.

The ability of intelligent hubs to generate network statistics and segment a network into multiple networks provides LAN administrators and network managers with a powerful performance measurement tool. When network usage increases to the point where collisions become excessive, you will more

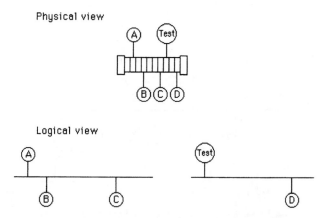

Figure 9.3 Ethernet testing. Many intelligent hubs permit users to logically subdivide the network, enabling test equipment to be used without adversely affecting the operation of stations not being tested.

than likely use an intelligent hub to segment an existing network. This provides you with the ability to balance traffic between workstations and from workstations to one or more servers.

Multiple Hubs/Single LAN

Figure 9.4 shows how an intelligent hub can be used to segment a saturated Ethernet network. The top portion of the illustration shows the physical view of the multiple hubs that may be necessary to obtain the required number of ports for constructing a large Ethernet network. In this example, it was assumed that each hub module is capable of supporting four ports. The interconnection of two ten-module hubs thus permits up to 80 devices to be connected to a single Ethernet network. For some hubs, the connection of one hub to another requires the use of a port on each hub, reducing the maximum number of devices that can be serviced by two ten-module hubs to 78.

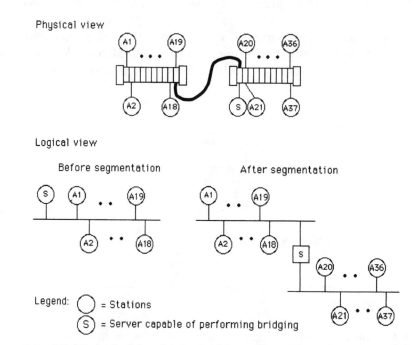

Figure 9.4 Multiple hub/multiple LAN configuration. A saturated Ethernet network can be segmented into two or more networks to increase performance.

The lower portion of Figure 9.4 illustrates the logical view of the network before and after its segmentation. In this example, it was assumed that as a result of a review of traffic statistics, we decided to segment the network so that 19 stations are located on one segment and 18 stations are located on the other segment. By adding a network interface card (NIC) to the server, we can connect that device to both networks. If the server supports bridging operations, internetwork connectivity between workstations on each network is obtained. Otherwise, if internetwork communication is required and the server cannot provide this capability, you can probably obtain a bridge module that can be inserted into a hub.

Two additional configurations available with intelligent hubs that warrant discussion are single hub/multiple LAN and multiple hub/multiple LAN configurations.

Single Hub/Multiple LAN

With a sophisticated backplane design, most intelligent hubs support networks using different protocols, topologies, and types of wiring. When bridge and router modules are available for insertion into a hub chassis, you can not only support multiple LANs from a single hub, but also enable stations on one LAN to communicate with stations on another LAN, located even hundreds or thousands of miles from the hub.

The top portion of Figure 9.5 shows from a physical perspective the use of a single hub to support multiple LANs. The lower portion of the figure shows the logical view, in which Ethernet and Token-Ring networks are supported through a common hub. With a bridge module installed in the hub, you can obtain an inter-LAN communications capability. In addition, the filtering capability built into most intelligent hubs provides you with a mechanism to control the flow of information between LANs, as well as between any LAN segments you may wish to create. This capability provides you with another mechanism to manage an enterprise network through the network management system of an intelligent hub.

Distributed Multiple Hubs/Single LAN

The fourth configuration obtainable through the use of intelligent hubs is an extension of the previously discussed single hub/single LAN configuration. That is, multiple hubs used to construct a single LAN can provide you with alternative network testing and control locations if you locate hubs in differ-

Physical view

Logical view

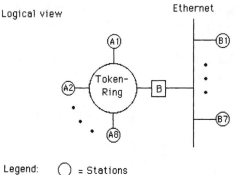

Legend: ◯ = Stations
         B = Bridge

Figure 9.5 Single hub/multiple LAN configuration.

ent areas within a building or throughout a college campus. For example, you could locate an intelligent hub in the wiring closet on each floor of a building and cable each hub together to form a building-wide network. In reality, as your network expands, you will probably subdivide your network, based on the number of stations located on each floor and use bridge modules inserted in the hub to connect each network. Now that we have an appreciation for the functionality and capability of intelligent hubs, let's turn our attention to the operation and use of switching hubs.

9.2 Switching Hubs

The incorporation of microprocessor technology into hubs can be considered as the first step in the development of switching hubs. Through additional programming, the microprocessor could examine the destination address of each frame; however, switching capability required the addition of a switching fabric design into the hub. Once this was accomplished, it became possible to use the microprocessor to read the destination address of each frame and initiate a switching action based upon data stored in the hub's memory, which associates destination frame addresses with hub ports.

There are two basic types of switching hubs, with the major difference between each type resulting from the layer in the ISO Reference Model where switching occurs. A layer 2 switch looks into each frame to determine the destination MAC address while a layer 3 switch looks further into the frame to determine the destination network address. Thus, a layer 2 switch operates at the MAC layer and can be considered to represent a sophisticated bridge while a layer 3 switch resembles a router. Both layer 2 and layer 3 operations will be covered as we examine the operation and use of switching hubs.

In this section we will first examine the rationale for switching hubs by noting the bottlenecks associated with conventional and intelligent hubs as network traffic grows. Once this is accomplished, we will focus upon the operation and usage of different types of switching hubs.

Rationale

The earliest types of Ethernet LANs were designed to use coaxial cable configured using a bus topology. The development of the hub-based 10BASE-T local area network offered a number of networking advantages over the use of coaxial cable. Some of those advantages included the use of twisted-pair cable, which is easier to use and less expensive than coaxial cable, and the ability to reconfigure, troubleshoot, and isolate network problems. By simply moving a cable connection from one port to another network, administrators can easily adjust the usage of a hub or interconnect hubs to form a new network structure. The connection of test equipment to a hub, either to a free port or by temporarily removing an existing network user, could be accomplished much easier than with a coaxial-based network. Recognizing these advantages, hub manufacturers added microprocessors to their hubs, which resulted in the introduction of a first generation of intelligent Ethernet hubs.

The first generation of intelligent hubs used the capability of a built-in microprocessor to provide a number of network management functions network administrators could use to better control the operation and usage of their network. Those functions typically include tracking the network usage level and providing summary statistics concerning the transmission of frames by different workstations, as well as providing the network administrator with the ability to segment the LAN by entering special commands recognized by the hub.

Bottlenecks

Both conventional and first-generation intelligent hubs simply duplicate frames and forward them to all nodes attached to the hub. This restricts the flow of data to one workstation at a time, since collisions occur when two or more workstations attempt to gain access to the media at the same time.

Conventional hubs, to include the first generation of intelligent hubs, create network bottlenecks, because all network traffic flows through a shared backplane. This results in every workstation connected to the hub competing for a slice of the backplane's bandwidth. For example, consider the hub illustrated in Figure 9.6, in which up to seven workstations and a file server contend for access to the network. Since only one device can transmit at any point in time, the average slice of bandwidth that each device receives is 1.25 Mbps (10 Mbps/8). The actual data transfer capability is less, since attempts by two or more workstations to simultaneously transmit can result in collisions that cause jam signals to be placed on the network, precluding other workstations from transmitting data during the duration of those signals. As more users are added to a network through the interconnection of hubs, network performance will continue to decrease as the potential for congestion increases. Thus, manufacturers of Ethernet products, as well as network administrators, focused their efforts upon developing different tools and techniques to alleviate network congestion.

Congestion-Avoidance Options

There are several techniques you can consider to alleviate network congestion. Those techniques include splitting a network into two, with each segment con-

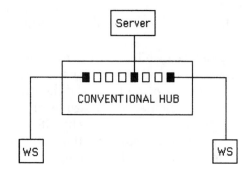

Figure 9.6 When using a conventional hub, congestion occurs when several workstations vie for access to a server.

nected to a separate server port, using bridges and dual servers, employing a router to develop a collapsed backbone network linking multiple network segments, or using one or more intelligent switches.

Network Segmentation

One of the earliest methods used to alleviate network congestion was obtained through the use of a server with an internal bridging capability. Splitting the network infrastructure into two and connecting each resulting segment to an NIC installed in a server provides the capability to reduce traffic on each segment, in comparison to traffic previously carried on a nonsegmented network.

Figure 9.7 illustrates the segmentation of a network into two on one server. NetWare, as well as other LAN operating systems, includes a capability to move packets between cable segments. This enables users on each segment to transmit and receive information from users on other segments, as well as maintain access to a common server. If server usage is low but network usage is high, this method of network subdivision represents a cost-effective method for reducing the effect of network congestion upon LAN performance.

In examining Figure 9.7, note that a workstation on each network segment can simultaneously transmit data to the server or receive data from the server. Thus, segmentation not only reduces network congestion, but in addition can double throughput if the server is capable of supporting sustained transmission to or receiving data from workstations on both segments.

Bridging

The major problem associated with the use of a server for network segmentation is the fact that it must perform internal bridging in addition to its file

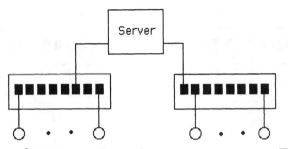

Figure 9.7 Network segmentation using a common server. Through the use of a file server that can move packets between segments, you obtain the ability to subdivide a network.

server operations. This usually limits the ability of the server to support network segments with a large number of workstations. In addition, the workstations on the connected segments still contend for the services of a common server. Thus, the use of a stand-alone bridge is usually the next step to consider when the level of network usage adversely affects LAN performance, and segmentation through the use of a file server is not a viable option.

Figure 9.8 illustrates the use of a bridge for network segmentation. Although the segmentation shown in Figure 9.8 is similar to the segmentation shown in Figure 9.7, there are several distinct differences between the two methods. First, the stand-alone bridge requires file servers to be located on one or more network segments. Secondly, since a stand-alone bridge is performing the required bridging functions, more workstations can be placed on each network segment than when a file server performs bridging operations. Workstations on each segment can simultaneously access the server on each segment, permitting network throughput to double when such traffic is localized to each segment.

Using a Router

Although primarily thought of as a mechanism to interconnect geographically dispersed networks, routers can be used as switching devices to interconnect network segments located within one geographical area, such as a building or campus. The networking architecture associated with the use of a router in this manner is referred to as a collapsed backbone, since the older bus-structured Ethernet LAN is replaced by LAN segments that communicate

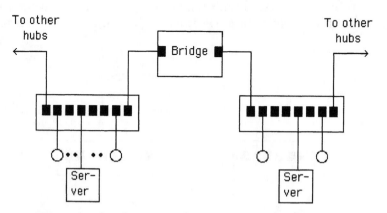

Figure 9.8 Using a bridge for network segmentation. The use of a bridge and one or more servers on each interconnected segment can significantly increase network capacity by localizing more traffic on each segment.

with one another through the router. Until 1994, the primary device used in the center of a collapsed backbone network was a router. Since then, switching hubs have gradually taken over the role of routers for reasons we will discuss later in this chapter.

Figure 9.9 illustrates a collapsed backbone formed through the use of a router. Note that you can locate servers on network segments for which server access is limited to workstations on the segment, and connect servers that are accessed by workstations on two or more segments to separate router ports. Thus, a router provides you with the ability to distribute network traffic based upon server access requirements. In addition, the construction of a collapsed backbone offers other benefits over distributed networks. Those advantages include the centralization of complexity and economy of operations. Rather than dispersing routers, locating a single router near a network technical control center can make network management easier. Then, if a routing problem arises, you may not have to send a technician to every location where hubs and servers are installed, since router management software may be able to pinpoint the problem. Since one router may be able to replace a number of less capable devices, you may also obtain some economic benefits from the use of a single router.

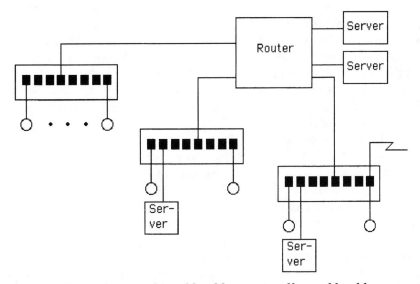

Figure 9.9 Collapsed router-based backbone. A collapsed backbone topology based upon the use of a router enables servers to be distributed based upon network access requirements.

Three additional benefits associated with the use of a router for creating a collapsed backbone network are security, protocol support, and the control of broadcast traffic. Many routers have a sophisticated filtering capability, permitting you to program templates that enable only predefined applications from predefined network users to access other network segments or servers connected to the router. Concerning protocol support, many routers can support multiprotocol transmission. Thus, you could connect a router port to a mainframe and pass SNA traffic between the mainframe and workstations on different network segments, as well as switching other protocol traffic between workstations and different types of servers. Since the use of a router results in a hierarchical network structure where frames are transported based upon network addresses, this provides the ability to restrict broadcast traffic generated on one segment to that segment. Thus, service advertisements commonly generated by different types of servers can be localized to the segment where they are located instead of flowing onto other segments where they would consume bandwidth.

Although the advantages associated with the use of routers to create a collapsed backbone are considerable, their use has several disadvantages. Those disadvantages include the complexity and cost of routers, as well as the latency or delay time associated with moving packets from one network segment to another segment. Concerning router latency, although all devices have a degree of latency, the delay associated with routers greatly exceeds that of bridges. The reason for this is the fact that routers operate at the network layer while bridges operate at the data link layer. This means that a bridge can inspect the beginning of each frame to determine its destination. In comparison, a router must look into each frame to determine the destination network address. Thus, the processing rate of a router is generally 50 to 75 percent of the processing rate of a bridge.

Another problem associated with the use of routers is the *eggs in one basket* syndrome, since the failure of the router results in the inability of many network users to access servers or send messages to users on other network segments. The latter problem has been addressed by router manufacturers through redundant logic and power supplies, as well as the use of modular components that can be easily swapped out without bringing down the router when a component failure occurs. Although the latter problem is applicable to intelligent switching hubs, this device addresses some of the problems associated with the use of routers, as well as—through improved functionality—permits switching hubs to provide an enhanced level of overall network performance. Thus, let's focus our attention upon the operation and use of switching hubs in the remainder of this chapter.

Switching Hub Operations

Switching hubs can be categorized in three main ways—by their method of operation, their support of single or multiple addresses per port, and the layer in the ISO Reference Model where switching occurs. The method of operation is commonly referred to as the switching *technique,* while the address-per-port support is normally referred to as the switching *method.*

The third main way of categorizing a switching hub is based upon the type of address used as a switching decision criteria—data link layer MAC addresses or network layer network addresses. Since switching hubs that support layer 3 switching actually represent a switch with a built-in routing capability, we will discuss layer 3 switches as a separate entity. Thus, we will first examine layer 2 switching hubs before focusing our attention upon layer 3 switches.

Layer 2 Switching

A switch that operates at the data link layer is a multiport bridge that reads MAC destination addresses and uses those addresses as a decision criterion for determining where to switch each frame. When operating at the data link layer, a switching hub provides several distinct advantages over the use of conventional and intelligent hubs. First, a switching hub does not transmit or regenerate data onto every port. Instead, unicast data flow is restricted to a routing from one port to a second port. This precludes a network user from operating a monitor and observing the flow of data on the network. Hence, switching hubs, although not necessarily secure devices, provide a more secure environment than a shared Ethernet LAN.

A second advantage of switching hubs is their ability to support simultaneous communication sessions. For example, consider a simple four-port switching hub with port numbers 1, 2, 3, and 4. If a user on port 1 is switched to a server on port 3, and another user on port 2 is switched to a server on port 4, you obtain two very short-duration, simultaneous communications sessions. Thus, in this example, bandwidth is double that of a conventional hub. If the switching hub supports only 10BASE-T operating rates, the four-port switch provides a maximum of two simultaneous cross-connections, doubling potential bandwidth to 20 Mbps. As we will note later in this chapter, many switching hubs incorporate full-duplex, Fast Ethernet, and Gigabit Ethernet technology, providing bandwidth many orders of magnitude beyond that obtainable from the use of a conventional hub.

Switching Techniques There are three switching techniques used by switching hubs—cross-point, also referred to as cut-through or *on the fly,* store-and-forward, and a hybrid method which alternates between the first two methods, based upon the frame error rate. As we will soon note, each technique has one or more advantages and disadvantages associated with its operation.

Cross-Point A cross-point switch examines the destination address of each packet entering the port. It then searches a predefined table of addresses associated with ports to obtain a port destination. Once the port destination is determined, the switch initiates the cross-connection between the incoming port and the outgoing port. Figure 9.10 illustrates cross-point/cut-through switching.

As previously noted in this chapter, a layer 2 switch can be considered to represent a more sophisticated type of bridge capable of supporting multiple simultaneous cross-connections. Thus, it should come as no surprise that a cross-point switch uses a backward learning algorithm to construct a port-destination address table. That is, the switch monitors MAC source addresses encountered on each port to construct a port-destination address table. If the destination address resides on the same port the frame was received from, this indicates that the frame's destination is on the current network and no switching operation is required. Thus, the switch discards the frame. If the destination address resides on a different port, the switch obtains the port destination and initiates a cross-connection through the switch, transferring the frame to the appropriate destination port where it is placed onto a network where a node with the indicated destination address resides. If the destination address is not found in the table, the switch floods the frame onto all ports other than the port it was received on. Although flooding adversely affects the capability of a switch to perform multiple simultaneous cross-connections, the majority

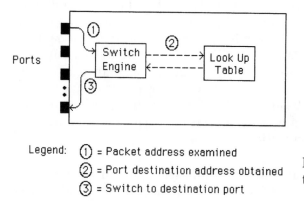

Legend: ① = Packet address examined
② = Port destination address obtained
③ = Switch to destination port

Figure 9.10 Cross-point/cut-through switching.

of this type of activity occurs when a switch is powered on and its port-address table is empty. Thereafter, flooding occurs periodically after an entry is purged from the table due to aging and a new request to a purged destination occurs, a new station becomes a recipient of traffic, or when a broadcast address is encountered.

Cross-point switching minimizes the delay or latency associated with placing a packet received on one port onto another port. Since the switching decision is made once the destination address is read, this means the full packet is not examined. Thus, a cross-point switch cannot perform error checking on a packet. This limitation does not represent a problem for most networks due to extremely low error rates on local area networks. However, when errored packets are encountered, they are passed from one network segment to another. This results in an unnecessary increase in network use on the destination segment, as a store-and-forward switch would simply discard packets containing one or more bit errors.

Latency Considerations A cross-point switching method only requires a small portion of a frame to be stored until it is able to read the destination address, perform its table lookup operation, and initiate switching to an appropriate output port. Due to this, latency is minimized.

Latency functions as a brake on two-way frame exchanges. For example, in a client/server environment the transmission of a frame by a workstation results in a server response. Thus, the minimum wait time is 2 * latency for each client-server exchange, lowering the effective throughput of the switch. We can compute the minimum amount of latency associated with a cross-point switch as follows. At a minimum, the switch must read 14 bytes (8 bytes for the preamble and 6 bytes for the destination address) before being able to initiate a search of its port-destination address table. At 10 Mbps we obtain:

$$96 \text{ μs} + 14 \text{ bytes} * 8 \text{ bits/byte} * 100 \text{ ns/bit}$$

or $\quad 9.6 \times 10 + 112 * 100 * 10^{-9}$

or $\quad 20.8 * 10^{-6}$ seconds

Here 96 μs represents the Ethernet interframe gap at an operating rate of 10 Mbps, while 100 ns/bit represents the bit duration of a 10-Mbps Ethernet LAN. Thus, the minimum one-way latency not counting switch overhead of a cut-through layer 2 switch is $20.8 * 10^{-6}$ seconds, while the round-trip minimum latency would be twice that duration.

Store-and-Forward A store-and-forward switching hub stores the full incoming packet in a buffer. This enables the switch to perform a CRC check to determine if the received packet is error-free. If it is, the switch uses the destination address of the packet to perform a table lookup to obtain the destination port address. Once that address is obtained, the switch performs a cross-connect operation and forwards the packet to its destination. Otherwise, the frame is considered to have one or more bits in error and will be discarded. Besides checking the CRC a store-and-forward switch will examine the entire frame. This enables other errors, such as runts and extended lengths (giant) frames to be caught and sent to the great bit bucket in the sky instead of being forwarded.

The storage of frames by a store-and-forward switch permits filtering against various frame fields to occur. Although a few manufacturers of store-and-forward intelligent switching hubs support different types of filtering, the primary advantage advertised by such manufacturers is data integrity and the ability to perform translation switching, such as switching a frame between an Ethernet network and a Token-Ring network. Since the translation process is extremely difficult to accomplish on the fly due to the number of conversions of frame data, most switch vendors first store the frame, resulting in store-and-forward switches supporting translation between different types of connected networks. Concerning the data integrity capability of store-and-forward switches, whether or not this is actually an advantage depends upon how you view the additional latency introduced by the storage of a full frame in memory as well as the necessity for error checking. Concerning the latter, switches should operate error-free, so a store-and-forward switch only removes network errors, which should be negligible to start with.

When a switch removes an errored frame, the originator will retransmit the frame after a period of time. Since an errored frame arriving at its destination network address is also discarded, many persons question the necessity of error checking by a store-and-forward switching hub. However, filtering capability, if offered, may be far more useful as you could use this capability, for example, to route protocols carried in frames to destination ports far easier than by frame destination address. This is especially true if you have hundreds or thousands of devices connected to a large switching hub. You might set up two or three filters instead of entering a large number of destination addresses into the switch. When a switch performs filtering of protocols, it really becomes a router. This is because it is now operating at layer 3 of the OSI Reference Model.

Figure 9.11 illustrates the operation of a store-and-forward switching hub. Note that a common switch design is to use shared buffer memory to store entire frames, which increases the latency associated with this type of switching hub. Since the minimum length of an Ethernet frame is 72 bytes, then the

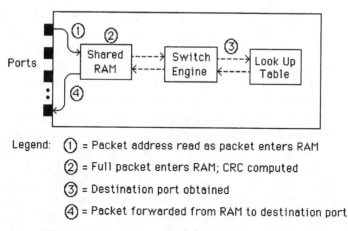

Legend: ① = Packet address read as packet enters RAM

② = Full packet enters RAM; CRC computed

③ = Destination port obtained

④ = Packet forwarded from RAM to destination port

Figure 9.11 Store-and-forward switching.

minimum one-way delay or latency, not counting the switch overhead associated with the lookup table and switching fabric operation, becomes:

$$96 \ \mu s + 72 \ \text{bytes} * 8 \ \text{bits/byte} * 100 \ \text{ns/bit}$$

or $9.6 * 10^{-6} + 576 * 100 * 10^{-9}$

or $67.2 * 10^{-6}$ seconds

Once again, 9.6 μs represents the 10-Mbps Ethernet interframe gap, while 100 ns/bit is the bit duration of a 10-Mbps Ethernet LAN. Thus, the minimum one-way latency of a store-and-forward Ethernet switching hub is .0000672 seconds, while a round-trip minimum latency is twice that duration. For a maximum-length Ethernet frame with a data field of 1500 bytes, the frame length becomes 1526 bytes. Thus, the one-way maximum latency at 10 Mbps becomes:

$$96 \ \mu s + 1526 \ \text{bytes} * 8 \ \text{bits/byte} * 100 \ \text{ns/bit}$$

or $9.6 * 10^{-6} + 12208 * 100 * 10^{-9}$

or   .012304 seconds

Hybrid A hybrid switch supports both cut-through and store-and-forward switching, selecting the switching method based upon monitoring the error rate encountered by reading the CRC at the end of each frame and comparing its value with a computed CRC performed on the fly on the fields protected by the CRC. Initially the switch might set each port to a cut-through mode of operation. If too many bad frames are noted occurring on the port the switch will automatically set the frame processing mode to store-and-forward, permitting the CRC comparison to be performed before the frame being forwarded. This permits frames in error to be discarded without having them pass through the switch. Since the switch, no pun intended, between cut-through and store-and-forward modes of operation occurs adaptively, another term used to reference the operation of this type of switch is adaptive.

The major advantages of a hybrid switch are that it provides minimal latency when error rates are low and discards frames by adapting to a store-and-forward switching method so it can discard errored frames when the frame error rate rises. From an economic perspective, the hybrid switch can logically be expected to cost a bit more than a cut-through or store-and-forward switch as its software development effort is a bit more comprehensive. However, due to the competitive market for communications products upon occasion its price may be reduced below competitive switch technologies.

Switching Methods Switching hubs can be classified with respect to their support of single or multiple addresses per port. The support of a single address per port is referred to as *port-based* switching, while the support of multiple addresses per port is referred to as *segment-based* switching.

Port-Based Switching A port-based switching hub can be considered to operate similar to an $n \times n$ matrix switch, reading the destination address of incoming frames from a single device connected to the port and using that address through a table lookup process to initiate a cross-connect to a destination port.

Figure 9.12 illustrates an example of port-based switching. Since each connected node is isolated from other nodes except when simultaneously contending for access to the same destination port, the resulting network throughput can be considerably higher than a shared Ethernet network. For example, user 1 could communicate with server 1, user 2 with server 2, and so on, all simultaneously. In this *best case* example, with n users and n servers, the operating rate through the switch becomes $n \times 10$ Mbps, or n times the operating rate of a conventional 10BASE-T Ethernet network.

It is important to compare the maximum potential throughput through a switch with its rated backplane speed. If the maximum potential throughput is less than the rated backplane speed, the switch will not cause delays based upon the traffic being routed through the device. For example, consider a 64-port switch that has a backplane speed of 400 Mbps. If the maximum port rate

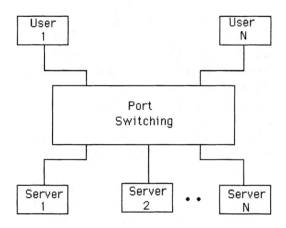

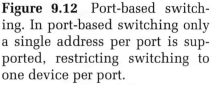

Figure 9.12 Port-based switching. In port-based switching only a single address per port is supported, restricting switching to one device per port.

is 10 Mbps, then the maximum throughput assuming 32 active cross-connections were simultaneously established becomes 320 Mbps. In this example the switch has a backplane transfer capability sufficient to handle the worst-case data transfer scenario. Now let's assume that the maximum backplane data transfer capability was 200 Mbps. This would reduce the maximum number of simultaneous cross-connections capable of being serviced to 20 instead of 32 and adversely affect switch performance under certain operational conditions.

Since a port-based switching hub only has to store one address per port, search times are minimized. When combined with a pass-through or cut-through switching technique, this type of switch results in a minimal latency to include the overhead of the switch in determining the destination port of a frame.

Segment-Based Switching A segment-based switch permits switched connectivity between multiple LAN segments, by supporting multiple addresses per port. The key difference between a segment-based switch and a port-based switch is in their ability to support multiple addresses per port. A port-based layer 2 switch only supports one MAC address per port. In comparison, a segment-based layer 2 switch supports multiple addresses per port, enabling it to support the direct connection of a single workstation or server as well as the connection of a segment to each port on the switch.

Figure 9.13 illustrates an example of a segment-based switching hub. Note that ports that support the connection of a segment must support switching for multiple MAC addresses. In examining the segment-based switching example illustrated in Figure 9.13, also note that workstations on each segment contend for access to *n* servers. Since a group of users is connected to the switching hub via a conventional hub, throughput is limited by the conventional hubs. In this example, two hubs would limit throughput of the network to 20 Mbps if a user on each segment accessed a different server. In comparison, a port-based switching hub can provide a higher throughput, since each network user is directly connected to a port on the switch. The primary advantage of a segment switching hub is cost, since a few ports can be used to support network segments containing a large number of LAN users.

Switching Processor The construction of intelligent switches varies both between manufacturers as well as within some vendor product lines. Most switches are based upon the use of either reduced instruction set computer (RISC) microprocessors or application-specific integrated circuit (ASIC) chips, while a few products use conventional complex instruction set computer (CISC) microprocessors.

   Although there are a large number of arguable advantages and disadvantages associated with each architecture from the standpoint of the switch manufacturer that are beyond the scope of this book, there are also some key considerations that warrant discussion with respect to evolving technology, such as virtual LANs. Both RISC and CISC architectures enable switches to be programmed to make forwarding decisions based upon either the data link

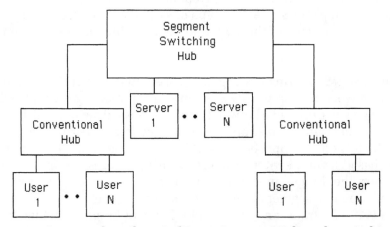

Figure 9.13 Segment-based switching. A segment-based switching technique requires each port to support multiple MAC addresses.

layer or network layer address information. In addition, when there is a need to modify the switch such as to enable it to support a vLAN standard when the standard is promulgated, this architecture is easily upgradable.

In comparison to RISC- and CISC-based switches, an ASIC-based device represents the use of custom-designed chips to perform specific switch functions in hardware. Although ASIC-based switches are faster than RISC- and CISC-based switches, there is no easy way to upgrade this type of switch. Instead, the vendor will have to design and manufacture new chips and install the hardware upgrade in the switch.

In early 1998 most switches used an ASIC architecture, as its speed enabled the support of cut-through switching. While ASIC-based switches provide the speed necessary to minimize latency, readers should carefully check vendor upgrade support as most vLAN standards can be expected to require modifications to existing switches.

Now that we have an appreciation for the general operation and use of switching hubs, let's obtain an appreciation for the high-speed operation of switch ports, which enables dissimilar types of networks to be connected and which can result in data flow compatibility problems along with methods used to alleviate such problems.

High-Speed Port Operations There are several types of high-speed port connections intelligent switches may support. Those high-speed connections include 100-Mbps Fast Ethernet, 1-Gbps Gigabit Ethernet, 100-Mbps FDDI, 155-Mbps ATM, full-duplex Ethernet and Token-Ring, and fat pipes, with the latter referencing a grouping of ports treated as a transmission entity. Another common name used in place of the term fat pipe is trunk group. The most common use of one or more high-speed connections on an intelligent switching hub is to support highly used devices, such as network servers and printers as well as for obtaining a backbone LAN connection capability. Figure 9.14 illustrates the use of an Ethernet switch, with two 100BASE-T Fast Ethernet adapters built into the switch to provide a high-speed connection from the switch to each server. Through the use of high-speed connections the cross-connection time from a server to client when the server responds to a client query is minimized. Since most client queries result in server responses containing many multiples of characters in the client query, this allows the server to respond to more queries per unit of time. Thus, the high-speed connection can enhance client/server response times through a switch. In examining Figure 9.14, let's assume a small query results in the server responding by transmitting the contents of a large file back to the client. If data flows into the switch at 100 Mbps and flows from the switch to the client at 10 Mbps, any buffer area in the switch used to provide temporary storage for speed incompatibilities between ports will rapidly be filled and eventually overflow, resulting in the loss of frames which, when compensated for by retransmission, compounds the problem. Thus, a mechanism is required to regulate the flow of data into and out of switch ports. That mechanism is known as flow control, and specific methods used to implement flow control will be covered later in this chapter when we discuss switch features.

Thus for now we can note that the intelligent switching hub or LAN switch is a highly versatile device that may support single or multiple devices per port and whose operation can vary based upon its architecture. By providing the capability for supporting multiple simultaneous cross-connections, the LAN switch can significantly increase network bandwidth, and its ability to support high-speed network connections enhances its versatility. Now that we have a basic appreciation for the operational characteristics of generic Ethernet LAN switches, we can use that information as a base and focus our attention upon the operation of Ethernet switches.

Switch Operations   Although features incorporated into Ethernet switches considerably differ between vendors as well as within vendor product lines, upon occasion we can categorize this communications device by the operat-

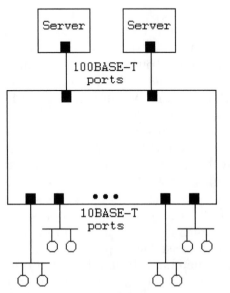

Figure 9.14   Using high-speed connections to servers.

TABLE 9.1 Types of Ethernet Switches Based
upon Port Operating Rates

All ports operate at 10 Mbps.
Mixed 10-/100-Mbps port operation.
All ports operate at 100 Mbps.
Mixed 10-/100-/1000-Mbps port operation.
All ports operate at 1000 Mbps.

ing rate of the ports they support. Doing so results in five basic types of Ethernet switches which are listed in Table 9.1. Switches that are restricted to operating at a relatively low data rate are commonly used for departmental operations, while switches that support a mixed data rate are commonly used in a tiered network structure at a higher layer in the tier than switches that operate at a low uniform data rate. Concerning the latter, when used in a tiered network structure the lower uniform operating rate switch is commonly used at the lower level in the tier.

Multi-Tier Network Construction

Figure 9.15 illustrates the generic use of a two-tiered Ethernet switch–based network, with the switch at the higher tier functioning as a backbone connectivity mechanism, which enables access to shared servers commonly known as global servers by users across departmental boundaries, while switches in the lower tier facilitate access to servers shared within a specific department. This hierarchical networking structure is commonly used with a higher-speed Ethernet switch such as a Fast Ethernet or Gigabit Ethernet switch, or with other types of backbone switches, such as FDDI and ATM, as well as with other types of lower-tier switches. One common variation associated with the use of a tiered switch–based network is the placement of both departmental and global servers on an upper-tier switch. This placement allows all servers to be colocated in a common area for ease of access and control and is commonly referred to as a server farm. However, if an upper-tier switch should fail, access to all servers could be affected, representing a significant disadvantage of this design. A second major disadvantage is the fact that all traffic has to be routed through at least two switches when a server farm is constructed. In comparison, when servers primarily used by departmental employees are connected to a switch serving departmental users, most traffic remains local to the local switch at the bottom of the tier.

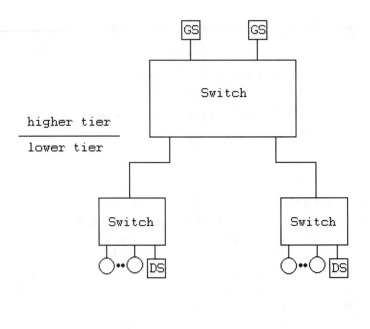

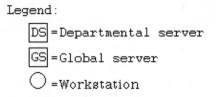

Figure 9.15 Generic construction of a two-tiered Ethernet switch–based network.

With the introduction of Gigabit Ethernet switches it becomes possible to use this type of switch in either a multitier architecture as previously shown in Figure 9.15 or as a star-based backbone. Concerning the latter, Figure 9.16 illustrates the potential use of a Gigabit Ethernet switch that supports a mixture of 100-Mbps and 1-Gbps ports. In this example the Gigabit Ethernet switch is shown being used to support two fat pipes or trunk groups, with one trunk group consisting of four 100-Mbps ports, while the second group consists of two 100-Mbps ports. To enable each grouping requires the use of switches from the same vendor since the establishment of fat pipes or trunk groups is a proprietary feature and not yet standardized.

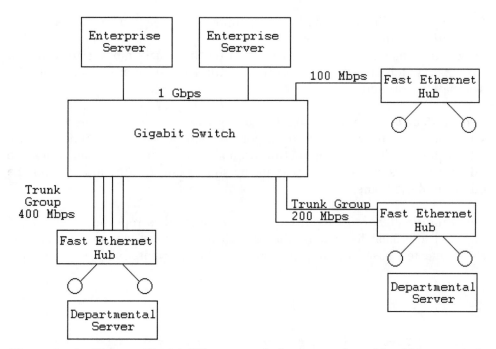

Figure 9.16   Using a Gigabit Ethernet switch as a star-based backbone switch.

In examining Figure 9.16 note that enterprise servers are connected to the Gigabit switch, while department servers are connected to 100-Mbps Fast Ethernet hubs. By connecting 10BASE-T switching hubs to Fast Ethernet hubs you could extend the star into a star-tiered network structure.

Basic Architecture

Regardless of the operating rate of each port on an Ethernet switch, most devices are designed in a similar manner. That is, most switches consist of a chassis into which a variety of cards are inserted, similar in many respects to the installation of cards into the system expansion slots of personal computers. Modular Ethernet switches that are scalable commonly support CPU, Logic, matrix, and port cards.

CPU Card   The CPU card commonly manages the switch, identifies the types of LANs attached to switch ports, and performs self and directed switch tests.

Logic Module   The logic module is commonly responsible for comparing the destination address of frames read on a port against a table of addresses it is responsible for maintaining, and instructing the matrix module to initiate a cross-bar switch once a comparison of addresses results in the selection of a destination port address.

Matrix Module   The matrix module of a switch can be considered to represent a cross-bar of wires from each port to each port as illustrated in Figure 9.17. Upon receipt of an instruction from a logic module, the matrix module initiates a cross-connection between the source and destination port for the duration of the frame.

Port Module   The port module can be considered to represent a cluster of physical interfaces to which either individual stations or network segments are connected based upon whether the switch supports single or multiple

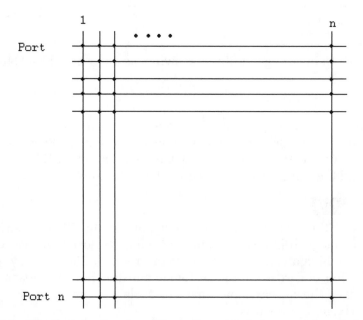

Figure 9.17   The key to the operation of a switch is a matrix module which enables each port to be cross-connected to other ports. The matrix module of a switch with n ports can be considered to represent an $n \times n$ star-wired backplane.

MAC addresses per port. Some port modules permit a mixture of port cards to be inserted, resulting in, as an example, 10 and 100 Mbps as well as full-duplex connections to be supported. In comparison, other port modules are only capable of supporting one type of LAN connection. In addition, there are significant differences between vendor port modules concerning the number of ports supported. Some modules are limited to supporting two or four ports, while other modules may support six, eight, or ten ports. It should be noted that many switches support other types of LAN port modules such as Token-Ring, FDDI, and even ATM.

Redundancy In addition to the previously mentioned modules, most switches also support single and redundant power supply modules and may also support redundant matrix and logic modules. Figure 9.18 illustrates a typical Ethernet modular switch chassis showing the installation of 11 modules to include five 8-port modules to form a 40-port switch.

Switch Features

There are literally an ever expanding number of features being incorporated into Ethernet switches. Those features range from providing such basic functions as port and segment switching to methods developed by some vendors to prevent erroneous frames from being transferred through the switch in a cut-through mode of operation. In this section we will review 19 distinct switch features, which are summarized in alphabetical order in Table 9.2.

The table of features presented was constructed not only to list features you should note, but, in addition, as a mechanism to facilitate the evaluation of switches. That is, you can indicate your requirement for a particular feature and then note whether or not that requirement can be satisfied by different vendor products by replacing *Vendor A* and *Vendor B* by the names of

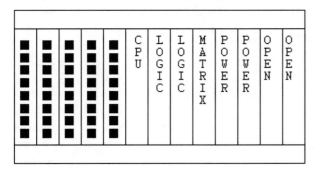

Figure 9.18 A typical Ethernet modular switch chassis containing a mixture of port, CPU, logic, matrix, and power cards.

TABLE 9.2 Ethernet Switch Features

Feature	Requirement	Vendor A	Vendor B
Address table size support			
Addresses/port	_____	_____	_____
Addresses/switch	_____	_____	_____
Aging settings	_____	_____	_____
Architecture			
ASIC-based	_____	_____	_____
CISC-based	_____	_____	_____
RISC-based	_____	_____	_____
Autonegotiation ports	_____	_____	_____
Backplane transfer capacity	_____	_____	_____
Error prevention	_____	_____	_____
Fat pipe and trunk group	_____	_____	_____
Filtering/forwarding rate support			
Filtering rate	_____	_____	_____
Forwarding rate	_____	_____	_____
Flow control			
Backpressure	_____	_____	_____
Software drivers	_____	_____	_____
802.3x flow control	_____	_____	_____
No control	_____	_____	_____
Full-duplex port operation	_____	_____	_____
Jabber control	_____	_____	_____
Latency	_____	_____	_____
Management	_____	_____	_____
Mirrored port	_____	_____	_____
Module insertion	_____	_____	_____
Port buffer size	_____	_____	_____
Port module support	_____	_____	_____
Spanning tree support	_____	_____	_____
Switch type			
Port-based switch	_____	_____	_____
Segment-based switch	_____	_____	_____
Switching mode			
Cut-through	_____	_____	_____
Store-and-forward	_____	_____	_____
Hybrid	_____	_____	_____
Virtual LAN support	_____	_____	_____

TABLE 9.2 (*Continued*)

Feature	Requirement	Vendor A	Vendor B
Port-based	———	———	———
MAC-based	———	———	———
Layer 3–based	———	———	———
Rule-based	———	———	———

switches you are evaluating. By duplicating this table, you can extend the two rightmost columns to evaluate more than two products. As we examine each feature listed in Table 9.2, our degree of exploration will be based upon whether or not the feature was previously described. If the feature was previously described in this chapter, we will limit our discussion to a brief review of the feature. Otherwise we will discuss its operation in considerable detail.

Address Table Size Support   The ability of a switch to correctly forward packets to their intended direction depends upon the use of address tables. Similarly, the capability of a switch to support a defined number of workstations depends upon the number of entries that can be placed in its address table. Thus, the address table size can be viewed as a constraint that affects the ability of a switch to support network devices.

There are two address table sizes you may have to consider—the number of addresses supported per port and the number of addresses supported per switch. The first address table constraint is only applicable for ports that support the connection of network segments. In comparison, the total number of addresses recognized per switch represents a constraint that affects the entire switch. Many Ethernet switches support up to 1024 addresses per port for segment-based support. Such switches may only support a total of 8192 addresses per switch. This means that a 16-port switch with 8 fully populated segments could not support the use of the 8 remaining ports as the switch would run out of address table entries. Thus, it is important to consider the number of addresses supported per port and per switch as well as match such data against your anticipated requirements.

Aging Settings   As explained earlier in this book when we discussed the operation of bridges, MAC addresses and their associated ports are stored with a time stamp value. This provides the bridge with the ability to purge old entries to make room for new entries in the port-address table. Since a switch is a multiport bridge, it also uses a timer to purge old entries from its port-address table. Some switches provide users with the ability to set the aging time within a wide range of values or to disable aging. Other switches have a series of predefined aging values from which a user can select.

Architecture   As previously noted, there are three basic methods used to construct LAN switches. Those methods include the use of application-specific integrated circuits (ASICs), complex or conventional instruction set computers (CISCs), and reduced instruction set computers (RISCs). Although the use of an ASIC-based architecture commonly results in a very low latency and high level of performance, upgrades are difficult to accomplish as such circuits must be replaced. In comparison, both conventional microprocessor and RISC-based switches use instructions in replaceable ROM. Although the differences may appear trivial, if an ASIC-based switch, for example, requires an upgrade to comply with a pending vLAN standard you would probably require a technician to visit your site to perform the upgrade. In comparison, you might be able to simply download a new software release from the vendor's World Wide Web site or electronic bulletin board to update a RISC- or CISC-based switch.

Autonegotiation Ports   To provide a mechanism to migrate from 10 Mbps to 100 Mbps, National Semiconductor developed a chip set known as NWay, which provides an automatic data rate sensing capability as part of an autonegotiation function. This capability enables a switch port to support either a 10- or 100-Mbps Ethernet attachment to the port; however, this feature only works when cabled to a 10-/100-Mbps network adapter card. You may otherwise have to use the switch console to configure the operating rate of the port or the port may be fixed to a predefined operating rate.

Backplane Transfer Capacity   The backplane transfer capacity of a switch provides you with the ability to determine how well the device can support a large number of simultaneous cross-connections, as well as its ability to perform flooding. For example, consider a 64-port 10BASE-T switch with a backplane transfer capacity of 400 Mbps. Since the switch can support a maximum of 64/2 or 32 cross connects, the switch's backplane must provide at least a 32 * 10 Mbps or 320 transfer capacity. However, when it encounters an unknown destination address on one port, the switch will output or flood the packet onto all ports other than the port the frame was received on. Thus, to operate in a nonblocked mode the switch must have a buffer transfer capacity of 64 * 10 Mbps or 640 Mbps.

Error Prevention   Some switch designers recognize that the majority of runt frames (frames improperly terminated) result from a collision occurring during the time it takes to read the first 64 bytes of the frame. On a 10-Mbps Ethernet LAN this is equivalent to a time of 51.2 μs. In a cut-through switch environment when latency is minimized, it becomes possible to pass runt frames to the destination. To preclude this from happening, some switch designers permit the user to introduce a 51.2-μs delay, which provides sufficient time for the switch to verify that the frame is of sufficient length to have a high degree of probability that it is not a runt frame. Other switches that operate in the cut-through mode may simply impose a 51.2-μs delay at 10 Mbps to enable this error prevention feature. Regardless of the method used, the delay is only applicable to cut-through switches that support LAN segments, as single user ports do not generate collisions.

Fat Pipe and Trunk Group   A fat pipe is a term used to reference a high-speed port. When 10BASE-T switches were first introduced, the term actually referenced a group of two or more ports operating as an entity. Today a fat pipe can reference a 100-Mbps port on a switch primarily consisting of 10-Mbps operating ports or a 155-Mbps ATM port on a 10-/100- or 100-Mbps switch. In addition, some vendors retain the term fat pipe as a reference to a group of ports operating as an entity while other vendors use the term trunk group to represent a group of ports that function as an entity. However, to support a grouping of ports operating as a common entity requires the interconnected switches to be obtained from the same company as the method used to group ports as proprietary.

Filtering and Forwarding Rate Support   The ability of a switch to interpret a number of frame destination addresses during a defined time interval is referred to as its filtering rate. In comparison, the number of frames that must be routed through a switch during a predefined period of time is referred to as the forwarding rate. Both the filtering and forwarding rates govern the performance level of a switch with respect to its ability to interpret and route frames. When considering these two metrics, it is important to understand the maximum frame rate on an Ethernet LAN, which was discussed earlier in this book.

Flow Control   Flow control represents the orderly regulation of transmission. In a switched network environment, there are a number of situations for which flow control can be used to prevent the loss of data and subsequent retransmissions, which can create a cycle of lost data followed by retransmissions. The most common cause of lost data results from a data rate mismatch between source and destination ports. For example, consider a server connected to a switch via a Fast Ethernet 100-Mbps connection, which responds to a client query when the client is connected to a switch port at 10 Mbps.

Without the use of a buffer within the switch, this speed mismatch would always result in the loss of data. Through the use of a buffer, data can be transferred into the switch at 100 Mbps and transferred out at 10 Mbps. However, since the input rate is 10 times the output rate, the buffer will rapidly fill. In addition, if the server is transferring a large quantity of data the buffer could overflow, resulting in subsequent data sent to the switch being lost. Thus, unless the length of the buffer is infinite, an impossible situation, there would always be some probability that data could be lost.

Another common cause of lost data is when multiple source port inputs are contending for access to the same destination port. If each source and destination port operates at the same data rate, then only two source ports contending for access to the same destination port can result in the loss of data. Thus, a mechanism is required to regulate the flow of data through a switch. That mechanism is flow control.

All Ethernet switches this author is familiar with have either buffers in each port, or centralized memory that functions as a buffer. The key difference between switch buffers is in the amount of memory used. Some switches have 128K, 256 Kbytes, or even 1 or 2 Mbytes per port, whereas other switches may support the temporary storage of 10 or 20 full-length Ethernet frames. To prevent buffer overflow four techniques are used—backpressure, proprietary software, IEEE 802.3x flow control, and no control. Thus, let's examine each technique.

Backpressure   Backpressure represents a technique by which a switch generates a false collision signal. In actuality, the switch port operates as if it detected a collision and initiates the transmission of a jam pattern. The jam pattern consists of 32 to 48 bits that can have any value other than the CRC value that corresponds to any partial frame transmitted before the jam.

The transmission of the jam pattern ensures that the collision lasts long enough to be detected by all stations on the network. In addition, the jam signal serves as a mechanism to cause nontransmitting stations to wait until the jam signal ends before attempting to transmit, alleviating additional potential collisions from occurring. Although the jam signal temporarily stops transmission, enabling the contents of buffers to be output, the signal also adversely affects all stations connected to the port. Thus, a network segment consisting of a number of stations connected to a switch port would result in all stations having their transmission capability suspended, even when just one station was directing traffic to the switch.

Backpressure is commonly implemented based upon the level of buffer memory used. When buffer memory is filled to a predefined level, that level serves as a threshold for the switch to generate jam signals. Then, once the buffer is emptied beyond another lower level, that level serves as a threshold to disable backpressure operations.

Proprietary Software Drivers   Software drivers enable a switch to directly communicate with an attached device. This enables the switch to enable and disable the station's transmission capability. Currently, software drivers are available as a NetWare Loadable Module (NLM) for NetWare servers, and may be available for Windows NT by the time you read this book.

IEEE 802.3x Flow Control   During 1997 the IEEE standardized a method that provides flow control on full-duplex Ethernet connections. To provide this capability, a special pause frame was defined that is transmitted by devices that want to stop the flow of data from the device at the opposite end of the link.

Figure 9.19 illustrates the format of the pause frame. Since a full-duplex connection has a device on each end of the link, the use of a predefined destination address and operation code (OpCode) defines the frame as a pause frame. The value following the OpCode defines the time in terms of slot times that the transmitting device wants its partner to pause. This initial pause time can be extended by additional pause frames containing new slot time values or canceled by another pause frame containing a zero slot time value. The PAD field shown at the end of the pause frame must have each of its 42 bytes set to zero.

Under the 802.3x standard, the use of pause frames is autonegotiated on copper media and can be manually configured for use on fiber links. The actual standard does not require a device capable of sending a pause frame to actually do so. Instead, it provides a standard for recognizing a pause frame as well as a mechanism for interpreting the contents of the frame so a receiver can correctly respond to it.

The IEEE 802.3x flow control standard is applicable to all versions of Ethernet from 10 Mbps to 1 Gbps; however, the primary purpose of this standard is to enable switches to be manufactured with a minimal amount of memory. By supporting the IEEE 802.3x standard, a switch with a limited amount of

Destination Address 01–C2–80–00–00–01 (6 bytes)	Source Address (6 bytes)	Type 8808 (2 bytes)	OpCode 0001 (2 bytes)	Pause.time (slot times) (2 bytes)	PAD (42 bytes)

Figure 9.19   The IEEE 802.3x pause frame.

memory can generate pause frames to regulate inbound traffic instead of having to drop frames when its buffer is full.

No Control Many switch vendors rely upon the fact that the previously described traffic patterns that can result in buffers overflowing and the loss of data have a relatively low probability of occurrence for any significant length of time. In addition, upper layers of the OSI Reference Model will retransmit lost packets. Thus, many switch vendors rely upon the use of memory buffers and do not incorporate flow control into their products. Whether or not this is an appropriate solution will depend upon the traffic you anticipate flowing through the switch.

Full-Duplex Port Operation If a switch port only supports the connection of one station, a collision can never occur. Recognizing this fact, most Ethernet switch vendors now support full-duplex or bidirectional traffic flow by using two of the four wire connections for 10BASE-T for transmission in the opposite direction. Full-duplex support is available for 10BASE-T, Fast Ethernet, and Gigabit Ethernet connections. Since collisions can occur on a segment, switch ports used for segment-based switching cannot support full-duplex transmission.

In addition to providing a simultaneous bidirectional data flow capability, the use of full duplex permits an extension of cabling distances. For example, at 100 Mbps the use of a fiber cable for full-duplex operations can support a distance of 2000 meters, while only 412 meters is supported using half-duplex transmission via fiber.

Due to the higher cost of full-duplex ports and adapter cards, you should carefully evaluate the potential use of FDX before using this capability. For example, most client workstations will obtain a minimal gain through the use of a full-duplex capability since humans operating computers rarely perform simultaneous two-way operations. Thus, other than speeding acknowledgments associated with the transfer of data, the use of an FDX connection for workstations represents an excessive capacity that should only be considered when vendors are competing for sales, and as such, they provide this capability as a standard. In comparison, the use of an FDX transmission capability to connect servers to switch ports enables a server to respond to one request while receiving a subsequent request. Thus, the ability to use the capability of FDX transmission is enhanced by using this capability on server-to-switch port connections.

Although vendors would like you to believe that FDX doubles your transmission capability, in actuality you will only obtain a fraction of this advertised throughput. This is because most network devices, to include servers that are provided with an FDX transmission capability, only use that capability a fraction of the time.

Jabber Control   A jabber is an Ethernet frame whose length exceeds 1518 bytes. Jabbers are commonly caused by defective hardware or collisions, and can adversely affect a receiving device by its misinterpretation of data in the frame. A switch operating in the cut-through mode with jabber control will truncate the frame to an appropriate length. In comparison, a store-and-forward switch will normally automatically drop a jabbered frame.

Latency   When examining vendor specifications, the best word of advice is to be suspicious of latency notations, especially those concerning store-and-forward switches. Many vendors do not denote the length of the frame used for latency measurements, while some vendors use what might be referred to as creative accounting when computing latency. Thus, let's review the formal definition of latency. Latency can be defined as the difference in time (t) from the first bit arriving at a source port to the first bit output on the destination port. Modern cut-through switches have a latency of approximately 40 μs, while store-and-forward switches have a latency between 80 and 90 ms for a 72-byte frame, and between 1250 and 1300 ms for a maximum-length 1500-byte frame.

For a store-and-forward Ethernet switch an entire frame is first stored. Since the maximum length of an Ethernet frame is 1526 bytes, this means that the maximum latency for a store-and-forward 10-Mbps Ethernet switch is:

$$\frac{1526 \text{ bytes} * 8 \text{ bits/byte}}{10 \text{ Mbps}} \quad \text{or } 1.2208 \text{ ms}$$

plus the time required to perform a table lookup and cross-connection between source and destination ports. Since a 10-Mbps Ethernet LAN has a 9.6-μs gap between frames, this means that the minimum delay time between frames flowing through a cut-through switch is 20.8 μs. Figure 9.20 illustrates the composition of this delay at a 10-Mbps operating rate. For a store-and-forward switch, considering the 9.6-μs gap between frames results in a maximum latency of 1230.4 μs plus the time required to perform a table lookup and initiate a cross-connection between source and destination ports.

Management   The most common method used to provide switch management involves the integration of RMON support for each switch port. This enables an SNMP console to obtain statistics from the RMON group or groups

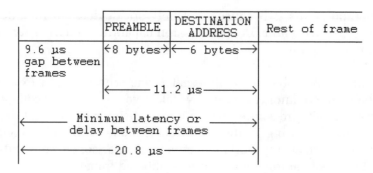

Figure 9.20   Switch latency includes a built-in delay resulting from the structure of the Ethernet frame.

supported by each switch. Since the retrieval of statistics on a port-by-port basis can be time-consuming, most switches that support RMON also create a database of statistics to facilitate their retrieval.

Mirrored Port   A mirrored port is a port that duplicates traffic on another port. For traffic analysis and intrusive testing, the ability to mirror data exiting the switch on one port to a port to which test equipment is connected can be a very valuable feature.

Module Insertion   Modular switches support two different methods of module insertion—switch power down and hot. As their names imply, a switch power down method requires you to first deactivate the switch and literally bring it down. In comparison, the ability to perform hot insertions enables you to add modules to an operating switch without adversely affecting users.

Port Buffer Size   Switch designers incorporate buffer memory into port cards as a mechanism to compensate for the difference between the internal speed of the switch and the operating rate of an end station or segment connected to the port. Some switch designers increase the amount of buffer memory incorporated into port cards to use in conjunction with a flow control mechanism, while other switch designers may use port buffer memory as a substitute for flow control. If used only as a mechanism for speed compensation, the size of port buffers may be limited to a few thousand bytes of storage. When used in conjunction with a flow control mechanism or as a flow control mechanism, the amount of buffer memory per port may be up to 64, 128, or 256 Kbytes, perhaps even up to 1 or 2 Mbytes. Although you might expect more buffer memory to provide better results, this may not necessarily be true. For example, assume a workstation on a segment is connected to a port that has a large buffer with just enough free memory to accept one frame. When the workstation transmits a sequence of frames only the first is able to be placed into the buffer. If the switch then initiates flow control as the contents of its port buffer is emptied, subsequent frames are barred from moving through the switch. When the switch disables flow control, it is possible that another station with data to transmit is able to gain access to the port before the station that sent frame one in a sequence of frames. Due to the delay in emptying the contents of a large buffer, it becomes possible that subsequent frames are sufficiently delayed as they move through a switch to a mainframe via a gateway that a time-dependent session could time out. Thus, you should consider your network structure in conjunction with the operating rate of switch ports and the amount of buffer storage per port to determine if an extremely large amount of buffer storage could potentially result in session time-outs. Fortunately, most switch manufacturers limit port buffer memory to 128 Kbytes, which at 10 Mbps results in a maximum delay of

$$\frac{128 * 1024 * 8 \text{ bits/byte}}{10 \text{ Mbps}}$$

or .10 seconds. At 100 Mbps, the maximum delay is reduced to .01 second, while at 1 Gbps the delay becomes .001 second.

Port Module Support   Although many Ethernet switches are limited to supporting only Ethernet networks, the type of networks supported can considerably differ between vendor products as well as within a specific vendor product line. Thus, you may wish to examine the support of port modules for connecting 10BASE-2, 10BASE-5, 10BASE-T, 100BASE-T LANs, and Gigabit Ethernet devices. In addition, if your organization supports different types of LANs or is considering the use of switches to form a tier-structured network using a different type of high-speed backbone, you should examine port support for FDDI, full-duplex Token-Ring, and ATM connectivity. Many modular Ethernet switches include the ability to add translating bridge modules, enabling support for several different types of networks through a common chassis.

Spanning Tree Support   Ethernet networks use the spanning tree algorithm to prevent loops that, if enabled, could result in the continuous replication of frames. In a bridged network, spanning tree support is accomplished by the use of bridge protocol data units (BPDUs), which enable bridges to select a root bridge and agree upon a network topology that preclude loops from occurring. Since a switch in effect represents a sophisticated bridge, we would want to preclude the use of multiple switches from forming a loop. For example, consider Figure 9.21, which illustrates the use of two switches to interconnect two LANs. If both switches were active, a frame from the client connected on LAN A destined to the server on LAN B would be placed back onto LAN A by switch S1, causing a packet loop and the replication of the packet, a situation we want to avoid. By incorporating spanning tree support into each switch, they can communicate with one another to construct a topology that does not contain loops. For example, one switch in Figure 9.21 would place a port in a blocking mode while the other switch would have both ports in a forwarding mode of operation.

To obtain the ability to control the spanning tree, most switches permit a number of parameters to be altered from their management console. Those parameters include the forwarding delay that governs the time the switch will wait before forwarding a packet, the aging time the switch waits for the receipt of a hello packet before initiating a topology change, the Hello time interval between the transmission of BPDU frames, and the path cost assigned to each port.

Switch Type   As previously discussed, a switch will either support one or multiple addresses per port. If it supports one address per port, it is a port-based switch. In comparison, if it supports multiple addresses per switch, it is considered to be a segment-based switch, even if only one end station is connected to some or all ports on the switch.

Switching Mode   Ethernet switches can be obtained to operate in a cut-through, store-and-forward, or hybrid operating mode. As previously discussed

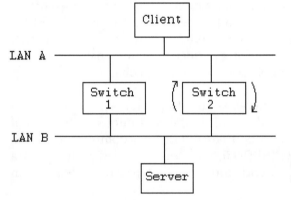

Figure 9.21   The need for loop control.

in this chapter, the hybrid mode of operation represents toggling between cut-through and store-and-forward based upon a frame error rate threshold. That is, a hybrid switch might initially be set to operate in a cut-through mode and compute the CRC for each frame on-the-fly, comparing its computed values with the CRCs appended to each frame. When a predefined frame error threshold is reached, the switch would change its operating mode to store-and-forward, enabling erroneous frames to be discarded. Some switch vendors reference a hybrid switch mode as an error-free cut-through operating mode.

Virtual LAN Support A virtual LAN can be considered to represent a broadcast domain created through the association of switch ports, MAC addresses, or a network layer parameter. Thus, there are three basic types of vLAN creation methods you can evaluate when examining the functionality of an Ethernet switch. In addition, some vendors now offer a rules-based vLAN creation capability, which enables users to have an almost infinite number of vLAN creation methods with the ability to go down to the bit level within a frame as a mechanism for vLAN associations.

Switched-Based Virtual LANs

As briefly mentioned in our review of switch features, a virtual LAN or vLAN can be considered to represent a broadcast domain. This means that transmission generated by one station assigned to a vLAN is only received by those stations predefined by some criteria to be in the domain. Thus, to understand how vLANs operate requires us to examine how they are constructed.

Construction Basics A vLAN is constructed by the logical grouping of two or more network nodes on a physical topology. To accomplish this logical grouping you must use a vLAN-aware switching device. Those devices can include intelligent switches, which essentially perform bridging and operate at the MAC layer, or routers, which operate at the network layer, or layer 3, of the OSI Reference Model. Although a switching device is required to develop a vLAN, in actuality it is the software used by the device that provides you with a vLAN capability. That is, a vLAN represents a subnetwork or broadcast domain defined by software and not by the physical topology of a network. Instead, the physical topology of a network serves as a constraint for the software-based grouping of nodes into a logically defined network.

Implicit versus Explicit Tagging The actual criteria used to define the logical grouping of nodes into a vLAN can be based upon implicit or explicit tagging. Implicit tagging, which in effect eliminates the use of a special tagging field inserted into frames or packets, can be based upon MAC address, port number of a switch used by a node, protocol, or another parameter that nodes can be logically grouped into. Since many vendors offering vLAN products use different construction techniques, interoperability between vendors may be difficult, if not impossible. In comparison, explicit tagging requires the addition of a field into a frame or packet header. This action can result in incompatibilities with certain types of vendor equipment as the extension of the length of a frame or packet beyond its maximum can result in the inability of such equipment to handle such frames or packets. Based upon the preceding, the differences between implicit and explicit tagging can be considered akin to the proverbial statement "between a rock and a hard place." Although standards can be expected to resolve many interoperability problems, network managers and administrators may not have the luxury of time to wait until such standards are developed. Instead, you may wish to use existing equipment to develop vLANs to satisfy current and evolving organizational requirements.

Port-Grouping vLANs As its name implies, a port-grouping vLAN represents a virtual LAN created by defining a group of ports on a switch or router

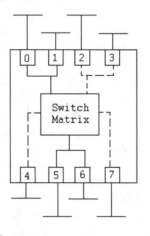

Legend: ☐n =port n

⊥ =network segment

vLAN1 = ports 0, 1, 5, 6
vLAN2 = ports 2, 3, 4, 7

Figure 9.22 Creating port-grouping vLANs using a LAN switch.

to form a broadcast domain. Thus, another common name for this type of vLAN is a port-based virtual LAN.

Operation   Figure 9.22 illustrates the use of an intelligent LAN switch to create two vLANs based upon port groupings. In this example the switch was configured to create one vLAN consisting of ports 0, 1, 5, and 6, while a second vLAN was created based upon the grouping of ports 2, 3, 4, and 7 to form a second broadcast domain.

Advantages associated with the use of LAN switches for creating vLANs include the ability to use the switching capability of the switch, the ability to support multiple stations per port, and internetworking capability. A key disadvantage associated with the use of a port-based vLAN is the fact they are limited to supporting one vLAN per port. This means that moves from one vLAN to another affect all stations connected to a particular switch port.

Supporting Inter-vLAN Communications   The use of multiple NICs provides an easy-to-implement solution to obtaining an inter-vLAN communications capability when only a few vLANs must be linked. This method of inter-vLAN communications is applicable to all methods of vLAN creation; however, when a built-in routing capability is included in a LAN switch, you would probably prefer to use the routing capability rather than obtain and install additional hardware.

Figure 9.23 illustrates the use of a server with multiple NICs to provide support to two port-based vLANs. Not only does this method of multiple vLAN support require additional hardware and the use of multiple ports on a switch or wiring hub, but, in addition, the number of NICs that can be installed in a station is typically limited to two or three. Thus, the use of a large switch with

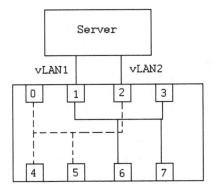

Figure 9.23 Overcoming the port-based constraint where stations can only join a single vLAN. By installing multiple network adapter cards in a server or workstation, a LAN device can become a member of multiple vLANs.

hundreds of ports configured for supporting three or more vLANs may not be capable of supporting inter-vLAN communications unless a router is connected to a switch port for each vLAN on the switch.

MAC-Based vLANs Figure 9.24 illustrates the use of an 18-port switch to create two virtual LANs. In this example, 18 devices are shown connected to the switch via six ports, with four ports serving individual network segments. Thus, the LAN switch in this example is more accurately referenced as a segment switch with a MAC or layer 2 vLAN capability. This type of switch can range in capacity from small 8- or 16-port devices capable of supporting segments with up to 512 or 1024 total addresses to large switches with hundreds of ports capable of supporting thousands of MAC addresses. For simplicity of illustration we will use the 6-port segment switch to denote the operation of layer 2 vLANs as well as their advantages and disadvantages.

In turning our attention to the vLANs shown in Figure 9.24, note that we will use the numeric or node addresses shown contained in circles as MAC addresses for simplicity of illustration. Thus, addresses 1 through 8 and 17 would be grouped into a broadcast domain representing vLAN1, while addresses 9 through 16 and 18 would be grouped into a second broadcast domain to represent vLAN2. At this point in time you would be tempted to say "so what," as the use of MAC addresses in creating layer 2 vLANs resembles precisely the same effect as if you used a port-grouping method of vLAN creation. For example, using an intelligent hub with vLAN creation based upon port grouping would result in the same vLANs as those shown in Figure 9.24 when ports 0, 1, and 4 are assigned to one vLAN and ports 2, 3, and 5 to the second.

To indicate the greater flexibility associated with the use of equipment that supports layer 2 vLAN creation, let's assume users with network node addresses 7 and 8 were just transferred from the project associated with vLAN1 to the project associated with vLAN2. If you were using a port-grouping method of vLAN creation, you would have to physically recable nodes 7 and 8 to either the segment connected to port 2 or the segment connected to port 3. In comparison, when using a segment switch with a layer 2 vLAN creation capability, you would use the management port to delete addresses 7 and 8 from vLAN1 and add them to vLAN2. The actual effort required to do so might be as simple as dragging MAC addresses from one vLAN to the other when using a graphical user interface (GUI) to entering one or more commands when using a command line management system. The top of Figure 9.25 illustrates the result of the previously mentioned node transfer. The lower portion of Figure 9.25 shows the two vLAN layer 2 tables, indicating the movement of MAC addresses 7 and 8 to vLAN2.

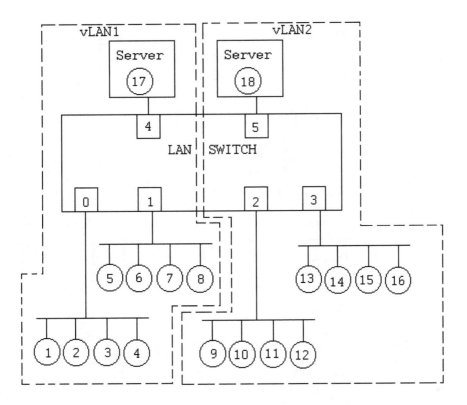

Legend:

$\boxed{n}$ = port n

$\bigcirc\!\!\!\!n$ = MAC address

Figure 9.24 Layer 2 vLAN. A layer 2 vLAN uses MAC addresses to construct broadcast domains that form a virtual LAN.

Although the reassignment of stations 7 and 8 to vLAN2 is easily accomplished at the MAC layer, it should be noted that the partitioning of a segment into two vLANs can result in upper-layer problems. This is because upper-layer protocols, such as IP, require all stations on a segment to have the same network address. Some switches overcome this problem by dynamically altering the network address to correspond to the vLAN on which the station resides. Other switches without this capability restrict the creation of MAC-

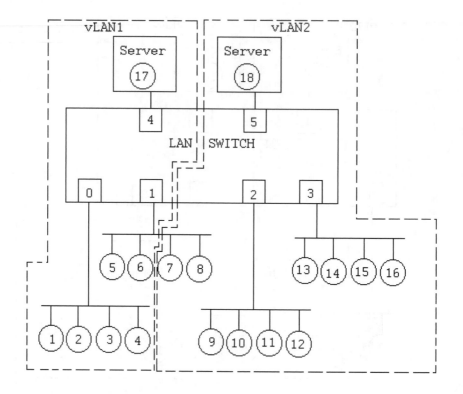

Legend: [n] = port n

(n) = MAC address n

vLAN1 = 1, 2, 3, 4, 5, 6, 17

vLAN2 = 7, 8, 9, 10, 11, 12, 13, 14, 15, 16, 18

Figure 9.25 Moving stations when using a layer 2 vLAN.

based vLANs to one device per port, in effect limiting the creation of vLANs to port-based switches.

Interswitch Communications Similar to the port-grouping method of vLAN creation, a MAC-based vLAN is normally restricted to a single switch; however, some vendors include a management platform that enables multiple switches to support MAC addresses between closely located switches. Unfortunately, neither individual nor closely located switches permit an expansion of vLANs outside of the immediate area, resulting in the isolation of the virtual LANs from the rest of the network. This deficiency can be alleviated in two ways. First, for inter-vLAN communications you could install a second adapter card in a server and associate one MAC address with one vLAN while the second address is associated with the second vLAN. While this method is appropriate for a switch with two vLANs, you would require a different method to obtain interoperability when communications are required between a large number of virtual LANs. Similar to correcting the interoperability problem with the port-grouping method of vLAN creation, you would have to use routers to provide connectivity between MAC-based vLANs and the rest of your network.

Router Restrictions When using a router to provide connectivity between vLANs, there are several restrictions you must consider. Those restrictions typically include a requirement to use a separate switch port connection to the router for each virtual LAN and the inability to assign portions of segments to different vLANs. Concerning the former, unless the LAN switch either internally supports layer 3 routing or provides a trunking or aggregation capability that enables transmission from multiple vLANs to occur on a common port to the router, one port linking the switch to the router will be required for each vLAN. Since router and switch ports are relatively costly, internetworking of a large number of vLANs can become expensive. Concerning the latter, this requirement results from the fact that in a TCP/IP environment routing occurs between segments. An example of inter-vLAN communications using a router is illustrated in Figure 9.26.

When inter-vLAN communications are required, the layer 2 switch transmits packets to the router via a port associated with the virtual LAN workstation requiring such communications. The router is responsible for determining the routed path to provide inter-vLAN communications, forwarding the packet back to the switch via an appropriate router-to-switch interface. Upon receipt of the packet the switch uses bridging to forward the packet to its destination port.

Returning to Figure 9.26, a workstation located in vLAN1 requiring communications with a workstation in vLAN2 would have its data transmitted by the switch on port 5 to the router. After processing the packet the router would return the packet to the switch, with the packet entering the switch on port 6. Thereafter, the switch would use bridging to broadcast the packet to ports 2, 3, and 7 where it would be recognized by a destination node in vLAN2 and copied into an appropriate NIC.

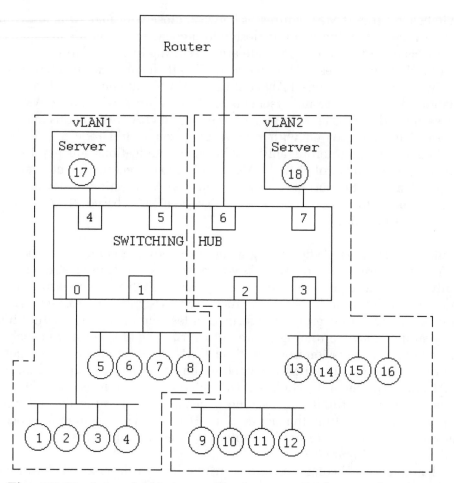

Figure 9.26 Inter-vLAN communications require the use of a router.

Layer 3–Based vLANs A layer 3–based vLAN is constructed using information contained in the network layer header of packets. As such, this precludes the use of LAN switches that operate at the data link layer from being capable of forming layer 3 vLANs. Thus, layer 3 vLAN creation is restricted to routers and LAN switches that provide a layer 3 routing capability.

Through the use of layer 3 operating switches and routers, there are a variety of methods that can be used to create layer 3 vLANs. Some of the more common methods supported resemble the criteria by which routers operate, such as IPX network numbers and IP subnets, AppleTalk domains, and layer 3 protocols.

The actual creation options associated with a layer 3 vLAN can vary considerably based upon the capability of the LAN switch or router used to form the vLAN. For example, some hardware products permit a subnet to be formed across a number of ports and may even provide the capability to allow more than one subnet to be associated with a network segment connected to the port of a LAN switch. In comparison, other LAN switches may be limited to creating vLANs based upon different layer 3 protocols.

Subnet-Based vLANs   Figure 9.27 illustrates the use of a layer 3 LAN switch to create two vLANs based upon IP network addresses. In examining the vLANs created through the use of the LAN switch, note that the first vLAN is associated with the subnet 198.78.55, which represents a Class C IP address, while the second vLAN is associated with the subnet 198.78.42, which repre-

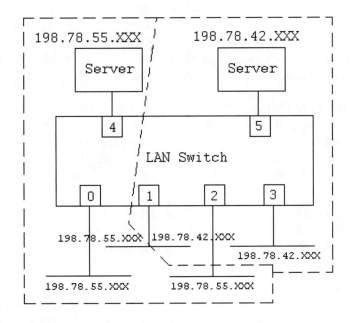

vLAN1 = subnet 198.78.55
vLAN2 = subnet 198.78.42

Figure 9.27   vLAN creation based upon IP subnets.

sents a second Class C IP address. Also note that since it is assumed that the LAN switch supports the assignment of more than one subnet per port, port 1 on the switch consists of stations assigned to either subnet. While some LAN switches support this subnetting capability, it is also important to note that other switches do not. Thus, a LAN switch that does not support multiple subnets per port would require stations to be recabled to other ports if it was desired to associate them to a different vLAN.

Protocol-Based vLANs   In addition to forming vLANs based upon a network address, the use of the layer 3 transmission protocol as a method for vLAN creation provides a mechanism that enables vLAN formation to be based upon the layer 3 protocol. Through the use of this method of vLAN creation, it becomes relatively easy for stations to belong to multiple vLANs. To illustrate this concept, consider Figure 9.28, which illustrates the creation of two vLANs based upon their layer 3 transmission protocol. In examining the stations shown in Figure 9.28, note that the circles with the uppercase *I* represent those stations configured for membership in the vLAN based upon the use of the IP protocol, while those stations represented by circles containing the uppercase X represent stations configured for membership in the vLAN that uses the IPX protocol as its membership criteria. Similarly, stations represented by circles containing the characters I/X represent stations operating dual protocol stacks, which enable such stations to become members of both vLANs.

Two servers are shown at the top of the LAN switch illustrated in Figure 9.28. One server is shown operating dual IPX/IP stacks, which results in the server belonging to both vLANs. In comparison, the server on the upper right of the switch is configured to support IPX and could represent a NetWare file server restricted to membership in the vLAN associated with the IPX protocol.

Rule-Based vLANs   A recent addition to vLAN creation methods is based upon the ability of LAN switches to look inside packets and use predefined fields, portions of fields, and even individual bit settings as a mechanism for the creation of a vLAN.

Capabilities   The ability to create vLANs via a rule-based methodology provides, no pun intended, a virtually unlimited vLAN creation capability. To illustrate a small number of the almost unlimited methods of vLAN creation, consider Table 9.3, which lists eight examples of rule-based vLAN creation methods. In examining the entries in Table 9.3, note that in addition to creat-

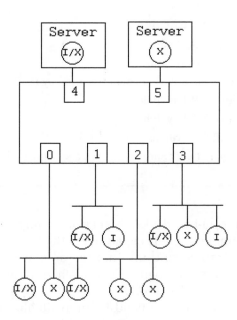

I = vLAN1 membership X = vLAN2 membership
I/X = membership in both LANs

Legend:

    ☐n☐ = port n

    Ⓘ = IP Protocol used by station

    Ⓧ = IPX Protocol used by station

    Ⓘ/Ⓧ = IPX and IP Protocols used by station

Figure 9.28 vLAN creation based upon protocol.

ing vLANs via the inclusion of specific field values within a packet, such as all IPX users with a specific network address, it is also possible to create vLANs using the exclusion of certain packet field values. The latter capability is illustrated by the next to last example in Table 9.3, which forms a vLAN consisting of all IPX traffic with a specific network address but excludes a specific node address.

TABLE 9.3   Rule-Based vLAN Creation Examples

All IP users with a specific IP subnet address.

All IPX users with a specific network address.

All network users whose adapter cards were manufactured by the XYZ Corporation.

All traffic with a specific Ethernet-type field value.

All traffic with a specific SNAP field value.

All traffic with a specific SAP field value.

All IPX traffic with a specific network address but not a specific node address.

A specific IP address.

Multicast Support   One rule-based vLAN creation example that deserves a degree of explanation to understand its capability is the last entry in Table 9.3. Although you might be tempted to think that the assignment of a single IP address to a vLAN represents a typographical mistake, in actuality it represents the ability to enable network stations to dynamically join an IP multicast group without adversely affecting the bandwidth available to other network users assigned to the same subnet, but located on different segments attached to a LAN switch. To understand why this occurs, let me digress and discuss the concept associated with IP multicast operations.

IP multicast references a set of specifications that allows an IP host to transmit one packet to multiple destinations. This one-to-many transmission method is accomplished by the use of Class D IP addresses (224.0.0.0 to 239.255.255.255), which are mapped directly to data link layer 2 multicast addresses. Through the use of IP multicasting, a term used to reference the use of Class D addresses, the need for an IP host to transmit multiple packets to multiple destinations is eliminated. This, in turn, permits more efficient use of backbone network bandwidth; however, the arrival of IP Class D–addressed packets at a network destination, such as a router connected to an internal corporate network, can result in a bandwidth problem. This is because multicast transmission is commonly used for audio and/or video distribution of educational information, videoconferencing, news feeds, and financial reports, such as delivering stock prices. Due to the amount of traffic associated with multicast transmission, it could adversely affect multiple subnets linked together by a LAN switch that uses subnets for vLAN creation. By providing a registration capability that allows an individual LAN user to become a single-user vLAN associated with a Class D address, Class D packets can be routed to a specific segment even when several segments have the same subnet. Thus, this limits the effect of multicast transmission to a single segment.

Switch Usage

The basic use of a stand-alone switch is to support a workgroup that requires additional bandwidth beyond that available on a shared bandwidth LAN. Figure 9.29 illustrates the use of a switch to support a workgroup or small organizational department. As a workgroup expands or several workgroups are grouped together to form a department, most organizations will want to consider the use of a two-tiered switching network. The first or lower-level tier would represent switches dedicated to supporting a specific workgroup to include local servers. The upper tier would include one or more switches used to interconnect workgroup switches as well as to provide workgroup users with access to departmental servers whose access crosses workgroup boundaries. Since the upper-tier switch or switches are used to interconnect

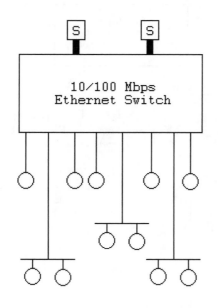

Legend:

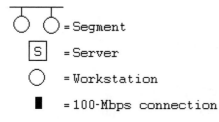

= Segment

$\boxed{\text{S}}$ = Server

○ = Workstation

■ = 100-Mbps connection

Figure 9.29 Support for a small department or workgroup.

workgroup switches, the upper-tier switches are commonly referred to as backbone switches. Figure 9.30 illustrates a possible use of one backbone switch to interconnect two workgroup switches.

Since the backbone switch provides an interconnection between workgroup switches as well as access to departmental servers, the failure of a backbone switch would have a much more significant effect upon communications than the failure of a workgroup switch. Thus, you should consider using a backbone switch with redundant power supplies, common logic, and other key modules. Then, the failure of one module at worst would only make one or a

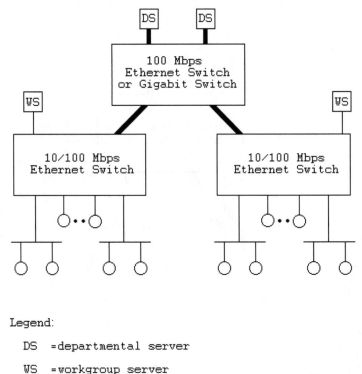

Figure 9.30 Creating a two-tiered switch-based network.

few port connections inoperative. If you acquire one or a few additional port modules you would then have the ability to recable around a port failure without having to wait for a replacement module to be shipped to your location.

When using one or more backbone switches, it is important to note that these switches directly affect the throughput between workgroups as well as the transfer of information to and from departmental servers. Due to this, most organizations will use dedicated 100-Mbps or Gigabit Ethernet switches for backbone operations. If this type of switch is not available at an economical cost, an alternative is to use a 10-/100-Mbps switch with enough 100-Mbps ports to provide connections from workgroup switches as well as to departmental servers.

Although the use of a 100-Mbps backbone Ethernet switch can provide sufficient bandwidth for most applications, it cannot provide what is referred to as a Quality of Service (QoS) in which bandwidth is reserved for the use of high-priority communications that requires a dedicated path through a switch whenever communications occurs. Examples of data streams requiring a QoS include videoconferencing, audio/telephone communications, and other types of time-dependent transmissions usually lumped under the term multimedia. Although the use of Ethernet switches may provide an acceptable level of performance under light switching loads, as traffic increases file transfers and interactive query-responses could adversely affect multimedia applications. In such situations, the use of ATM switches should be considered as it could provide sufficient bandwidth for the delivery of time-dependent traffic for most organizations.

Organizational Switching Building upon the departmental switching previously illustrated in Figure 9.30, you can use routers to interconnect geographically dispersed departments. Doing so can result in an organizational Ethernet switching network that could span different locations in the same city, different cities, one or more states, a country, or the entire globe. Figure 9.31 illustrates the attachment of one router to a backbone switch, connecting the backbone at one location to a wide area network. Although the actual use of one or more routers will be governed by our specific networking requirements, Figure 9.31 illustrates how you can connect one switch-based network to other switch-based networks.

As you design your network infrastructure you should consider the use of one or more Ethernet switch features previously discussed in this chapter to enhance the performance of your network. For example, you may wish to use full-duplex ports for local and departmental server connections. In addition, by the time you read this book economical Gigabit switches should be avail-

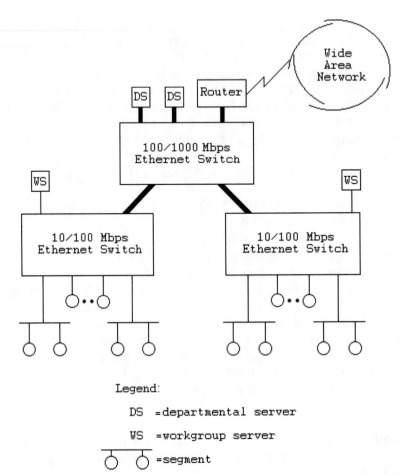

Legend:

DS =departmental server

WS =workgroup server

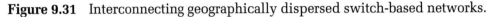 =segment

○ =workstation

━ =100-Mbps connection

Figure 9.31   Interconnecting geographically dispersed switch-based networks.

able whose use could provide you with another option to consider when constructing a tiered network structure.

Layer 3 WAN Switching

In concluding this chapter we will briefly turn our attention to layer 3 switching. Although we previously discussed layer 3 switching when we examined the operation and use of vLANs, until now we only glossed over the technology required to perform switching at the network layer. Thus, in this concluding section covering our examination of LAN switches, we will turn our attention to layer 3 switches designed for WAN transmission.

When we discuss layer 3 switching, we are really talking about a wide range of products that operate at the network layer. Some products are LAN switches with a built-in simplistic routing capability, which enables the switch to look into each frame to the network layer and make switching decisions based upon the type of protocol or network address as previously discussed during our examination of virtual LANs. Other layer 3 switching products are actually designed to forward packets at extremely high data rates beyond the capabilities of conventional routers. As such they are manufactured for providing transmission over a wide area network in comparison to layer 3 LAN switches that provide a network layer vLAN creation capability on a local area network.

Layer 3 WAN switching was introduced by Ipsilon Networks during 1996 and shortly followed by other vendors that introduced their own methods for using network addresses for high-speed WAN switching. In addition to Ipsilon Networks, IP switching technique examples of other layer 3 techniques include Cisco System's Tag Switching, 3Com's Fast IP, and IBM's Aggregate Route-Based IP Switching (ARIS). Some techniques are restricted to supporting IP switching while other techniques support IP and IPX or essentially any network protocol.

The key to layer 3 WAN switching is for the switch to first identify a flow. Here the term flow represents a conversation between two end stations through a network. Then, information specific to the flow, such as possible resource requirements, has to be shared with all intermediate devices between flow points. Thus, all routers and switches between source and destination must be capable of supporting a single method of layer 3 forwarding across a WAN.

Although the driving force for layer 3 WAN switching is currently the Internet, it is this author's belief that the eventual use of Gigabit Ethernet by organizations will also require layer 3 WAN switching when geographically separated LANs are connected. While the use of layer 3 WAN switches for intranets may not be practical until the next millennium, hopefully by that time standards will be in place that will allow equipment to interoperate.

chapter ten

Managing the Network

With a little bit of luck, a small network without a significant amount of usage may require a limited amount of effort by the network manager or administrator to tailor the network to the requirements of the organization. As networks grow in complexity, the necessity to manage the network increases to the point where network management tools and techniques become indispensable for obtaining an efficiently and effectively run network.

This chapter will focus upon the tools and techniques required to effectively manage a network. First, we will examine the Simple Network Management Protocol (SNMP) and its Remote Monitoring (RMON) management information base (MIB). Once this is accomplished, we will focus upon the use of products that can provide us with some of the tools we may require to both effectively manage the transmission of information on the network, as well as observe the operation of file servers attached to the network.

Although an Ethernet network is a layer 2 transport facility, it is commonly used to transport a variety of higher-layer protocols. Thus, any discussion focused upon the management of Ethernet would be remiss if it did not cover at least one tool you can use to observe the state of higher-layer activity on an Ethernet network. Recognizing this fact, we will conclude this chapter by examining the use of a software product that can be used to provide a valuable insight concerning the utilization of an Ethernet network to include the type of traffic transported and status of different devices on the network.

10.1 SNMP

The Simple Network Management Protocol (SNMP) was originally developed as a mechanism for managing TCP/IP and Ethernet networks. Since the first SNMP Internet Draft Standard was published in 1988, the application and utilization of SNMP has considerably expanded, and an enhanced version, which added authentication, access controls, and a few other features, was introduced in 1993. Through the use of SNMP, you can address queries and commands to network nodes and devices that will return information concerning the performance and status of the network. Thus, SNMP provides a mechanism to isolate problems, as well as analyze network activity, which may be useful for observing trends that if unchecked could result in network problems.

Basic Components

SNMP is based upon three components—management software, agent software, and management information bases (MIB), the latter representing databases for managed devices. Management software operates on a network management station (NMS) and is responsible for querying agents using SNMP commands. Agent software represents one or more program modules that operate within a managed device, such as a workstation, bridge, router, or gateway. Each managed agent stores data and provides stored information to the manager upon the latter's request. The MIB represents a database that provides a standard representation of collected data. This database is structured as a tree and includes groups of objects that can be managed. Concerning the latter, the first MIB, referred to as MIB-I, included 114 objects organized into eight groups. Table 10.1 lists the groups supported by the first MIB defined by the Internet Standards Organization to include a brief description of each group.

In examining the MIB-I groups listed in Table 10.1, it is important to note that SNMP represents an application layer protocol. That protocol runs over the User Datagram Protocol (UDP), which resides on top of the Internet Protocol (IP) in the TCP/IP protocol stack. Figure 10.1 illustrates the relationship of SNMP protocol elements to Ethernet with respect to the OSI Reference Model.

In examining Figure 10.1, note that SNMP represents the mechanism by which remote management operations are performed. Those operations are transported via UDP, which is a connectionless service that can be viewed as providing a parallel service to the Transmission Control Protocol (TCP), which also operates at layer 4 of the ISO Reference Model. At layer 3, the Internet Protocol provides for the delivery of SNMP, controlling fragmentation and reassembly of datagrams, the latter a term used to reference portions of a message. Located between IP and layer 4 is the Internet Control Message Protocol (ICMP). ICMP is responsible for communicating control messages and error reports between TCP, UDP, and IP.

In addition to being transported via UDP, SNMP can be transported via Novell's IPX, within Ethernet frames and through the use of AppleTalk and OSI transports. In 1992, a new MIB, referred to as MIB-II, became an Internet

TABLE 10.1 MIB-I Groups

Group	Description
System	Provides vendor identification to include configuration in information and time since the management portion of the system was last reinitialized.
Interfaces	Provides single or multiple network interfaces that can be local or remote, and designates the operating rate of each interface.
AddressTranslation Table	Provides a translation between the network address and physical address equivalences.
Internet Control Message Protocol (ICMP)	Provides a count of ICMP messages and errors.
Transmission Control Protocol (TCP)	Provides information concerning TCP connections, transmissions, and retransmissions to include maintaining a list of active connections.
User Datagram Protocol (UDP)	Provides a count of UDP datagrams transmitted, received, or undelivered.
Exterior Gateway Protocol (EGP)	Provides a count of interrouter communications, such as EGP locally generated messages, EGP messages received with and without error, and information on EGP neighbors.

standard. MIB-II included the eight groups of MIB-I previously listed in Table 10.1, as well as two new groups—Common Management Information and Services Over TCP (CMOT) and SNMP. When the effort to run ISO's management on top of TCP/IP was abandoned, CMOT was essentially dropped as an active group. The addition of an SNMP group permits SNMP to track everything to include its own traffic and errors.

Operation

SNMP has a core set of five commands referred to as protocol data units (PDUs). Those PDUs include GetRequest, GetNextRequest, SetRequest, GetResponse, and Trap.

The NMS issues a GetRequest to retrieve a single value from an agent's MIB, while a GetNextRequest is used to *walk* through the agent's MIB table. When an agent responds to either request, it does so with a GetResponse.

The SetRequest provides a manager with the ability to alter an agent's MIB. Under SNMP Version 1, there was no method to restrict the use of this command, which if used improperly could corrupt configuration parameters and

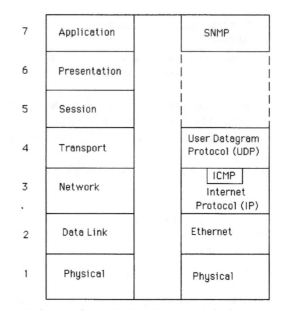

7	Application		SNMP
6	Presentation		
5	Session		
4	Transport		User Datagram Protocol (UDP)
3	Network		ICMP / Internet Protocol (IP)
2	Data Link		Ethernet
1	Physical		Physical

Figure 10.1 Relationship of SNMP protocol elements to Ethernet.

impair network services. Recognizing this problem, many vendors elected not to support the SetRequest command in their SNMP agent software. The introduction of SNMP Version 2 added authentication as well as encryption, resulting in a network management message received by an agent to be recognized if it was altered, as well as to be verified that it was issued by the appropriate manager. This permits the SetRequest to be supported without fear of an unauthorized person taking control of a portion of a network, or an agent returning false information.

Since SNMP is a polling protocol, a mechanism was required to alert managers to a situation that requires their attention. Otherwise, a long polling interval could result in the occurrence of a serious problem that might go undetected for a relatively long period of time on a large network. The mechanism used to alert a manager is a Trap command, issued by an agent to a manager.

Under SNMP Version 2, two additional PDUs were added—GetBulkRequest and InformRequest. The GetBulkRequest command supports the retrieval of multiple rows of data from an agent's MIB with one request. The InformRequest PDU enables one manager to transmit unsolicited information to another manager, permitting the support of distributed network management, which until SNMP V2, was performed in a proprietary manner.

One of the problems associated with the development of MIBs was the provision within the standard that enables vendors to extend their database of collected information. Although the tree structure of the MIB enables software to be developed by one vendor to read another vendor's extension, doing so requires some effort and on occasion results in interoperability problems. To reduce a degree of interoperability, the Remote Monitoring (RMON) MIB was developed as a standard for remote-LAN monitoring. RMON provides the infrastructure that enables products from different vendors to communicate with a common manager, permitting a single console to support a mixed vendor network.

10.2 Remote Monitoring

Remote Monitoring (RMON) represents a logical evolution of the use of SNMP. RMON provides information required for managing network segments that can be located in your building or on the other side of the world.

Operation

RMON operations are based upon software or firmware operating either in managed devices or managed stand-alone hardware probes. Managed devices can include such programmable hardware products as bridges, routers, gateways, hubs, workstations, minicomputers, and mainframes that are connected to a network. Through appropriate software, each managed device responds to network management station (NMS) requests transported via the SNMP protocol. Although a stand-alone probe can be considered to represent a managed device, it differs slightly from the previously mentioned devices in that it is firmware-based and is restricted to performing one set of predefined tasks—RMON operations.

Whether an RMON agent is a managed device or managed stand-alone probe, it captures predefined data elements and will either send statistics and alarms to a network management station upon request for statistics, or generate a trap command upon occurrence of a preset threshold being exceeded, resulting in the generation of an alarm condition that the NMS will then pool.

Figure 10.2 illustrates the relationship between a network management station and a series of managed devices consisting of RMON agents or probes. The MIB provides a standard representation of collected data, as well as defines groups of objects that can be managed. At the NMS, one or more application programs control the interaction between the NMS and each managed

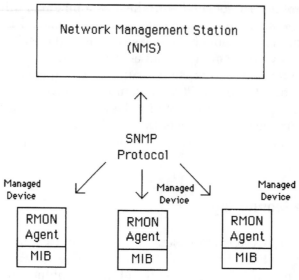

Figure 10.2   RMON operation.

device, as well as the display of information on the NMS and generation of reports. Other functions performed by NMS applications can include password protection to log on to and take control of the NMS, support for multiple operators at different locations, forwarding of critical event information via e-mail or beeper to facilitate unattended operations, and similar functions.

The RMON MIB

Remote network monitoring devices or probes represent hardware and software designed to provide network managers and administrators with information about different network segments to which they are attached. The remote networking monitoring MIB is defined in RFC 1271, and consists of objects arranged into nine groups. Table 10.2 lists each MIB group and provides a brief description of the function of each group. All groups in the MIB listed in Table 10.2 are optional and may or may not be supported by a managed device.

Both the statistics and history groups can provide valuable information concerning the state of the Ethernet segment being monitored. The statistics group contains 17 entries for which countervalues are maintained, while the history group contains 11 entries for which countervalues are maintained. In addition,

TABLE 10.2 Remote Network Monitoring MIB Groups

Group	Description
Statistics	Contains statistics measured by the RMON probe for each monitored interface.
History	Records statistical samples from a network for a selected time interval and stores them for later retrieval.
Alarm	Retrieves statistical samples on a periodic basis from variables stored in a managed device, and compares their values to predefined thresholds. If the monitored variable exceeds a threshold, an alarm event is generated.
Host	Contains statistics associated with each host discovered on a network.
HostTopN	A group used to prepare reports that describe the hosts that had the largest traffic or error counts over an interval of time.
Matrix	Stores statistics of traffic and errors between sets of two addresses.
Filter	Permits packets to be matched based upon a filter equation.
Packet Capture	Permits packets to be captured after they flow through a channel.
Event	Controls the generation and notification of events from the managed device.

the history group includes the real-time maintenance of an integer value that denotes the mean physical layer network utilization in hundredths of a percent.

Table 10.3 provides a comparison of the measurements performed by the statistics and history RMON groups. Although both groups provide essentially the same information, there are some significant differences between the two. The first major difference is the fact that the statistics from the statistics group take the form of free-running counters that start from zero when a valid entry is received, and provide information concerning the recent operational state of the segment. In comparison, the statistics in the history group provide information more useful for long-term segment trend analysis. Recognizing these differences, the statistics group tracks different packet lengths, while the history group ignores packet lengths and tracks network utilization.

Since a managed device or probe is essentially useless if a segment becomes isolated from the organizational network due to a router or bridge failure or cabling problem, some vendors provide Ethernet RMON probes with redundant access capability. This capability is normally provided through the use of a built-in backup modem or ISDN support. Another common feature offered with some stand-alone probes is a multisegment support capability. This fea-

TABLE 10.3   Comparing Statistics and History Group Measurements

	Statistics	History
Drop Events	Yes	Yes
Octets	Yes	No
Packets	Yes	Yes
Broadcast Packets	Yes	Yes
Multicast Packets	Yes	Yes
CRC Alignment Errors	Yes	Yes
Undersize Packets	Yes	Yes
Oversize Packets	Yes	Yes
Fragments	Yes	Yes
Jabbers	Yes	Yes
Collisions	Yes	Yes
Packets 64 octets in length	Yes	No
Packets 65–127 octets in length	Yes	No
Packets 128–255 octets in length	Yes	No
Packets 256–511 octets in length	Yes	No
Packets 512–1025 octets in length	Yes	No
Packets 1024–1518 octets in length	Yes	No
Utilization	No	Yes

ture enables a single probe to be used to provide support for up to four network segments, assuming cabling distances permit. Figure 10.3 illustrates the use of a multisegment RMON probe to capture and report statistics for two Ethernet segments at one location to an NMS at a remote location.

Managing Remote Networks

To illustrate the use of a network management platform to remotely monitor two Ethernet LANs, this author used Network General's Foundation Manager program. Figure 10.4 illustrates the selection of this program's Remote Quick-Stats bar, which enables you to specify an IP address of a probe on the remote network you wish to monitor. Once this is accomplished, the program will use that address to access the probe and retrieve predefined MIB elements such as the distribution of packet lengths shown in the upper left portion of Figure 10.4. In fact, if you compare the last seven entries in Table 10.3 with the con-

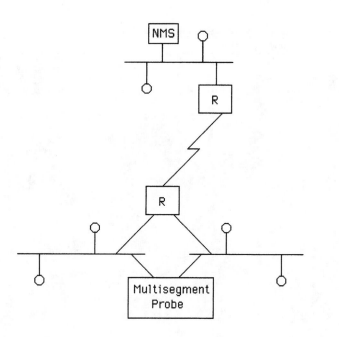

Legend:

NMS = Network management station
R   = Router

Figure 10.3   Using a multisegment RMON probe.

tents of Figure 10.4, you will note that the packet distribution shown in Figure 10.4 and the usage meters in that illustration correspond to those seven statistics entries in the table.

One of the key features of Foundation Manager is its ability to provide users with the capability to remotely monitor up to eight networks at one time and simply click on an icon to change the display of statistics from one monitored network to another. This capability is shown in Figure 10.5 where the first two of eight QuickStat buttons are darkened to indicate two remote LANs are being monitored. Here the second QuickStat button is associated with an Ethernet LAN in San Antonio, and clicking on the first button would immediately bring up the statistics screen for Sacramento that was previously shown in Figure 10.4.

In examining the screens shown in Figures 10.4 and 10.5, you will note both provide the same key metrics for each monitored network. Those metrics include the distribution of packets, network usage, traffic in terms of frames,

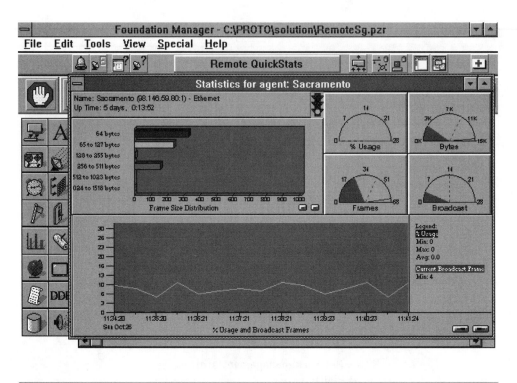

Figure 10.4 Using Network General's Foundation Manager QuickStats feature enables you to view key statistics concerning the operational state of a remote network.

and bytes and broadcasts. In addition, the lower portion of each screen provides a graph over time of the percentage of network utilization and broadcast traffic. Thus, at a glance you can visually note the current use of the monitored network and whether or not a metric indicates a potential or existing problem that requires closer examination.

10.3 Other Network Management Tools

Now that we have an appreciation for SNMP and RMON, we can turn our attention to the use of other network management tools that can assist us in our network management functions. To provide a foundation for discussing network management functions, we will first examine the use of a specific

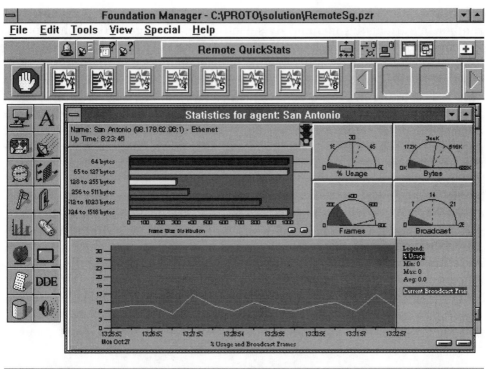

Figure 10.5 Through the use of up to eight QuickStat buttons, Foundation Manager can be used to monitor up to eight remote networks.

vendor product that will demonstrate the management capabilities of many intelligent hubs. Once this is accomplished, we will discuss in detail a core set of network management functions you can use as a mechanism to evaluate the suitability of different vendor products. As we will shortly note, upon occasion no one product will satisfy all of your management requirements and you may have to turn to multiple products to view both network and server operations. Thus, we will conclude this chapter by examining the use of network management tools you can use to observe network and server performance.

Fibermux LightWatch

The Fibermux LightWatch network management system is a Windows-based product that supports point-and-click operations of a mouse. To illustrate its capability, let us assume our network consists of three hubs connected to one another in a triangular manner. By selecting the program's Hierarchy option, we can display our network topology as illustrated in Figure 10.6.

The Fibermux LightWatch network management system permits users to obtain a detailed physical view of each hub, including the modules installed. This is illustrated in Figure 10.7, which shows the physical view of hub A. Note that this view immediately tells an observer that two modules are unused—they are represented by blank panels in the hub. Thus, a simple point-and-click operation can provide a wealth of information about the modules and the capacity of each hub in our network.

Statistics and Alarms

One of the key features of LightWatch is its ability to generate and display a variety of statistics, both on a composite hub basis and for individual ports on each hub. In addition, LightWatch provides users with the ability to assign thresholds to different measurements and generate alarms when those thresholds are exceeded.

Figure 10.8 illustrates the port statistics display screen generated for hub A in our network. Figure 10.9 illustrates the alarm display screen for hub A. Note that the latter permits you to set the threshold values for six events, and to

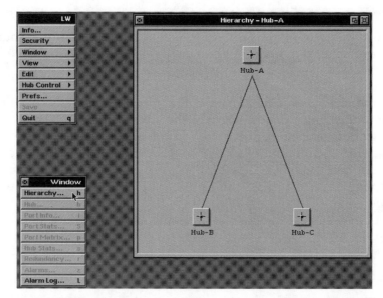

Figure 10.6 LightWatch network topology display obtained by selecting the Hierarchy option.

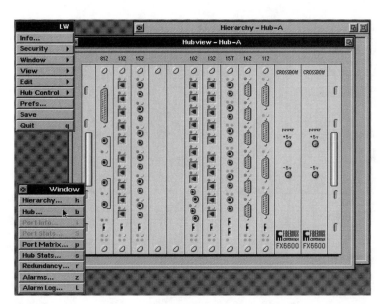

Figure 10.7 Viewing the physical layout of hub modules.

assign a major or minor alarm to a threshold event when a threshold value occurs or is exceeded. By carefully monitoring the statistics generated by Light-Watch, and by setting appropriate thresholds, you can enhance the control of your network to the point where you can actually manage the network, instead of just responding to user complaints. Intelligent hubs provide you with the ability to be proactive rather than reactive in controlling your network.

In our discussion of LightWatch, we briefly examined the network management capability of a specific vendor product. Our primary focus of attention was on the use of a hub for network management, and our discussion was essentially limited to the statistics and alarm generating capabilities of one product. In concluding this section, we will expand on our knowledge of network management by briefly examining its main functional areas and the major activities associated with each area. This will form a foundation for our examination of several popular software products that perform most of the major activities associated with network management.

Network Management Functions

There is a core set of five functions associated with network management. Those functions are configuration, performance, fault, accounting, and security management. Each functional area manages a set of activities.

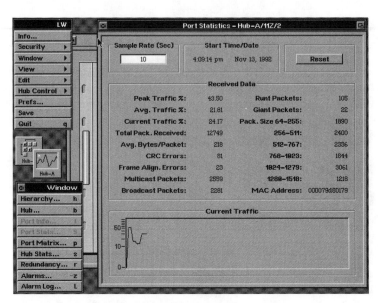

Figure 10.8 LightWatch port statistics screen.

Figure 10.10 illustrates the functional areas commonly associated with network management and the set of activities managed by each area.

Configuration Management

The process of configuration management covers both the hardware and software settings required to provide an efficient and effective data transportation highway. Thus, configuration management consists of managing the physical hardware—including cables, computers, and network adapters—along with the logical network configuration governed by the installation of the network operating system, the selection of a network protocol or stack of protocols, and the manner in which users can access server facilities. The latter concerns the setup of the network, including permissions and routings that enable users to access different servers. Although this may appear to involve security management, it is mainly focused on the setting and distribution of network passwords and the assignment of file permissions. Thus, logical configuration management permits a user to reach a network facility once he or she is connected to the network, while security management involves the ability of a user to gain access to the network and to different facilities made available by configuration management.

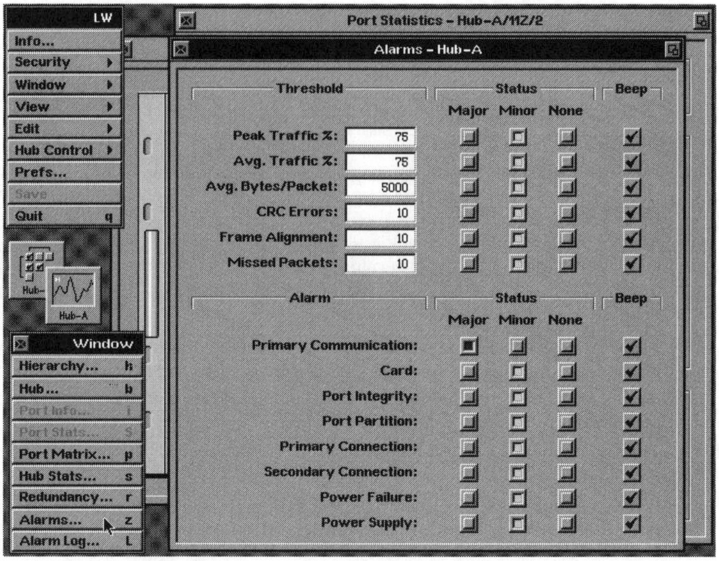

Figure 10.9   LightWatch alarm screen.

Performance Management

Performance management involves those activities required to ensure that the network operates in an orderly manner without unreasonable service delays. This functional area is concerned with the monitoring of network activity to ensure there are no bottlenecks to adversely affect network performance.

Monitored network activity can include the flow of data between stations and between stations and servers; the use of bridges, routers, and gateways; and the utilization of each network segment with respect to its total capacity. By performing these tasks, you will obtain information that will enable you to adjust the use of network hardware and software, as well as to consider a variety of network segmentation options that can eliminate potential network bottlenecks before they occur.

Fault Management

Networks have their less desirable moments in which components fail, software is configured incorrectly, and other problems occur. *Fault management* is the set of functions required to detect, isolate, and correct network problems.

A large number of hardware and software products are now marketed to provide a fault management capability for cables, hardware, and network soft-

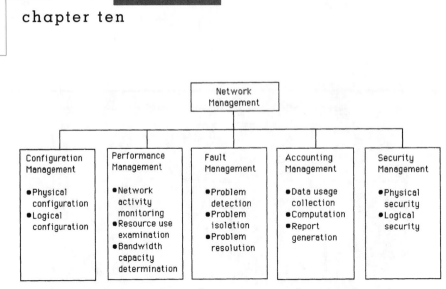

Figure 10.10   Network management functional areas.

ware. The most common type of diagnostic device is a *time domain reflectometer,* which generates a pulse and uses its reflected time delay (or absence of a reflection) to isolate cable shorts and opens. LAN protocol analyzers allow you to test individual Ethernet adapters, and to monitor network performance and isolate certain types of network problems, such as jabbering. Both hardware-based LAN protocol analyzers and many software products provide a LAN frame decoding capability. This helps you determine whether the flow of frames and frame responses provides an insight into network problems. For instance, a station might be rejecting frames because of a lack of buffer space, which could easily be corrected by reconfiguring its software.

Accounting Management

Accounting management is a set of activities that enables you to determine network usage, generate usage reports, and assign costs to individuals or groups of users by organization or by department. Normally, the network operating system provides a raw set of network usage statistics, and you will need one or more other software packages to generate appropriate reports and assign costs to usage. While cost assignment is commonly used in wide area networks and for electronic mail usage, it is not commonly used to distribute the cost of using local area networks. Instead, accounting management is normally employed to answer such questions as, "What would be the effect on the network if the engineering department added five new employees?" In this situation, accounting management data might provide you with network usage statistics for the engineering department, including total department usage as well as individual and average station usage data. Using these statistics in conjunction with performance monitoring, you could then determine the probable effect of the addition of new employees to the network.

Security Management

As discussed in our overview of configuration management, security management involves primarily the assignment of network access passwords and access permissions to applications and file storage areas on the network. Other aspects of security management involve the physical placement of stations in areas where access to those stations is restricted, and the selection and control of specialized hardware and software security products. These products can range in scope from programs used to encipher and decipher electronic mail messages to network modems that can be programmed to perform a series of operations: prompt users for a code when they dial into the network, disconnect the user, and then dial a number predefined as associated with the user code.

Most network management products provide excellent coverage of a subset of the five core functional areas, but few products actually cover all functional areas. Most users will normally consider the use of two or more products to perform all five network management functions. In the remainder of this chapter, we will examine the use of software products marketed by Triticom of Eden Prairie, Minnesota, Frye Computer Systems of Boston, Massachusetts, now a part of Seagate Software, and Cinco Networks of Pleasanton, California, now a part of Network General. These products can be used to manage Ethernet networks.

Triticom EtherVision

One of the more popular Ethernet monitors is a program marketed by Triticom of Eden Prairie, Minnesota, under the trademark EtherVision. This program is designed to operate on a workstation, and must be used with a specific type of Ethernet/IEEE 802.3 adapter—a Novell NE/2, NE1000, or NE2000, a 3Com Etherlink II, a Western Digital EtherCard, or a Pure Data PDI8023, PDI 8023-16, or PDUC8023. At the time this book was written, EtherVision supported 14 adapter cards and Triticom was in the process of adding program support for additional vendor adapter cards. Only the workstation executing EtherVision requires a specific Ethernet/IEEE 802.3 adapter card; all other workstations, servers, and other devices on the network can use any vendor adapter card. EtherVision's rationale for requiring a specific vendor's adapter card is based on the necessity to write software that accesses MAC layer buffers in the adapter, so that the program can read frames transmitted on the network. These frames form the basis for numerous network-operation statistics generated by the program.

Main Menu

The starting point for the use of EtherVision is the program's main menu. This menu contains a list of eight actions; these can be selected either by pressing the first letter of the listed options or by moving a highlight bar over an action and pressing the Enter key.

Options you can select from the main menu enable you to perform a variety of operations:

◆ Monitor network traffic

◆ Enable and disable a variety of alarms

◆ Assign names, alarms, and filters to station addresses

◆ Enable and disable network event logging

◆ Test the cable connected to the workstation's adapter

◆ Control the configuration options of the program

◆ Generate different types of reports

◆ Quit to DOS

By examining the use of several program options, we can obtain an appreciation for how EtherVision can assist you in managing your network.

Traffic Monitoring

By selecting the Monitor Traffic option from the program's main menu, you can monitor either source or destination addresses on a real-time basis. Figure 10.11 shows the screen display when the monitoring of source addresses is selected. As indicated, the display consists of five distinct areas.

The top bar across the screen in Figure 10.11 shows both the date and time when monitoring began and the current time. The main area of the display lists the source addresses of stations identified on the network and the number of frames counted for each station. At the time this screen display was printed, EtherVision was in operation for 40 seconds and had identified 22 stations on the network. Although station addresses are shown in Figure 10.11 in hexadecimal format, by pressing the F2 key you can toggle the station address display to its logical name or the vendor-adapter address. The highlighted bar over the top source address indicates that information about that address is dis-

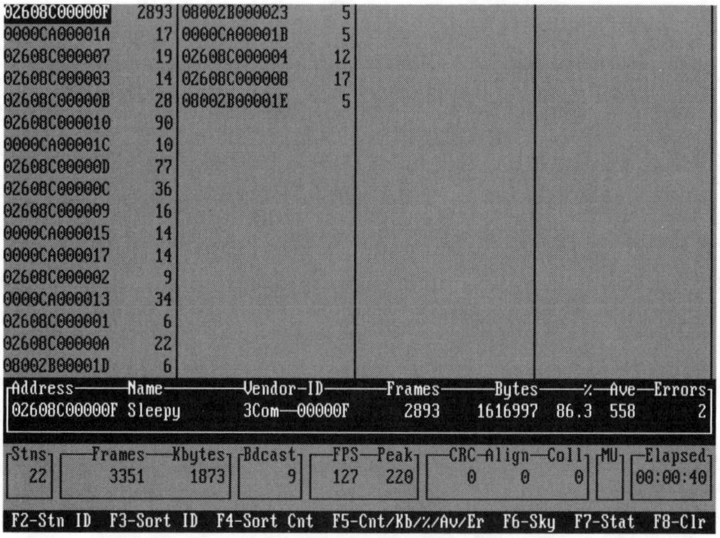

02608C00000F	2893	08002B000023	5
0000CA00001A	17	0000CA00001B	5
02608C000007	19	02608C000004	12
02608C000003	14	02608C00000B	17
02608C00000B	28	08002B00001E	5
02608C000010	90		
0000CA00001C	10		
02608C00000D	77		
02608C00000C	36		
02608C000009	16		
0000CA000015	14		
0000CA000017	14		
02608C000002	9		
0000CA000013	34		
02608C000001	6		
02608C00000A	22		
08002B00001D	6		

| Address | Name | Vendor-ID | Frames | Bytes | %—Ave—Errors |
| 02608C00000F | Sleepy | 3Com—00000F | 2893 | 1616997 | 86.3 558 | 2 |

| Stns | Frames | Kbytes | Bdcast | FPS | Peak | CRC-Align | Coll | MU | Elapsed |
| 22 | 3351 | 1873 | 9 | 127 | 220 | 0 | 0 | 0 | 00:00:40 |

F2-Stn ID   F3-Sort ID   F4-Sort Cnt   F5-Cnt/Kb/%/Av/Er   F6-Sky   F7-Stat   F8-Clr

Figure 10.11   EtherVision source address monitoring.

played in the third area on the screen display, which shows the hexadecimal address, logical name, and vendor-ID for the address highlighted. Note that in the first 40 seconds of monitoring, the station named Sleepy was anything but, accounting for 86.3 percent of all network traffic. If the network utilization continued to be relatively high for a long monitoring period and some users complained about poor response time, you would probably want to determine what the user with the logical name of Sleepy was doing. Perhaps a one-time download of a large file occurred and there is no cause for alarm.

The fourth area of the screen shown in Figure 10.11 provides summary information concerning all stations that have been identified. Here, we see 22 stations were identified, and together they transmitted 3351 frames and 1873 K of information. A total of nine frames were broadcast to all stations, and the frames per second (FPS) and peak frames per second activity were 127 and 220, respectively. During the monitoring period there were no CRC errors, frame alignment errors, or collisions, nor were there any missed or unprocessed (MU) frames.

A missed or unprocessed frame typically results from data arriving too fast for the adapter to keep up with network traffic. The adapter used by a station running EtherVision must function in a promiscuous mode of operation. This means that the adapter must pass every frame read from the network to the higher-level network layers, instead of passing only frames that have the adapter's destination address. This is required since EtherVision must process each frame to compute a variety of network statistics.

When one or more stations on the network request a long file transfer, it becomes possible that the processor of the computer running EtherVision may not be able to process frames as they are read from the network. Thus, missed or unprocessed frames may indicate the need to operate EtherVision on a workstation that has a faster microprocessor to obtain more reliable statistics.

The last area of the display shown in Figure 10.11 indicates the function keys and their assignments, and enables you to select different action options. For example, pressing the F2 key changes the display of identified network adapters to logical names or a vendor-ID display format, while pressing the F8 key clears the display and resets all counters and the elapsed time to zero.

Skyline Displays

To obtain detailed information about network utilization, you would press the F6 key from the traffic monitoring display. This provides you with the ability to view the program's skyline display of network utilization and the FPS carried by the monitored network.

Figure 10.12 shows the EtherVision skyline display of network utilization, and Figure 10.13 shows the skyline display with respect to the FPS rate of data flow on the network. In examining Figure 10.12, note that the display shows intervals for a 60-second monitoring period. By pressing the F5 key, you can change the monitoring period of the display to one hour—a more realistic period for examining network utilization. Since the network utilization in Figure 10.12 only slightly exceeded 10 percent, if this low level of utilization continued for a longer period of time it would indicate that you could expand your network through the addition of workstations before considering the use of bridges to subdivide the network.

The FPS display shown in Figure 10.13 provides you with a general indication of traffic flow on your network. However, by itself this display does not provide you with meaningful information, because it does not indicate the average frame size nor the distribution of frames by their length. This information can be obtained by pressing the F7 key to generate the program's statistics screen.

Statistics Display

Figure 10.14 illustrates the display of EtherVision's Statistics screen. Note that this screen provides you with summary information concerning frame counts, distribution of frame sizes, network utilization, and frame errors. Although

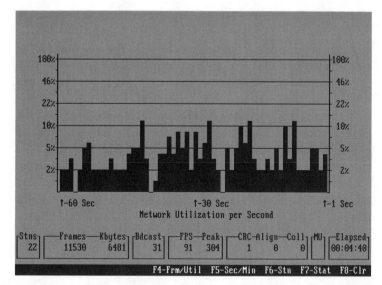

Figure 10.12   EtherVision Network Utilization skyline display.

this screen provides information similar to Foundation Manager's QuickStats display previously shown in Figure 10.4 and 10.5, there are key differences between that program and EtherVision that deserve a brief discussion. Foundation Manager is an SNMP RMON manager, capable of monitoring up to eight remote LANs. In comparison, EtherVision requires you to run the program on a station on the network to be monitored and does not support remote monitoring. Thus, you would use Foundation Manager or a similar product if you need to monitor remote networks while EtherVision or a similar product could be used to monitor a local network. Returning to our discussion of EtherVision, note that in the Frame Counts window, the average computed frame size is displayed, while the Frames Per Second window displays the average and peak frames per second monitored on the network. By using this data, you can compute and verify the data in the Network Utilization window and compute the effect of adding additional workstations to the network. For example, the peak FPS rate is 304 for 22 stations, or approximately 14 FPS per workstation. Adding 10 workstations with similar operational characteristics to existing workstations can be expected to increase the network traffic flow by 140 FPS. Since the average frame size is 561 bytes, 10 additional workstations can be expected to result in 561 bytes × 8 bits per byte × 140 FPS, or less than 630,000 bps of network traffic.

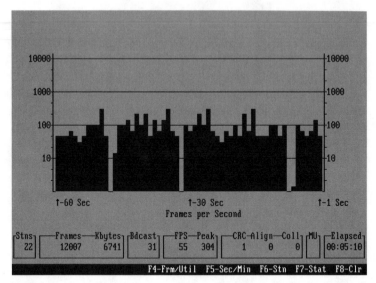

Figure 10.13 EtherVision Frames per Second skyline display.

Alarms

The key to the effective management of a network is the ability to generate alarms when important predefined events occur. EtherVision provides network administrators with the ability to generate several key alarms, without which you would have to monitor several screens constantly. You can avoid this cumbersome process by using the program's Network Alarms/Options screen, illustrated in Figure 10.15. The Network Alarms/Options screen illustrated in Figure 10.15 allows you to enable or disable five alarms and to set the threshold value for three alarms. When an alarm is enabled and the event occurs or an alarm threshold is exceeded, the alarm status will be displayed on the top line of any EtherVision screen you are using, as well as being written to the program's Network Event Log.

The network idle time alarm will be triggered when EtherVision senses no traffic for the specified period of time. Since NetWare file servers periodically transmit IPX frames to make servers aware of each other, a Novell-based Ethernet LAN will always have at least some traffic at periodic intervals. Thus, the occurrence of a network idle time alarm can inform you of a serious network problem, such as the failure of a server or a faulty adapter in the computer operating EtherVision.

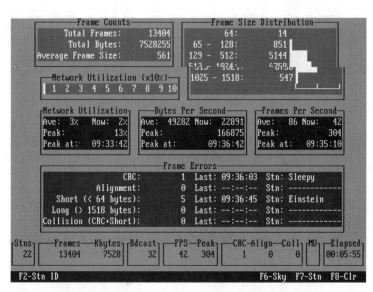

Figure 10.14 EtherVision Statistics display.

The network utilization alarm allows you to determine whether your network is approaching or has reached a level of saturation that warrants its subdivision. Normally, a utilization level that periodically exceeds 50 percent on an Ethernet/IEEE 802.3 network indicates a level of use that warrants the subdivision of the network and its connection via a bridge.

The frame error alarm goes off when it reaches a specified number of frame errors. Since the error rate on a LAN is typically 1 in a billion bits, or 1×10^{-9}, you can use this alarm to determine whether your network has an acceptable error level. To do so, you would view the Statistics screen when a frame error alarm occurs to determine the number of bits that have been transmitted during the time it took until the frame error alarm was generated. With this information, you could determine whether your LAN's bit error rate (BER) is at an acceptable level. For example, assume the total number of frames in the frame count window in the Statistics display was 100,000,000 when the frame error count reached 100 and generated an alarm. Also assume, for simplicity, that the average frame size in the Statistics display was 1000 bytes. An average of 100,000,000/100, or 1,000,000 frames, flowed on the network for each frame error. Since we assumed that each frame has an average length of 1000 bytes, 1,000,000 frames × 1000 bytes per frame × 8 bits per byte, or 8,000,000,000 bits,

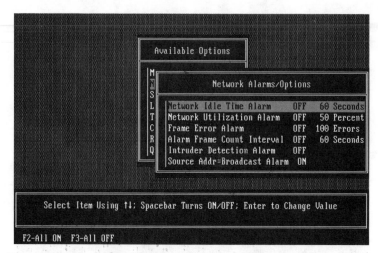

Figure 10.15   EtherVision Network Alarms/Options screen.

are transmitted per frame error. This is equivalent to a BER of 1/8,000,000,000, or 1.25×10^{-8}, which is about what we would expect from a LAN that performs well, and that has properly connected cables routed a safe distance from sources of electromagnetic interference.

The alarm count interval can be used to generate an alarm when enabled and set to a specific time period. Then, if the number of frame errors specified by the frame error alarm occurs within the specified alarm period, an alarm frame count interval alarm will go off.

The intruder detection alarm operates by triggering an alarm when a new station enters the network that was not defined to the program by the assignment of a logical name. When we examine the Station Options screen, we will see how logical names are assigned to each station address. The last alarm shown in Figure 10.15 is Source Addr=Broadcast Alarm. Since all source addresses must be unique, this alarm occurs when a source address with its broadcast bit set is detected.

Station Options Display

Through EtherVision's Station Options display screen you obtain the ability to assign names, filters, and alarms to specific hardware adapter addresses. Figure 10.16 illustrates the display of the program's Station Options screen.

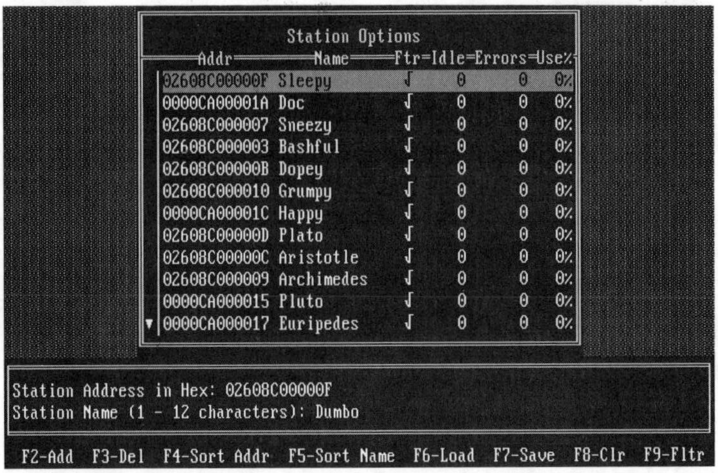

Figure 10.16 EtherVision Station Options display.

In examining Figure 10.16, note that the highlighted bar is positioned over the top address, which was previously assigned the logical name Sleepy. In this example, we are in the process of changing the station's name to Dumbo. By moving the highlight bar over different station addresses and/or pressing appropriate function keys, you can control the assignment of names, alarms, and filters to stations. For example, F2 permits you to add or change a name, F3 prompts you to delete the name currently selected by the highlight bar, and so on. When assigning names, you can specify a filter (Ftr) for each station. Then, during monitoring, only those stations marked for filtering will be displayed on the program's monitoring screen. For a large network, filtering enables you to examine groups of stations, such as the accounting department's workstations. In addition to station filtering, you can use the Station Options display to set an idle alarm from 1 to 9,999, an error alarm of 1 to 9,999, and a usage alarm based on a percentage of network activity for each station. Thus, you can use the Station Options display to isolate a problem condition on a specific station or group of stations.

Network Event Logging Display

Figure 10.17 illustrates EtherVision's Network Event Logging screen. From this screen, you can enable and disable the logging of events to the program's

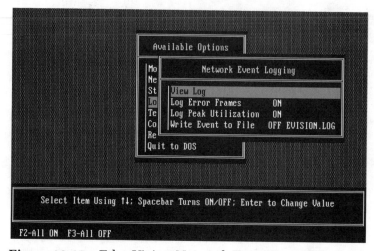

Figure 10.17 EtherVision Network Event Logging screen.

log file and select the logging of error frames and peak utilization data. In addition, from this screen you can view the event log.

Figure 10.18 displays a portion of the network event log, which can be scrolled through a window on your display. Since we previously enabled the logging of both frame errors and peak utilization, the contents of the log reflect both types of activities. In examining Figure 10.18, note that "Frame Short" refers to any frame shorter than the minimum length of 64 bytes—a condition usually caused by a collision. Although collisions normally occur on an Ethernet/IEEE 802.3 network, a situation in which one station has a large number of collisions associated with its transmission may indicate a faulty adapter. Thus, from an examination of Figure 10.18 it appears that the adapter used on the station whose logical address is Sleepy may be in need of an awakening action, during which the adapter is tested, and if it continues to generate short frames, replaced.

As indicated by our short review of EtherVision, it permits you to perform most of the major functions associated with network management. Regardless of which management tool you use, you should always ensure that you have one available. The periodic use of an appropriate network management tool provides you with a detailed view of network activity, which can be invaluable in performing your network management functions.

Figure 10.18 EtherVision network event log.

NetWare Management

While EtherVision provides you with a detailed view of your network's traffic and utilization of bandwidth, it overlooks one important component of your network. That component is your server. Since a large majority of Ethernet and IEEE 802.3 networks are based on Novell's NetWare operating system, we will focus our attention on NetWare management in this section, examining a software product from Frye Computer Systems of Boston, Massachusetts, (now owned by Seagate Software) as well as a built-in capability of Novell NetWare to provide a view of your network server. The first product provides detailed information about the operational characteristics of the file servers in your network, and the second product provides a more limited view of the server in some areas while providing additional information concerning certain server software characteristics.

Frye Utilities for Networks

NetWare Management is more fully known as the Frye Utilities for Networks, which name probably served as the rationale for the selection of the executable program name of FUN. Running under DOS, or as a DOS session under Windows 3.X, Netware Management is easy to install; it fully supports Novell NetWare 2.1+ and 3.1+.

Once loaded, NetWare Management provides you with the ability to use 11 program modules, ranging in scope from detailed information about your file server to such trivial information as the version of NetWare you are using. The program includes a NetWare loadable module (NLM), which consists of hooks into NetWare that gather the appropriate information a NetWare file server computes. The FUN module then sends messages to the NetWare-extracted parameters to provide you with a detailed insight into your Novell network. Since the best way to illustrate the utility of a program is to take a look at some program module screens, let's do so.

Server General Display   Figure 10.19 shows the General display screen of the program's server module. Note that the right side of the screen shows a graph of server utilization, defined as the fraction of CPU time for which the file server is doing productive work. Although this graph and several of the data elements and their values listed in the left part of the screen can be extremely valuable in isolating performance problems, utilization is unfortunately shown only for the past 30 seconds on the graph. In addition, the value of several of the listed performance parameters on the left portion of the screen is displayed almost in real time but is not accumulated over time. For example, Disk I/O Pending shows the number of disk operations that are currently in the server's queue. A large number indicates a high level of disk activity, and if the number stays relatively high for a long period of time, it tends to indicate that server performance could be improved by the replacement of your current hard disk with another that has a faster access time.

Because the program is unable to log utilization statistics over a long period of time, you will probably want to run this program periodically during the busiest hour of the day. For most organizations, the hour in which peak network usage occurs is typically the hour preceding lunch, or around 3 to 4 P.M. on a Tuesday or Thursday. Through the periodic monitoring of server and network utilization statistics, you will be able to determine whether an undesirable level of performance is due to the bandwidth constraints of network cabling and adapter cards or to the capability of the server. For example, monitoring of the network might indicate a network utilization level of 10 or 15 percent, but you might be receiving complaints from users concerning network performance. By using the Frye Utilities for NetWare, you might determine that the server utilization level is 60 to 70 percent, indicating that an improvement in overall network performance could be accomplished by either adding an additional server or obtaining a faster

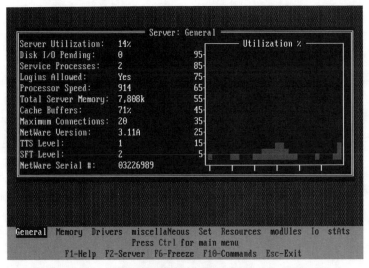

Figure 10.19   Frye Utilities Server General display.

platform for server software to operate upon. Alternatively, you might want to increase RAM in the server if further investigation indicates that paging of modules and the time delay associated with paging are causing poor network response.

Server Statistics Display   Figure 10.20 illustrates the Frye Utilities Server Statistics display screen. At first glance this display may appear to represent no more than a simple accumulation of server statistics, and you may feel that, while interesting, such statistics are of limited value. However, the statistics displayed can be very valuable when combined with knowledge about your server's directory structure and other information. For example, the ratio of file reads to directory searches can indicate whether network users are familiar enough with your server's directory structure to make efficient use of the files on the server. A low ratio probably indicates that network users are having difficulty finding the files they need, in which case you may wish to consider rearranging or renaming directories, or publicizing your server's directory structure and the contents of each directory.

User Program Module   Figure 10.21 illustrates the General Information screen of the program's Users module. The left portion of the screen allows

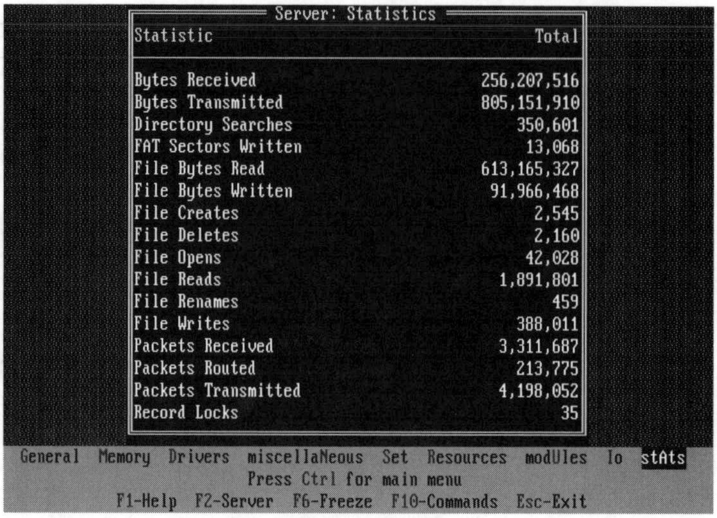

Figure 10.20 Frye Utilities Server Statistics display.

you to move the highlight bar over each network user name; the right portion of the screen displays information about the selected user name. By moving the highlight bar, you can easily view general information about each network user, and using the left and right arrow keys permits you to access the Groups, Security, and other Users module screens. While most of the displays generate interesting information, this information is normally known to the network administrator and is not earth-shattering by any means. Where Frye Computer's NetWare Management excels is in the comprehensive series of reports that it can generate and that you can direct to your screen, printer, or disk.

Program Report Capability Figure 10.22 illustrates the Select Report display of the program's Reports module, and Figure 10.23 illustrates the Select Configuration Report display of the program's Configuration module. As you will note from the names of the reports listed in the two displays, you can generate a rather large number of reports to provide information about server resources, disk usage, workstation and server network statistics, and about the setup of your NetWare file server.

To illustrate the potential value of the program's report capability, we will select the Node Statistics Report from Figure 10.22, directing the report to our display.

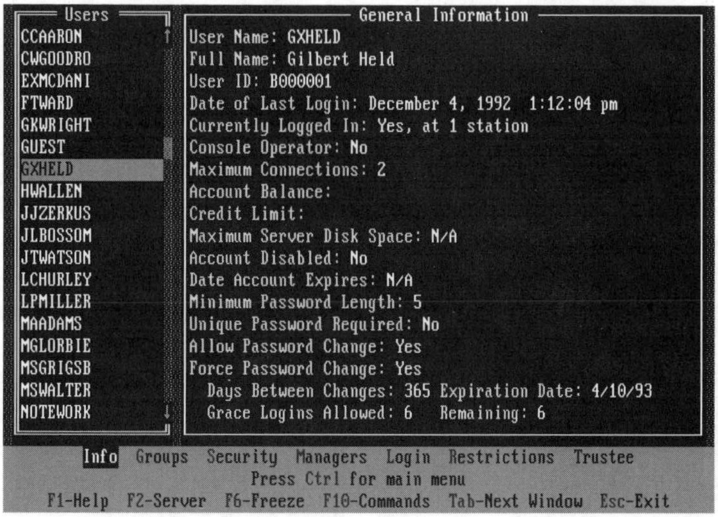

Figure 10.21 Frye Utilities General Information screen of Users module.

Figure 10.24 displays one screen of the resulting Node Statistics Report, showing only a portion of the SPX statistics and then all of the IPX statistics for one workstation. A large number of packets lost because of a lack of available event control blocks (ECBs) normally indicates a potential network slowdown. More seriously, a number of malformed ECBs probably indicates an application that does not use direct IPX calls properly.

One of the best features of Frye Computer's NetWare Management is its manual's comprehensive reference section. If you have fought your way through Novell manuals, you'll find the Frye reference section refreshing: it defines and explains most NetWare terms in alphabetical order. In fact, it's probably quite worthwhile to read the manual's reference section, because it explains NetWare parameters and the effect of their settings on your network's performance.

The NetWare Monitor

One of the programs included in NetWare is the MONITOR, which operates on the server console or on a workstation with the NetWare RCONSOLE command. Although this program is no substitute for a comprehensive network management system, it does provide a significant amount of information that can facilitate the management of your network. Thus, in concluding this section we will focus our attention on the use of this NetWare program.

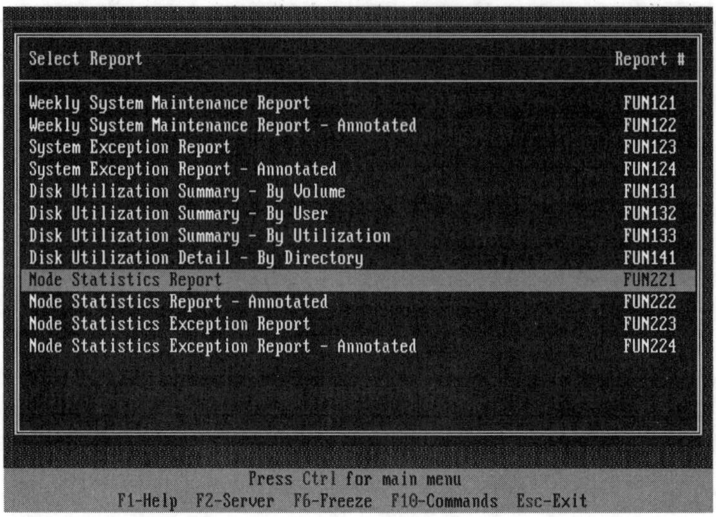

Figure 10.22 Frye Utilities Select Report screen of Report module.

NetWare Monitor Main Screen Display   Figure 10.25 illustrates the main screen display resulting from loading the NetWare MONITOR program. The first line in the top window indicates how long the file server has been in operation. Note that in the left portion of the top window, server utilization is shown numerically. Unlike the previously described Frye Computer NetWare utility program, which displays utilization over a small period of time, the MONITOR program indicates utilization on a real-time basis. Similarly, other information displayed by the MONITOR program is also displayed on a real-time basis.

The top window in Figure 10.25 displays information about fast computer memory (cache buffers) used to store information normally kept on disk, service processes, connections, and other operations. Service Processes encompass such tasks as a read or write. The higher this number, the busier the server—a large number normally indicates a high utilization level. The Connections in Use parameter simply refers to the number of workstations that are logged into the network; however, these users may be performing only local workstation functions, so this number does not provide an indication of network activity. The Open Files parameter indicates the number of files on the server that users have opened. Like the Connections in Use parameter, this information does not indicate a direct level of performance, since a user could open a file and then go to lunch.

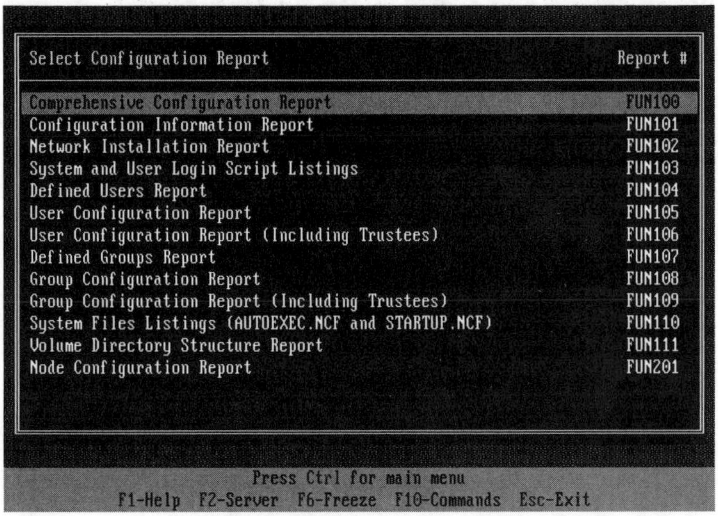

Figure 10.23   Frye Utilities Select Configuration Report screen of Configuration module.

The lower window shown in Figure 10.25 contains a menu of options you can select through the use of the MONITOR program. You can select an option by moving the highlight bar over an option and pressing the Return key. For example, pressing the Return key when the highlight bar is over Disk Information results in a screen display similar to the one illustrated in Figure 10.26.

Server Memory Statistics Display   The top window shown in Figure 10.26 displays specific information about the use of your server's memory. The lower window provides specific information about a variety of NetWare resources. In this example, we moved the highlight bar over REMOTE.NUM: AES Events. It was assumed that we wanted to obtain information on an NLM named "REMOTE." When you press the Enter key, the lower portion of your display changes, as shown in Figure 10.27. In examining the contents of the lower window labeled "Resource Information," note that it informs us that a NetWare asynchronous event scheduler (AES) event resulted in one remote console being in use. This tells us that one workstation is functioning as a remote console. If you are the Network Administrator, this information might be of considerable value, because the Remote Console user has very similar capabilities to the NetWare Supervisor with respect to the functions and network control

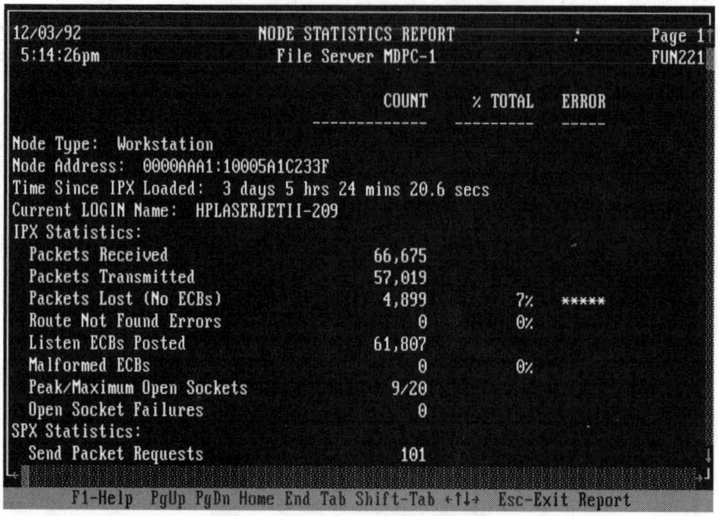

```
12/03/92                    NODE STATISTICS REPORT              :        Page 1
 5:14:26pm                    File Server MDPC-1                          FUN221

                                      COUNT     % TOTAL    ERROR
                                    ----------  --------   -----
Node Type:  Workstation
Node Address:  0000AAA1:10005A1C233F
Time Since IPX Loaded:  3 days 5 hrs 24 mins 20.6 secs
Current LOGIN Name:  HPLASERJETII-209
IPX Statistics:
  Packets Received                  66,675
  Packets Transmitted               57,019
  Packets Lost (No ECBs)             4,899       7%     *****
  Route Not Found Errors                 0       0%
  Listen ECBs Posted                61,807
  Malformed ECBs                         0       0%
  Peak/Maximum Open Sockets           9/20
  Open Socket Failures                   0
SPX Statistics:
  Send Packet Requests                 101

    F1-Help  PgUp PgDn Home End Tab Shift-Tab ←↑↓→  Esc-Exit Report
```

Figure 10.24 A portion of the Node Statistics Report directed to the screen.

he or she can perform. By selecting different resources, you can display other information about NetWare resources on a real-time basis. Understanding the top window in both Figures 10.26 and 10.27, labeled "Server Memory Statistics," requires a degree of knowledge concerning NetWare terminology and operations. For example, the Alloc Memory Pool (allocate memory pool), which currently represents just 2 percent of server memory, may appear small. However, NetWare uses this memory area for storing small objects for short periods of time, and expands it automatically from the total server memory as needed. The cache buffers indicate the amount of server memory currently used as disk cache buffers. Although the percentage will vary, if it falls below 25 percent of server memory, it will significantly degrade server performance or even cause the server to crash. Thus, this parameter should be monitored as an indicator of whether server memory requires expansion. In this example, it obviously does not require expansion.

The movable memory area is used for large, dynamically allocated objects. Objects placed in this memory area can be moved to provide larger amounts of contiguous memory for tables, such as File Allocation buffers that expand dynamically. In comparison, nonmovable memory is an area used for loading NLMs into memory and allocating large memory buffers that do not change in size. Since server resources like the MONITOR are initiated by loading an NLM, nonmovable memory may require expansion if too many

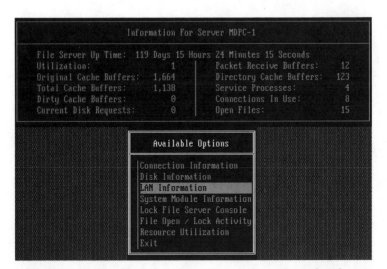

Figure 10.25   NetWare Monitor main screen display.

NLMs require simultaneous operation. For example, Frye's NetWare Management program represents another NLM which, when loaded, uses non-movable server memory.

LAN Driver Information   Perhaps one of the more valuable groups of data obtainable from the Available Options menu is under the LAN Information option. This option displays a window labeled "LAN Driver Information," which lists the LAN drivers active on your server, such as Ethernet or Token-Ring drivers. Next, selecting an appropriate driver displays a new window containing a series of LAN driver statistics, from which you can obtain specific information about the operation of one or more LANs connected to a Novell NetWare server. To illustrate the wealth of information, let us assume that you are using Novell's 3C503 Ethernet LAN driver. Table 10.4 lists 10 of the 27 statistics you can obtain from Novell's 3C503 LAN driver.

The Reset Count increments each time a hard transmit error, bad network error, or a hardware receive mismatch occurs, and the network board is reset to a known state. A large Reset Count may indicate an adapter card problem.

The Carrier Sense Lost Count increments when the transmitter on the card loses the carrier. This condition occurs when the cable connection to the network is lost. If this count periodically increases, it may indicate a loose cable.

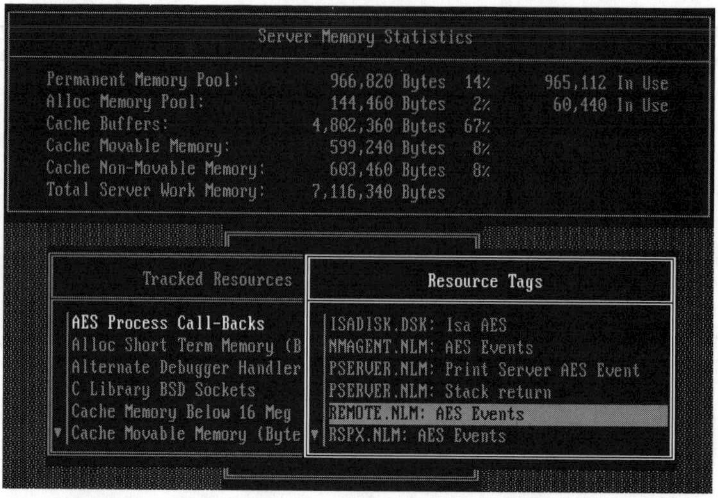

Figure 10.26   Server Memory Statistics display.

The Enqueued Sends Count increments each time the driver cannot transmit a packet and is thus forced to place the packet in a queue until the transmitter is available. A large count indicates network congestion.

When a collision occurs on a network board or in the cabling, the Excess Collisions Count is incremented. A large number of collisions may indicate that network traffic is too heavy to be efficiently carried, or that nodes are spaced too far from one another. The latter condition expands the length of the collision window, and may indicate a need to recable a portion of the network.

When a packet is addressed to a network board that cannot accept it because of a full receive buffer, the Receiver Missed Packet Count is incremented. Some adapter cards include the ability to select different size receive buffer areas. If the Receiver Missed Packet Count is high, you may wish to consider expanding the receive buffer area on your adapter card if that card has that capability.

The Total Collision Count increments in tandem with each network collision. When this count increases rapidly, it indicates a very high level of network activity. If the count increases rapidly only during short periods of time, it indicates that you may wish to consider splitting your network.

The Transmit Timeout Count is incremented each time the network card interrupts the file server with a "send bit" lost message. This indicates the oc-

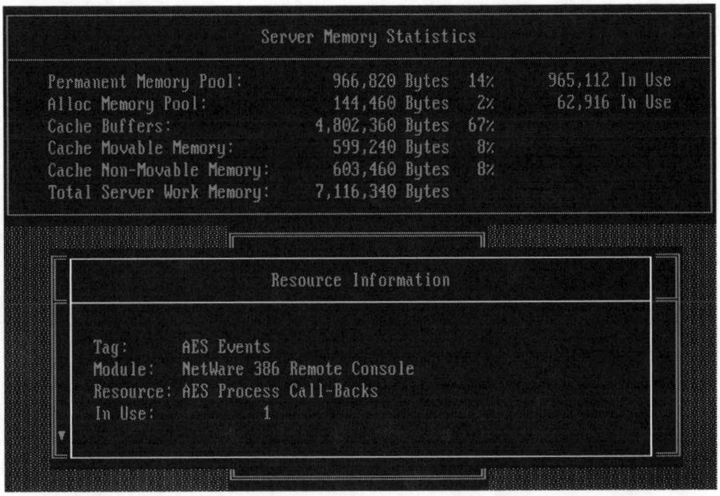

Figure 10.27 Obtaining information as a resource.

currence of a hardware problem resulting from faulty cabling, a malfunctioned adapter card, or a missing terminator.

The Underrun Error Count can be considered the inverse of the Enqueued Sends Count. That is, the Underrun Error Count increments when the buffer on the adapter card is full, and the card cannot accept additional packets until the buffer is serviced and cleared.

The last two counts listed in Table 10.4 indicate the number of MAC and LLC packets. By comparing these two counters, you can determine the relationship between information and control frames flowing on the network.

Cinco Networks WebXRay

As previously discussed in this chapter, it is important to note that Ethernet is a layer 2 transport protocol that operates at the data link layer of the ISO Reference Model. This means that different types of protocols can be transported over Ethernet, which is both a key advantage of the network as well as the cause of many network-related problems. In this concluding section we will turn our attention to the use of Cinco Network's WebXRay network monitoring and troubleshooting tool, which can be of considerable assistance when looking at IP traffic. Due to the growing role of the Internet and corporate

TABLE 10.4 Novell 3C503 LAN Driver Statistics

- Reset Count
- Carrier Sense Lost Count
- Enqueued Sends Count
- Excess Collisions Count
- Receiver Missed Packet Count
- Total Collisions Count
- Transmit Timeout Count
- Underrun Error Count
- Number of Ethernet 802.2 Packets Received
- Number of Ethernet 802.3 Packets Received

intranets, most Ethernet LANs carry a considerable amount of IP traffic, and the use of this program can provide a valuable tool for examining the state of different IP machines and the traffic they transmit and receive.

Overview

Figure 10.28 illustrates the WebXRay Dashboard, which provides a meter gauge view of IP statistics when the program is initialized. The top gauge displays the IP versus network load in terms of the number of packets per second. The next gauge indicates IP versus network utilization. In examining Figure 10.28 note that at the time the display was captured IP was contributing 39 percent of network utilization, with all traffic resulting in a network utilization level of 42 percent. This indicates that IP is the predominate protocol transported on the monitored network and any need to restructure the network due to high levels of utilization will have to consider the architecture of IP and its addressing.

Autodiscovery

One of the key features of WebXRay is its autodiscovery capability. Through the use of this feature you can use the program to identify all hosts on a segment as well as the IP services they are currently configured to support.

Figure 10.29 illustrates the WebXRay Topology Discovery dialog box. Into this box you enter the IP subnet address and the range for the last digit of the IP address you wish to search for. Since the WebXRay program uses the Ping application to locate hosts, it also provides you with the ability to set the timeout value for each ping. In the example shown in Figure 10.29, we will search

Figure 10.28 Cinco Network's WebXRay's Dashboard provides a meter or gauge display, which enables the role of IP traffic on a network to be visually noted.

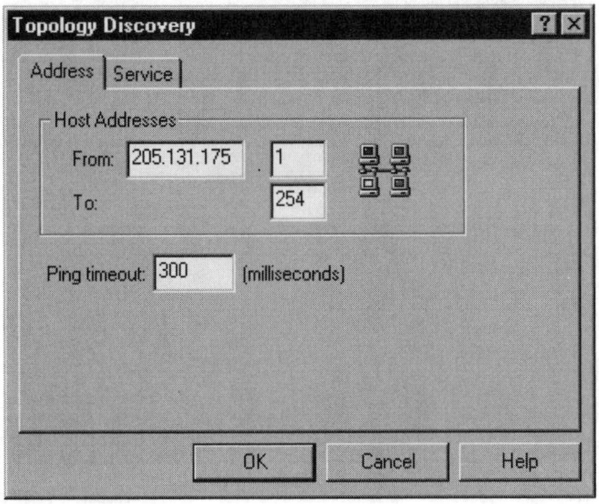

Figure 10.29 Through the Topology Discovery dialog box you can configure WebXRay to search for a specific range of host addresses.

the entire segment by using the last digit address range of 1 through 254 since 0 means this net and 255 is a broadcast address. A word of caution is in order concerning the entry of a Ping timeout value and host search range. If you set a very large Ping timeout value, a full search of a network segment for a large number of services per host can take a considerable amount of time.

To specify the services you wish to discover, you would click on the service tab of the Topology Discovery dialog box, generating a display similar to the one shown in Figure 10.30. In Figure 10.30 the selected services for DNS, FTP, HTTP, SNMP, and Telnet are shown checked. This means that the autodiscovery program will search each possible host address on the segment for the range of network values specified to determine if a host supports the services of interest.

Once you click the OK button in Figure 10.30 the autodiscovery process commences. As each node on the segment is discovered, its domain name will be displayed. If the domain name cannot be found, the IP address of the discovered node will be shown. Figure 10.31 illustrates a portion of the autodiscovery process at a point in time when 17 nodes were discovered on the segment being monitored. As you might surmise, the autodiscovery feature represents a valuable mechanism to discover unknown machines users may have set up without informing management as well as services on those systems that might require a reconfiguration of a router's access list or firewall.

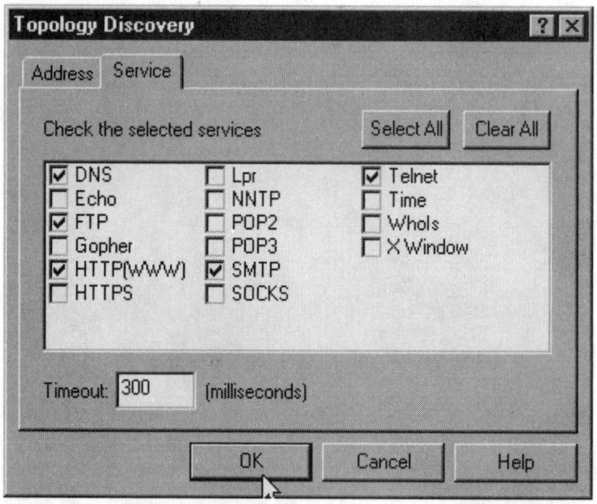

Figure 10.30 Through the Service tab in the Topology Discovery dialog box you can select the TCP/IP services you wish the WebXRay program to scan for during its autodiscovery process.

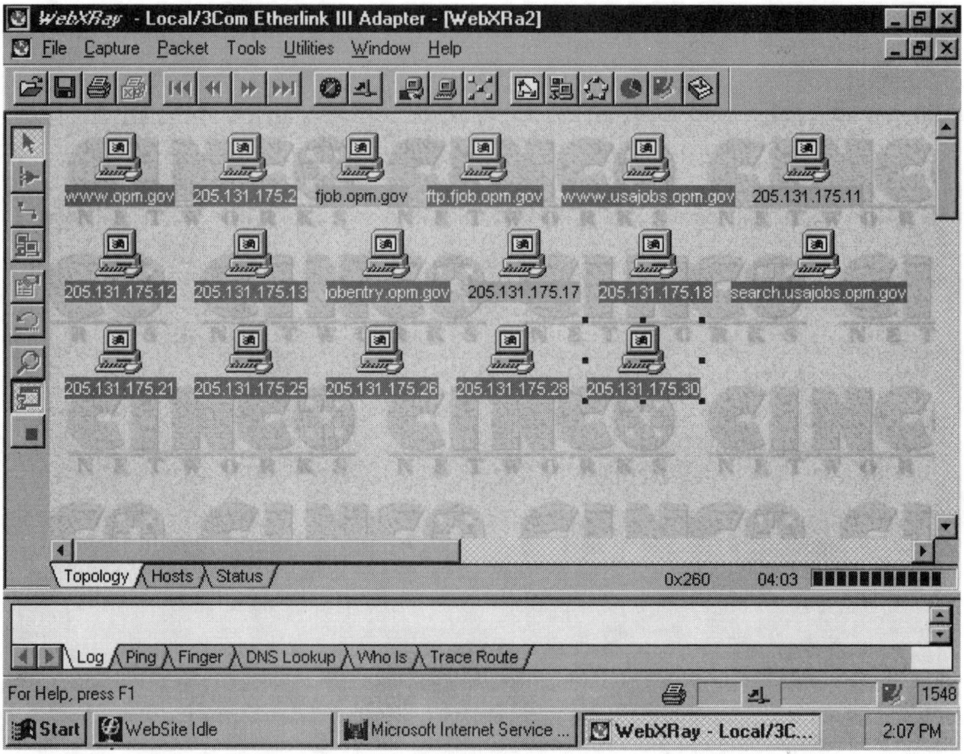

Figure 10.31 During the autodiscovery process WebXRay displays the domain name or IP address of each host discovered.

Thus, a periodic autodiscovery process is usually a very valuable procedure for employing on a large network.

Once the autodiscovery process is completed you can determine the status of each service for each node discovered. To do so, you would click on the status tab at the bottom of the map window shown in Figure 10.31. This action will result in the display of the service window which is shown in Figure 10.32. In examining Figure 10.32 note that a happy face means the node or service is up and available, a question mark indicates that the status of the service is unknown, while a minus sign enclosed in a circle means that the service is not available for the network node. Since we previously indicated we wanted to restrict our service queries to specific types of services, those services with question marks primarily represent services we did not have the program query.

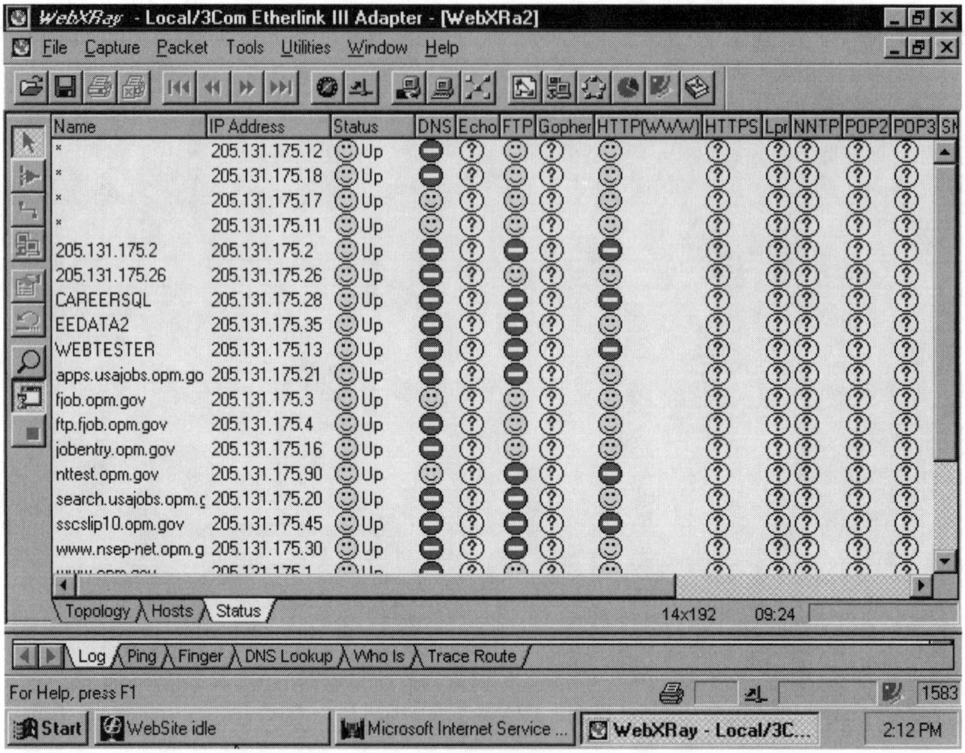

Figure 10.32 The WebXRay Service window indicates the status of different TCP/IP services or applications for each autodiscovered node on a segment.

As indicated by our examination of WebXRay, this program is well-suited for determining the effect of IP on your LAN and discovering nodes and the services they are configured to support. As such, WebXRay provides an additional insight into the activity on an Ethernet network that can be of considerable assistance in obtaining information on the operations and utilization of the network.

Summary

As indicated by our review of the operation and utilization of several management tools, the ability to determine the operational state of your network may require the use of more than one product. Vendor products, like people, do some things better than other things and may not do certain performance-related tasks at all. Since the health of a network depends on the capability of the wiring infrastructure and adapter cards to transfer information, as well as the ability of the server to process information requests, you will more than likely require the use of separate products to examine each network performance area. Otherwise, the examination of one area may provide you with misleading information about the actual level of performance of your network.

chapter eleven

The Future of Ethernet

When a book is devoted to a well-defined technology, it is always important to discuss the future of that technology. This is especially true with respect to Ethernet, since many readers are employees of organizations that have invested or plan to invest tens to hundreds of thousands of dollars or more in acquiring network adapter cards and hubs, installing cabling, obtaining software, and teaching employees to use a network operating system. Thus, a logical question readers may have involves the safety of their current or planned investment in Ethernet technology. That is, what can you expect in the evolution of Ethernet technology, and will the introduction of new technology result in the obsolescence of your existing or planned Ethernet network? Although there is no simple answer to this multifaceted question, since the effect of technological advances is highly dependent on organizational communications requirements, we can examine trends in networking and Ethernet technology. This will provide us with a foundation of knowledge from which we can express some general observations about a previous or planned investment in an Ethernet network.

11.1 Ethernet Trends

In attempting to project the future of Ethernet, we should consider a variety of variables in addition to technological developments. Some of the major variables we must consider are the cost of technology, the performance it provides, and the potential to use existing technology in a more productive manner. The latter may minimize or reduce a requirement to migrate to new technology. In this section, we will focus our attention on the cost and performance of existing and evolving Ethernet technology, as well as the emerging use of wireless transmission for LAN communications.

Network Adapter Card Cost

Just a half-dozen years ago, the average price of an Ethernet adapter card was approximately $1000, while the cost of a personal computer was between $3000 and $4000. Excluding the cost of cabling and a network operating system, an Ethernet adapter card represented an approximate 25- to 33-percent increase in the cost of a personal computer. By early 1998 you could acquire an Intel Pentium II–based personal computer with 32 M of RAM, SVGA support, and an SVGA monitor for approximately $2500. At the same time, the average cost of a 10-/100-Mbps dual-speed Ethernet adapter card was under $100, so the additional cost to network a personal computer was only approximately 4 percent of an organization's hardware budget. Clearly, the cost of obtaining an Ethernet network communications capability was extremely nominal by 1998.

Future Price Direction

Not only has the cost of Ethernet hardware significantly declined over the past few years, but advances in chip fabrication technology indicate that price declines are far from being over. In 1992 Zenith Data Systems introduced several notebook computers with a built-in Ethernet communications capability on the computer's motherboard. Additional computer manufacturers now provide a built-in Ethernet networking capability for their products, enabling portable computer users to simply plug a 10BASE-T jack into their computer's plug upon return to the office to obtain access to the corporate network.

According to several trade press articles, the inclusion of an Ethernet chip set on nonportable personal computers adds less than $20 to the cost of the computer. This can be expected to make an Ethernet networking capability on personal computers as pervasive as the inclusion of a parallel port. In comparison, alternative network adapter cards, such as Token-Ring and FDDI, range in cost from $300 to $400 for a 16-Mbps Token-Ring adapter to $400 to $550 for an FDDI adapter. Ethernet can thus be expected to continue to hold a significant cost advantage over competing local area network adapter cards. This should extend the use of Ethernet networks far into the foreseeable future.

In the area of desktop personal computers, it is almost a common occurrence to note approximately 25 percent of all advertisements now include either a built-in NIC or a 10-/100-Mbps adapter bundled with memory, an SVGA video adapter, and other computer features. Thus, not only is Ethernet recognized as the de facto network of choice, but, in addition, a significant number of PCs are now being bundled with Ethernet adapters.

Although the cost of Gigabit Ethernet adapter cards was relatively expensive in comparison to 10-/100-Mbps adapters, the cost of the former is rapidly declining. First introduced at prices above $2000, by early 1998 some Gigabit Ethernet adapters were priced below $1500. However, it is important to note that currently available Gigabit Ethernet adapters are based upon relatively expensive optical technology. Once copper standards are promulgated, you can reasonably expect production of adapters using that media to achieve significant levels of production that can result in economics of scale, which lowers the cost of production. This in turn will eventually result in declining prices for 1000BASE-T adapter cards as the market for this product grows.

Wireless Ethernet

The growth in the use of laptops, notebooks, and personal digital assistants resulted in the development of several types of communications products designed to support mobile communications. Some products, such as docking stations and miniature adapter cards enclosed in a housing the size of a cigarette package, require the mobile computer to be moved to a fixed location to be connected to an organization's network. Here the mobile computer might be inserted into a docking station previously connected to the LAN. As an alternative, a computer user could connect the parallel port of the mobile computer to a miniature adapter that was on their desk and was previously connected to the network. For either situation, the mobile computer would lose its mobility whenever a user wanted to access the LAN. Recognizing this problem, several manufacturers developed products that untether network communications, enabling mobile computing to remain relatively mobile while providing access to LAN facilities.

Operations

Similar to any transmission system, a wireless LAN requires a transmitter, receiver, and transmission media, the latter represented by the air instead of a cable used by conventional LANs. The actual use of the air in a wireless LAN falls into two technologies—radio frequency (RF) and infrared.

Although many vendors refer to their products as wireless LANs, in actuality the wireless capability is used to extend the communications capability of an existing network. This is accomplished by connecting an access point to an existing LAN. The access point functions as a specialized network node, containing either an RF or infrared transmitter/receiver (T/R), which enables it to communicate with one or more clients that have either an RF or infrared T/R. Figure 11.1 illustrates the relationship between an access point, its clients, and an Ethernet network.

The key difference between the use of infrared and RF technology concerns the support of roaming. Infrared is a line-of-sight communications technology and does not permit a user to move around an office. Although infrared is suit-

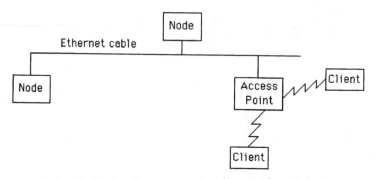

Figure 11.1   Components of a wireless LAN.

able for use where conventional cabling is impractical, such as a reception desk in the middle of a hotel atrium, it is impractical if users wish to have mobility. For this reason all Ethernet wireless LAN equipment manufacturers were currently limiting their equipment to RF technology when this book was written. However, within the use of RF, there are two competing methods used by different vendors.

RF Methods

The use of radio frequency for communications requires the selection of frequencies in the electromagnetic spectrum that will not cause interference with equipment designed to operate in other portions of the electromagnetic spectrum. In addition, since several corporations might want to establish wireless LANs in the same building, the power of the signal must be limited. The first constraint resulted in the selection of the industrial, scientific, and medical (ISM) bands of the electromagnetic spectrum for transmission of RF signals. The ISM bands include frequency ranges at 902 MHz to 928 MHz, and 2.4 GHz to 2.484 GHz. The channels in which transmitters operate in the 900-MHz band are limited to 500-KHz bandwidth, while channels are limited to 1-MHz bandwidth. Transmission in these bands does not require an FCC license, as FCC rules result in compliance with the second constraint by limiting transmission power. This is accomplished by requiring frequency transmission to occur using a *spread spectrum* method of modulation.

Spread Spectrum Modulation

Spread spectrum modulation results in the transmission of a low-power signal occupying a large portion of a radio band. Originally, spread spectrum modulation was developed as a mechanism to protect communications from eavesdropping and interference. By using a low amount of power and hopping from one frequency to another based upon a predefined algorithm, an enemy receiver was lucky to pick up very small portions of communications. The development work resulting in spread spectrum frequency–hopping communications provided the foundation for two spread spectrum techniques used with wireless LANs—frequency-hopping spread spectrum (FHSS) and direct-sequence spread spectrum (DSSS).

Under the FHSS technique, the radio transmitter hops from one frequency to another at a specific rate in a specific sequence. Since only the intended receiver knows the transmitter's hopping sequence, only that receiver can correctly receive the transmitted signal. Currently, each vendor using an FHSS transmission technique develops its own proprietary hopping algorithm; however, each algorithm is similar in that it precludes two transmitters hopping to the same frequency at the same time.

Under FCC rules, FHSS transmitters cannot spend more than 0.4 seconds on any one channel every 20 seconds in the 902-MHz band, and every 30 seconds in the 2.4-GHz band. In addition, FCC rules require transmitters to hop through a minimum of 50 500-KHz channel bandwidths in the 902-MHz band, and 75 1-MHz channel bandwidths in the 2.4-GHz band.

The second method of spread spectrum communications, DSSS, operates by adding redundant data, bits referred to as *chips,* to transmission over a wide band of the frequency spectrum. This results in a bandwidth larger than needed to transmit data, enabling chips to spread the signal, with the spread of the signal governed by the number of chips per bit. At any given time, two or more components of the signal are being received concurrently at many different frequencies.

To successfully *unspread* the transmitted signal and generate a signal the network can understand requires the receiving devices to have the correct decoding algorithms to interpret received data. Otherwise, the received data over the spread spectrum will appear to represent noise.

FCC rules for DSSS transmission requires 10 or more redundant data bits to be added to each signal. This limits the maximum throughput of DSSS transmitters to approximately 2 Mbps when using the 902-MHz band, and 8 Mbps in the 2.4-GHz band. In comparison, FHSS transmitters are limited to a maximum throughput of 2 Mbps when operating in the 2.4-GHz band.

Due to the growth in the use of notebooks, personal digital assistants, and pagers, we can logically expect the use of wireless LANs to increase. In fact, several network management products can now be obtained with the ability to send alert messages and alarms via different types of wireless interfaces. Although wireless LANs may not replace conventional LANs, their use can be expected to increase as network users become more mobile within their working environment.

11.2 Network Performance Considerations

At the time this book was written there were a wide range of options available for supporting what some persons refer to as legacy 10-Mbps Ethernet LANs. Today you can consider using LAN switches, a faster backbone infrastructure, or a combination of switches and a fast shared backbone. In addition to pure Ethernet solutions you can consider the use of ATM and FDDI as a backbone. With all these potential solutions a logical question readers may wish to ask themselves is whether they need a 100- or 1000-Mbps local area network to satisfy their current and future data transmission requirements. Even if the answer is yes, this answer, as we will soon note, may not mean that your previous investment in Ethernet technology is obsolete.

Supplementing an Existing Network

To demonstrate how more modern and higher operating rate local area network technology can be used to supplement existing Ethernet equipment, let us assume that your organization previously installed a series of Ethernet networks on floors within a building, using 10BASE-T bridges and wiring through floor risers to interconnect users on each "floor"-based network. Under this networking scenario, it is quite possible that the initiation of a file transfer operation by two or more network users accessing a server on a third network via a 10BASE-T bridge would adversely affect other internet transmission until the file transfer operations are completed.

To see this potential for internet congestion, consider Figure 11.2, in which three "floor" LANs are connected with three 10BASE-T bridges wired together, perhaps using the riser within the building. Let us assume that stations A and C initiate file transfers to the server S_n located on network C. If each network operates at 10 Mbps, the traffic offered to the middle bridge is 20 Mbps. However, since each network operates at 10 Mbps, the best performance possible for the middle bridge is to route the file transfer data at 10 Mbps to the server. Now suppose that station D on network B attempts to access the server S on network C. Frames generated by that station must contend with frames generated by workstations A and C for service by the bridge. It is thus quite possible for interactive queries, as well as file transfer operations across networks, to be adversely affected by existing file transfer operations.

Using a Backbone Network

Although one potential solution to internet congestion is to install new networks capable of supporting higher data transfer operations, doing so might

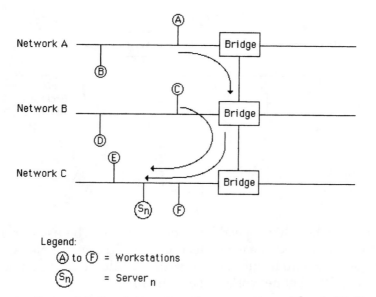

Legend:

(A) to (F) = Workstations

(Sn) = Server n

Figure 11.2 Potential for internetwork congestion. The initiation of file transfer operations from two or more workstations to a server on a third workstation can create network congestion.

require both new adapter cards and new network wiring. A far less expensive potential solution to internet congestion is to use a higher operating rate local area network to serve as a backbone net.

Figure 11.3 shows the use of an FDDI backbone network to interconnect the three previously installed Ethernet networks. Since the FDDI network operates at 100 Mbps, its use is equivalent to a high-speed interstate highway linking country roads together. That is, inter-LAN traffic is facilitated by a high-speed backbone LAN in the same manner that interroad traffic is facilitated by an interstate highway. Once a frame is bridged onto the FDDI network, it flows at 100 Mbps, enabling more frames to be carried between linked local area networks per unit time than possible when a 10BASE-T network is used as a backbone network.

Unless your organization is already using FDDI, its installation cost can be relatively expensive in comparison to 100BASE-T technology. Thus, many organizations will more than likely consider the use of a 100BASE-T shared media hub or even a 1-Gbps buffered distributor to form a network backbone.

In early 1998, the cost of an 8-port 100-Mbps shared Ethernet hub was under $500, providing a most economical method for creating a higher-speed

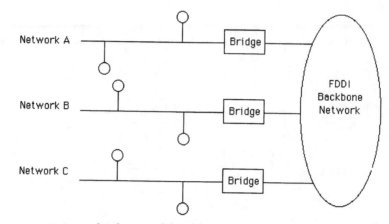

Figure 11.3 Using a high-speed backbone network. The use of a 100-Mbps FDDI network as a backbone to connect separate Ethernet LANs can remove a large degree of potential internet congestion while permitting the previous investment in Ethernet networks to be maintained.

backbone network for bridging between LANs. Figure 11.4 illustrates how you could use a low-cost 100-Mbps shared Ethernet hub as a backbone for connecting legacy 10BASE-T networks. Note that this network configuration also preserves your investment as all cabling and network adapters to the left of each bridge remain as is. Since the cost of a 100-Mbps shared Ethernet hub is equivalent to the cost of a few FDDI adapters, this represents a low-cost mechanism to retain your network infrastructure.

In examining Figure 11.4, note that transmission from any bridge port to the 100-Mbps shared Ethernet hub is regenerated onto all other hub ports. However, the use of bridges on each network connection serves as a filter, barring repeated frames from flowing onto networks they are not intended for. Thus, although each network could be directly connected to a hub port, the use of bridges can significantly enhance network performance by limiting repeated frames from destination networks they are not actually directed to.

Using a Switching System

Another solution to network congestion can be obtained through the use of a 100BASE-T Fast Ethernet switch or creating a tiered hub-based switching network.

Figure 11.5 illustrates the use of a Fast Ethernet hub-based switch. In this example, network servers are connected to the 100-Mbps Fast Ethernet ports,

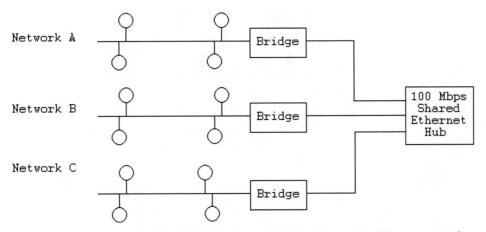

Figure 11.4   Using a 100-Mbps shared Ethernet hub as a backbone provides a very low-cost mechanism for supporting inter-LAN communications.

while existing 10BASE-T hubs are connected to the switching hub using 10BASE-T adapters operating at 10 Mbps. Note that the switching hub can provide two simultaneous cross-connections to the two file servers, boosting available bandwidth in comparison to the situation where file servers are located on a common network. In addition, through the use of a 100-Mbps connection each query response is completed quicker than if communications occurred on a shared 10-Mbps network.

The configuration illustrated in Figure 11.5, which this author labeled as a tiered network, can also be considered to represent a collapsed backbone. Although a switching hub using two Mbps Fast Ethernet port connections to two file servers is shown, there are many other network connections that can be considered to protect your investment in 10-Mbps Ethernet technology while providing a mechanism to reduce network congestion. You can consider the use of switching hubs with a fat pipe or full-duplex capability, or the use of a router as an alternative to the use of a switching hub. Readers are referred to the next section in this chapter as well as to Chapter 9 for additional information concerning methods by which switching hubs can be used to reduce or eliminate network congestion.

Although the use of switching hubs or routers can provide a mechanism to alleviate network congestion, another method you can consider is the bottleneck between workstations, servers, and the network. That bottleneck is the LAN adapter card. Many times the use of an enhanced adapter card may solve

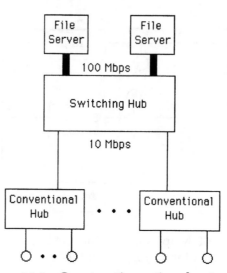

Figure 11.5 Constructing a tiered network.

a network congestion problem many consultants would have you believe requires the use of a more expensive solution.

Using Enhanced Adapter Cards

One of the key limits to the ability of a workstation to transfer large quantities of data is the type of network adapter card used in a workstation. A typical low-cost Ethernet adapter card may have a data transfer rate of only 200,000 to 400,000 bytes per second. Such adapters are capable of transmitting and receiving data at only approximately 10 to 20 percent of the transfer rate of a 10BASE-T network. While this transfer rate is usually more than sufficient for most client/server operations, it becomes a bottleneck for long file transfers and for devices such as bridges, routers, and gateways that may require a higher transfer rate capability. The selective use of enhanced Ethernet adapter cards may provide you with the ability to increase network performance and reduce or eliminate network bottlenecks.

Two types of Ethernet adapter cards you may wish to consider for workstations that have a large amount of file transfer operations or for bridges, routers, and gateways are bus mastering and parallel processing adapter cards.

Bus Mastering Cards A bus mastering card is designed to perform I/O data transfers directly to and from the memory of the computer in which it is installed. To accomplish this, a bus mastering card includes circuitry known as a *direct memory access* (*DMA*). The adapter card can initiate a DMA transfer, which permits data to be moved directly to or from memory, while the processor on the adapter card performs other operations. The net effect of bus mastering is to increase the transfer capability of the adapter card by 50 to 100 percent.

Parallel-Tasking Cards   Standard Ethernet adapter cards perform networking operations in a fixed sequential manner. Although a bus mastering adapter permits memory access operations to be performed in parallel with some network operations, greater efficiencies are obtainable with the use of parallel-tasking Ethernet adapters. One such adapter is Etherlink III, manufactured by 3Com Corporation, which has the capability to transfer data at approximately 500,000 bytes per second.

To demonstrate the efficiency of parallel-tasking, the top portion of Figure 11.6 shows the operation of a pair of standard Ethernet adapters used to transmit and receive data. As indicated, each operation has to be completed before the next can be begun.

The lower portion of Figure 11.6 shows the tasks performed for the transmission of information between two parallel-tasking Ethernet adapter cards. As noted by the time chart, the performance of many tasks in parallel reduces the time required to transfer information, which enhances the transfer rate of the adapter card.

100-Mbps Adapter Operations   Although the use of appropriate 10BASE-T adapter cards may by themselves prolong the ability to operate at 10 Mbps, when upgrading to 100-Mbps Fast Ethernet or another network, you must also carefully consider the capability of adapter cards. For example, assume your organization's 10BASE-T network is heavily saturated and additional applications to include multimedia are on the horizon. Although upgrading to a 100BASE-T network might initially satisfy your organization's networking requirements, it is quite possible that access contention to a video server, even at 100 Mbps, could result in delays that distance the delivery of video. In this situation you might consider installing a full-duplex 100BASE-T adapter card in the video server and connecting the server to a 100-Mbps switching hub.

Figure 11.7 illustrates one version of the Grand Junction Network Fast NIC 100 EISA adapter card. The adapter card illustrated in Figure 11.7 contains a pair of connectors for fiber-optic cabling, supporting transmission and recep-

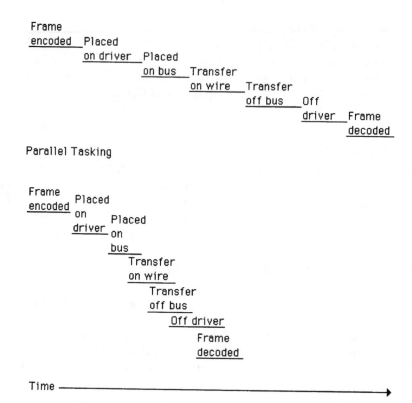

Figure 11.6 Serial-tasking versus parallel-tasking Ethernet adapters. The use of parallel-tasking Ethernet adapter cards permits the overlapping of many operations, thus reducing the time needed to transfer information and increasing the data transfer capability of the adapter.

tion of data at distances up to 1312 feet (400 meters) between the adapter and a switch port, and up to 6558 feet (2 kilometers) if supporting collision-free full-duplex operations. In examining Figure 11.7, note that the bottom edge connectors of the adapter are designed to the Extended Industry Standard Architecture (EISA) specification, providing a true 32-bit path between the adapter card and the computer bus. This extended path becomes critical to support sustained data transfers, since a full-duplex operation can result in up to a 200-Mbps throughput between a station that has this NIC installed and a full-duplex switch port.

Figure 11.7 Grand Junction Networks Fast NIC 100 EISA. The Grand Junction Fast NIC 100 EISA 100BASE-FX adapter supports a 200-Mbps throughput at distances up to 6558 feet (2 km) in a collision-free full-duplex mode of operation. (Photography courtesy of Grand Junction Networks, Inc.)

You can use the Grand Junction Networks' Fast NIC 100 EISA or compatible adapter with both 100-Mbps hubs as well as switching hubs, providing a mechanism to extend high-performance Ethernet networking to a large base of users. Figure 11.8 illustrates the Grand Junction Networks' FastHub 100, the first 100BASE-T conventional hub to be commercially marketed. This hub functions similar to a 10-Mbps 10BASE-T hub, repeating a received signal onto all ports. However, unlike a 10BASE-T hub, the FastHub 100 operates at 100 Mbps.

The FastHub 100 illustrated in Figure 11.8 is the vendor's 100BASE-FX model, which supports 12 multimode fiber optic cable pairs. The 100BASE-FX hub supports a transmission distance of up to 1000 feet (305 meters) between any two stations in an unbridged 100BASE-FX network with one repeater, while the use of two repeaters reduces the transmission distance to 688 feet (210 meters). In comparison, the vendor's 100BASE-TX hub, which supports category 5 UTP cabling, permits a 328-foot (100-meter) maximum

Figure 11.8 The Grand Junction FastHub 100 (100BASE-FX model) supports the use of 12 multimode fiber-optic cable pairs to workstations, hubs, or servers, each cable operating at 100 Mbps. (Photograph courtesy of Grand Junction Networks, Inc.)

cabling distance, and a 688-foot (210-meter) maximum distance between any two stations in an unbridged 100BASE-T network with two repeaters.

You can use up to two Grand Junction FastHub 100 hubs as a top-level tier for constructing a network to support up to 750 switched Ethernet users and 30 100BASE-T connected servers. To do so you would connect a Grand Junction FastSwitch 10/100 to each FastHub port. The Grand Junction FastSwitch 10/100 is a switching hub that supports up to 24 dedicated 10-Mbps ports and one dedicated 100-Mbps port to workstations or servers, and up to four 100-Mbps 100BASE-T shared ports, ideal for connecting servers. When used with the firm's FastHub, the FastSwitch 10/100 resulting configuration capability permits 25 ports to be used for dedicated switching, and one port for shared usage.

Figure 11.9 illustrates the construction of a tiered Fast Ethernet–based network using Grand Junction 100BASE-T hubs and switching hubs. Through the use of two 100BASE-T hubs, you can support the interconnection of up to 30 of the vendor's FastSwitch switching hubs at the lower tier. Each

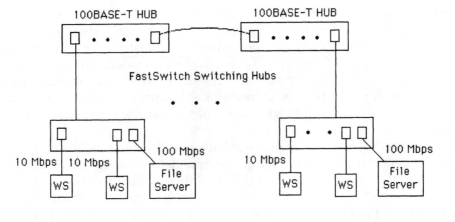

Figure 11.9   Constructing a tiered Fast Ethernet-based network.

FastSwitch switching hub in turn can support up to 25 ports for dedicated switching, and one port for shared switching. Thus, the use of this vendor's hardware enables you to construct an Ethernet network containing up to 750 switched workstations and 30 file servers. Note that this network design enables multiple users on each switching hub to simultaneously access the file server on the hub, since a Fast Ethernet connection is used to connect each file server to the hub. In addition, each workstation in the network requiring access to a workstation or server on a different switching hub can access the hub through the top tier 100BASE-T hubs.

1000-Mbps Adapter Operations   When considering the use of Gigabit Ethernet the methodology of the manner by which data is moved between the computer and adapter as well as the bus supported by the adapter are extremely important design features you must consider. Today you can consider two types of PCI bus. One bus has a 32-bit width, while the other has a 64-bit width. Both can operate at a bus speed of either 33 or 66 MHz. Multiplying the bus width in bytes by the bus speed provides an indication of the raw or theoretical byte transfer rate of the adapter, while multiplying the bus width in bits by the bus speed provides an indication of the theoretical transfer rate of the bus. However, from a practical standpoint the overhead associated with frame copying, buffer alignment, checksum computations, and other overhead functions commonly reduces the efficiency of an Ethernet adapter to approximately 60 percent of its theoretical transfer rate. Using the preceding as a guide, Table 11.1 indicates the realistic bit transfer rates you can expect from the use of four types of PCI bus adapters. In examining the entries in Table 11.1, it is important to note that if you are using a 32-bit PCI card in a computer with a 33-MHz bus, at best you will probably achieve a data transfer capability approximately 63 percent of the transfer supported by Gigabit Ethernet.

Since the 60-percent efficiency previously used to compute the probable bit rate column entries in Table 11.1 is a representative average of different vendor products, one way to enhance the capability of the use of Gigabit Ethernet is to use more efficient adapters. However, this is normally only true if you are using a 32-bit PCI card in a computer whose bus operates at 33 MHz. If you are using a computer whose bus operates at 66 MHz or you are using a 64-bit PCI card from Table 11.1 you will note that the probable bit rate can be expected to be 1.273 Gbps or 2.534 Gbps. Even if the manufacturer of the Gigabit Ethernet NIC uses a highly inefficient buffering method that reduces throughput by 20 percent, the data transfer capability of the adapter should be more than 1 Gbps. Thus, when considering a Gigabit Ethernet adapter it is probably more important to consider the bus width and bus speed than vendor claims of design efficiency.

Multimedia and Video Separation

Throughout 1997 you probably noted a considerable number of articles about the use of multimedia and video image applications on local area networks. What most of these articles had in common was the fact that the data transfer capability of Ethernet and Token-Ring networks could not support more than one or a few users simultaneously accessing the multimedia and video image applications that reside on a server, nor could it support the transfer of images

TABLE 11.1 Gigabit Ethernet PCI Bus Considerations

Bus Width (bits)	Bus Speed (MHz)	Theoretical Byte Transfer Range (MB/s)	Theoretical Bit Rate (Gbps)	Probable Bit Rate (Gbps)
32	33	132	1.056	0.634
32	66	264	2.112	1.273
64	33	264	2.112	1.273
64	66	528	4.224	2.534